Media Literacy

Media Literacy

Keys to Interpreting Media Messages

FOURTH EDITION

Art Silverblatt, Andrew Smith, Don Miller,
Julie Smith, and Nikole Brown

 PRAEGER

AN IMPRINT OF ABC-CLIO, LLC
Santa Barbara, California • Denver, Colorado • Oxford, England

BH

Library of Congress Cataloging-in-Publication Data

Silverblatt, Art.
  Media literacy : keys to interpreting media messages / Art Silverblatt, Andrew Smith, Don Miller, Julie Smith, and Nikole Brown. — Fourth edition.
     pages cm
  Includes index.
  ISBN 978-1-4408-3091-4 (hardback : alk. paper) — ISBN 978-1-4408-3092-1
(e-book) — ISBN 978-1-4408-3115-7 (pbk. : alk. paper) 1. Media literacy. I. Title.
  P96.M4S594   2014
  302.23—dc23   2014001562

ISBN: 978-1-4408-3091-4 (cloth)
       978-1-4408-3115-7 (paper)
EISBN: 978-1-4408-3092-1

18 17 16 15 14   1 2 3 4 5

This book is also available on the World Wide Web as an eBook.
Visit www.abc-clio.com for details.

Praeger
An Imprint of ABC-CLIO, LLC

ABC-CLIO, LLC
130 Cremona Drive, P.O. Box 1911
Santa Barbara, California 93116-1911

This book is printed on acid-free paper ∞
Manufactured in the United States of America

11/13/14

To my Media Literacy Buddies:

- *Respected ML scholars and colleagues: Frank Baker, Liz Thoman, Kathleen Tyner, Renee Hobbs, and Marieli Rowe*
- *Partners: Yupa Saisanan Na Ayudhya, Sara Gabal, Kit Jenkins, Jessica Brown, and my DIMLE co-authors*
- *My young ML scholars: Zoey Wong, Ahmed (Naz) Nasr El Din, Naoko Onishi, Bobbie Watson, and Chris Penberthy*
- *The co-authors of this fourth edition: Julie Smith, Andrew A. Smith, Don Miller, and Nikole Brown*
- *And, of course, Margie, Leah B., Ozzie, and Chub.*

—Art

For N. L. Nilsson,
Because.

—Julie Smith

To my mentor, Art Silverblatt, for helping me to
see the world in a different way.

To my parents, William and Deborah Smith, for always
encouraging me to pursue what I love.

And to my wife, Sarah, for being everything I could have
ever hoped for in another human being.

—Andrew Allen Smith

To Bob: Your faith, love, and support is immeasurable.

To Morrie: You've changed my life in ways that I hadn't
even imagined possible. I love you both.

To Art: Thanks for the opportunity! You are an incredible mentor.

—Don Miller

To my mother, Karan Brown—

Who always said I was special for having dreams, but the
only reason I had them was because of her.

—Nikole Brown

Contents

Preface to the Fourth Edition

Media Literacy: Keys to Interpreting Media Messages offers a critical approach that will enable students to better understand the information conveyed through the channels of mass communication—print, photography, film, radio, television, and digital media. One of the principal goals of *Media Literacy* is to enable students to realize a healthy independence from the pervasive influence of the media.

The organization of the fourth edition remains the same as the previous editions. Part 1 (chapter 1) presents an introduction to the discipline of media literacy. Part 2 (chapters 2–7) presents a theoretical framework for the critical analysis of media texts—the Keys to Interpreting Media Messages. Part 3 (chapters 8–11) applies this methodological framework to the following media formats: journalism, advertising, American political communications, and digital media communications. Part 4 (chapters 12 and 13) considers a range of mass media issues (violence in the media, media and children, media and social change, and global communications), and a discussion of potential outcomes, once individuals have become media literate.

However, since the first edition of this text was published in 1995, much has happened in the world of media. The text reflects recent developments, particularly in the realm of digital literacy. In addition, many examples (particularly the chapters on American Political Communications and Digital Media Communications) in earlier editions are outdated and have been replaced by current examples.

PART I

INTRODUCTION

I

Introduction to Media Literacy

*When children 4–6 were asked in a survey, "Which do you like better,
TV or your daddy," 54 percent said "TV."*[1]

The media have assumed a large role in the lives of the average American
family. For instance:

- Only 59 percent of adults talk with other family members during the
  course of an evening.[2]
- Only 34 percent of parents spend time with their children during the
  evening.[3]
- The average American married couple spends only 4 minutes a day
  in "serious" conversation.[4]
- Parents spend an average of 5.5 minutes per day in "meaningful conversation" with their children.[5]

At the same time:

- Watching TV is the dominant leisure activity of Americans, consuming more than double the amount of time we spend socializing.[6]
- The average American watches more than 70 days of nonstop viewing
  per year.[7]
- 40 percent of Americans always or often watch television while eating
  dinner.[8]
- 25 percent of Americans fall asleep with the TV on at least three
  nights a week.[9]

And remember that television represents only *one* media system.

The traditional definition of literacy applies only to print: "having a knowledge of letters; instructed; learned." In light of the emergence of the channels of mass communications (i.e., print, photography, film, radio, television, and digital media), this definition of literacy must be expanded. The National Telemedia Council defines media literacy as "the ability to choose, to understand—within the context of content, form/style, impact, industry and production—to question, to evaluate, to create and/or produce and to respond thoughtfully to the media we consume. It is mindful viewing, reflective judgment."[10]

At the National Conference on Media Literacy sponsored by the Aspen Institute in December 1992, the groups' representatives settled on a basic definition of media literacy: "It is the ability of a citizen to access, analyze, and produce information for specific outcomes."[11]

This author's definition of media literacy builds on the preceding ideas but emphasizes the following elements:

1. *Media literacy promotes the critical thinking skills that enable people to make independent choices with regard to 1) which media programming to select and 2) how to interpret the information they receive through the channels of mass communication.*
   Media literacy is, first and foremost, a critical thinking skill that is applied to the source of most of the information we receive: the channels of mass communication. However, for a variety of reasons that will be discussed later in the chapter, we often blindly accept the information that we receive through the media—with disastrous results. We develop brand loyalties that have little to do with the quality of the product. We take the word (or pictures) of journalists to provide us with a clear understanding of our world. And we vote for candidates on the basis of "gut reactions" to political spots devised by clever political media consultants.

   Rather than tuning to a specific program, all too often the audience simply watches the *medium* ("I'm gonna watch TV"). Indeed, 40 percent of TV viewers don't bother to check the TV listings before turning on the set; instead, they simply flip through the channels to determine what they want to see (or what is least objectionable).[12] One of the criteria of becoming an educated person is developing the critical faculties to understand one's environment—an environment that, increasingly, is being shaped by the media. As Bill Moyers observes, "At stake is our sense of meaning and language, our sense of history, democracy, citizenship and our very notions of beauty and truth."[13]

2. ***Understanding the process of mass communication.***
   By itself, a medium is simply a channel of communication; consequently, it is neither good nor evil. A number of factors determine the impact of a media presentation, including an understanding of the elements involved in the process of media communications: 1) *media communicator,* who is producing the presentation; 2) the *function* (or purpose) behind the production of the presentation; 3) *comparative media*—the distinguishing characteristics of each medium; and 4) the intended *audience* (see Chapters 2–5).

3. ***An awareness of the impact of the media on individuals and society.***
   The media have transformed the way we think about the world, each other, and ourselves. Media presentations convey cumulative messages that *shape, reflect,* and *reinforce* attitudes, values, behaviors, preoccupations, and myths that define a culture. Within this context, media literacy education has had an impact on young students' behaviors and attitudes with regard to alcohol[14] and tobacco usage[15] and eating disorders.[16] In addition, media literacy "interventions" have helped curb aggressive and antisocial behaviors among third and fourth grade children.[17]

4. ***The development of strategies with which to analyze and discus media messages.***
   Media literacy provides strategies that enable individuals to decipher the information they receive through the channels of mass communications. These keys also provide a framework that facilitates the discussion of media content with others—including children, peers, and the people responsible for producing media programming.

5. ***An awareness of media content as a "text" that provides insight into our contemporary culture and ourselves.***
   As we will see in Chapter 4 (Cultural Context), media presentations often provide insight into the attitudes, values, behaviors, preoccupations, patterns of thought, and myths that define a culture. And conversely, an understanding of a culture can furnish perspectives into media presentations produced in that culture.

6. ***The cultivation of an enhanced enjoyment, understanding, and appreciation of media content.***
   Media literacy should not be considered as merely an opportunity to bash the media. Within this context, critical analysis can heighten your awareness of media at its best: insightful articles, informative news programs, and uplifting films.

Moreover, an understanding of media literacy principles should not detract from your enjoyment of programs, but rather enhance your appreciation of media content.

7. *In the case of media communicators: the ability to produce effective and responsible media messages.*

In order to be successful, professionals in the field of media must demonstrate an awareness of the mass communication process, as well as a mastery of production techniques and strategies. But in order to truly improve the media industry, media communicators must also be aware of the challenges and responsibilities involved in producing thoughtful programming that serves the best interests of the public.

OBSTACLES TO MEDIA LITERACY

One would think that the development of mass communication would eliminate the traditional barriers to literacy. After all, one must be educated in order to read. On the other hand, all that is required to watch television is a strong thumb to operate the remote control.

However, universal *access* to the media should not be confused with media literacy. Despite the pervasiveness of the channels of mass communication, media illiteracy remains a problem, for several reasons:

Elitism

In a study asking, "To what degree does the media have an effect on society?," 80 percent "Strongly Agreed" that media had an effect on society as a whole. At the same time, however, only 12 percent of these respondents "Strongly Agreed" that media had a personal impact on them.[18]

The implications of this survey are both intriguing and disturbing. Participants in the study apparently had no difficulty seeing the influence of the media on *other* people. However, these same people were unable to recognize the impact of the media on their *own* lives. And the more that people deny personal influence of mass media, the more susceptible they are to media messages.

A follow-up survey found that education was not a significant variable in this wide disparity between perceptions of the effects of media on others and on themselves.[19] People with college degrees were as likely as high school graduates to recognize the impact of the media on others, while at the same time discounting its effects on their own lives. One possible explanation for this finding is that educated people are embarrassed to admit that they watch *Judge Judy* or scan the *National Enquirer* while standing at the check-out counter, like everyone else. As a result, well-educated people (in the traditional sense) may be as susceptible to the influence of media messages as members of the general population.

Consequently, a first step in media literacy requires an admission that you are exposed to numerous messages daily through the media and that these messages can influence your attitudes, values, and behavior.

Affective Nature of Photography, Film, Television, Radio, and Digital Media

Imagine glancing up from this text and gazing out the window. Suddenly, you spot an unattended toddler wandering into the street. Your immediate reaction might include:

- Experiencing a sudden jolt as your nervous system carries this information to your brain.
- Feeling a tightening sensation in your stomach.
- Breaking out in an immediate sweat.
- Struggling to translate these feelings into words and actions to help the child.

In contrast with print, visual and aural stimuli initially touch us on an *affective*, or emotional, level. In his discussion of the impact of the visual image, art historian E. H. Gombrich observes,

> The power of visual impressions to arouse our emotions has been observed since ancient times. . . . Preachers and teachers preceded modern advertisers in the knowledge of the ways in which the visual image can affect us, whether we want it to or not. The succulent fruit, the seductive nude, the repellent caricature, the hair-raising horror can all play on our emotions and engage our attention.[20]

Because of the affective nature of visual and aural media, it may seem more natural (and considerably easier) to simply "experience" a song or film rather than undertake the arduous task of conceptualizing, articulating, and analyzing your emotional responses. Consequently, the level of discourse about media programming is often reduced to emotional responses; in the immortal words of Beavis and Butthead, programs are either "cool" or they "suck."

But while affective responses may initially discourage discussion, they can ultimately serve as a springboard for in-depth analysis and discussion. As a result, one effective strategy for the interpretation of media messages is to ask *why* you reacted as you did while watching a program. (For further discussion, see the section titled "Affective Response" in Chapter 2.)

Audience Behavior Patterns

During the communication process, audience members select the most pertinent bits of information to store and assimilate into meaning. However, audiences are often engaged in competing activities while receiving media messages. Because your primary attention may be focused on other activities (driving while listening to the radio, for instance), you may be susceptible to subtle messages that affect your attitudes and behaviors. Further, if you answer the phone or leave the room for a portion of a telecast, the text of information from which to select has been altered. As a result, you may be receiving an altogether *different* message than was originally intended by the media communicator. (For further discussion, see the discussion of audience in Chapter 2, Process.)

Audience Expectations

In many instances, the function of a media activity, or the purpose for which you decide to engage in it, has nothing to do with the critical analysis of media content. For instance, after a long, stress-filled day at school, you may turn on your television to wind down and put the day's events in perspective. This form of "electronic meditation" signals to others that you are not in the mood for conversation. Furthermore, on these occasions, you do not feel particularly inclined to analyze media content. And the only way to *discover* media messages is to *look* for media messages.

Nature of Programming

The American media system is a market-driven industry predicated on turning a profit. Feature films, popular music, and newspapers must attract and maintain an audience in order to remain in business. To illustrate, broadcast journalists are now pressured to present the news in an entertaining fashion. This trend toward "infotainment" has severely compromised the content of many news programs.

Nevertheless, programs that were never intended to instruct the public convey messages about how the world operates, provide models of acceptable and unacceptable behavior, and reinforce cultural definitions of success and failure.

Credibility of Media

Audiences are often predisposed to believe what appears in the media. One particularly dangerous media message is that information presented on television or in the newspaper must be *true,* simply because it appears in the media. To illustrate, a Times-Mirror Poll found that 50 percent of those who watched crime re-creation TV shows interpreted the footage as news, even though disclaimers appeared at the bottom of the TV screen declaring that the program are dramatic reenactment of a crime.[21]

In its ability to preserve a moment of time in space, photography creates the illusion of *verisimilitude,* or lifelike quality. We must remember, however, that photographs only present a *version* of reality. A photograph captures only a brief instant, without the context that gives it meaning. In addition, the audience's attention is confined to the space within the frame. We only see what the photographer or filmmaker *wants* us to see; we cannot see what is happening outside of the boundary of the camera lens. Further, because digital technology enables a photographer to alter images seamlessly, a photograph may not represent what was originally captured by the camera.

Indeed, the very presence of the media alters the event it is intended to capture. Consider the typical wedding. The photographer does not hesitate to interrupt the proceedings and whisk the newlyweds away from the celebration. Like trained seals, the bride and groom strike the conventional poses: holding the rose, cutting the cake, and standing in formation with assorted relatives. The entire occasion has been transformed into a photo session, to be enjoyed later, when the couple leafs through the photo album.

Within this context, one of the fundamental tenants of media literacy, as identified by Canadian Association for Media Literacy, is that "All media are constructions of reality":

> This is arguably the most important concept. The media do not simply reflect external reality. Rather, they present carefully crafted constructions that reflect many decisions and are the result of many determining factors. Media Literacy works towards deconstructing

these constructions (i.e., to taking them apart to show how they are made).[22]

Media-literate individuals have learned to examine the information presented through the media with a healthy skepticism and determine for themselves whether the content is accurate.

Complexity of the Language of Media

Media audiences generally can identify the sign and symbol system of media. For instance, although the narrative in a film is generally presented in chronological order, the filmmaker often manipulates its time sequence to establish relationships between people, locations, and events. Thus, a flashback is a formulaic narrative technique in which a past event is inserted in the narrative to show the influence of the past on the present.

However, as Mark Crispin Miller observes, audience members often underestimate the "language" of media production: "Most Americans still perceive the media image as transparent, a sign that simply says what it means and means what it says. They therefore tend to dismiss any intensive explication as a case study of reading too much into it."[23]

For example, many children are unable to detect spatial and temporal inferences depicted on screen. Daniel Anderson explains, "[Children's] failure to comprehend cinematic transitions cumulatively gives them a fragmented comprehension of lengthy televised narratives. With age and viewing experience, however, the child more rapidly and automatically makes the bridging inferences necessary to achieve connected comprehension."[24]

Understanding the different "languages" of media has become essential in the world of business. In 2009, the average American consumed approximately 34 gigabytes of data and information each day—an increase of about 350 percent over nearly three decades. At the same time, however, the amount of time that individuals spend reading has actually *declined* (Bilton). Consequently, many companies now place a value on employees who have the ability to interpret, construct, and disseminate messages using the different "languages" of media, such as film, television, audio, and the Internet.

In addition, a familiarity with various production elements (i.e., editing, color, lighting, shot selection) can enhance your understanding and appreciation of media content. (For additional discussion of *production elements,* see Chapter 9, Advertising.)

LEVELS OF MEANING: MANIFEST AND LATENT MESSAGES

Manifest messages are direct and clear to the audience. We generally have little trouble recognizing these messages when we are paying full attention to a media presentation. For instance, have you ever noticed how many commercials *tell* you to do something?

- "Insist on Blue Coal" (Radio broadcast, 1947)
- "American Express: Don't leave home without it"
- "Just Do It" (Nike)

But in addition, media presentations may contain *latent messages.* Latent messages are indirect and beneath the surface, and consequently often escape our immediate attention. Latent messages may reinforce manifest messages, or they may suggest entirely different meanings. For example, "G.I. Joe" commercials promote a line of war toys. But at the same time, the G.I. Joe ad campaign conveys latent messages equating violence with masculinity and glorifying war.

Cumulative Messages

Cumulative messages occur with such frequency over time that they form new meanings, independent of any individual production. Consistent messages with regard to gender roles, racial and cultural stereotypes, and measures of success recur throughout many media presentations. As an example, Dwayne Johnson (aka "The Rock") is a popular action-film hero. However, his macho image, characteristic of countless other media figures, including John Wayne, Sylvester Stallone, and the Marlboro Man, sends an aggregate message about the ideal of masculinity.

Point of View

In any media presentation, the story can be told from a range of perspectives, or *points of view:*

- The media communicator
- The characters in the presentation
- The prevailing point of view of the period in which it was produced
- Your own point of view

Point of view has an impact on: 1) how a story is told; 2) what information is conveyed; and 3) how the audience responds to the information being presented.

Identifying the prevailing point of view in a media presentation enables you to filter the information and come to your own conclusions. As an example, Fox television supports a conservative political agenda, while MSNBC generally presents programming from a progressive point of view. But there is nothing wrong with watching an ideological channel like MSNBC news, so long as you know what it *is* and what it *isn't*. The danger lies in thinking that these ideological channels are presenting objective news. (For further discussion, see Chapter 10, American Political Communications.) The Keys to Interpreting Media Messages provide you with tools to identify the point of view of the program, media communicator, or primary character in the presentation.

Affective Strategies

As mentioned earlier, visual and aural media (photography, film, television, radio, and digital media) are particularly well suited to emotional appeals. Media communicators can influence the attitudes and behavior of audiences by appealing to their emotions. For instance, some advertisers sell products by appealing to primal emotions such as guilt or the need for acceptance.

In addition, production elements such as color, shape, lighting, and size convey meaning by evoking emotional responses in the audience. Thus, media communicators convey meaning through their production choices, involving the use of lighting, music, and connotative words and images.

Embedded Values

Media literacy analysis can furnish perspectives into the values of media communicators by identifying the *preferred reading* of the narrative. Media communicators establish a preferred reading, in which the text dictates the responses of the audience. The preferred reading asks the audience to assume the role, perspective, and orientation of the heroes and heroines, who may be surrogates for the media communicator.

Production elements such as music, lighting, and angle distinguish the heroes from the villains, and consequently direct how the audience is to respond to these characters. In this way, the sympathies of the audience are aligned with his/her values and beliefs.

Word choice can also furnish perspectives into the attitudes of the media communicator toward the subject of the presentation. To illustrate, consider the following headlines for two newspaper stories reporting on a car-bombing incident that took place in Baghdad in 2003, during the war in Iraq:

"Five Consecutive Martyrdom Operations Rock Baghdad"[25]

"Bloodied Baghdad; Four Coordinated Suicide Car Bombings Kill 34, Wound 224"[26]

In the first headline, which appeared in an Egyptian government-owned newspaper, the word "martyrdom" is an indication that the media communicator regarded this action as morally justifiable. In contrast, the term "suicide bombings," which appeared in *Newsday*, a mainstream American publication, reveals that the reporter considered this to be a brutal and senseless attack.

NOTES

1. Berkeley Pop Culture Project, *The Whole Pop Catalog* (Berkeley: Avon Books, 1991), 547.
2. Joe Schwartz, "Is There Life before Bed?" *American Demographics* (March 1990): 12.
3. Ibid.
4. NBC, 1991.
5. Media Reform Info Center, "TV Facts," http://www.enviroweb.org.
6. "No Excuse: We All Have More Free Time Than We Think, Experts Say," *St. Louis Post-Dispatch,* June 6, 1997: A-2.
7. Shelly Freierman, "Drilling Down; We're Spending More Time Watching TV," *New York Times,* January 9, 2006.
8. See Frank Baker, "Media Use Statistics: Resources on Media Habits of Children, Youth and Adults," www.frankwbaker.com/mediause.htm.
9. Ibid.
10. Harper's Index, January 1996, http://www.harpers.org.
11. Presented at the Aspen Institute, "National Leadership Conference on Media Literacy," Queenstown, Maryland, 7-9 December 1992.
12. Frank Absher, "Media on Media," *St. Louis Journalism Review* (October 1999): 3.
13. Bill Moyers, *The Public Mind: Consuming Images,* Public Broadcasting Service, November 8, 1989.

14. Erica Austin and Kristine Johnson, "Effects of General and Alcohol-Specific Media Literacy Training on Children's Decision Making about Alcohol," *Journal of Health Communication* 2 (1997): 17–42.

15. Richard Beltramini and Patrick Bridge, "Relationship between Tobacco Advertising and Youth Smoking: Assessing the Effectiveness of a School-Based, Antismoking Intervention Program," *Journal of Consumer Affairs* 35.2 (Winter 2001): 263–267.

16. Dianne Neumark-Sztainer et al., "Primary Prevention of Disordered Eating among Preadolescent Girls: Feasibility and Short-term Effect of a Community-based Intervention," *Journal of the American Dietetic Association* (December 2000), http://www.findarticles.com/cf_0/m0822/12_100/68739951/p1/article.jhtml?term=neumark-sztainer+%22primary+prevention+of+disordered+eating+among+preadolescent+girls%22 (July 31, 2003).

17. Thomas Robinson et al., "Effects of Reducing Children's Television and Video Game Use on Aggressive Behavior," *Archives of Pediatric Adolescent Medicine* 155.1 (2001): 17–23.

18. James Tiedge, "Public Opinion on Mass Media Effects: Perceived Societal Effects and Perceived Personal Effects," paper presented at Speech Communication Association Convention, Minneapolis, 1980.

19. James Tiedge, Arthur Silverblatt, Michael J. Havice, and Richard Rosenfeld, "The Third-Person Effects Hypothesis: Scope, Magnitude, and Contributing Factors," *Journalism Quarterly* 68 (Spring–Summer 1991): 141–54.

20. E. H. Gombrich, "The Visual Image," in *Media and Symbols: The Forms of Expression, Communication, and Education.* Publication of the National Society for the Study of Education, Vol. 73, Pt. 1, ed. David R. Olson (Chicago: University of Chicago Press, 1974), 244.

21. Thomas B. Rosensteil, "Viewers Found to Confuse TV Entertainment with News," *Los Angeles Times,* August 17, 1989: I-17.

22. "Key Concepts of Media Literacy, the Association for Media Literacy," Ontario Ministry of Education, 1987.

23. David Considine and Gail Haley, *Visual Messages: Integrating Imagery into Instruction* (Englewood, Colorado: Teacher Ideas Press, 1992), 3.

24. Daniel R. Anderson, "Online Cognitive Processing of Television," in *Psychological Processes and Advertising Effects,* ed. Linda F. Alwitt and Andrew A. Mitchell (Hillsdale, NJ: Lawrence Erlbaum Associates, 1985), 191.

25. "Five Consecutive Martyrdom Operations Rock Baghdad," *Al Gumhuria,* October 23, 2003.

26. Mohamad Bazzi, "Bloodied Baghdad; Four Coordinated Suicide Car Bombings Kill 34, Wound 224," *Newsday,* October 23, 2003.

PART 2

KEYS TO INTERPRETING MEDIA MESSAGES

The Keys to Interpreting Media Messages provide a theoretical framework for the systematic analysis of *media messages* (that is, the underlying themes or ideas contained in a media presentation).

Think of these keys as a series of lenses. Each lens will provide you with fresh insights into media-carried content. Depending on the specific focus of study, one key may be more useful than others. Obviously, certain production elements would not be relevant to an analysis of newspapers. Use only those keys that will be most applicable to the particular media format.

But in all cases, what determines the validity of the interpretation is the following: 1) the analysis must be systematically applied, and 2) the analysis must be supported with concrete examples from the *media presentation* (i.e., films, television episodes, newspaper articles, video games, or advertisements).

2

Process

OVERVIEW: ELEMENTS OF COMMUNICATION

In order to become media literate, you must first develop an understanding of the communication process.

Communication is an active, dynamic experience that demands your fullest attention and energy. The moment that someone approaches you and initiates a conversation, you become engaged in a rapid sequence of activities:

- Receiving a message
- Selecting relevant information
- Forming appropriate responses
- Responding to the message

Immediately after you have formed an appropriate response, the roles are reversed: you shift from audience to communicator, and vice versa.

In order for people to communicate effectively, a relationship of mutual trust and respect must be established. The communicator and audience formulate a communication contract that governs their conduct. Both parties agree to abide by the rules. For instance, the participants implicitly agree to maintain a comfortable distance from one another during conversations (neither too close nor too distant). There is also an unwritten understanding that one person should not dominate the conversation. Any violation of these agreements results in an instant breakdown of the social contract. For example, if you feel that the person with whom you are conversing isn't really listening to you or doesn't respect what you have to say, then the conversation is doomed.

There are *three* primary types of communication:

1. *Intrapersonal communication* takes place within ourselves. It is the basis of all forms of communication, because until we know what it is that we want to say, we will not be able to communicate effectively with other people.
2. *Interpersonal communication* is based upon face-to-face interaction with another person.
3. *Mass communication* is that in which messages are communicated through a channel of communication (e.g., radio or television) to a large group of people who may not be in direct contact with the communicator.

The Communications Model

The basic *communications model* consists of the following elements:

- The *communicator* is the person who delivers the message.
- The *message* is the information being communicated.
- The *channel* refers to the passage through which the information is being conveyed. For example, your voice, eyes, and facial expressions are the channels employed in interpersonal communication. In mass communication, the media—newspapers, photographs, film, radio, television, and the Internet—serve as the channels of information to large groups of people who are separated in time and/or space from the media communicator.
- The *audience* consists of the person or people who receive the message.

Communication Elements: Feedback and Interference

Two elements are critical to the communications process: *feedback* and *interference.*

Feedback offers audience members the opportunity to ask questions or comment, in order to better understand what the communicator is trying to say. Feedback can also be used to reassure the communicator. When listeners nod their heads, smile, or repeat key phrases, they are letting the communicator know they are alert, interested, and involved in the conversation.

Interference refers to those factors that can hinder the communications process. Interference can occur at all points of the communications model:

- *Communicator interference* arises when the communicator obstructs the message. As an example, people may have difficulty expressing themselves clearly at times. Communicator interference can also occur when the communicator does not know exactly what he/she wants to say. In this instance, the communicator might ramble on until the listener eventually loses interest. Communicator interference also takes place if the communicator is not *self-aware*. For instance, you may be angry with a friend but are unwilling to admit it—even to yourself. As a result, you may be sending mixed messages—denying that you are angry at the same time that your behavior is contentious and abrupt.

- *Channel interference* occurs when a glitch in the channel distorts the message. For example, if you have laryngitis, your audience may be unable to understand your speech. In mass communications, channel interference occurs when your television screen suddenly goes blank, or your computer freezes while you are on the Internet.

  Channel interference may also result from using an *inappropriate* channel to send a particular type of message. As we will discuss later in the chapter (see "Comparative Media"), a particular medium may not be the most effective channel to convey specific types of information. For instance, corporations may spend enormous amounts of money on promotional videos, when the detailed information they are trying to convey would be more suitable in print.

- *Environmental interference* refers to distractions within the setting in which the information is received. For example, we have all attended movies in which people behind us have talked throughout the picture, or have had our view blocked by a tall person seated in front of us.

- *Audience interference* occurs when audience members obstruct the communication process. For example, *attention span* may be a factor in audience interference. As mentioned earlier, communication is an active process that demands concentration and energy. Occasionally we'll just take a break and tune out the speaker. This option is particularly tempting when we are presented with information outside of our personal frames of reference. Healthy teenagers and adults can sustain attention for about 20 minutes. At the same time, focused attention—the kind that is the result of a distraction, whether it be a ringing telephone or a television commercial—typically only lasts about eight *seconds*.[1]

  Finally, audience members often filter messages through their *egos*. That is, they only hear those aspects of a conversation that pertain to them, ignoring the rest of the message. Audience members are not always paying strict attention while the other person is speaking. Instead, they are busily formulating their responses or are anxiously awaiting their chance to talk.

Psychological Principles: Comprehension of Information

The following psychological principles explain ways in which members of the audience process information:

- *Selective exposure* refers to how an individual's personal values and interests affect his/her selection of information. People often seek out information with which they agree while avoiding information that does not fit their preexisting views. Reporter Franco Ordonez provides the following example:
  - The television remote control has become a de facto ballot in today's hyper-polarized world of politics. Turn the dial to the left to watch MSNBC and it's more likely you lean left. Turn it to the right to tune in Fox, and it's more likely you lean right. Which cable news channel people watch has become a bona fide indicator of what they think about taxes, health care, immigration and the size and scope of the federal government. . . .
  - Take the big debate this year over the role of the federal spending in the economy. Just 19 percent of Fox viewers think that increasing government spending would help the economy, while 79 percent think increasing the debt in the process would hurt the economy. MSNBC viewers lean the other way, with 55 percent saying more spending would help and 43 percent saying the debt would hurt the economy.[2]
- *Selective perception* is the phenomenon in which people's interpretation of content is colored by their predispositions and preconceptions. To illustrate:
  - Individuals who consume alcohol are more likely to remember seeing anti-drunk-driving PSAs and moderation ads than individuals who don't drink.
  - Those who do not consume alcohol are *less* likely to remember seeing anti-drunk-driving PSAs and moderation ads.
  - Those who smoke will be more likely to remember seeing anti-smoking messages than non-smokers.

○ Individuals who do not smoke will be *less* likely to remember seeing antismoking messages.[3]

Taken further, individuals may reject information that conflicts with their preconceived ideas. This would account for charges of bias against the media from both ends of the political spectrum. Conservatives rail against the "liberal media," while progressives decry the "conservative press." As a result, media messages must be modified in order to be equally effective with different segments of the population.

- *Selective retention* occurs when a person selectively remembers (or forgets) information. People tend to tune out conversations when they are exposed to subject matter in which their interest level is low. For instance, if you decide to talk about a subject I know nothing about (e.g., nuclear physics), I will focus my attention elsewhere, where I am more comfortable. An individual's recall of information may be influenced by a number of other factors as well: whether the person was distracted at the time, a sense of nostalgia (reconstructing past events so that they appear more positive), or the impulse to minimize unpleasant thoughts or experiences.
- *Cultural insulation* is one of the unintended consequences of the evolution of digital media; people are becoming immersed in a few selected areas of personal interest, remaining completely uninformed and disinterested in other cultural spheres. That is, individuals now know more and more about less and less. For example, if you are only interested in country music, you are never in a position to be exposed to hip-hop. As a result, audience members are not introduced to perspectives of other groups.

  Cultural insulation can undermine the very foundation of culture, which is built on common understandings, experiences, and values. To illustrate, James O'Neill, a professor at South Puget Sound Community College, gave his class a cultural indicators test to determine his students' general knowledge of American culture. O'Neill found that his students no longer have a shared cultural heritage, simply answering "I don't know" up to 86 times in a test containing 100 questions.

  An essential aspect of media literacy involves looking beyond the materials that have been directed at your particular demographic group in order to get a broader perspective. For instance, it can be worthwhile to watch MSNBC for a liberal ideology, while Fox News provides a conservative perspective on events.

DIFFERENCES BETWEEN INTERPERSONAL AND MASS COMMUNICATION

While the principles discussed above apply to all forms of communication, some significant differences exist between interpersonal and mass communication.

Mass Communications Model

When Marshall McLuhan declared, "The medium is the message," he was suggesting that the media have reconfigured the traditional communications model. The channels of mass communications have now assumed a primary role in determining content, choice of communicator, and the audience (see Table 2.1).

To illustrate, the medium of television dictates the choice of *communicator* in news programming. Anchorpersons must be likable, convincing, and attractive. To that end, the Fox News network keeps stylists on staff whose task is to make its anchors and reporters more appealing to a young audience.[4] In the process, journalistic ability has become subordinate to performance skills.

The characteristics of a medium also affect the content—or *messages*—in news presentations. Print journalism lends itself to the detailed presentation of complex issues. Consequently, newspaper coverage of a story tends to be issues oriented, providing detailed context and background.

In contrast, television is less successful in its ability to present the context, interpretation, and implications of these incidents. However, because of the visual properties of television, television news is an ideal medium for showing events in the process of unfolding. Thus, in order to take advantage of the visual capabilities of the medium, television news generally emphasizes *events* rather than *issues*.

Table 2.1   Mass Communications Model

Communications Model	Mass Communications Model
Communicator	Channel
Message	Communicator
Channel	Message
Audience	Audience

In addition, TV news is influenced by the entertainment sensibility of television. News producers tend to select stories that are dramatic and sensational, and have an identifiable cast of characters and a clear narrative structure (with a beginning, middle, and conclusion).

Finally, the choice of medium has a significant impact on the *audience*. To illustrate, in 2011, 66 percent of Americans designated television as their primary source of news. However, people under 30 cite the Internet as their primary news source, while newspapers are the choice of people 65 and older.[5]

Feedback in Mass Communications

The advent of digital media technology has resulted in more direct lines of feedback than had previously been the case in media communications.

Before the age of digital media technology, media communicators had no immediate way of knowing whether the audience was truly involved in the communication process. Much of the feedback in the mass communication process was delayed (e.g., letters to the editor, petitions, or phone calls), indirect (e.g., revenue from sales or critical responses, such as the Oscars) or cumulative (reflecting a collective opinion). But although ratings systems like the Nielsen system present numerical information about how many people watch a particular program, these ratings cannot measure whether the audience actually *enjoy* the program.

However, the interactive feature of digital media gives audience members the opportunity to respond immediately to media programming. Indeed, programs like *American Idol* incorporate audience response into the presentation, as viewers vote for their favorite performers.

Saturation of the Mass Media

In interpersonal communications, the speaker enjoys direct, personal access to the audience; however, the size of this audience is limited. In contrast, a media communicator can reach a vast audience simultaneously with a uniform message. For example, after the signing of the Treaty of Ghent, which officially ended the War of 1812, it took nearly two months for the news to reach America. In contrast, when the Japanese earthquake/tsunami occurred in March 2011, Al Jazeera and NHK from Japan provided a live feed of the event as it happened.

But although mass communications is unrivaled at providing a *breadth* of information, there are limits to the *depth* of information it can furnish.

Clearly, some media are more limited than others. But whether it is a two-minute news report or a two-hour documentary, media presentations operate within strict time frames that may or may not meet the informational requirements of the subject.

Ability to Preserve a Message

In interpersonal communication, information is exchanged on an informal basis. Consequently, we may forget precisely what we said. Or we may choose to reinterpret the conversation on the basis of what we *meant* to say—particularly if we said something silly or embarrassing.

In contrast, media presentations (e.g., newspapers, DVDs, CDs) are characterized by a degree of permanence, so that they can be scrutinized and re-examined by the audience. As a result, mass communicators are highly accountable for the material that they produce and must be prepared to accept responsibility for their work.

Media as Collaborative Process

Unlike interpersonal communications, the production of a newspaper, news broadcast, or ad campaign often requires a production team. For example, a Hollywood film project comprises the following crew members:

- The *producer* is responsible for the business arrangements (e.g., financing, business planning, insurance, contracts, and personnel).
- The *scriptwriter* develops the screenplay. He/she may be solely responsible for the original treatment, or be part of a team. In addition, additional writers may be brought in to revise a script that has been obtained by a producer or studio.
- The *director* is the film's principal creative authority, responsible for the presentation of the script on screen.
- *First and second assistant directors* assist with cast and crew management, crowd control, and coordination of the schedule.
- The *continuity* department is charged with making sure that the props, clothing, and makeup remain consistent. This can be a difficult task, given that scenes are often filmed out of sequence.
- The *cast* includes the stars, supporting players, bit players, and uncredited extras. Additional cast members consist of stunt doubles, who perform dangerous shots, and stand-ins, who work with the crew to set up the proper camera positions and lighting for the performers.

- The *cinematographer* is responsible for the artistic and technical quality of the film, including lighting, framing, and color values.
- The *production designer,* or art director, is responsible for set design.
- The *editor* assembles, arranges, and selects the footage, often in concert with the director.

Other crew members include a gaffer (chief electrician), best boy (gaffer's assistant), grips (who haul heavy lights), costume designer, music director, sound editors, and the publicity team.

Because members of the crew may hold different opinions about content and approach, compromise is a large part of the decision-making process. As a result, the final presentation may be disjointed and confusing.

However, one of the major changes in the evolution of digital media production is that in many productions, one person can shoot and edit video, produce animation, and incorporate graphics into the production.

Media as Industry

Most media programming is extremely expensive to produce. For instance, the cost of making the blockbuster film *Titanic* (1997) exceeded $200 million —more than the cost of building the actual ocean liner.

As a result, many producers are reluctant to take artistic risks, relying instead on "bankable" stars and genres. Instead of challenging the audience artistically, major studios tend to bankroll films that rely on violence, sex, and flashy music. In addition, sequels, comic-book adaptations, and franchise films cater to a well-established audience and provide studios with less risk. Indeed, 14 of the top 20 domestic-grossing films of all time were assured of a built-in audience by employing this strategy.

However, individuals now have access to sophisticated media technology on their laptops that, not long ago, was available only in professional studios. This equipment can cut down on production costs and give individuals more room to experiment with form and content.

The first key to interpreting media messages—*process*—consists of the following elements:

- **Media communicator**
- **Function**
- **Comparative Media**
- **Affective Response**
- **Audience**

MEDIA COMMUNICATOR

Identifying the Media Communicator

It can be very difficult for the audience to determine the identity of the media communicator. In interpersonal communications, the communicator and audience are in direct and immediate contact. In contrast, in mass communications, the media communicator is separated both in time and space from the audience, and therefore is largely unknown to the audience. An old movie that you watch on television may have been produced 40 years ago, by someone you never met, who lived in another part of the world.

Although we generally assume that the person in front of the camera or microphone is the person who is responsible for what is being said, this performer or model is very often instructed on what to say by someone who is unseen by the audience. Indeed, these on-camera performers are rather like ventriloquist dummies—simply mouthing the words penned by a team of scriptwriters. Consequently, identifying the background and worldview of this invisible media communicator can furnish valuable perspective into the content and outlook of the media production.

The media communicators (i.e., the people who appear on-screen) generally embody the characteristics of their audience. As Bill Shine, the executive vice president for programming at Fox News, explains, "We reflect who the audience is. Our audience knows us, and we know them."[6]

One of the major challenges facing these media communicators is producing programming for an audience with a different background and mindset. To illustrate, the *Dork Diaries* is a popular book targeting a "tween" audience between the ages of 9 and 12. Reporter Leslie Kaufman provides the following description:

> The *Dork Diaries* are the journals of the socially aspiring, fashion-impaired Westchester Country Day School student Nikki Maxwell. Each volume chronicles one month of the major crises in Nikki's eighth-grade life, like a lack of invitations to cool parties, her crush on Brandon and her tangles with the school snob MacKenzie Hollister— or as Nikki calls her, that "KILLER SHARK" in "sparkly nail polish." Nikki lays it all out with humor, lots of embedded illustrations and plenty of CAPITALIZATION and exclamation points!!!!![7]

Surprisingly, the author of the books is Rachel Renée Russell, a divorced former bankruptcy lawyer with two daughters who are in their twenties. Moreover, although Russell is African American, the heroine of the series

(Nikki) is white. At 53 years of age, Russell is many years removed from her own tween years. However, she relies on her memories to "channel" her "Inner-Dork": "I never had a date through high school, and my father had to pay a family friend $50 and loan him the Cadillac to get me a date for the prom," she said with a laugh.[8]

Identifying the backgrounds of media communicators can also provide insight into the possible *motives* behind their contributions to a media presentation. To illustrate, the following polls and studies that appeared in newspapers and magazines were sponsored by groups that had a vested interest in their results:

- Americans believe the best learning and information source today is the Internet. (Sponsored by Internet provider Prodigy.)
- The majority of Americans polled plan to travel during the holidays. (Sponsored by online travel service Expedia.com.)
- More Americans are afraid of getting sick from germs in a public restroom than in any other place. (Sponsored by Kimberly-Clark, makers of tissues, towels, and soaps used in public restrooms.)
- More than half of all Americans say their legs ache several days a week. (Sponsored by Futuro, makers of support hose.)
- More than 75 percent of American women want more choices in birth control. (Sponsored by Ortho-McNeil, makers of prescriptive birth control.)
- Two out of three doctors who offer nutritional advice to their patients recommend that said patients eat more yogurt. (Sponsored by the Dannon Yogurt Company.)[9]

Although the surveys may indeed be accurate, discovering the motives of these media communicators, at minimum, calls their findings into question.

The Architects

Identifying the media communicator often extends beyond recognizable Hollywood stars and directors to individuals who arrange for producing and distributing media presentations.

To illustrate, the *Hollywood Reporter's* 2012 list of "The Most Powerful People in Hollywood" included some recognizable names, to be sure: Anderson Cooper, Bob Costas, Stephen Colbert, Sean Hannity, and Rachel Maddow.

However, a surprising number of names on this list may be unfamiliar:

- Jeff Fager, CEO, CBS News
- Steve Capus, President, NBC News
- Jim Bell, Executive Producer, NBC's *Today Show* and 2012 London Olympics
- James Goldston, Senior VP Content and Development, ABC News[10]

This list, which is admittedly subjective, includes executives from behind-the-scenes occupations such as agents, accountants, and investors. These executives determine not only *what* appears in the media but *who* appears as well.

To illustrate, Media Rights Capital (MRC) is a powerful Hollywood talent agency that has been financing and producing films and television programs since 2006, founded by Mordecai Wiczyk, Ariel Emanuel, Patrick Whitesell, and Asif Satchu. For example, in 2011, MRC made a "rent-a-studio" arrangement with Universal, in which the film studio agreed to distribute 20 MRC pictures over five years. In addition, Media Rights Capital was also responsible for programming the CW's Sunday-night lineup during the 2008–2009 season through a time-leasing arrangement. Without an agency like Media Rights Capital, many writers, actors, and musicians would labor in complete anonymity.

In addition, identifying the media communicator often extends beyond individuals to the owners who are responsible for the production and distribution of media presentations. (For more discussion of ownership patterns, see Chapter 5, Structure, and Chapter 8, Journalism.)

Table 2.2 Media Literacy Tips: Media Communicator

The following questions are useful in considering the role of the media communicator:

CHECK MARK Who is responsible for creating the media production?

CHECK MARK What are the demographic characteristics of the media communicator(s)?

- Age
- Income
- Race/Ethnicity
- Gender

CHECK MARK How do these characteristics affect the content and outlook of the media production?

POINT OF VIEW

A media presentation can provide insight into the point of view of the media communicator.

Point of View in Print

Writers can present information from a range of perspectives:

- The *first-person* point of view presents the action as interpreted by one character. To illustrate, Herman Melville's classic American novel *Moby Dick* begins, "Call me Ishmael." The reader's understanding of this epic whale hunt is colored by the outlook of Ishmael, an obscure member of the crew.
- The *second-person* point of view makes the reader the primary participant in the story. This perspective makes use of the pronoun "you."
- The *third-person* point of view describes the activities and internal processes of one character. In the third person point of view, which commonly employs the pronouns "he," "she," or "they," the author is privy to the thoughts and activities of this character but retains some critical distance and is therefore not accountable for the behavior for the character.
- The *omniscient,* or all-knowing, point of view enables the author to enter the heads of any and all of the characters, so that the reader has a comprehensive exposure to the people and events depicted in the work. This point of view is used frequently in journalism, which creates the appearance of objectivity in news coverage.

While writers generally try to maintain a consistent perspective, they may occasionally adopt a *panoramic* point of view, in which the perspective is constantly shifting. For instance, during the climactic whale-hunting scene of *Moby Dick,* the novel suddenly shifts to an omniscient narrator. The audience somehow overhears Captain Ahab's dialogue, even though Ishmael is stationed in a different boat. Journalists may also adopt this panoramic point of view by incorporating their own (first-person) perspective into the "objective," third-person account through production techniques such as connotative words and images, space, and editing decisions.

Point of View in Film and Television

In video and film, the point of view of the camera determines what the audience sees on screen. A shift in camera proximity (i.e., close-ups or

POINT OF VIEW—*The Lady in the Lake*

In *The Lady in the Lake* (1947), a battered Philip Marlowe (Robert Montgomery) checks his wounds in the mirror with Audrey Totter (Adrienna Fronsett). In this experiment in subjective camera techniques, the camera assumes the perspective of Marlowe. This fleeting image in the mirror provides the only opportunity in the film for the audience to see Marlowe.

wide-angle shots) provides the audience with a new way to think about the subject.

Film and television can *approximate* the first-person perspective through use of the *extreme close-up* camera shot (XCU). Gifted actors can express their innermost thoughts and emotions to the audience through subtle facial reactions such as a lifted eyebrow or wry smile.

In addition, filmmakers and videographers can create a *literal* first-person point of view by employing a *subjective camera technique.* For instance, in *The Lady in the Lake* (1947), the camera assumed the perspective of the protagonist, Philip Marlowe (Robert Montgomery), so that the audience saw the world through the eyes of the main character. The only time that Marlowe appears in front of the camera occurs when he passes in front of a mirror, and his reflection is caught by the camera. This first-person perspective was effective—for a brief period. However, without a focal character to watch, the film was disorienting. For example, the fight scene degenerated into a burlesque in which the camera spun around (as "Marlowe" was hit). The effect was to make the audience dizzy.

Obviously, the second person ("you") perspective is nearly impossible to achieve in television and film, unless you actually appear on screen. However, TV and filmmakers can simulate the second-person perspective by selecting performers who are supposed to represent you. The "man in the street" approach in advertising casts normal, everyday people to embody your concerns and interests. In addition, audience participation programs encourage people (like you) to express their concerns.

The *medium shot* (MS) is analogous to the third-person perspective in print, in that it simply records the actions and interactions of characters. This shot frequently takes in several actors in the frame. A third-person perspective can also be attained by shooting over the shoulder of one participant and then the other. Herbert Zettl explains,

Are we now using the camera subjectively, with the viewer alternately associating with the person not seen on the screen? Not really. Even if the person on the screen (A) speaks directly to the camera, we know from the context that person A's target is not us, the viewers, but person B. . . . We are not in any way involved in the exchange . . . and are, therefore, not enticed to participate in the event or to assume person B's role.[11]

Film and television employ several different production techniques to simulate the omniscient perspective employed in print. The *extreme long shot* (XLS) is frequently employed at the beginning of a scene to provide the visual context for the subsequent action. This shot takes in a wide expanse of visual information. The viewer can see a great deal within the frame and thus has a measure of control in terms of what to watch. In addition, the director can use the *omniscient* camera, which moves freely in time and space. This technique enables the director to focus on characters in different settings (unbeknown to the other characters).

In addition, "ultra-tram" technology enables viewers to see the world in entirely new ways. For instance, in televised golf matches, lipstick cameras placed near the ball give the audience an unfettered look at a Tiger Woods tee shot. Moreover, super slow motion provides intimate examination of shots. And "under the hoop" floor cams now enable the fans of TV poker to peek at the hands of all of the players.

Television news also employs an omniscient point of view. Media technology enables the television news industry to transmit reports instantaneously from around the globe. This omniscient perspective contributes to the impression that the broadcast journalist is all knowing, and that the information contained in the broadcasts is unimpeachable.

Another way to identify the point of view is to examine the *preferred reading* of the video or film presentation. The media communicator establishes a preferred reading, in which production elements establish cues and clues that dictate how the audience responds to the events and characters in the narrative. To illustrate, the music that accompanies the appearance of the hero is often warm and stirring, while the music associated with villains is often discordant and abrasive. Likewise, the choice of costume colors is different for protagonists and villains. In this way, audience members are encouraged to assume the point of view of the preferred reading.

Of course, audience members may choose to negotiate their own meaning, based upon their own experiences. But this perspective would be a departure from the preferred reading of the narrative. (For further discussion of audience interpretation, see the discussion of "Audience" later in this chapter.)

The simplest way to determine the point of view in a film or television program is to ask: *Whose story is this?* In the romance genre, the main character generally is facing the camera when the couple embrace. The main character is the one receiving the attention from the other character, and the audience vicariously assumes the position of the subordinate character.

FUNCTION

A simple communication activity may be motivated by many purposes, or *functions.*

Media communicators have a clear understanding of the purpose(s) behind their presentations.

Examples of functions include:

- *Expression* occurs when speakers inform the listener of their frame of mind—what they are thinking at that moment, how they are feeling, or their attitudes toward people and issues. As E. H. Gombrich observes, "A speaker can inform his partner of a state of affairs past, present or future, observable or distant, actual or conditional."[12]
- *Description* can involve elaboration on general statements, providing concrete examples and details.
- *Instruction* refers to occasions in which the purpose is either 1) to inform others about a subject with which they are unfamiliar, or 2) to furnish *additional* information about a subject with which the audience is already acquainted. Examples include giving directions to the airport or watching the evening news on television.
- *Information exchange* refers to occasions in which all parties benefit by sharing knowledge.
- *Persuasion* is a function in which the communicator's objective is to promote a particular idea or motivate the audience to change specific behaviors or attitudes. The ultimate purpose of persuasion is *control.* Advertising attempts to persuade you to think positively about a product and, ultimately, to purchase the advertiser's brand.
- *Humor* is a social mechanism that brings people together. Jokes, stories, and gossip divert people's attention from the pressing matters of the day. Sharing laughter is also a time-honored way to break

down social barriers. Accomplished public speakers often begin with an amusing anecdote that makes the audience feel comfortable. And in political communications, humor is an effective strategy to attack a person or undermine an opponent's position.

- *Creative expression* is used by novelists, painters, and experimental videographers, who express themselves through their art and share their artistic vision with the audience. Thanks to digital technology, independent artists and nonprofessionals have the means to produce, edit, and distribute their works of art.

- *Exploration* may occur when a communicator is not clear what he/she wants to say. Stalling techniques (like interspersing "uh" and "you know" between words) gives the speaker a bit of space to figure out where he/she is going next. However, we still say things that we wish we could take back.

Mass communicators typically present polished information that has been prepared in advance. However, with many hours to fill and a limited amount of programming, media communicators are frequently forced to ad lib. Reporters remain talking on-air even when there is nothing new to report. Max Frankel observes that this reliance on "oral media" has altered the level of discourse in the media:

> In the oral media, thoughts fly from the top of the head, causing even smart people to sound ignorant. The camera permits no pauses, even for feigned reflection. To escape the gaps in their knowledge, television ad-libbers seek safety in mere opinion, speculation, and prophecy, which can be contradicted but not easily proved false.[13]

- *Ritual,* as it pertains to communication, is a verbal or written exchange that has an underlying social significance. As an example, international students often express bewilderment over Americans' habit of greeting people with, "How are you?" and then moving on without waiting for a reply. However, what the students have mistaken for superficiality is actually a cultural ritual, in which people are making a formal connection with one another. "Small talk" is a similar ritual intended to make social situations more comfortable.

- A surprising amount of our communication is devoted to performance. Think about the dynamics that occur in singles bars. Although the manifest function of a speaker may be informational (e.g., "What's your major?"), the latent function is to impress the other person.

This function also carries over into the world of mass media. Production elements reinforce the themes, mood, or messages of the media presentation. All too often, however, media communicators include dazzling special effects and elaborate camera movements to impress the audience with their expertise.

- *Emotional catharsis* includes spontaneous expressions of love, passion, anger, pain, happiness, or the release of tension. These expressions may not be coherent or planned—what did you say the last time that someone dented the fender of your car? —but your outburst can be quite effective.

  Media figures—whether they are interviewers or interviewees— are trained to control these revealing outbursts. However, when people are under constant media scrutiny, restraint is not always possible. These moments provide brief but candid glimpses behind the images that are so carefully cultivated for public view.

- *Disengagement* occurs when you withdraw from communication. At times, your objective may be to *discourage* extended conversation. Perhaps you are in a hurry but find yourself in an awkward or tedious conversation. In this instance, you might adopt strategies designed to terminate discussion—by responding in monosyllabic answers or furnishing verbal cues intended to accelerate the conversation (e.g., "And then. . . ?")

- *Profit* is a major consideration in the construction of media presentations because the American media system is a market-driven system. At times, profit is a manifest function, but even when profit is not a manifest function, it is very likely to be a latent function.

  Because the principal function of most children's programming is to entertain, young audience members may be unaware that its underlying purpose (i.e., latent function) is to generate product sales. Media lawyer Chris Kelleher points out that children's programs on public television also has a latent profit function:

> Once a show gets some traction to it, then they negotiate with toy manufacturers to make and distribute the characters. One of the biggest offenders in the "tie in" department is PBS, with Barney, Teletubbies and Arthur. Although PBS's roots are in "educational TV," these characters have generated millions in sales for the toy companies through never ending exposure on "non commercial" TV. PBS then gets a cut of the profits.[14]

Latent Functions

Latent function refers to instances in which the media communicator's intentions are not immediately obvious to the audience. For instance, we have all been involved in an information exchange in which it eventually becomes clear that the other person is not really interested in our opinions but instead is intent on converting us to his/her point of view. In this case, the latent function is *persuasion.*

In the digital landscape, it is often difficult to ascertain whether there is a latent function behind a particular communication. Journalist Nick Bilton provides the following example:

> Today, when celebrities and people with large followings on social networks promote a product or service, it's often impossible to know if it's an authentic plug or if they were paid to say nice things about it.
>
> Take Miley Cyrus, the 20-year-old pop star who was traveling around America last week promoting her new album. One morning she posted on Twitter: "Thanks @blackjet for the flight to Silicon Valley!" The details of the arrangement between BlackJet, a Silicon Valley start-up that arranges for private jet travel, and Ms. Cyrus are unclear. But Dean Rotchin, chief executive of BlackJet, said "she was given some consideration for her tweet." Ms. Cyrus did not respond to a request for comment.[15]

It is astounding to discover how frequently the manifest function is irrelevant—or at least, subordinate—to other, latent purposes, like impressing the audience or making a profit. As an example, *America's Army* is a popular online video game produced by the Army, in which players interact during the training stages of the game and watch videos about those soldiers' experiences in the real Army. But in addition to its entertainment function, the game doubles as a recruiting tool for the United States Army. Chris Chambers, the deputy director of the Army Game Project explains, "We are out there meeting young people on the Internet and introducing them to the Army. [The Web site pages, action figures and virtual characters] put a real face on what has been a generic story about the Army."[16]

And alarmingly, another latent function of this video game is the promotion of assault weapons. Indeed, popular video games such as the *Call of Duty* franchise belong to a genre that First Lieutenant John Selbert refers to as "gun porn."[17] For instance, the most recent entry in the *Call of Duty* franchise, Black Ops II, featured weapons made by Barrett and Browning.

Ryan Smith, who contributes to the Gameological Society, an online gaming magazine, declares, "It (is) almost like a virtual showroom for guns."[18]

Often, the manifest function is designed to *divert* the audience's attention away from the principal latent purpose behind a message. According to author Stuart Ewan, these latent commercial functions ultimately undermine the meaning initially ascribed to "sacred" images such as elected officials and the American flag: "All people make images sacred as a way of commenting on their world and ascribing meaning to culture. Now this has been transformed into merchandise—the general meaning is lost."[19]

At times, the latent function can be very subtle, escaping the attention of the young audience. To illustrate, Miranda Cosgrove, the star of the popular Nickelodeon program *iCarly,* was a featured "presenter" at the 2010 MTV Video Music Awards. The manifest function behind Ms. Cosgrove's appearance was her celebrity status, which added to the luster of the event. But at the same time, the latent function behind her presence was to introduce her to the MTV audience, which is generally older than fans of Nickelodeon (Nickelodeon, MTV, and Ms. Cosgrove's music label are all owned by Viacom International).

Multiple Functions

Multiple functions occur when a communications exchange serves more than one function at a time. Although multiple functions are often harmonious, at times the functions may work at cross purposes. For instance, shows that feature political satire like *The Daily Show* and *Bill Maher* encompass two functions simultaneously—to entertain and inform. However, efforts to accomplish both purposes can backfire, meaning that the program is not funny, while the content has been misrepresented to get a laugh.

Undefined Functions

The absence of a clearly defined function can result in a muddled, directionless presentation. For instance, we have all attended movies in which it seems the director could not make up his/her mind whether the film should be a comedy or tragedy. And as a result, it is neither.

COMPARATIVE MEDIA

Each medium is defined by a set of distinctive characteristics that make it uniquely well suited to present certain types of information. For instance, radio obviously cannot employ visuals in transmitting information. However, the radio producer can appeal to the listeners' imaginations through creative use of words and sound effects.

Consequently, one of the principles of media literacy involves the value of a *balanced media diet,* in which the audience uses media in combination to take advantage of the distinctive attributes of each medium. As discussed earlier, the stories selected for broadcast news are unparalleled at showing events as they unfold. In contrast, print stories contain essential detail and context. Consequently, using *both* media provides the audience with a comprehensive understanding of the news story.

In addition, a medium may lend itself to certain learning styles. For instance, dyslexia is a condition that impairs the brain's ability to process symbols. Consequently, dyslexic individuals, who struggle with written communication, often gravitate toward visual communications, such as photography and video.

The following considerations can be helpful in assessing the characteristics of a medium:

The *senses* involved in receiving information affect people's ability to assimilate certain kinds of information, as well as the ways in which they respond to the content.

- The *pace* of the presentation, which refers to the rhythm or rate at which information should be assimilated.
- The *environment* in which the medium is presented. The physical surroundings affect how an individual comprehends and responds to a media presentation.
- *Dissemination patterns* refer to 1) the amount of time it takes for information to be conveyed through a particular medium, and 2) the route that it takes to get to the public.

Print

Print is a tangible medium. Books are bound, collected, and passed from generation to generation. Although the primary sense used in reading is sight, readers also employ the sense of touch; you can hold printed material in your hands, smell the paper, and, in the case of newspapers, feel newsprint rubbing off on your hands. Printed material can be re-read and examined in depth. In addition, authors' names generally appear in their published work, so that they are responsible for the accuracy of their statements.

Print is a portable medium. You can take your book with you anywhere—the library, in the park, or on the subway. The major factor in location is adequate lighting.

To all outward appearances, you may be simply lounging about with a book in your hands at this moment. However, reading is a physical activity that demands an intense level of concentration and energy.

Reading is generally a primary experience. Unless you are reading a story aloud to a small child, you tend to read silently, by yourself. Reading requires relative solitude. Try reading this textbook while engaged in other activities (driving or talking on the phone, for instance). Then see if you can clearly summarize the major points in the chapter. One activity or the other will surely suffer.

Print lends itself to the detailed presentation of information and discussion of complex issues. Print also enables the author to describe internal states of consciousness: not merely what people are *doing* but what they are *thinking* as well. For instance, Henry James's novel *Portrait of a Lady* examines the interior life of the heroine, Isabelle Archer, and the principal inhabitants of her world. The following passage, detailing a chance meeting between Isabelle's husband Osmond and the nefarious Madame Merle, offers James the opportunity to discuss the subtext behind this simple, everyday encounter:

In the manner and tone of these two persons, on first meeting at any juncture, and especially when they met in the presence of others, was something indirect and circumspect, as if they had approached each other obliquely and addressed each other by implication. The effect of each appeared to be to intensify to an appreciable degree the self-consciousness of the other. Madame Merle of course carried off any embarrassment better than her friend; but even Madame Merle had not on this occasion the form she would have liked to have—the perfect self-possession she would have wished to wear for her host. The point to be made is, however, that at a certain moment the element between them, whatever it was, always leveled itself and left them more closely face to face than either ever was with anyone else. This was what had happened now. They stood there knowing each other well and each on the whole willing to accept the satisfaction of knowing as a compensation for the inconvenience—whatever it might be—of being known.[20]

In print, the author clearly establishes the pace in which the material is received. The density of information and sentence structure determines the optimum reading rate. As you doubtless noticed, Henry James's novels demand careful attention. James's style is characterized by long, complex narrative prose with frequent interpolations. On the other hand, the spare writing style and colorful graphics of *USA Today* enable readers to skim the paper, so that they can incorporate this task into their busy routines. And finally, news delivered via Twitter is restricted to 160 characters, which drastically affects the presentation of content.

However, readers do exercise an element of control over the pace. If you decide to put this text down now, there is very little that the author can do about it. If you decide to read more rapidly or skip entire paragraphs, that is ultimately your choice.

The dissemination schedule for print is comparatively deliberate. Daily newspapers operate on a 24-hour news cycle. Magazines may come out once a week or even bimonthly. Although it normally takes a year or more for a book to be written, edited, published, and distributed, publishers are now able to release an e-book on a popular subject before interest in the subject subsides. For example, four days after the death of Osama bin Laden in 2011, two retellings of the mission were released, published by Glenneyre Press and Belodon Labs.

Photography

We live in a visual environment. We see billboards in crowds, wear images on our clothes, and see images in a variety of public places, as well as at home. Posting images on Facebook furnishes a record of our daily activities. And thanks to cell phones, we now carry cameras with us wherever we go.

A photograph possesses an almost mystical quality; looking at photographs can stir memories, bringing the past into the present. Indeed, a person achieves a measure of immortality through photographic images. Examine a picture from your childhood. Although you have changed, your image remains forever young. Although photographs have a distinct feel and smell, the primary way in which we appreciate photographs is through the sense of sight. As mentioned earlier, we tend to respond to visually oriented media in an *affective,* or emotional, way. Consequently, the image-maker can use the visual tools at hand to create a mood that subtly conveys media messages.

Photographs provide documentation of identity. Pictures have become particularly precious in contemporary culture, when, in so many cases, the extended family is no longer in close proximity. Photos preserve significant rites of passage in a family, such as birthdays, holidays, graduations, and weddings.

In photography, the pace is primarily determined by the audience. The viewer determines how much time he or she chooses to devote to examining a photograph. However, the skilled photographer is able to direct the attention of the viewer to certain aspects of the photograph through the selection and arrangement of the subject matter. (For additional discussion of photography, see Chapter 7, Production Elements.)

The dissemination schedule for photographs has changed radically, from a delay of days in traditional chemical photographic processing to the immediate "grabbing" and downloading of a digital image.

Film

Like photography, film is an affective medium that generates an immediate emotional response from the audience. The illusion of motion in film seemingly brings the film images to life, adding another layer of *verisimilitude* (or lifelike quality) to the medium. Because movement is a defining characteristic of film, plots that emphasize action—people doing things—play particularly well on screen.

As a result, film narratives tend to emphasize plot, which is based on conflict—what Thrall, Hibbad, and Holman refer to as "the interplay of one force upon another."[21]

Unfortunately, many feature films are merely celebrations of movement, filled with car chases and wanton acts of violence. But at its best, films use plot to furnish insight into character and theme; that is, the events in the story cause the main characters to undergo significant changes or come to important realizations about themselves and the world depicted in the film. Adding the element of sound to the visuals makes film a particularly effective communication vehicle.

Watching a film is a primary experience. In contrast with other media, you must travel to a designated area—a movie theater. One of the attractions of going to the movies is simply getting away from the pressures and routines of home. The theater is dark and comfortable. The sound and images on the large screen can be overwhelming, moving you into a new realm of experience.

In addition, attending a movie is a social occasion. Who can forget their first date at the movies—the tension about whether to hold hands, sharing popcorn, and what to talk about after the show? Members of the audience are involved in a communal experience—responding to the program at the same moment. On the other hand, the audience can serve as a major distraction, when cell phones ring or the people behind you are chattering, as though they're at home in their living rooms watching TV.

The pace of film is primarily determined by the filmmaker. We cannot stop the film if we decide to buy popcorn or visit the restroom. Movies are intended to be viewed in their entirety, in one sitting. The audience may be bored or overwhelmed by the pace of a film, but it has very little choice in the matter, other than leaving the theater.

The dissemination schedule for film is the most deliberate of all media. A Hollywood film project can take over three years from conception to exhibition in theaters. This process consists of four distinct stages:

- *Preproduction* includes all the preliminary creative, developmental, and planning stages, including the writing of the script, the negotiation for film rights, casting the film, contract negotiations with the performers' agents, building of studio sets, and deciding on locations. This stage generally requires between three months and two years.
- *Production* involves shooting the primary film footage, with accompanying recorded dialogue. This phase normally lasts between 30 and 80 days. Each day of shooting covers approximately three pages of the script and generates two or three minutes of final used footage.
- The *postproduction* stage includes editing, dubbing voices, sound mixing, creating and adding the musical score, addition of special effects, studio previewing, and reshooting of specific scenes. This stage can require three months to one year.
- The *promotion* stage consists of distribution, exhibition, and publicity. Many films never make it to this stage and are never released.

Film content is likely to undergo many transformations during this protracted process, so that it may not even resemble the original screenplay. This prolonged process makes it difficult for a filmmaker to gauge whether a film will be topical by the time it is released.

In recent years, the domestic film industry in the United States has declined. Although the number of films released in 2011 increased by 7 percent, domestic box office revenue fell by 4 percent.[22] This drop in attendance is the result of several factors: the competition of CD sales; improvements in home viewing, such as big-screen televisions and high-definition quality; and the reduced time between a film's theatrical run and

Bollywood film star Aishwarya Rai performing during the Bollywood Awards in 2000. (AP/ Wide World Photos)

its availability for home viewing. In addition, the availability of high-speed Internet, accompanied by a lax enforcement of copyright regulations, has contributed to an increase in "piracy," in which consumers purchase first-run films for home use.

However, the international film industry continues to flourish. Worldwide box-office film sales rose by 6 percent in 2012.[23] The most prolific center of filmmaking in the world now is Bombay, India. Over one thousand films per year come out of "Bollywood."[24]

Another center of film production is "Chinawood." China's box office grew by 35 percent in 2011 and Chinese investors are seeing potential in producing their own content. Thus, "Chinawood" investors are developing a $1.78 billion proposal that would create studio infrastructure to compete with the United States and India and create films that appeal to a Chinese audience.[25]

Radio

Radio is an integral part of our everyday experience. In 2011, 93 percent of all American consumers over 12 years old listened to the radio during the course of a week. The average radio consumer spends more than 14 hours per week listening to the radio.[26] Almost all Americans own at least one radio, and the average per household is 5.6 radios.[27]

Radio is continuous and accessible 24 hours per day. The clock radio puts people to sleep at night and wakes them up in the morning. Consequently, radio has assumed a remarkable personal significance in our lives. Hearing an old song on the radio may awaken memories of a summer long ago, perhaps, or of old friends, or a first romance. In that sense, it often is not the song that we are reacting to (in fact, upon reflection, we may actually dislike the particular tune). However, the media program has become internalized as a part of our personal experience, and we feel nostalgic about a program because it has put us in touch with ourselves and our pasts.

In addition, radio is a very portable medium. Most workday radio listening occurs away from the home. Between the hours of 7:00 a.m. and 7:00 p.m., the majority of radio listening occurs in the car, at work, or in some location other than the listeners' homes.

Digital technology has had a pronounced influence on radio. E-radio (radio delivered through the Internet) connects listeners to traditional radio stations through the Internet. In 2012, Clear Channel's online audience increased by 117 percent.[28] (For more discussion of the assimilation of radio and the Internet, see "Media History: A Systems Approach," in Chapter 3.)

Radio relies entirely upon the listener's sense of hearing. Consequently, we must use our imaginations to envision what is being described over the air. On one level, this can be liberating—enabling us to project our own mental pictures onto the events. Old-time baseball announcers like Ronald "Dutch" Reagan (who later became the fortieth president of the United States) relayed Western Union accounts of the action over the radio, learning to take advantage of the imaginative possibilities of the medium. Rather than simply announcing the progress of the game, they embellished the report with fictitious details, sweeping emphasis, and artificial crowd noise to dramatize the action.

In radio, the pace of the presentation is controlled by the communicator. Radio announcers are trained to speak slowly and distinctly, with a pleasing modulation of tone. In addition, the pace of radio is also influenced by a third agent—the station manager. A computer software program enables studio engineers to compress a speaker's presentation, speeding up the delivery of the speaker, eliminating pauses, and removing what is known as "redundant" data from within words. By shortening a long syllable, engineers can free up to four minutes per hour for additional commercials. However, accelerating the pace of the presentation can alter its meaning as well. Alex Kuczyanski notes, "The new device has angered radio denizens like (Rush) Limbaugh, who says he uses pauses for emphasis, much like an actor raises an eyebrow on stage."[29] Moreover, condensing the presentation can make the presentation difficult to follow, which affects how the audience interprets messages.

Although radio is separated in space from its audience, the medium operates live, in "real time." For instance, morning radio is designed to help get you to work on time, by insuring that their weather and traffic reports are timely and accurate. The disc jockey takes dedications from fans and makes references to local celebrities, events, and landmarks. As a result, radio audiences develop intense loyalties to particular stations and radio personalities. Radio listeners may listen to two or three stations but are loyal to one in particular.[30]

However, as a cost-saving measure, radio programs now originate from a central hub, with one announcer serving a large, transregional audience.

The dissemination schedule for radio is immediate; as soon as radio broadcasters become aware of a story, they can put it on the air. This immediacy, combined with the easy accessibility of radio, makes this medium a primary source of information in times of crisis.

Listening to the radio is primarily a secondary activity. While we are engaged in other primary activities at home, school, or work, the radio serves as background, as a mood enhancer or as a companion. For example, while the car radio is on, our principal attention is (or should be) to keep the vehicle on the road. Consequently, because the radio audience is focusing its primary attention elsewhere, listeners may be susceptible to media messages conveyed through radio broadcasts.

Television

For the first time, the amount of time that Americans have spent watching television is exceeded by time devoted to digital media. Indeed, for the first time, the amount of time that the American viewer has spent watching television has declined (from four hours and 38 minutes in 2012 to four hours and 31 minutes in 2013).[31]

One reason for this drop-off is that younger viewers enjoy alternative programming on the Internet, such as YouTube. In addition, many of these viewers are watching television programs online.

However, television remains a major channel of communication; in 2011, 96.7 percent of American households had television sets.[32] Television is on the air for 24 hours per day. And although cable television requires a subscription fee, broadcast television remains free; anyone with a television can tune in.

Like film, television combines sight, sound, motion, and color. TV hits us on an *affective* level, presenting images that move us emotionally.

Television is primarily an in-home experience, experienced by a single individual or small group. Because complete darkness is not essential for viewing, people are often engaged in competing activities while they are watching television. Approximately 75 percent of all TV viewers are engaged in at least one other activity while watching or listening to TV.[33] This may help to account for the formulaic nature of television; its predictability and simplicity enables the audience to follow the narrative while multitasking (e.g., talking on the phone, reading, or cleaning the house).

As a result, television is an ideal medium for showing events in the process of unfolding. The standard format for TV programming is the series, in which episodes are installments in a much longer, more complex story.

The television set has been incorporated into the interior design of the home, much as the medium has become integral to our daily activities. Think about the primary television viewing area in your home. The furniture is arranged around the television set; indeed, it is often difficult for people to face one another without craning their necks. Television has emerged as a prominent member of the family.

The ongoing nature of television also contributes to a unique personal dynamic between the performers and the audience. As an example, Ellen DeGeneres's daytime talk show is simply entitled *Ellen,* reflecting the public's personal relationship with the star—they are on a first-name basis with the performer.

Thanks to digital technology, audiences now assume a major responsibility for the pace of television programming. With digital recorder (DVR) penetration at 39.7 percent of American households, viewers can pause or repeat a sequence, as well as record programs.

The dissemination schedule for television is now almost instantaneous. For instance, during the "Arab Spring" uprisings of 2011, live coverage of demonstrations taken from cell phones and uploaded via satellite enabled the public to witness the events as they were unfolding. However, as discussed earlier, print media was more suitable for presenting the context, interpretation, and implications of this incident.

Historically, the technological differences between film and television resulted in a different aesthetic between the two media. Television was characterized by an intimate production style; instead of showing vast exteriors, television programs were limited to presenting interior sets.

In addition, as Herbert Zettl notes, television was an expressive medium that was well-suited to focus on relationships: "Film derives its energy from landscapes as well as people; in television, it is primarily people with all their complexity who power a scene, while the landscape aspects take a back seat."[34] As a result, television programs employed more close-ups than were commonly found in film. For example, in the soap opera genre, the significance is not so much on the action but on the *reaction* of the characters. And consequently, the style of soap operas focused on the effects of various events on relationships between characters and on the larger soap opera community.

The arrival of digital video and high-resolution HDTV has reduced these historical aesthetic differences between video and film. Recent breakthroughs in technology have made it possible to capture movies using high-definition digital video cameras with fidelity comparable to 35-millimeter film and to project them digitally in theaters with no loss of image quality. Once grainy and pixilated, video technology now recreates (and enhances) real life visuals with startling realism. According to Rob Sabin, this new video technology will revolutionize filmmaking:

> For filmmakers, exhibitors and moviegoers alike, digital cinema promises, over time, the single most significant enhancement of the movie experience since *The Jazz Singer* introduced sound in 1927. A shift to digital cameras will allow dramatic reductions in costs and new possibilities in special effects. On the distribution end, digital projection could open avenues for the exhibition of less commercial films, creating more choices for consumers. And it will allow movie lovers to see, for the first time in history, exactly what the director sees in his final cut, without the degradation of image that is inevitable with film prints.[35]

As a result, it is inevitable that the style of television programming soon will resemble the production techniques employed in film.

Hybrid Media

We now have entered the world of *digitized hybrid media,* such as the presentation of film on huge flat-screen television sets, iPads, and small cell phones. For instance, flat-screen television sets, high-definition television (HDTV), and sophisticated sound systems have transformed the experience of watching a film. Although the size and quality of the presentations approach what you encounter at the film theater, the home environment and the pace of viewing approximate the experience of watching television. For instance, the home audience can pause a film and replay portions of the movie. Even the dissemination schedule has been affected; a filmmaker can produce and release a presentation online within a much shorter time frame.

Moreover, the information itself is shaped by the characteristics of the medium—some information is more suitable for one medium than another. Thus, as digitized hybrid media continue to evolve, it will be worth paying attention to the ways in which these new hybrids affect the types of films being produced.

At the same time, amateur video shot on cell phones is commonly found on sites such as YouTube—not just footage of events caught by amateur citizen journalists, but people who shoot entertainment programming and documentaries on their cell phones. Significantly, the audiences for these videos do not seem particularly troubled by this "amateur style."

Digital Media

The year 2013 was the first in which American adults spent more time each day using digital media than watching television. The average adult spent five hours and nine minutes daily with digital media, an increase of 38 minutes over 2012. Much of this increase was attributable to time spent on mobile devices; U.S. adults spent, on average, two hours and 21 minutes per day on mobile devices for activities other than phone calls—an increase of 46 minutes from 2012.[36]

Digital media is the *ultimate* hybrid, combining the distinctive characteristics of written communication, images, graphics, sound, and motion. Digital technology facilitates the convergence of these channels. Unlike the other mass media, interactive communications is *nonlinear,* replicating the impulses and thought patterns that characterize human interpersonal communications. As a result, the individual exercises extraordinary control over the *pace* of the presentation. To illustrate, if you log on to a Web page on President Franklin Roosevelt, you may discover a hyperlink that takes the audience to another Web page that focuses exclusively on the American Depression. From there, you may select a link focusing on another related topic, such as "Films of the Depression." And so on. . . .

In the 1950s, the UNIVAC computer took up an entire room. Today, with the introduction of the computer chip, computers have become increasingly portable. But at the same time, your cell phone is exponentially more powerful than that original UNIVAC.

One of the remarkable characteristics of interactive technology is the accelerated *dissemination schedule* of digital media. Information is nearly instantaneous; indeed, it is ironic how impatiently we now wait for the few seconds required to "grab" graphics or find reference information on the Internet.

Digital communication is unique in its ability to provide both *depth* and *breadth* of information. Entire libraries are literally at our fingertips. Consequently, it is no coincidence that the audience for online news is particularly interested in categories of information that newspapers and television do not cover in depth: science, health, finance, and technology.[37]

Many interactive media communicators have yet to take full advantage of the potential of this medium. Many digital media communicators lack a clear objective (or *function*) for choosing interactive media as the channel of communication. Companies often operate according to the *double negative* syndrome with respect to interactive media. That is, although they can see no good reason to put up a Web site, they are afraid *not* to, for fear of falling behind their competition. As a result, Web sites are often simply repetitions of print fliers, failing to take full advantage of the unique properties of this medium.

Occasionally, digital media communicators try to dazzle the audience with their technical wizardry—the *function* being to impress the audience. However, the inclusion of glitzy effects simply to impress the audience can actually *interfere* with the communication process.

Media communicators must learn to take advantage of this medium's unique ability to present different types of information, all within one site. Thus, detailed information can be conveyed through its use of print. Graphics can help illustrate or clarify complex statistical information. And photographs and video can provide a record of events.

In addition, digital communicators can use these different media in combination to accommodate different learning styles of individuals. For instance, people who are most comfortable remembering visual information may rely on the video and audio features of the site.

AFFECTIVE RESPONSE

As discussed earlier, we respond to visual and aural media on an *affective,* or emotional, level. Emotional appeals in film, videos, and computer games influence the attitudes and behaviors of audience members.

A media presentation can provide a healthy emotional release for audiences. For instance, when we watch scary movies, the theater becomes a safe place to confront our wildest fears. As Wes Craven, director of the *Scream* series of horror films, observes,

It's like boot camp for the psyche. In real life human beings are packaged in the flimsiest of packages, threatened by real and sometimes horrifying dangers, events like the Columbine (school massacre). But the narrative form puts those fears into a manageable series of events. It gives us a way of thinking rationally about our fears.[38]

According to Walt Disney, the true Disney experience—and a key to its success—is that the films put children in touch with a range of their emotions:

> What is the difference between our product and the other? . . . Giving it "heart." Others haven't understood the public. We developed a psychological approach to everything we do here. We seem to know when to "tap the heart." Others have hit the intellect. We can hit them in an emotional way. Those who appeal to the intellect only appeal to a very limited group.[39]

To illustrate, *101 Dalmatians* (1961 and 1996) touches a range of very intense feelings in young audience members. The first few scenes are filled with warmth and affection, as two Dalmatians (Pongo and Perdita) meet and fall in love. The audience then witnesses the formation of a family, featuring the antics of 15 puppies. But at this point, the young audience reacts with sadness, grief, and anger, as the puppies are kidnapped by villainess Cruella De Vil. The puppies are imprisoned in an old mansion, where they wait to be slaughtered so that their fur can be converted to a coat for Cruella. But by the conclusion of the film, as the puppies are rescued and order is restored, the children experience an emotional catharsis. These feelings of relief and happiness complete the emotional cycle.

The effective media communicator has learned to anticipate how the audience should react at each point of the presentation and then strives to elicit that particular response. Hollywood director George Cukor, whose work included *The Women, Holiday,* and *Dinner at Eight,* was not known for his technical expertise. Instead, he surrounded himself with the best available cast and crew and, stationing himself by the camera, acted as his *own* audience while the action unfolded. If he was moved by the scene, he was satisfied. If not, he would gather his experts around him to discuss strategies that would produce the intended response.

Because the story is geared toward the climax, the feelings that we experience in the process often fade from memory. However, one useful way to approach the analysis of media presentations is to think along with the media communicator. How does the media communicator want you to be feeling at particular points in the plot? Sad? Happy? Scared? Insecure? Envious?

The next step involves investigating *why* the media communicator is attempting to elicit that intended emotional response from the audience. In that regard, considering the *function* of the affective appeal can furnish perspective into the media presentation.

Advertisers frequently use affective appeals to influence the attitudes and behaviors of the audience. For instance, in 2012, AT&T launched an ad campaign aimed at discouraging teenagers from texting while driving. The ad begins with the image of a simple text, "where r u," while the narrator, with difficulty, relates his story of how sending that simple text resulted in brain damage to the speaker. The camera then cuts to shots of the narrator struggling to walk, while he explains that he didn't think that texting while he was driving would drastically change his life. As media literacy educator Julie Smith explains, "The scenes are difficult to hear and watch, which was AT&T's intent. Our affective response to the ad is designed to change our texting behavior."[40]

Affective response is also employed as a dramatic device in novels, films, and video games. Rather than simply talking about a subject, the media communicators are able to evoke the same emotional reactions among individuals in the audience as the feelings being expressed by the characters on-screen. This empathy with the characters serves to enhance audience members' understanding of themes and messages.

For instance, the 1956 version of *Invasion of the Body Snatchers* begins with the town doctor (the prototypical 1950s authority figure) paying a house call on a family. A boy runs to the car, screaming, "My mother's not really my mother." The camera then cuts to an emotionless zombie on the front porch, who calls to her "son" to come to the house. This revelation is particularly chilling to young children who (according to psychoanalytic attachment theory) often experience separation anxiety at that age. Young audience members project these primal feelings onto the screen, making the film that much more terrifying.

Finally, paying attention to your affective responses during a media program can furnish valuable perspective into your personal belief system. A good illustration can be found in Charlotte Brontë's novel *Jane Eyre*. Jane is a governess who goes to work in the household of a gentleman named Rochester. The two fall in love and plan to marry. However, as the wedding day approaches, Jane becomes aware of strange and disturbing noises in the attic. It is clear that whatever is in the attic is some dreaded secret that, if uncovered, might jeopardize their future together.

Should Jane clear up this mystery before she weds Rochester, or should she marry Rochester and *then* make a trip to the attic? Is marriage an institution of refuge, where people blindly seek comfort regardless of consequence? Should people marry for security or love (or both)? What is the role of trust in relationships? Your emotional response can serve as the basis for critical self-analysis.

AUDIENCE

Audience Identification

The better you know your audience, the more effectively you can tailor the message to his/her predispositions, values, and beliefs. However, media communicators have no direct contact with their audience. Consequently, they must devote considerable attention and resources to develop a clear sense of their audience.

Some media programming targets both a *manifest* and *latent* audience simultaneously. For instance, Saturday morning commercials are directed at children. However, a secondary target audience consists of *parents,* who are pressured to purchase these products for their children.

Over time, a media market becomes so large that it is no longer necessary to appeal to every viewer, moving from a *broadcasting* to a *narrowcasting* philosophy. To illustrate, the overall television audience is so enormous that ESPN does not have to attract every television viewer to make a profit; it merely has to reach all sports fans. (For more discussion of narrowcasting, see the section in Chapter 3 titled "Media History: A Systems Approach.")

This narrowcasting strategy enables the media communicator to tailor media presentations to the background and interests of particular sub-groups. For example, various cable television channels specialize in topics such as politics, classic movies, history, sports, fashion, and pornography. Cable stations also cater to minority groups, including African Americans, women, and kids.

Thus, audience identification can furnish insight into the communications strategy, style, and content of a media presentation. And conversely, examining the communications strategy, style, and content of a media presentation can provide insight into its intended audience. To illustrate:

- *Strategy.* Proctor and Gamble has long maintained its marketing strategy around its connection with mothers. However, in 2010, 69 percent of men said they change just as many diapers as their wives. Moreover, 4 percent said they assumed primary responsibility for this chore. In response, Pampers directed an ad campaign at fathers, featuring New Orleans Saints quarterback Drew Brees.[41]

- *Style.* In 2013 a number of ads for products as varied as Chinet disposable plates and Martha White baking mixes appropriated social media terms such as "fans," "friend request," "like," "social network," and "status update." According to columnist Stuart Elliott, this use of language is an example of *borrowed interest,* a tactic in which "brands seek to associate themselves with elements of popular culture that are pervasive enough to be familiar to the proverbial everybody."[42]
- *Content.* Newspapers such as the *Miami Herald* conduct reader-preference surveys to identify what the audience *wants* to know—a far cry from the news imperative of the *New York Times,* providing what the audience "needs" to know. Surveys reveal that a large segment of the population wants "entertaining and enjoyable local news presented by personalities who deliver it in a caring way."[43] Consequently, in their drive to make the news entertaining to the audience, entertainment has become news.

Further, according to economist Jesse M. Shapiro, "The data suggests [sic] that newspapers are targeting their political slant to their customers' demand and choosing the amount of slant that will maximize their sales."[44]

Digital Media Communications Model

In this rapidly evolving media landscape, the mass communications model discussed earlier must be reconfigured yet again. Because of the interactive nature of digital media, producers must take their audience into consideration at an earlier stage of the communication process.

Thanks to innovations in media technology such as the DVR, the audience can decide for themselves what—and when—to consume media programming.

Further, in many instances, the audience now determines the choice of *media communicator.* Producers now recruit youthful hosts who can "relate" to the young audiences they wish to attract—even if they are not the most qualified candidates for the position. To illustrate, executives at the History Channel sent out a memo to producers, suggesting that they recruit younger historians "with better hair" as on-air sources for their programs. The memo goes on to say that the historians being interviewed don't have to be the preeminent scholars in the field but, instead, must be "telegenic . . . experts who are in their 40s or younger."[45]

Moreover, producers now can bypass the traditional media gatekeepers (e.g., CBS or the *New York Times*) and distribute their work directly over the Internet. For instance, Netflix has produced *House of Cards,* a popular television series that viewers can access directly from its Web page. Advertisers are now producing and distributing their own television commercials over the Internet without going through traditional ad agencies.

Businesses are operating on a business model in which their Web sites provide virtual arenas for the audience, who contribute the content themselves. For instance, YouTube is a video-sharing platform, in which the content consists of videos that are uploaded and shared by its audience. These Web sites provide an alternative to corporate media communicators as a source of information and entertainment. Courtney Holt, executive vice president for digital music at MTV, declares, "The tools for programming are in the hands of consumers. Right now it almost feels like a fanzine culture, but it's going to turn into mainstream culture. The consumer is looking for it."[46]

Indeed, the newsmakers themselves are now able to circumvent the traditional media gatekeepers to reach the audience directly. Columnist David Carr provides the following example, the case of Edward Snowden:

> The jailbreak on information reached a pinnacle less than two weeks ago, when Glenn Greenwald, a columnist for *The Guardian,* broke the news of systematic surveillance by the National Security Agency, after he was chosen by Edward Snowden as a conduit for a big leak. . . . And the video that accompanied (the interview) . . . allowed Mr. Snowden to make his own case before he was defined by media and government. . . .[47]

Ironically, in the Digital Media Communication Model, the message often is the *final* consideration. In the digital communications model, the audience dictates choices in programming. For instance, because the typical moviegoer is between the ages of 18 and 24, studios and distributors steer away from subjects that would be of interest to mature audiences. Film studios frequently rely on the input of focus groups, made up of their target audience, before deciding on the finished product—much to the chagrin of the filmmakers. Agent Bob Broder explains, "Too many times a writer is asked to add or change an element or character of a show, even if it makes no creative sense, merely in an attempt to reach a specific demographic."[48]

One of the distinguishing features of the Digital Media Communications Model is that content moves from *narrowcasting* to *microcasting.*

That is, messages can be customized to the interests of each member of the audience. For example, digitized window displays in malls are programmed to identify the pedestrians passing their store and promote items that may be of particular interest to that customer. (For further discussion, see Chapter 9, Advertising.)

AUDIENCE BEHAVIOR PATTERNS

In 2013, U.S. adults spent almost half of their day engaged in media activities—on average, 11 hours and 52 minutes.[49]

What are these individuals doing while they are receiving media messages? Audience behavior patterns refer to an individual's aggregate experience while exposed to media content.

Competing Activities

Audience members are frequently multitasking while receiving media messages (driving while listening to the radio, for instance). According to a 2011 Nielsen survey, approximately 75 percent of all TV viewers engage in another activity while watching television. Forty percent of tablet and smartphone owners multitask, and approximately 14 percent of e-book readers do as well.[50] Colleen Fahey Rush, executive vice president for research at MTV Networks, notes, "Our research showed that people somehow managed to shoehorn 31 hours of activity into a 24-hour day. That's from being able to do two things at once."[51]

Significantly, although your brain can become more proficient at carrying out multiple tasks, your performance levels are never as high as when these tasks are carried out independently. A study using magnetic resonance images of brain activity reveals that engaging in competing activities impairs an individual's ability to perform *either* task effectively. Because of this divided attention, you may not be giving critical attention to either activity. Consequently, you may be susceptible to a wave of messages that can affect your attitudes and behaviors. Despite their years of training, young people can be overwhelmed by this barrage of images, sounds, and messages. Andrew Blau declares,

> There is more media produced than can ever be seen. . . . Even young people who can multitask in ways that make older heads spin will not be able to keep up with the growing amount of media available on the growing number of surfaces, devices, and screens of all kinds.[52]

A young girl multitasking with multiple forms of media. (Marcio Eugenio/ Dreamstime.com)

Studies indicate that approximately one-third of the audience changes to another channel or turns off the television at least once during the course of a one-hour television show.[53] These types of interruptions alter the narrative; if you miss the ending of a police drama, tuning out before the criminals are caught, you may be left with the message that crime *does* pay.

Significantly, multitasking often involves several media-related activities:

- About 80 percent of teens regularly use more than one media type at a given time.[54]
- More than 60 percent of teens say they regularly go online while watching TV.[55]
- Nearly 60 percent use instant messaging and about 35 percent listen to the radio while watching TV.[56]
- 29 percent of Americans watching television were also using Facebook concurrently.[57]
- 17 percent of Americans were engaged in three media activities concurrently: television, Internet, and a mobile device.[58]

Indeed, a 2013 study found that Twitter conversations sometimes *cause* people to turn on the TV. Twitter messages were found to cause a "significant increase" in television ratings.[59]

As a result of this merging of images, printed text, dialogue, and music, you may be receiving an altogether *different* message than was intended by either media communicator.

The media are so pervasive that sometimes we don't realize how these channels have been incorporated into our everyday lives. A media log is a way to keep a daily record of your exposure to media.

You might well find that the following variables play a role in your media behavior:

- Media Formats

We are accustomed to thinking of media appearing in conventional formats: on the television screen, newspaper page, or movie theater. However, these media now appear in a variety of formats, including billboards and T-shirts. In addition, media messages appear in unusual settings, such as grocery stores and elevators. Be sensitive to the various media surrounding you. In the course of a single day, how much time did you spend with:
  - Print
  - Photography
  - Radio
  - Film
  - Television
  - Computer
  - Mobile Device
  - Other

In addition to the established media systems cited above (e.g., photography, film, television), what other media did you encounter?
  - Billboards
  - T-shirts
  - Video Games
  - Other

- Multiple Media

People are frequently involved in more than one media activity at a time (e.g., listening to the radio while you are reading this book). This barrage of media affects the amount of attention you can devote to any one message. Multiple media may even combine to form a separate, independent meaning.

- ○ How much of your time was devoted to multiple media?
- ○ Which media were used in combination?

As a result you may be susceptible to subtle messages that can affect your attitudes and behaviors.
- ○ How much of your media time involved competing activities?
- ○ What activities competed with your media time?

- • Voluntary vs. Involuntary Media

Voluntary media consists of times when *you* choose a particular medium or program. Involuntary media refers to the times when someone *else* has made a media selection, and you are exposed to messages beyond your control (e.g., someone blasting the radio in the next room while you are trying to sleep).

Involuntary media activity is also *embedded within* a voluntary media activity. For instance, for every "half-hour" news broadcast, up to eight minutes are devoted to advertisements.[60] Other examples include the information that scrolls across the bottom of your television screen, the station logo on the bottom of the screen, and the ads that comprise the backgrounds at sporting events.

With this in mind:
- ○ How much of your media activity was voluntary?
- ○ How much media activity was involuntary?
- ○ How much involuntary media activity was *embedded* in voluntary media?

- • Weekend vs. Weekday Activity

Media activities are often closely associated with our daily routines. Consequently, because our routines often change during the weekends, so does our media usage:

Do you devote more or less time to media-related activities during the weekend?

Are your choices of specific types of media (television, radio, etc.) different?

How many of your weekend social activities revolve around the use of media?

AUDIENCE INTERPRETATION OF MEDIA CONTENT

What role does the audience play in the comprehension of media content?

Two schools of thought provide explanations with respect to the responsibility of the audience in the comprehension of content: 1) the hegemonic model and 2) reception theory.

The *hegemonic model* is based on the premise that the media communicator establishes a *preferred reading,* in which the text dictates the responses of the audience. (See the previous discussions in this chapter of "Media Communicator" and "Point of View.") The audience, then, assumes a *passive* role in the communications process.

In contrast, reception theory posits that the audience assumes an active role in interpreting the information they receive through mass media. According to this construct, audience members may *negotiate* a meaning that is entirely different from the preferred reading dictated by the media communicator. The responses of an individual are based upon his/her unique experience. As art historian E. H. Gombrich explains,

> The information extracted from an image can be quite independent of the intention of its maker. A holiday snapshot of a group on a beach may be scrutinized by an intelligence officer preparing for a landing, and the Pompeiian mosaic might provide new information to a historian of dog breeding.[61]

In addition, members of subcultures may react to a media presentation in a characteristic fashion, based on the shared experiences of the group. For instance, women are often more sensitive to messages about violence against females in film than men.

Thus, according to reception theory, when considering the ways in which the audience comprehends media content, it is important to consider the following questions:

- What values, experiences, and perspectives are shared by members of the audience?
- Do these shared values, experiences, or perspectives influence their understanding or interpretation of the presentation?
- How do the experiences and perspectives of the *individual* audience member affect his/her interpretation of the presentation?

In addition, reception theory addresses the issue of *taste*—why certain people derive pleasure from particular media presentations.

Which perspective on audience interpretation is correct—the hegemonic model or reception theory? *Probably both.* Although audience members are encouraged to assume the point of view of the preferred reading, they also negotiate their own meaning based on their individual backgrounds, orientations, and experiences.

AUDIENCE—RECEPTION THEORY

What is the role of the audience with regard to the interpretation of media content? According to reception theory, audience members assume an active role in interpreting, or "negotiating," the information they receive through mass media, based on their particular experiences and backgrounds.

The following variables affect how an individual interprets media content:

- *Background*
- How much does the audience already know about the subject?
- *Interest level*
- How interested is the audience in the subject? How attentive is the audience?
- *Predisposition*
- What is the attitude of the audience toward the subject (positive or negative) going into the conversation?
- *Priorities*
- What issues are of particular concern to the audience? Why?
- *Demographic Profile*
  - National origin
  - Gender
  - Race
  - Ethnic origin
  - Age
  - Education
  - Income
- *Psychological Profile*
  - Self-concept
  - Primary relationships
  - Significant life experiences
  - Ways of relating to others
  - Ways of dealing with emotions
  - Personal aspirations

- *Communications Environment*
  - What is the size of the audience?
  - What are audience members *doing* while they are receiving the information?
- *Stage of Development*
- Have you ever re-read a novel and reacted differently than you did the first time? The content did not change, but *you* did. As people grow older, their experiences influence their perception of what they see. In addition, the maturation process alters how people interpret their world—including media content.

SUMMARY

Keys to Interpreting Media Messages: Process

Communications is a very complex activity. This process is even more challenging in mass communications, when the communicator is removed in time and space from the audience. However, in both cases, the successful communicator:

- Understands the communication process
- Recognizes the purpose of the communication
- Is self-aware
- Understands the message (knows what he/she wants to say)
- Understands the characteristics of the channel that he/she uses
- Can identify his/her audience
- Uses feedback to insure that the audience comprehends the message

Applying the following questions related to **Process** can provide insight into media messages:

A. **Media Communicator**
   1. Who is responsible for creating the media production?
   2. What are the demographic characteristics of the media communicator(s)?
   3. How do these characteristics affect the content and outlook of the media production?
B. **Function**
   1. What is the purpose behind the production?

2. Does the media communicator want you to think or behave in a particular way as a result of receiving the information?
3. Does the production contain any of the following?
   a. Latent functions
   b. Multiple functions
   c. Undefined functions

C. **Comparative Media**
   1. What are the medium's distinctive characteristics?
   2. In what ways does the choice of medium affect:
      a. The communication strategy?
      b. The communication style?
      c. The content?

D. **Affective Response**
   1. How does the media communicator want you to be *feeling* at particular points in the plot?
      a. Why does the media communicator want you to be feeling this way?
      b. Is the media communicator successful in eliciting this intended emotional response?
   2. Do your affective responses provide insight into media messages? Explain.
   3. Do your affective responses provide insight into *your* personal belief system? Explain.

E. **Audience**
   1. Audience Identification
      a. For whom is the media presentation produced?
      b. Is there more than one intended audience?
      c. What values, experiences, and perspectives are shared by the audience?
      d. What does the *communication strategy, content,* and *style* of a media presentation reveal about the intended audience?
   2. Audience Behavior Patterns
      a. What are audience members doing while they are receiving media messages?
      b. What is the environment in which the audience is receiving media messages?
      c. In what ways does the behavior of the audience affect how the messages are received?
   3. Audience Interpretation of Media Content
      a. Do these shared values, experiences, or perspectives influence their understanding or interpretation of the presentation?

    b. How do the experiences and perspectives of the *individual* audience member affect his/her interpretation of the presentation?

    c. How does the choice of audience influence the *strategy, style,* and *content* of the media presentation?

    d. Do the *strategy, style,* and *content* of the media presentation provide insight into the intended audience(s)?

NOTES

1. Dianne Dukette and David Cornish, *The Essential 20: Twenty Components of an Excellent Health Care Team* (RoseDog Books, 2009), 72–3.
2. Franco Ordonez, "Fox, MSNBC Viewers See World Differently," McClatchy Newspapers, July 27, 2012.
3. Ekaterina Ognianova and Esther Thorson, "Evidence for Selective Perception in the Processing of Health Campaign Messages," paper submitted to the Communication Theory & Methodology Division of the Association for Education in Journalism and Mass Communication for its 1998 conference.
4. Frank Absher, "Hair Brain," *St. Louis Journalism Review* (November 1998), 3.
5. Pew Research Center, September 22, 2011, www.pewresearch.org.
6. Leslie Kaufman, "The Grown-Up behind a Tween Phenomenon," *New York Times,* March 25, 2013.
7. Ibid.
8. Jeremy W. Peters, "Enemies and Allies for 'Friends,'" *New York Times,* June 20, 2012.
9. "Survey Readers Beware: Ridiculous Claims Ahead," *St. Louis Post Dispatch Everyday Magazine,* Monday, December 17, 2001.
10. The Hollywood Reporter, www.hollywoodreporter.com.
11. Herbert Zettl, *Sight, Sound, Motion: Applied Media Aesthetics* (Belmont, CA: Wadsworth, 1990), 225.
12. E. H. Gombrich, "The Visual Image," in *Media and Symbols: The Forms of Expression, Communication, and Education,* publication of the National Society for the Study of Education, Vol. 73, Pt. 1, ed. David R. Olson (Chicago: University of Chicago Press, 1974), 242.
13. Max Frankel, "What's Happened to the Media?" *New York Times Magazine,* March 21, 1999: 38–40.
14. Interview with Chris Kelleher, September 23, 1999, St. Louis, Missouri.
15. Nick Bilton, "Disruptions: Celebrities' Product Plugs on Social Media Draw Scrutiny," *New York Times,* June 9, 2013.
16. Maria Aspan, "A Game with Real Soldiers," *New York Times,* September 18, 2006: C-6.
17. Interview with Zoey Wang, October 10, 2013, Webster University, St. Louis, Missouri.

18. Barry Meier and Andrew Martin, "Real and Virtual Firearms Nurture a Marketing Link," December 24, 2012.

19. Bill Moyers, *The Public Mind: Consuming Images,* Public Broadcasting Service, November 8, 1989.

20. Henry James, *Portrait of a Lady* (New York: The Modern Library, 1966), 239.

21. William Flint Thrall, Addison Hibbard, and C. Hugh Holman, *A Handbook to Literature* (New York: The Odyssey Press, 1960), 357.

22. Brooks Barnes, "A Year of Disappointment at the Movie Box Office," *New York Times,* December 25, 2011.

23. Ben Child, *The Guardian,* December 29, 2011.

24. Shelly Freierman, "Wooing the World," *New York Times,* March 25, 2013: B-7.

25. Andrew Pulver, "China to Build $1.27bn Hollywood Co-Production Film Studio," *The Guardian,* May 1, 2012, http://www.guardian.co.uk/film/2012/may/01/china-hollywood-film-studio-chinawood.

26. Radio Advertising Bureau, "Radio Marketing Guide 2011," http://www.rab.com/public/marketingGuide/marketingGuide.pdf.

27. Rebecca Pirrto, "Why Radio Thrives," *American Demographics* 16 (May 1994), n5, 40 (7).

28. Ben Sisario, "Aggregators Help Radio Reach Online Audiences," *New York Times,* August 5, 2012.

29. Alex Kuczyanski, "Radio Squeezes Empty Air Space for Profit," *New York Times,* January 6, 2000.

30. Pirrto, "Why Radio Thrives."

31. Cotton Delo, "Digital Devices Now Get More Than Five Hours Per Day, According to eMarketer," *Ad Age Digital,* August 1, 2013, http://adage.com/article/digital/americans-spend-time-digital-devices-tv/243414/.

32. Media Reform Info Center, "TV Facts," http://www.enviroweb.org.

33. Shan Li, "Smartphone and Tablet Owners Multitask While Watching TV, Survey Finds," *Los Angeles Times,* October 13, 2011.

34. Herbert Zettl, *Sight Sound Motion: Applied Media Aesthetics* (Belmont, CA: Wadsworth, 1990), 95.

35. Rob Sabin, "The Movies' Digital Future Is in Sight and It Works," *New York Times,* November 26, 2000.

36. Delo, "Digital Devices Now Get More Than Five Hours Per Day."

37. Pew Research Center Biennial News Consumption Survey, "Event-Driven News Audiences."

38. David Blum, "Embracing Fear as Fun to Practice for Reality," *New York Times,* October 30, 1999.

39. Bob Thomas, *Walt Disney: An American Original* (New York: Simon and Schuster, 1976), 278.

40. Interview with Art Silverblatt, February 11, 2013, Webster University, St. Louis, Missouri.

41. Andrew Adam Newman, "Pampers Tries Marketing Diapers to Dads," *New York Times,* June 28, 2010, http://article.wn.com/view/2010/06/30/Pamper_Celebrates _a_SportsFilled_Fathers_Day_With_Super_Bow/

42. Stuart Elliott, "Ads That Speak the Language of Social Media," *New York Times,* March 25, 2013.

43. Bill Carter, "Shrinking Network TV Audiences Set Off Alarm and Reassessment," *New York Times,* November 22, 1998.

44. Austan Goolsbee, "Lean Left? Lean Right? News Media May Take Their Cues From Customers," *New York Times,* December 7, 2006: C-3.

45. Jim Rutenberg, "Younger Historians, with Better Hair," *New York Times,* August 5, 2002: C-7.

46. Jeff Leeds, "The New Tastemakers," *New York Times,* September 3, 2006: B-1.

47. David Carr, "Big News Forges Its Own Path," *New York Times,* June 17, 2013.

48. Susan Stellin, "Media Talk: Putting Readers in the Assignment Desk," *New York Times,* January 22, 2001.

49. Delo, "Digital Devices Now Get More Than Five Hours Per Day."

50. Li, "Smartphone and Tablet Owners Multitask While Watching TV, Survey Finds."

51. Sharon Waxman, "At an Industry Media Lab, Close Views of Multitasking," *New York Times,* May 15, 2006.

52. Andrew Blau, "Deep Focus," National Alliance for Media Arts and Culture, January 2005, 15.

53. Waxman, "At an Industry Media Lab, Close Views of Multitasking."

54. Kevin Downey, "Huge Challenge for Advertisers to Get Noticed," *Media Life,* September 25, 2003.

55. Ibid.

56. Ibid.

57. "Infographic: The Hours We Spend on Facebook, Tumblr, Pinterest, & Social Media," Marketing Land, November 29, 2012, http://marketingland. com/infographic-hours-facebook-tumblr-pinterest-social-media-27473.

58. Ibid.

59. Brian Stelter, "Study Links TV Viewership and Twitter Conversations," *New York Times,* August 6, 2013.

60. Andrew Adam Newman, "Pampers Celebrates a Sports-Filled Father's Day With Super Bowl XLIV MVP Drew Brees and Family at Yankee Stadium," Wn.com. http://article.wn.com/view/2010/06/30/Pampers_Celebrates_a _SportsFilled_Fathers_Day_With_Super_Bow/

61. Gombrich, "The Visual Image."

3

Historical Context

Media presentations derive their significance from the events of the day. Clearly, the primary goal of the journalist is to record events that have political or social significance. But entertainment programming and advertising are also influenced by current events. A historical approach to media analysis offers a way to put prominent events and figures of the day into meaningful perspective.

LINES OF INQUIRY: HISTORICAL CONTEXT

Historical context can follow nine lines of inquiry:

1. *A media presentation can add to our understanding of historical events.*

   In general, individuals look to news programming on the Internet and in newspapers and on television to keep abreast on the day's events. But in addition, many people look to entertainment programming like Comedy Central's *The Daily Show, The Colbert Report,* and *South Park* as their principal source of political news. Indeed, a 2009 *Time Magazine* poll found that *The Daily Show's* Jon Stewart was regarded as America's "most-trusted newscaster" by 44 percent of participants, easily outdistancing the network anchors (29 percent voted for NBC's Brian Williams, 19 percent for ABC's Charles Gibson, and 7 percent for CBS's Katie Couric).[1]

   Because many popular media presentations derive their meaning from the historical events of the day, older media presentations can furnish perspective into the historical period in which it was produced.

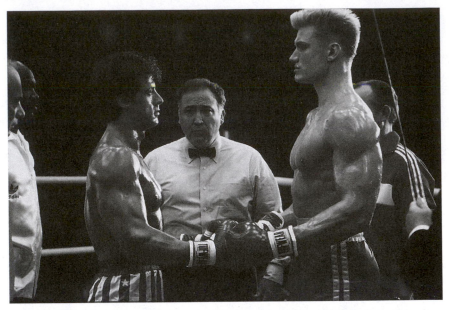

Rocky Balboa (left, played by Sylvester Stallone) preparing to fight Ivan Drago (played by Dolph Lundgren) in *Rocky IV* (1985). (MGM/UA/Photofest)

To illustrate, in the 1985 film *Rocky IV,* the sports drama of the previous Rocky films was enhanced by the tension of the Cold War, which was reaching its climax in the Reagan-era 1980s. In the film, Rocky travels to the Soviet Union to fight Ivan Drago, a tall, blonde, chiseled Communist. The production values of the film, which was directed by Sylvester Stallone, reveal how Americans felt about the Soviet empire during that time period. Drago trains in a stark, sterile medical environment. He is shown with syringes, implying that he cheats. His training montages are shot with a red-filtered light and Drago even wears red boxing trunks. Drago is portrayed as a robotic figure controlled by his trainers and the government, reflecting the lack of individualism characteristic of Soviet society.

In contrast, Rocky trains outdoors in the countryside with natural elements. He chops trees. He pulls wagons. He exercises in a warmly lit barn.

Rocky is portrayed as a kind-hearted, warm, and natural individual who even helps a couple move their wagon when it is stuck in the snow. Rocky wins the boxing match and in the process, the Soviet crowd begins to chant Rocky's name in a symbolic political revolution.

2. *Conversely, an understanding of historical events can furnish perspective into a media presentation.*

   A 1993 ad for Clorox bleach is a mystery—unless you are acquainted with events that occurred when the ad appeared. The ad declared that "putting a few drops of Clorox into drinking water" made it suitable for drinking—a use not normally associated with bleach. This ad only makes sense when placed within the historical conflict of "the great American Midwestern flood" of 1993, in which flooded water purification treatment plants were temporarily contaminated.

   Thus, a knowledge of this event clarifies what otherwise would be a puzzling media presentation.

3. *A media presentation can serve as a barometer of current attitudes toward historical events.*

   Traditionally, media programming has been a source of commentary on historical events. John Leland cites the following examples:

   > In the 18th century, songwriters responded to current events by writing new lyrics to existing melodies. "Benjamin Franklin used to write broadside ballads every time a disaster struck," said Elijah Wald, a music historian, and sell the printed lyrics in the street that afternoon. This tradition of responding culturally to terrible events had almost been forgotten, Mr. Wald said, but in the wake of Hurricane Katrina, it may be making a comeback, with the obvious difference that, where Franklin would have sold a few song sheets to his fellow Philadelphians, the Internet allows artists today to reach the whole world.[2]

4. *Recognizing historical references can furnish clues into themes and messages contained in media presentations.*

   Popular films, music, and television programs frequently contain historical references. For instance, the HBO series *Homeland* (2011–) is the story of a U.S. Marine, held captive for eight years in Iraq, who returns home to his wife and country. Friends and colleagues voice concern over the soldier's strange behavior, and a seasoned CIA Middle East analyst suspects that he may have been "turned" against America by terrorists while imprisoned. Reporter Todd VanDerWerff observes that a familiarity with the Iraq war enhances the audience's understanding of the series:

   > Even though a viewer could watch and enjoy the show without a strong knowledge on the history of the Iraq War, references to the

"War on Terror" and even the creation of the Department of Homeland Security itself inform much of the show's plotlines and themes. The character of the Vice-President on the show has striking similarities to Dick Cheney, and one storyline specifically focuses on the death of a child in a Middle East school zone by a drone attack, a combat method that has been authorized and employed extensively by President Barack Obama. The show's producers both worked on the Fox show *24*, which presented a very black and white viewpoint of the War on Terror whereas *Homeland* asks hard questions about how some of this "war" is being managed and executed. References to the tragic events of 9/11 influence the storyline and motivations of most of the characters.[3]

5. *In countries with restricted civil liberties, media communicators are able to comment on public affairs issues in an indirect fashion.*
For instance, film critic A. O. Scott has focused attention on Iranian filmmakers who, between 1990 and 2005, produced movies that skillfully commented on political and cultural conditions of his homeland:

> The range of themes these filmmakers and their colleagues were able to explore, and the kinds of images they could use were limited by a strict but not entirely inflexible system of censorship. These restrictions resulted in a series of remarkable films about children and also—because of taboos on how men and women could be shown interacting indoors—in a cinematography of open-air natural landscapes and vividly evoked urban neighborhoods.[4]

6. *Tracing the history of media presentations over time can provide insight into changes within a culture.*
In the article on Iranian filmmakers discussed above, A. O. Scott continues,

> The flowering of Iranian cinema in the 1990s was itself evidence of a cultural and political thaw, a tentative premonition of the current demand for change. . . . You see class divisions, the cruelty of the state, the oppression of women and their ways of resisting it, traditions of generosity and hospitality, and above all a passion for argument. . . . The Iranian cinema of recent years offers a foreshadowing of what is happening now, beyond the screen.[5]

7. *At times, media presentations can forecast historical events.*

   Because the American media industry relies so heavily on current events and trends as the source of media programming, entertainment programming frequently anticipates historical events. As an example, by analyzing the positive or negative sentiments expressed in Twitter messages, social scientists have been able to predict the performance of the stock market.[6]

8. *Examining a media program from a different era can furnish perspective into the cultural attitudes, values, and behaviors of the period in which it was produced.*

   For example, the sitcom *The Mary Tyler Moore Show* (1970–1977) provides considerable insight into the feminist movement of the period. The lyrics of the theme song announces that this is an initiation story about an unmarried professional female who has left home in quest of success and happiness:

   > *You can have a town, why don't you take it You're gonna make it after all.*

This introduction serves as a microcosm of the women's movement in the early seventies. Although there is considerable uncertainty on this journey, both she and the audience will discover that her personal qualities will enable her to meet these challenges. (Mary can take a "nothing day" and "make it all seem worthwhile.")

Further, the series presents a worldview in which women can achieve almost anything. Thus, the heroine is embarking on an adventure, filled with excitement and expectation. ("*You can have a town, why don't you take it?*")

Significantly, the lyrics of the theme song changed after the first few episodes. Initially, the song posits that Moore "might make it after all," reflecting both hope and uncertainty. But soon the lyrics declared, "*You're gonna make it after all,*" expressing a new confidence in the feminist worldview.

The phenomenon of the "remake" also furnishes perspective on the interests, preoccupations, and values that characterize different eras. To illustrate, *Invasion of the Body Snatchers* has been remade three times: in 1978, 1993, and 2006. The original version was a product of the Cold War era, in which the Invaders were metaphors for the Communist threat. The 1978 adaptation comments on the impact of the Vietnam War and Watergate on public confidence in the government. Don Miller explains,

The 1978 re-make took place after the Viet Nam War and Watergate, when the public's mistrust of the American government was deep-seated. In one scene, the protagonist, Matthew Bennell (Donald Sutherland) contacts Washington D.C. for help, only to discover that his call has been intercepted; the person on the other end of the line knows Bennell's name before he announces it. In the worldview of *Invasion of the Body Snatchers,* the pod people have taken over the government and are monitoring Bennell's activities.[7]

The 2006 version was made in a climate of suspicion of the government. In addition to public questions about the motives behind the Iraq War, President George W. Bush had admitted that secret CIA prisons were located outside of the United States and therefore not accountable to domestic laws. Thus, in this remake, a U.S. spacecraft, the Invasion, crash lands on earth, containing a foreign substance that infects the population and takes over their bodies when they fall into REM sleep. A CDC researcher helps spread the virus more quickly by placing it into flu shot "vaccines."

9. *Media presentations can distort historical events.*

In entertainment programming, historical events may be altered for dramatic purposes. To illustrate, film critics Manohla Dargis and A. O. Scott cite some of the inaccuracies in Oscar-nominated films for 2013:

Connecticut congressmen did not vote against the 13th amendment in 1865, as shown in Steven Spielberg's *Lincoln.* Iranian Revolutionary Guards did not chase a plane carrying six American Embassy workers down a Tehran airport runway in 1980, as they do in the climax of Ben Affleck's *Argo.* And a freed slave in 1858 did not lay waste to a Mississippi plantation called Candyland to free his German-speaking wife, as in Quentin Tarantino's brazenly fantastical *Django Unchained.*[8]

Docudramas frequently romanticize a historical period for entertainment purposes, while glossing over the social and economic conditions that precipitated the historical event. These dramatizations generally focus on the impact of historical events on the personal lives of the characters.

Although these entertainment media programs are not intended to serve as historical documents, the audience often believes that a docudrama presents an accurate account of events—with dangerous consequences. Media historian Michael Parenti observes,

In the minds of many Americans, movie and television dramas are the final chapter of history, the most lasting impression they have of what the past was like, what little of it they may have been exposed to. For the most part, make-believe history is an insipid costume epic, a personalized affair, the plotting, strutting, and yearnings of court figures and state leaders. Tyrants become humanly likable as the social realities of their tyranny are ignored. The revolutionary populace is represented as tyrannical and irrational, while the sources of their anger and misery remain unexplained. Conflicts and wars just seem to happen, arising out of personal motives and ambitions. In these ways make-believe history reinforces the historical illiteracy fostered in the schools and in political life in general.[9]

But according to media scholars Ian I. Mitroff and Warren Bennis, TV news often presents information in isolation, without the historical context that provide meaning:

With very few exceptions, most issues on network television news are presented in a completely historical context or no context whatsoever. Most news issues, especially local items, merely appear; they drop in from out of the blue. . . . The overall effect is one of dazzling confusion. Little or no attempt is made to present a larger view in which the issues could be located in a coherent framework. . . .[10]

Moreover, newspapers face space limitations that restrict their ability to present the full historical context necessary for a comprehensive understanding of the events of the day. Television news is even more limited, with news stories rarely exceeding two minutes in length. As a result, it may be necessary to read additional articles or books on the topic to get a full picture of events. (For more discussion, see Chapter 8, Journalism.)

However, examining the historical events depicted in both news and entertainment media presentations can serve as a useful springboard for additional research, in response to the following questions:

- Does the media program present an accurate portrait of events?
- Are the causes leading to the events in the presentation clear?
- Does the information in the narrative provide a complete picture of the historical period?
- What (if anything) was left out of the narrative?
- What consequences (if any) are depicted in the narrative?

MEDIA HISTORY: A SYSTEMS APPROACH

We all recall, with horror, high school history classes that required the memorization of assorted names and dates for a multiple choice or true-false exam. Although cramming for an exam may have some character-building value, it serves no particular educational purpose; soon after the examination, we forget those names and dates that we had struggled so valiantly to master.

A *systems* approach to the history of media is designed to place events within a broader historical context. Details such as names and dates acquire meaning, in terms of how they fit into (and influence) these historical patterns. And by recognizing patterns that have emerged, you will be better prepared to understand present conditions and anticipate future developments.

Biological Systems

One very useful analogy for the analysis of media history involves the study of biological systems. Biologists regard living creatures as systems composed of smaller *interrelated* and *interdependent* subsystems. For example, the cells of the human body have a life of their own, but they also interact to make up larger units, such as the digestive, reproductive, and respiratory systems. Each of these systems depends upon the others for selected, specialized functions; the respiratory system, for example, cannot serve the functions of the digestive system. These systems, in turn, are parts of a still larger system—the human body.

In like fashion, the mass media is a complex "system." Each medium is made up of interrelated and interdependent subsystems. For example, a newspaper is made up of a number of departments, such as the publisher, editorial department, news desk, features, and the advertising division. Each "subsystem" of the newspaper plays a distinct role in the publication of the paper. For instance, the advertising department determines how many news stories can be carried in a particular edition. But at the same time, these departments are interdependent. As an example, it is not uncommon for articles to be "cut" to accommodate the insertion of a last-minute advertisement. Moreover, an ongoing ethical dilemma facing newspaper editors involves how they should treat stories involving prominent clients, on whom the paper depends for advertising revenue.

At the same time, each medium (e.g., film, radio, or the Internet) is part of a larger system, commonly referred to as "the media." As is the case in biological systems, these media are also interrelated and interdependent.

Conglomerates frequently own different media (e.g., newspapers and television stations), sharing ownership philosophies and resources. For instance, NewsCorp owns television stations, newspapers, book publishing companies, and Internet sites. Through cross-promotion, Fox television programs subtly promote films, CDs, or other television programs produced by a NewsCorp subsidiary.

In addition, media systems frequently rely on one another for programming and information. To illustrate, nearly three-quarters of all radio stations rely on local newspapers as a primary source of news.[11]

Media subsystems may also have an overlapping influence on *style*. For instance, print journalism had a profound influence on the literary style of twentieth-century authors such as Ernest Hemingway. More recently, the medium of film has had an impact on modern literature; current novels are written in a very visual, plot-oriented style that can easily be adapted into film and television scripts.

Finally, "the media" are part of a network of interrelated social institutions that include church, schools, government, and family. Significantly, when Mikhail Gorbachev initiated social reforms in the Soviet Union in 1987, he began by ordering the privatization of the nation's radio and television industries (glasnost), which had an impact on other social institutions.

Principles of Evolution

Evolution refers to patterns by which species develop from earlier forms of life. According to scientists, life forms began as simple organisms. Over time, these organisms became more complex in order to adapt to new circumstances and environments. Those life forms unable to adapt, like the dinosaur, became extinct.

Natural selection is a related biological principle. During the process of evolution, the best features of an organism are retained and the unnecessary elements are eliminated. To illustrate, the appendix is an organ that has no current physiological function in humans. Scientists believe that at one time, this organ probably aided in cellulose digestion. In other animals, the appendix is much larger and provides a pouch off the main intestinal tract, in which cellulose can be trapped and be subjected to prolonged digestion. Dr. Mabel Rodrigues speculates that the appendix will gradually disappear in human beings, as our diet no longer includes cellulose.[12]

The major media systems follow a readily identifiable pattern of evolution:

I. *The Inception Stage*

This initial stage of development refers to the invention of the medium. This stage is generally *decentralized*. Individual inventors conducted their research in relative isolation. In some cases, individuals were working on the same invention simultaneously. For instance, radio was developed by a number of inventors from different countries:

- In 1887, German physicist Heinrich Hertz set up the first spark transmitter and receiver.
- In 1892, a French inventor, Edouard Branly, created a tube containing loose zinc and silver filings, with contact plugs on each end. The shavings would stick together after the first spark was received; a method of separating them for the next signal was necessary.
- In 1893, a Serbian, Nikola Tesla, carried out the first demonstration of wireless communication.
- In 1895, an Italian, Guglielmo Marconi, experimented with Hertzian waves and was able to send and receive messages over a mile and a quarter.
- In 1906, American William De Forest developed the audion, a device that made it easier to receive voice and music transmissions.

Similarly, three men were working on the invention of the television at the same time. In 1923, Russian Vladimir Zworkin invented the inconoscope (camera tube), and in 1926, the kinescope receiving unit. In 1925, John Logie Baird, a Scottish inventor, achieved the world's first real television picture in his laboratory, which used spinning disks to scan pictures. And in 1927, Philo Farnsworth, an American, transmitted the first electronic television image.

Moreover, "packet switching," the technological foundation of the Internet, was developed independently by two scientists, Donald Davies in England and Paul Baran in the United States, between 1966 and 1969.

At the inception stage, the inventors of these media systems were consumed with the scientific possibilities of their projects, never imagining the commercial implications of their work. Reporter Jeff Kisseloff notes,

The earliest pioneers (of television) vividly recall the thrill of exploration, of building something from nothing, to please not some corporate sponsor but themselves. Nobody knew what television was or would be, so there were no molds to fit into. Mostly, they proceeded on curiosity and raw intelligence and a willingness to experiment in an atmosphere that not only tolerated resourceful thinking but depended on it.[13]

Historical events often play a role in the development of media systems. For instance, World War I greatly accelerated the growth of the radio industry, as the armed forces began to rely on the communications capability of this medium. By the war's end, over 100,000 people had been trained in radio operations.

However, the development of television was *slowed* by the Great Depression and World War II, when nearly all resources were committed to the war effort. Between 1948 and 1952, the U.S. Federal Communications Commission (FCC) imposed a freeze on all new applications for TV stations, as well as the number of station licenses awarded, in order to give itself time to develop technical standards and procedures for the use of the airwaves.

The invention of the Internet was a product of the Cold War. In 1957, following the Soviet Union's launch of Sputnik (the first manmade satellite to orbit the Earth), the U.S. Defense Department's Advance Research Projects Agency (ARPA) was formed. By the mid 1960s, the U.S. Defense Department had become concerned about the vulnerability of its defense system. If a targeted area was decimated by a nuclear warhead, all of the defense information at that site would cease. Thus, the Arpanet project (from which the Internet eventually evolved) was created to facilitate rapid electronic distribution of defense information.

At the inception stage, programming is generally designed to demonstrate the capabilities of the medium. For instance, the early films of pioneer filmmakers Auguste and Louis Lumière in the early twentieth century were simply celebrations of movement. One was called *Train Coming into Station*; another showed workers leaving the Lumière Factory.

In like manner, one of the first television broadcasts, U.S. president Franklin Roosevelt's address during the 1939 World's Fair, demonstrated the immediate transmission of picture and sound.

II. *The Embryonic Stage*

As the commercial potential of a young medium becomes apparent, corporations agree to sponsor the research of these inventors and hobbyists. For instance, in 1920, Frank Conrad, an amateur radio operator and engineer for Westinghouse Electric, began broadcasting programs from his garage on amateur station 8XK in Wilkinsburg,

Dr. Frank Conrad, assistant chief engineer for Westinghouse Electric and Manufacturing Company, demonstrates the television motion picture projector on August 10, 1928. (Library of Congress)

Pennsylvania. The broadcasts generated such interest that Westinghouse built KDKA, the first broadcasting station.

Attempts to develop a media system into a profitable industry often become a race, as corporations became objects of dramatic patent wars and monopoly litigation. For instance, in 1919, Radio Corporation of America (RCA) was formed to head off the dominance of the British-dominated Marconi Company.

As television moved into the embryonic stage, RCA wanted to extend its radio monopoly to this new technology. Consequently, the corporation connived to wrest control from inventor Philo Farnsworth. Evan I. Schwartz explains,

In a bid to copy Farnsworth's idea, [RCA President David] Sarnoff sent his top engineer, Vladimir Zworykin, to Farnsworth's lab. Then Sarnoff himself paid a visit. Still unable to match Farnsworth's work in RCA's labs and unwilling to pay him royalties, Sarnoff tied Farnsworth up in a court battle that hamstrung the inventor for many years.

Even though the U.S. Patent Office eventually determined that Farnsworth was the true inventor of electronic television, the massive RCA publicity machine ensured that Sarnoff would receive credit for bringing television to the world. That PR campaign peaked with a much-ballyhooed demonstration of a TV at the 1939 World's Fair. "This started at the World's Fair, when Sarnoff announced that RCA was now introducing television—a series of untruths that were accepted by everybody and are still accepted, and are in the history books," says Russell Farnsworth (Philo's son).[14]

By 1932, NBC installed a television station in the newly built Empire State Building, and Zworykin was employed as director of RCA's electronic research laboratory.

During the embryonic stage, the media hardware (radio receivers, television sets, computers) is extremely expensive to produce, and as a result, is nearly prohibitive in cost for the average consumer. For instance, in the early 1950s, television sets sold for over $1,000; factoring in inflation, that is the equivalent of approximately $8,400 today. In like fashion, in 1985, the first color LCD home computers cost approximately $3,000, which would have amounted to $5,657.00 in 2012.[15]

As a result, programming during the embryonic stage is directed toward an elite, affluent audience. To illustrate, after Johann Gutenberg invented moveable type (the basis of the printing press) in 1454, the first printed documents were religious texts and government papers. Both audiences were literate, so they could read the materials and affluent enough to afford to buy these documents, which were expensive to produce. To cite another example, the first commercial radio programs consisted of opera and public information shows.

At the same time, the embryonic phase is characterized by experimentation in the style, structure, and content of programming, as the media communicators learn about the possibilities of the medium. Before the formulaic conventions of genres have been established, early work is characterized by innovations that are only seen again after the medium has been well established and the conventions have been thoroughly explored by media communicators. For instance, early filmmaker George Melies experimented with special effects in his work, including stop-action animation. In television, Ernie Kovacs was a comic genius who began experimenting with the medium in the 1940s, before the conventions of television had been established. Kovaks concocted elaborate gags involving camera angles, lenses, music, live audiences, and immediate transmission.

In many instances, media communicators were forced to find creative ways to work within the economic and technological limitations of the medium. Kisseloff provides the following example from the early days of television:

> Because no spare parts were available, Arch Brolly used a pickle jar to complete his transmitter and keep WBKB, Chicago's most important station, on the air during World War II. When Brolly's boss, the redoubtable Captain Bill Eddy, needed a camera base that could be raised and lowered, he created one from a barber chair. . . . When the producers of "Captain Video" needed a ray gun, Charles Polachek, the director, grabbed a spark plug, muffler, rearview mirror and ashtray from the automotive department, glued them together himself and called it the "opticom scillometer."[16]

III. *The Popular Stage*

At the popular stage of development, the size of the audience has expanded to the degree that a profitable mass audience exists.

- Photography was invented with the development of the daguerreotype in 1839. With the development of the "dry plate" (purchased and ready to use), photography emerged as a popular medium at the beginning of the twentieth century, with people taking personal "snap shots."
- Radio's "golden age" was the decade of the 1930s. In 1930, almost 50 percent of American households had radios. But by 1940, 90 percent of American homes had radios. During this decade, radio advertising revenues rose from $25 million to more than $70 million.[17]
- The 1940s was a period of unprecedented popularity for the film industry. Between 1942 and 1945, the American public spent approximately 23 percent of its total recreation dollar going to the movies. By the late 1940s, the weekly attendance at the cinema totaled ninety million people.[18]
- Television experienced a surge of popularity during the decade of the 1950s. For instance, in 1950, television sets were in 9 percent of American homes. By 1956, two-thirds of American households had at least one TV set. And by 1960, 90 percent of the country (45 million homes) owned at least one TV set.[19]

The Internet remained the territory of academics and government until the early 1990s, when the evolution of technology made computers smaller and more affordable for personal use. The development of the Web during the 1990s was astonishing. In December 1995, 16 million people worldwide were online. By 2001, that number had ballooned to 513.41 million.[20]

And in December 1994, there were approximately 1,579,000 subscribers to America Online. By December 1998, the number of subscribers to AOL had increased to 15,000,000.[21]

During the popular stage, the media "hardware" (i.e., television sets, radio receivers, or computers) becomes less expensive, making the purchase of the media equipment more affordable for the average consumer. One reason for this cost reduction can be attributed to mass production; making more units at one time cuts down on the cost of each individual unit. But in addition, industry executives discovered that the most fruitful revenue source was not the *hardware* (the media equipment), but rather the *software*. To illustrate:

- During the 1930s radio companies discovered that the greatest source of profit was not the radio receiver, but rather the revenue generated by the advertising. Consequently, it behooved the radio companies to lower the cost of the radio set in order to put a set in every consumer's hands. Indeed, in many radio contests during the Depression, the prizes were radio receivers—a shrewd strategy to put more radios in the hands of consumers.
- The original cost of a consumer video recorder was $800. The price of a VCR eventually dropped to under $100, as media companies generated their profits through the sale and rental of videotapes. This devaluation has also been enhanced by the introduction of a new technology (DVDs) that supplanted videotapes.
- The cost of a home computer has steadily dropped from its original home consumer cost of $2,000 in the 1990s. In 2006, the nonprofit project One Laptop Per Child announced plans to produce laptops for worldwide distribution at a cost of $150.[22] This type of drastic cost reduction creates a large and profitable market for computer software, as well as goods advertised over the Internet.

During the popular stage of development, the market is far from saturated. Consequently, in order to insure a profit, it is necessary to attract as much of the mass audience as possible, through a *broadcasting strategy*. (For more discussion, see Chapter 2.)

For instance, in the early 1950s, not everyone had a TV set yet, and those who did generally had one set for the entire family, which was stationed in the "TV room." As a result, variety programs like the *Ed Sullivan Show* flourished during the 1950s. This genre featured acts that appealed to the interests and tastes of different segments of the mass audience. Thus, in the course of 90 minutes, the *Ed Sullivan Show* would feature puppet shows for the kids, opera singers for "cultured" adults, and Elvis for the teenagers.

During this stage, popular genres are moved into the emerging medium. For instance, during television's golden era of the 1950s, quiz shows, soap operas, and westerns became popular television genres. (For more discussion of genre, see Chapter 6.)

Moreover, at this stage, the formula of a genre is established within the medium. Formula refers to patterns in *premise, structure, characters, plot, and trappings*. To illustrate, the evening talk show genre hit its stride with *The Tonight Show, Starring Johnny Carson,* which dominated the genre for 30 years (1962 to 1992).

During Carson's tenure, the standard formula of the evening talk show was established. The program time was reduced from 90 to 60 minutes. Each show featured a blend of comedians, musicians, and movie or television stars. In addition, the basic structure of each program was established:

- First, Carson presented a monologue. This session included joshing with sidemen, such as Ed McMahon and bandleader Doc Severinsen.
- Carson then moved over to the primary set, consisting of a desk, which the host sat behind, and a sofa for the announcer and guests.
- The pecking order of the guests was also established in order of celebrity. The most renowned guest would appear first; the end of the show was relegated to relative unknowns, such as young comics or authors.

IV. *The Mature Stage*

During the mature stage, media companies are absorbed by large conglomerates. Media presentations are regarded by these corporations as a product, like shoes, rugs, or any other consumer item. Decisions are made on the basis of its profit potential. (For more discussion, see Chapter 5, Structure.)

At this stage of development, the media market has become so large that it becomes profitable to pursue a *narrowcasting* strategy, appealing to minority interests and tastes. To illustrate, cable television features a wide range of channels that appeal to specialized interests, including news, old films, religious programming, cooking shows, and country music. Because of this huge mass audience base, it is no longer necessary to appeal to every viewer. Thus, Turner Classic Movies can realize a profit if it attracts all the old movie buffs within the mass audience. (For more discussion of narrowcasting, see Chapter 2.)

During this stage, competition emerges within each subcategory of programming. For instance, the competition for *The Tonight Show* on broadcast television alone now includes *Late Show with David Letterman* (CBS), *Conan O'Brien* (NBC), *Late, Late Show/Craig Ferguson* (CBS), and *Jimmy Kimmel Live* (ABC). In addition, talk shows appear in the morning and afternoon slots as well.

At this stage, media communicators often experiment with the established formula of genres in order to keep them fresh. Significantly, some of these innovations mirror experimentation that occurs at the embryonic stage of development. For instance, some of the "street activities" in the Letterman show are reminiscent of the Ernie Kovacs show discussed earlier.

International Media History

Although the media systems of various countries begin their evolutionary cycles at different times, the same stages of development apply. To illustrate, India's "golden age" of television was 2000 to 2005. During this period, the number of homes with televisions increased from 88 million to 105 million. Advertising spending on Indian television has increased, on average, by 21 percent a year between 1995 and 2005, when it reached $1.6 billion.[23]

In many countries in which the development cycle of the media began later than in the United States, the early stages of development were accelerated because of technological developments. As an example, thanks to satellite technology, the Indian television industry was able to circumvent the time-consuming and expensive stage of installing cable in individual sets. As Vikram Kaushik, the chief executive of Tata Sky, a satellite TV company, declares, "Everything that happened in the rest of the world in 10 years, is happening here in two years."[24]

Principles of Ecology

The principles of *ecology* offer a useful construct for understanding the complex relationship between media systems, particularly in the wake of the emergence of digital media.

Ecology refers to the biological principle of *coexistence*. In some cases, organisms are antagonistic to one another. Thus, in Africa, lions are predators who feast on a variety of animals, including buffalo, zebra, antelope, giraffe, and warthogs. In other instances, organisms operate in a state of *symbiosis*, in that both organisms prosper through their relationship with one another.

Phase I: New Medium as Threat

The emergence of a new medium poses a threat to existing media on several levels:

- *Programming.* An emerging medium "borrows" its programming from established media, creating an enormous vacuum in those media systems. To illustrate, in the early 1950s, radio began to lose its programming to the newest medium—television. Situation comedies such as *I Love Lucy* and *The Jack Benny Show* moved over to television, causing considerable panic within the radio industry. Other popular genres that moved from radio to television included soap operas, westerns, and quiz shows.
- *Audience.* The emergence of a new medium siphons the audience base from the established media systems. To illustrate, in 1946—the same year that television began daily broadcasts in New York—weekly film attendance in the United States had swelled to 90 million per week, which was equivalent to half of the population of the country. But by the following year, as the commercial television industry began to operate in earnest and the number of television sets in the United States increased to one million, movie attendance dropped to seventy million per week.[25]

To cite a more recent example, video games are eating away at television viewership. A 2005 article in *USA Today* explains,

If video killed the radio star in the 1980s, then it seems video games are trying to do the same thing to TV in this decade. . . . 24% of gamers reduced their TV watching over the past year and 18% expect to cut small-screen viewership next year. Video gamers watched 11.1% less TV than last year, dropping their weekly TV viewership to 16 hours, compared with 18 hours in 2004.[26]

These technical advances in digital media draw the audience away from the established media systems. David Carr explains,

Newspapers felt the pain of technological disruption first, when people had dial-up modems capable of transmitting modest, largely text-based data. As fatter pipes developed, music performed a jailbreak, leaving behind a maimed industry. And now, with the number of ever-faster connections spreading and the advent of the Flash player, television seems positioned as roadkill, with great big movie files soon to fall after that.[27]

- *Financial Base.* The competition of a new media system threatens the financial stability of established media. For instance, in the 1950s, the radio industry was faced with a financial crisis, as the sponsors of soap operas moved with the programs to finance their television counterparts.

    Likewise, in 2006, the film industry found itself in crisis as a result of the competition from "new media." Media critic Laura M. Holson explained,

The growth of new media threatens to undermine traditional businesses, while studios are flummoxed about how to take advantage of the new opportunities they represent. And movies and TV also face tough new competition from video games and online social networking sites. Even cell phones have become a favorite diversion among the young.[28]

Threatened by a loss of cultural control, members of elite culture dismiss the advent of new media systems as detrimental to the culture. In the eighteenth century, women were advised not to read novels for fear that it would make their brains soft. In 1859, poet Charles Baudelaire warned, "By invading the territories of art, this industry [photography] has become art's most mortal enemy."[29]

In like fashion, some psychologists recently have decried the effects of "Internet addiction." Reporter Virginia Heffernan points out that a "strange and influential self-evaluation questionnaire" by Dr. Kimberly Young, designed to measure this malady, actually stirs up anxiety and ill-feeling:

Dr. Young told me she believes the Internet is addictive in part because it "allows us to create new personalities and use them to fulfill unmet psychological needs"—which sounds worrying except that art, entertainment and communications systems are designed explicitly to permit self-exploration and satisfy psychological needs.

The way the test loads the cultural dice in favor of reality over fantasy should make hearts sink. In the hierarchy of the test, any real-world task or interaction, no matter how mundane or tedious, is more important—and, worse, ought to be more fulfilling—than online fantasy, research or social life. "Do you neglect household chores to use the Internet?" one question asks, and undone laundry is later cited as a warning sign. "How often do you block out disturbing thoughts about your life with soothing thoughts of the Internet?" goes another question. Can this really be science? (And might another psychologist find something to admire in a person who quiets his mind with mere thoughts of the Internet?)[30]

Initially, the established media react by trying to compete with the new medium on its own terms; unfortunately, this tactic only exposes its limitations. For instance, the traditional news cycle for print newspapers is approximately 12 hours. However, the Internet has virtually eliminated production and distribution time. Because of this "virtual deadline," the pressure to bring information to the public has played a major role in changing the standards and practices of traditional journalism. Instead of the traditional guidelines of requiring two sources to confirm the facts of a story, editors have reduced this procedure to one source—sometimes with disastrous results.

Another tactic of the established media industries is to make every effort to discourage the development of the new system. For instance, in the 1950s, American film studios exerted pressure to prevent their stars from appearing on television, forcing the new medium to recruit minor movie actors for their shows or develop its own stable of performers. In addition, in the early days of television, when the industry was struggling to find programming to fill its schedule, the studios refused to release their films for presentation on television. Finally, to counter the growing popularity of television, the film industry launched an aggressive publicity campaign with the slogan "Movies Are Better Than Ever!"

Another response to the diminishing profits is to demand that actors and directors lower their fees or risk having their projects dropped. In 2006, Twentieth Century Fox and Universal Pictures walked away from *Halo,* a movie based on the popular video game, after the executive producer, Peter Jackson, and others refused to reduce their salaries. Russell Crowe dropped out of negotiations to star in a movie being directed by Baz Luhrmann and produced by Twentieth Century Fox. Crowe explained, "I do charity work, but I don't do charity work for major studios."[31] Brian Grazer, an Academy Award winner who produced the blockbuster *The Da Vinci Code,* explained, "You are faced with a new reality. Do you want to stick to your price and be forced to stand in the parking lot instead of playing on the field? That is cause for conflict between talent and studios."[32]

Phase II: Specialization

Eventually, the established media systems fight for their survival by promoting their own distinctive characteristics. This specialization occurs in three ways:

Technological Innovations. In the 1950s, the film industry introduced a series of technical advances to compete with television, which was in its popular stage of evolution. Because television screens were only 13 inches in diameter, film studios produced movies in widescreen formats such as Cinemascope and Cinerama. Further, during this era, television programming was primarily delivered in black and white—color was introduced in 1954 but was expensive and exclusive until the 1960s. As a result, the film studios produced movies in Technicolor—a rich, super-saturated color that, again, provided a contrast with black-and-white TV sets. Further, the tiny speakers in TV sets could not deliver quality sound; in response, the film industry enhanced its audio delivery systems, including "Surround Sound." The film industry even resorted to technological gimmicks to attract audiences, producing movies in 3-D, "Smellorama," and "Psychorama."

During this period, radio responded to the threat of television with technical innovations. The early television sets were large and bulky, and required being near an electrical outlet. In response, the radio industry came up with the transistor, so that portable radios could accompany listeners anywhere—to the beach, or on a picnic. The car radio was another innovation that fit into the American lifestyle. Because Americans were spending an increasing amount of time driving, the car radio was a welcome companion that (unlike television) would not be a distraction for the motorist. The audience for radio multiplied.

Programming. Over time, the evolution of a new medium actually *liberates* the established media by forcing them to develop their own distinctive programming. For instance, the development of photography in the nine-teenth century ultimately freed painters to explore other realms of visual expression. Rather than striving for *verisimilitude* (i.e., accuracy or "truth-fulness") in landscapes and portraits, nineteenth-century impressionists like Monet and Manet were free to capture how the world appeared to the subjective human eye. In the twentieth century, Expressionism emerged as another school of art, in which the intention was to reveal the emotional state of the artist. Expressionistic painters like Wassily Kandinsky, Franz Marc, George Grosz, and Amedeo Modigliani expressed on canvas how they felt about what they saw and experienced.

During the 1950s, the film industry took advantage of the medium's capacity for size by displaying grand landscapes. And by extension, film could present grand *themes* as well. Film studios released a series of epic films, such as *The Ten Commandments* (1956) and *Ben-Hur* (1959), befit-ting the size of the screen.

In like fashion, radio was faced with a programming vacuum when quiz shows and westerns moved to television. In response, radio turned to a pro-gramming format for which the poor audio quality of television was unequipped—music. Thus the "Top 40" formats became popular in the 1950s.

Narrowcasting. Because established media are further advanced on the evolutionary cycle, they are in a position to direct their programming at target audiences, while the new media system is still establishing its mass audience base. Thus, while television was pursuing a *broadcasting* strat-egy in the 1950s, the film industry took advantage of the burgeoning teen market to produce films about adolescence, including *The Wild One* (1953) and *Rebel without a Cause* (1955). At the same time, films with "mature" themes like *Written on the Wind* (1956) and *Peyton Place* (1957) were designed to attract an adult audience.

Radio also targeted an adolescent audience through its new "Top 40" for-mat. Radio played a pivotal role in the popularity of rock and roll and its teen heartthrobs such as Elvis. As a result, despite the gloomy forecasts about the future of the radio industry, the number of radios in use in the United States increased, from 105,300,000 in 1952 to 183,800,000 in 1962.[33]

Phase III: Assimilation

Eventually, producers of established media systems realize not only that they can coexist with the new medium, but that the two media systems can actually flourish together. Reporter Brian Stelter recalls,

Blogs and social Web sites like Facebook and Twitter enable an online water-cooler conversation, encouraging people to split their time between the computer screen and the big-screen TV.

"The Internet is our friend, not our enemy," said Leslie Moonves, chief executive of the CBS Corporation, which broadcast both the Super Bowl and the Grammy Awards this year. "People want to be attached to each other."[34]

Assimilation can occur on the following levels:

- *Consolidation of Ownership.* The holdings of media conglomerates include book publishing companies, film studios, newspapers, and radio stations. Thus, Twentieth Century Fox is part of a media empire, Newscorp, that includes Fox television and the London *Times.* The distribution of media presentations has also become assimilated. As an example, the theatrical release of a film now is closely followed by presentation on cable television, and then DVD sales and rentals.
  In 2009, New Line joined forces with Time Warner studio, contributing nearly half of Warner's domestic box-office sales through mid-May 2011, thanks to films like *He's Just Not That into You,* a romantic ensemble, and *Friday the 13th,* a horror remake.
- *Technical Convergence.* Digital technology has had a transformative impact on established media systems. For instance, digital photography has replaced the traditional chemical process, capturing images through an electronic process.
  Recent breakthroughs in digital technology have made it possible to capture movies using high-definition digital video cameras with fidelity comparable to 35-millimeter film, and to project them digitally in theaters with no loss of image quality.
- *Programming.* Programming has also become assimilated across the media landscape. For instance, in 2010, nearly a quarter of consumers under 25 claimed that they watched most of their television content online.[35] Consequently, consumers are now able to download episodes of network television programs like *Desperate Housewives* and *Lost* on iPods through iTunes. Moreover, major film studios, including the Walt Disney Company, Twentieth Century Fox, Warner Brothers, and Universal Studios, have also added feature movies to the iTunes music store.

Merging of Styles. Because the aesthetic distinction between film and video has become much less pronounced, television directors increasingly are able to use filmic techniques in their productions.

Cycles

New technological developments can cause a medium to *repeat* the stages of the evolutionary cycles. For instance, digital photography moved the medium from the mature stage back to the *popular* stage, as consumers discovered the application of digital cameras and cell phones.

In like fashion, a medium may repeat the same ecological phases in response to the technological innovations of another medium. Just as the radio industry had to adapt to the arrival of television in the 1950s, the radio industry initially struggled to coexist with the Internet, which appropriated its technology, programming, format, and audience. Richard Siklos explains,

> While more than 9 out of 10 Americans still listen to traditional radio each week, they are listening less. And the industry is having to confront many challenges like those that have enticed Mr. Costa, including streaming audio, podcasting, iPods and Howard Stern on satellite radio.
>
> As a result, the prospects of radio companies have dimmed significantly since the late 1990's, when broadcast barons were tripping over themselves to buy more stations. Radio revenue growth has stagnated and the number of listeners is dropping. The amount of time people tune into radio over the course of a week has fallen by 14 percent over the last decade, according to Arbitron ratings.[36]

But once again, the radio industry looked to Phase II: Specialization in its battle for survival. As digital media devices have appropriated the music format, conventional radio stations have been left with an enormous programming hole. The radio industry responded through the format of talk radio, which offers a type of programming that is unique to this medium. In addition, the radio industry relied more on syndicated programs—not just to save money but as a way to attract a large audience. For instance, superstar Rush Limbaugh reaches 20 million listeners weekly through 500 radio stations.

The radio industry is already entering Phase III: Assimilation, using digital technology to increase the appeal of the medium. Radio is providing content for many of the venues created by digital media. For instance, individuals can access traditional radio stations on their mobile devices. In addition, "Radio on the Internet," such as Pandora.com, offers uninterrupted music in a format of your choice. This Internet site selects songs, providing a "surprise" element that the audience enjoys, and offers an exhaustive playlist that introduces the audiences to new songs.

SUMMARY

Historical context refers to those surrounding ways in which historical events influence our understanding of messages in media presentations. Applying the following questions related to *historical context* can provide insight into media messages:

1. What does the media production tell us about the period in which it was produced?
   a. When was this media production first presented?
   b. What events were occurring when the presentation was produced?
   c. How has the media presentation been influenced by the events of the day?
   d. Does the media presentation comment on the events of the day?
   e. How does an understanding of these events furnish perspective into the presentation?
2. Does an understanding of historical events provide insight into the media presentation?
   a. Media presentations made during a particular historical period
      1. What events were occurring when the presentation was produced?
      2. What prior events led to the climate in which this media presentation was produced?
      3. How did people react to the production when it was first presented? Why?
         a. How do people react to the production today?
         b. How do you account for any differences in reaction?
      4. How does an understanding of these events furnish perspective into the presentation?
   b. Historical References
      1. Are there historical references in the media production?
      2. How does an understanding of these historical references affect your understanding of the media presentation?

3. Does a media presentation furnish perspective into current attitudes toward historical events?
4. Did the media presentation anticipate or foreshadow any political or historical events? Explain.
5. Did the presentation play any role in shaping the events of the day? Explain.
6. In the case of *entertainment* programming, is the dramatization an accurate portrait of events? Compare the presentation with historically accurate accounts of the event or period.
    a. Are the causes leading to the events in the presentation clear?
    b. What were the consequences of the dramatized events?
7. In the case of a *news* story, how much historical context has been provided?
    Where would you find the answers to these unanswered questions?
8. In countries with restricted civil liberties, does media programming comment on political and cultural issues in an indirect fashion? Explain.
9. Can a media program from a different era furnish perspective into the cultural attitudes, values, and behaviors of the period in which it was produced? Explain.
10. Systems Approach to Media History: Evolution of Media Systems
    a. In what ways does the history of a medium fit into the following stages of evolution?
        1. The Inception Stage
            a. Decentralization
            b. Innovation
            c. Impact of historical events on the development of the medium
        2. The Embryonic Stage
            a. Corporate sponsorship
            b. Expensive technology
            c. Affluent, elite audience
            d. Programming
                1. Innovative
                2. Elite
        3. The Popular Stage
            a. Rapid growth of audience
            b. Technology becomes more affordable
            c. Formulas and conventions of genres are established
            d. Broadcasting approach to programming

    4. The Mature Stage
      a. Bought by mega-corporations
      b. Profit incentive affects programming
      c. Narrowcasting/microcasting approach to programming
      d. Innovations in programming—to "break through the clutter"
   b. In what ways (if any) does the history of this medium *depart* from the patterns discussed in the chapter? What are the implications of these departures?

11. Systems Approach to Media History: Phases of Media Ecology
In what ways does the history of a medium fit into the following phases?
    1. Phase I: New Medium as Threat
      a. Appropriating programming
      b. Siphoning audience base
    2. Phase II: Specialization
      a. Technology
      b. Programming
      c. Target audience
    3. Phase III: Assimilation
      a. Technical convergence
      b. Programming
      c. Consolidation of ownership
   b. In what ways (if any) does the history of these media *depart* from the patterns discussed in the chapter? What are the implications of these departures?

NOTES

1. David Knowles, "Poll: Jon Stewart Is America's Most Trusted Newsman," *Politics Daily,* http://www.politicsdaily.com/2009/07/23/poll-jon-stewart-is-americas-most-trusted-newsman/.
2. John Leland, "Art Born of Outrage in the Internet Age," *New York Times,* September 25, 2005.
3. Todd VanDerWerff, "Alex Gansa Walks Us through Homeland's First Season," January 26, 2012, avclub.com.
4. A. O. Scott, "Iran's Tensions, Foreshadowed in Its Cinema," *New York Times,* June 20, 2009.
5. Ibid.
6. Jon Gertner, "Social Media as Social Index," *New York Times,* December 17, 2010.
7. Don Miller, unpublished paper, Webster University, August 11, 2006.

8. Manohla Dargis and A. O. Scott, "Confronting the Fact of Fiction and the Fiction of Fact," *New York Times,* February 22, 2013.

9. Michael Parenti, *Make Believe Media* (New York: St. Martin's Press, 1992), 68.

10. Ian I. Mitroff and Warren Bennis, *The Unreality Industry* (New York: Oxford University Press, 1989), 13.

11. Needham, Harper & Steers Advertising, Washington, DC, conducted on the Associated Press Broadcasting Services, Yahoo! Internet Life.

12. Dr. Mabel Rodrigues, "Ask a Scientist," Zoology Archive, June 29, 2005, http://www.newton.dep.anl.gov/askasci/zoo00/zoo00015.ttm.

13. Jeff Kisseloff, "In the Television's Beginning, There Was Risk-Taking," *New York Times,* November 29, 1998.

14. Don Aucoin, "Televisionary Decades after the Fact, the World Is Just Tuning in to the Work of TV Inventor Philo T. Farnsworth," *Boston Globe,* September 7, 2002: C-1.

15. U.S. Department of Labor, Bureau of Labor Statistics, http://www.bls.gov.

16. Kisseloff, "In the Television's Beginning, There Was Risk-Taking."

17. Michael W. Gamble and Teri Kwai Gamble, *Introducing Mass Communication* (New York: McGraw-Hill Book Company, 1986), 166.

18. Kristin Thompson and David Bordwell, *Film History: An Introduction* (New York: McGraw Hill, 2002), 125.

19. Brad J. Bushman and Craig A. Anderson, "Media Violence and the American Public," *American Psychologist* (June/July 2001): 477.

20. "The History of the Internet and WWW. Part I: Statistics," http://www.netvalley.com/intvalstat.html.

21. "Ticker," *Brill's Content* (December 1998/January 1999): 140.

22. John Markoff, "For $150, Third-World Laptop Stirs a Big Debate," *New York Times,* November 30, 2006: A-1.

23. Vikas Bajai, "In India, the Golden Age of Television Is Now," *New York Times,* February 11, 2007: C-1.

24. Ibid.

25. David A. Cook, *A History of Narrative Film* (New York: W.W. Norton & Company, 1981), 411.

26. Gamers' TV Time Going Down the Tube," *USA Today,* August 8, 2005: D-1.

27. David Carr, "Idiosyncratic and Personal, PC Edges TV," *New York Times,* October 16, 2006: C-1.

28. Laura M. Holson, "Hollywood Puts the Squeeze on Talent," *New York Times,* November 6, 2006: C-1.

29. Helmut Gernsheim and Alison Gernsheim, *The History of Photography* (New York: McGraw-Hill Book Company, 1969), 243.

30. Virginia Heffernan, "Miss G.: A Case of Internet Addiction," *New York Times,* April 9, 2011.

31. Holson, "Hollywood Puts the Squeeze on Talent."

32. Ibid.

33. Shirley Biagi, *Media Impact* (Belmont, CA: Wadsworth Publishing Co., 1988), 105.

34. Brian Stelter, "Water-Cooler Effect: Internet Can Be TV's Friend," *New York Times,* February 24, 2010.

35. Jolie O'Dell, "TV Viewing's Shift to the Web," *Mash,* April 12, 2010, http://mashable.com/2010/04/12/tv-online/.

36. Richard Siklos, "Changing Its Tune," *New York Times,* September 15, 2006.

4

Cultural Context

What can we learn by studying a media presentation as a cultural "text"?

Anthropologists study ancient civilizations by unearthing artifacts as a way to reconstruct a portrait of the society. In the same way, the study of popular culture has a *hermeneutic,* or interpretive, function furnishing a means of understanding culture.

Russel B. Nye offers a comprehensive definition of *popular culture:*

> Popular culture describes those productions, both artistic and commercial, designed for mass consumption, which appeal to and express the tastes and understanding of the majority of the public, free of control by minority standards. They reflect the values, convictions, and patterns of thought and feeling generally dispersed through and approved by American society.[1]

Nye traces the origin of popular culture in the Western world to the industrial-democratic revolution of the eighteenth century. Democratization, urbanization, education, increased income and leisure time, and industrialization contributed to the emergence of a middle class (predominately white and male) that created a new market for popular art. Nye observes, "This mass society had leisure time, money, and cultural unity; it needed a new art—neither folk nor elite—to instruct and entertain it."[2]

Popular artists discovered that they could make a living by attracting a mass audience that would patronize their art. Popular art thus became a consumer product, not unlike a pair of shoes or a new rug. These new market considerations also altered the traditional relationship between the artist and the audience. To illustrate, imagine elite novelist James Joyce jogging around a track with a group of his admirers. If the audience is unable to keep up with Joyce, they are out of luck. Indeed, in novels such as *Ulysses* and *Finnegan's Wake,* Joyce is contemptuous of his audience, regarding them as incapable of appreciating the complexities of his work.

Now imagine popular filmmaker Steven Spielberg running the track with his fans. If he pulls ahead of the pack, he . . . *slows down.* In popular art, the burden of understanding shifts to the artist. Successful mass communicators must learn to anticipate the interests and concerns of the audience—to offer content that is interesting and challenging, without being so far afield that they lose their audience entirely.

This relationship between the popular artist and audience might best be characterized as *reciprocal.* Clearly, media presentations are beyond the immediate control of the audience; in that sense, the media is prescriptive. However, because the Western media is a market-driven industry rooted in popular culture, media communicators must be responsive to the needs and interests of their audience. Gifted media communicators intuitively sense what people are interested in and are able to anticipate potential questions and concerns.

According to Nye, *elite* art is defined by the following characteristics:

- *Exclusivity.* Elite art is intended to be enjoyed by a select few.
- *Aesthetic Complexity.* Technical and thematic complexity is regarded as a virtue.
- *Historical Context.* Elite art is part of a larger artistic tradition.
- *Innovation.* Elite art is unconventional and exploratory.[3]

Though useful, Nye's distinction between elite and popular art is far from absolute. Popular artists William Shakespeare, Charles Dickens, and Mark Twain were elevated to elite status after their deaths when it became evident that their popularity was in many respects due to the artistic merits of their work. To further confuse the issue, some programs in a popular genre become "classics," which have endured over time because the artists were able to work so skillfully within the accepted format. Examples would include the classic western film *Shane,* the detective novel/film *The Maltese Falcon,* and the radio/television situation comedy *I Love Lucy.*

Clearly, the media are channels of mass communication that carry elite art (e.g., operas, independent films, and PBS specials). However, it can be said that the majority of the content carried by the channels of mass communication meets Nye's definition of popular art.

In authoritarian countries with restrictive media control, the media also operate as a text. But instead of reflecting public attitudes, values, and preoccupations, the media in countries like North Korea provide insight into the attitudes and policies of the government that controls the message.

MEDIA AND POPULAR CULTURE

1. *In the U.S., media programming can be regarded as a text that reflects the attitudes, values, and behaviors that define a culture.*
The term "popular" connotes acceptance, approval, and shared values among large numbers of people. We admire the popular set because of who they *are* (attitudes and values) and for what they *do* (behaviors). This notion of popularity also applies to media presentations. People only watch programs that meet their approval. If we are truly offended by violent programs, we won't watch them. In America's market-driven media industry, programming with low ratings are soon cancelled.

    To illustrate, professional wrestling features classic confrontations between performers who embody popular cultural attitudes. During the Cold War era, American wrestlers adopted the personas of Russian villains, adopting names like as "Nikolai Volkoff" and "Krusher Khrushchev," parading around in fur hats and wearing the Soviet hammer and sickle. These wrestlers, who personified the Soviet Union, were routinely beaten by their all-American opponents. More recently, some professional matches reflect the resentment of the sizeable American Latino community over the current U.S. immigration policy. Reporter Michael Brick observes,

    > In the heart of the fight card, a deeper conflict played on the racial tensions and stereotypes of a downtrodden immigrant audience. Among the wrestlers, the vilest of the vile were the members of La Legión Extranjera, the Foreign Legion, gringos who openly disparaged the spectators, their language and their country. The invasion, in this sense, referred to the chance for the Mexican heroes to drive out the Foreign Legion. . . . With immigration policy and the violent Mexican drug wars consuming the attention of policy makers, the cartoonish confrontation of north and south in the ring has found an eager audience in California, home to 37 percent of the nearly 12 million Mexicans . . . living in the United States.[4]

2. *Media content reflects cultural preoccupations; that is, the relative importance that a culture places on particular issues.*
A preoccupation can be described as the value that an individual puts on another person, concept, or thing. The term suggests that

the subject of a preoccupation is the object of uncommon attention—sometimes out of control. The amount of attention given to a
person, concept, or thing in the media can be regarded as a measure
of cultural preoccupation. As an example, U.S. media programming
reveals the preoccupation with sex in American culture. To illustrate,
among the top 20 TV shows watched by teens in 2010:

- 70 percent contained sexual content of some kind;
- 45 percent contained sexual behavior itself; and
- 10 percent contained a reference to sexual risks or
  responsibilities.[5]

3. *Media content reflects cultural myths.*

Cultural myths are sets of beliefs that may not be true, but nevertheless
tell us about ourselves and our culture. As Foster Hirsch observes,
"A culture does not buy fantasies that have no connection to it."[6] For
instance, popular song titles often pay homage to a cultural myth that
might be entitled "The All-Sufficiency of Love," in which a person's
identity is totally dependent upon a partner (as opposed to self):

- "One Heart One Love"
- "All You Need Is Love"
- "Part of Me"
- "How Do I Live (Without You)?"
- "You Are My Everything"
- "All I Wanna Do (Is Keep on Loving You)"
- "One Love"
- "Lost without You"
- "Made to Love"

According to this cultural myth, romantic love is a mysterious, mystical
force that leads to loss of control ("I Can't Help Myself"). Thus, although
romantic love is dangerous ("Devil with the Blue Dress On," "Cupid's
Chokehold"), it is essential for survival.

Within this context, it's easy to understand the sense of urgency involved
in finding romance ("It's Now or Never"). The end of a relationship has
ramifications beyond the loss of your partner; you lose your identity, your
self-esteem, and your reason for living.

Over time, cultural myths (such as the all-sufficiency of love) can
assume a *mythic reality* as people buy into it. The danger presented by
mythic realities is that people sometimes make decisions on the basis of
these myths. For instance, an individual might react to the all-sufficiency
myth by marrying someone out of fear of being alone.

Table 4.1   Media and Popular Culture

Media Presentations	Reflect Reinforce Shape	Cultural	Attitudes Values Behaviors Preoccupations Myths

4. *Media presentations reflect cultural change.*
   Examining changes in media content over time can furnish per-spective into trends within the culture. To illustrate, the frequency with which gay couples appear on popular broadcast television programs reflects the growing acceptance of gay marriage through-out American society. As an example, in 2013, Expedia, an online travel agency, began running a commercial on television networks watched by general audiences, like CNN, History, MSNBC, and the National Geographic Channel, featuring a father planning a trip to attend his daughter's wedding to another woman. Michael Wilke, executive director of the AdRespect Advertising Educational Program, explains,

> As society becomes more diverse, there's more inclusive messaging, which reflects what society actually looks like. It's not about being inclusive to stand out, it's about being inclusive to blend in.[7]

Indeed, in 2013, NBC scheduled a new sitcom featuring a gay couple and their surrogate birth mother; the title of the series is *The New Normal.*

5. *Media presentations reflect cultural attitudes toward particular groups.*
   Popular films such as *Scoop, Brothers of the Head, Thank You for Smoking,* and *Superman Returns* depict reporters as drunks, crooks, or bumblers. This portrait of reporters reflects the American pub-lic's lack of confidence in the competence, integrity, and ethics of journalists. Joseph Saltzman, director of the Image of the Journalist in Popular Culture project, explains,

> The anger and lack of confidence most Americans have in the news media today is partly based on real-life examples they have seen and heard. But much of the image of the journalist as a money-grubbing, selfish, arrogant scoundrel is based on images from movies and television.[8]

The cast of the NBC sitcom *The New Normal*. (NBC/Photofest)

6. ***Popular culture not only reflects but also reinforces cultural attitudes, values, behaviors, preoccupations, and myths.***
Cumulative messages about issues such as violence, tobacco, and gender stereotypes are reinforced through the countless hours of media programming that, directly or indirectly, repeat the cultural script.

In an effort to drive up their ratings, talk radio hosts tap into prevailing social attitudes and, in the process, reinforce those attitudes in the audience. As an example, two New Jersey talk radio hosts generated controversy by inflaming attitudes about immigration:

> [Craig Carton and Ray Rossi, hosts of an afternoon radio show called *The Jersey Guys,*] started "Operation Rat a Rat/La Cucha Gotcha," a listener-participation game that encourages people to turn in friends, neighbors and "anyone suspicious" to immigration authorities. They introduced the segment with mariachi music and set the campaign to end on May 5 (Cinco de Mayo), a well-known Mexican holiday. . . . The phrase "La Cucha Gotcha" is meant to evoke the Spanish word for cockroach.
>
> At a news conference Thursday, Hispanic elected officials and others condemned the campaign as "dehumanizing," "poisonous," and "idiotic," threatening boycotts of the show's advertisers unless

the Jersey Guys apologize. "Scapegoating and stereotyping Latinos does nothing but give bigoted individuals a platform to make ethnic slurs and racist comments," said Assemblyman Wilfredo Caraballo of Newark, calling the campaign a "publicity stunt" that could incite violence against Hispanics.[9]

7. **The media does not merely reflect or reinforce culture but in fact shapes thinking.**

We all had to receive messages for the first time. In this sense, the media also plays a role in inculcating, or educating us in regard to cultural values, attitudes, behaviors, and preoccupations.

WORLDVIEW

When you watch television, play a video game, or read the newspaper, what kind of world is depicted?

Popular artists construct a complete world out of their imaginations. The premise, plot, and characters of fictional narratives are based on certain fundamental assumptions about how this world operates. Even when we watch nonfiction programming like the news, we receive overall impressions about worldview. Consequently, worldview can be a valuable key to discover manifest and latent messages contained in media programming.

Cultural Ideologies

What kind of culture or cultures populate the world of a media presentation? *Ideology* refers to the system of beliefs characteristic of an individual, group or culture. An ideology contains assumptions about how the world should operate, who should oversee this world, and the proper and appropriate relationships among its inhabitants.

Cultural Studies is a critical approach that focuses attention on the role of the media as a principal means by which ideology is introduced and reinforced in contemporary culture. One of the central tenets of Cultural Studies is that the media promote the dominant ideology of a culture. This imposition of an ideology within a culture is referred to as *hegemony*.

The media industry is owned by those people, groups, and interests that maintain economic and social control of the culture. The media create (or re-create) representations of reality that support the dominant ideology as a means of maintaining cultural control.

Alan O'Connor declares that the media serve as "processes of persuasion in which we are invited to understand the world in certain ways but not in others."[10] Media presentations contain their own *preferred readings,* based on the social position/orientation of the media communicator. In this way, the sympathies of the audience are aligned with the values and beliefs of this dominant culture. (For further discussion of preferred reading and the hegemonic model, see the discussion of audience in Chapter 2.)

As an example, author Naomi Wolf observes that the cumulative media messages about female sexuality cause young girls "to absorb the dominant culture's fantasies as [their] own":

The books and films [young girls] see [are] from the young boy's point of view his first touch of a girl's thighs, his first glimpse of her breasts. The girls sit listening, absorbing . . . learning how to leave their bodies and watch them from the outside. Since their bodies are seen from the point of view of strangeness and desire, it is no wonder that what should be familiar, felt to be whole, becomes estranged and divided into parts. What little girls learn is not the desire for the other, but the desire to be desired.[11]

According to Wolf, the cumulative messages about women contained in media presentations are clear: "The woman learns from these images that no matter how assertive she may be in the world, her private submission to control is what makes her desirable."[12]

Susan G. Cole warns that these messages can have disturbing repercussions:

In spite of hopes to the contrary, pornography and mass culture are working to collapse sexuality with rape, reinforcing the patterns of male dominance and female submission so that many young people believe this is simply the way sex is. This means that many of the rapists of the future will believe they are behaving within socially accepted norms.[13]

Generally speaking, the worldview of television continued to reflect the dominant ideology. According to the 2010 U.S. Census, females outnumbered males 143 million to 138 million.[14] But at the same time, an analysis of the 100 top-grossing movies of 2008 shows that men had 67 percent of the speaking roles; women had the remaining 33 percent.[15]

Significantly, in family films (in which the primary audience consists of young, impressionable boys and girls), males outnumbered females 3 to 1. Further, between 2006 and 2009, not one female character was depicted in G-rated family films in the field of medical science, as a business leader, in law, or in politics. In these films, 80.5 percent of all working characters are male and 19.5 percent are female, which is a contrast to real-world statistics, where women comprise 50 percent of the workforce.

Females are also underrepresented behind the camera. Across 1,565 content creators, only 7 percent of directors, 13 percent of writers, and 20 percent of producers are female. This translates to 4.8 males working behind the scenes to every one female.[16]

At the same time, while Latinos make up 17 percent of the U.S. population, only 5 percent of the prime-time characters in a 2010 study were Latino.[17]

The preeminence of dominant ideology in the media is further supported by a classic study by Gerbner and Signorielli, which identified the groups most frequently victimized by violence on prime time television (in order):

- Women of all ages (particularly young adult and elderly women)
- Young boys
- Non-whites
- "Foreigners"
- Members of the lower and upper class.[18]

In reality, the groups that are more likely to be victims of violence include teens and young adults, African Americans, low-income people, and immigrants. Sociologist Karen Sternheimer offers the following explanation for this disparity between the actual victims of violence and representations of violence in media programming:

[L]et's think about who is most likely to be featured in crime dramas. The victims on these shows tend to be (although are not always) sympathetic figures; after all, if we don't care about the victim, we might not care if their assailants are caught and brought to justice.

This might lead to highlighting white female victimization, both in crime dramas and in the news to appeal to a specific target audience. Historically the fear for white women and children's safety motivated the lynching of many black men and the passage of laws allegedly to protect women's virtue.

In seeking a middle-class audience, producers might also tend to focus on middle-class victims, people we might imagine are "just like us" and therefore their victimization hits closer to home. We might also feel more emotional connection to stories about elderly victims, which heighten the sense of outrage against a heartless perpetrator.

So crime shows have a lot of compelling reasons for telling slightly different crime stories than the ones that happen in real life. Drama, after all, is heightened reality, not reality.

But it's important to recognize that the abundance of crime dramas might distort our perception of who are most likely to be victims. Based on NCVS data, those who are young, black, male, and poor are disproportionally likely to be crime victims. Why do you think we have had an easier time viewing this group as the cause of crime, rather than as crime victims?[19]

Media Stereotyping

A stereotype is an oversimplified depiction of a person, group, or event. This term is derived from the Greek word *steros* (hard or solid), which underscores the inflexible, absolute nature of stereotypes.

Stereotyping is an *associative* process; that is, ideas about groups are based upon a shared understanding about a group. According to Western philosopher Friedrich Nietzsche, people often base their opinions about a person on one distinctive characteristic, which becomes the basis of the stereotype:

> In the eyes of people who are seeing us for the first time . . . usually we are nothing more than a single individual trait which leaps to the eye and determines the whole impression we make. Thus the gentlest and most reasonable of men can, if he wears a large moustache . . . usually be seen as no more than the appurtenance of a large moustache, that is to say a military type, easily angered and occasionally violent—and as such he will be treated.[20]

For example, take a moment to picture a "typical" scientist. . . .

Now, compare your profile to the following version of the stereotypical scientist, compiled through a *New York Times* survey: "A scientist is a short, unattractive, old man who is bald, has few friends, is clumsy, silly, and is hard to understand. In some cases, he is dangerous."[21]

If there is a general consensus of opinion, then we have a working stereotype.

Stereotyping is a natural coping mechanism. We make decisions based upon generalizations in order to function on an everyday basis. As an example, if you look outside and see dark clouds forming, you automatically take appropriate rain gear with you. But although *prejudging* can be a useful device (it can prevent you from getting wet, for example), *prejudice* is a reductive principle that interferes with people's ability to appreciate the unique characteristics of individuals. According to sociologist William B. Helmerich, this grouping principle is often inaccurate, negative, and dangerous: "Approximately one third of stereotypes can be said to have a good deal of truth to them, and that the accurate stereotypes are predominately positive, whereas those that seem highly inaccurate tend by and large to be negative."[22]

Racial stereotyping continues to play a powerful role in an individual's chances for success in America. Light-skinned immigrants in the United States make more money on average than those with darker complexions, and the chief reason appears to be discrimination. Professor Joni Hersch declared, "On average, being one shade lighter has about the same effect as having an additional year of education."[23]

The media industry is particularly well suited for stereotyping. Media communicators do not have the luxury of time to develop a unique set of characters; indeed, over the past 10 years, the amount of time in which a network television program could run before facing cancellation has been reduced from 13 to 4 weeks—which makes it difficult for the audience to become familiar with a full cast of complex, unique characters. Consequently, media communicators often use stereotypical characters that tap into the cumulative experience of the audience; audience members recognize a character who appears on screen because they have seen him or her (or a similar character) dozens of times before.

Media communicators also rely on stereotypes to compensate for their limited ability to collect information firsthand. To illustrate, in the course of the Iraq War, it became increasingly dangerous for Western correspondents to venture out of the fortified "Green Zone." Consequently, they relied on official military briefings for their information and hired untrained Iraqis to go out into the field and bring back stories. As a result, the news coverage of the war reflected only a general, second-hand understanding of the conflict.

Stereotyping Techniques. Media stereotyping techniques can be quite subtle. These stereotypical depictions appear very *normal* in media programs. No one in the presentation (and certainly not the protagonists) questions the truthfulness of the characterizations.

For instance, during the 2012 presidential election, Newt Gingrich incorporated a series of stereotypical characteristics into his assessment of Barack Obama's performance as president:

> You have to wonder what he's doing. I'm assuming that there's some *rhythm* to Barack Obama that the rest of us don't understand. Whether *he needs large amounts of rest,* whether he needs to go *play basketball for a while or watch ESPN,* I mean, I don't quite know what his *rhythm* is, but this is a guy that is a *brilliant performer* as an orator, who may very well get reelected at the present date, and who, frankly, happens to be a partial, part-time president.[24]

Editing decisions—what to omit or include in a media presentation—also reinforce stereotypes. The issue is not necessarily that a particular stereotypical behavior is depicted by the media, but, rather, that this characteristic consistently is the *only* dimension presented. For example, characteristics associated with the African American male stereotype—being silly, lazy, and confused—are central to comedy in general. Indeed, it is easy to find corresponding examples of buffoonery among white male performances. For instance, *The Hangover* is a film in which Alan (Zach Galifianakis) is a man/boy who tags along with his buddies on a bachelor

Zach Galifianakis in a scene from *The Hangover Part III* (2013). (Warner Bros./ Photofest)

party. This "slacker" is annoying, crude, and clueless. If these character traits were the *only* way that white males are presented in media presentations, then this characterization would perpetuate a cultural stereotype. The key, then, is to broaden the attributes associated with other groups in media presentations.

To be sure, new shows have broken through many of the African American stereotypes over the last decade. However, African Americans are still largely depicted in ways that support the traditional stereotype.

- African Americans are under-represented, including as "talking heads" or as users of computers;
- African Americans are over-represented in certain negative depictions, such as criminality or unemployment;
- African Americans are limited in their positive depictions and especially to sports or entertainment;
- African Americans are overly associated with seemingly intractable problems; and
- African Americans have important dimensions of their lives largely ignored, such as fatherhood or work lives.[25]

According to a report by the Opportunity Agenda, the perpetuation of this stereotype can lead to:

- Inflated views related to criminality and violence;
- Public support for punitive approaches to problems;
- General antagonism toward black males;
- Exaggerated views, expectations, and tolerance for race-based socio-economic disparities;
- A higher likelihood of being shot by police;
- Harsher sentencing by judges;
- Lower likelihood of being hired or admitted to school; and
- Lower odds of getting loans.[26]

To be sure, new shows have broken through many of the female stereotypes over the last decade. However, many of these programs present only the *appearance* of transcending stereotypes. To illustrate, many of the strong, independent female characters depicted in contemporary media presentations appear as exceptional figures. Thus, in *Kill Bill* (2003), filmmaker Quentin Tarantino presents the heroine as a trained warrior who easily dispatches waves of male antagonists. In other media presentations, heroines are supernatural figures—witches or super-heroines. Removing these strong females from the context of everyday experience makes them more acceptable to the general public.

Independent female characters are often cast in films either as villains or as victims, whose "femininity" has been compromised by their assertiveness. To illustrate, *The Devil Wears Prada* tells the story of Andy Sachs (Anne Hathaway), a young woman who finds a job in New York City as an assistant to Miranda Priestly, the ruthless editor of a top fashion magazine. Miranda's staff fears their boss—in part because she displays the assertive traits that characterize male CEOs. Priestly (played by Meryl Streep) is a satanic figure who abuses everyone around her. Indeed, the publicity poster of the film depicts fashionable high heels (belonging to Ms. Priestly); the heel is the devil's scepter. Columnist David Carr points out that making Miranda a villainess reflects the double standard that exists in American culture with regard to women in the workplace:

> One of the movie's running jokes occurs when Miranda Priestly, Ms. Wintour's cinematic doppelganger, arrives at work and flings all manner of jillion-dollar handbags and coats on the desk of her hapless assistant. . . . Male media stars can ingest illegal drugs, make obscene phone calls or hire prostitutes without apparent consequence, but the failure of a female media figure to say please when ordering coffee can lead to wholesale indictment.[27]

As the story progresses, Andy discovers that she has become a victim of her professional success. Like her mentor, Miranda, her achievements have been attained at the expense of her personal life. Carr observes, "However, the movie's . . . chief preoccupation—is Miranda Priestly . . . really happy?—seems entirely beside the point. It is a question that seems to come up only when the successful executive happens to wear a dress."[28]

It is therefore imperative that actors play roles that are not tied to their ethnicity or gender, and consequently broaden the depictions of these groups as they appear in the media.

Romantic Ideal

The worldview reflected in many popular media presentations reflect a *romantic ideal.* As Richard Harter Fogle observes, this ideal presumes an ordered universe: "The center of romanticism . . . lies in a . . .vision, in which everything is alive, related, and meaningful."[29]

In this ordered universe, nature is a microcosm of heaven, defined by an absolute value system:

- Truth
- Love
- Beauty
- Faith
- Justice

These values are unified and interchangeable; one virtue cannot exist in isolation from the others. Beauty is merely the external manifestation of the other, less tangible virtues. Justice ultimately prevails. Love triumphs, the truth is revealed, and faith is rewarded. Even in action/adventure films, violence is a necessary means of restoring and preserving this ideal order.

Within this context, the individualism that characterizes romanticism is a celebration of the divinity in human beings. As poet Walt Whitman declares in *Song of Myself,*

I celebrate myself and sing myself,
And what I assume you shall assume,
For every atom belonging to me as good belongs to you.[30]

An important issue in the romantic worldview is *control.* A formulaic plotline in many popular genres involves the protagonist taking charge of a chaotic situation, despite overwhelming odds. Control is a central issue in advertising as well. Beyond selling a particular product, a latent message in many ads is the promise that the product will enable the consumer to assume control of their lives. For instance, a television commercial for Chevrolet begins with a rock singer in the foreground. The song lyrics announce:

I get what I want
I go where I please. . . .

This latent message of control even extends to the worldview of broadcast news. No matter how catastrophic the news, the broadcast anchor is trained to present the information in a measured—and controlled—fashion.

However, women in media presentations often inhabit a world in which they are powerless. They live in fear of the elements, of men, and of their own natures. The only chance for happiness for these women is through male benevolence and protection.

To be sure, we are exposed to entertainment and informational programming that represents a departure from this romantic ideal. For instance, the horror genre presents a world of evil and chaos, in which human beings are powerless and vulnerable. This genre explores concerns that are fundamentally terrifying to humans: fear of death, of demons, of worlds beyond our understanding, and of our own Promethean delusions that are manifested in the creation of nuclear-inspired monsters (giant ants, for instance). However, order is generally restored at the conclusion, which re-establishes this romantic ideal—at least until the sequel is released.

Values Hierarchy

How can you identify the value system operating within the worldview of a media presentation?

Milton Rokeach defines the notion of values as "[a]n enduring belief that a specific mode of conduct or end-state of existence is personally or socially preferable to alternate modes of conduct or end-state of existence."[31]

The values system in a media presentation generally represents the culmination of layers of belief systems. The personal values of the media communicator are defined through membership in a number of subcultures: gender (male-female), ethnic/racial identity (e.g., African American, Jewish), stage of life (college student), and social class—all of which operate according to separate value systems. Thus, in order to identify a value system operating in a media production, it is of paramount importance to define its culture (or subcultures).

The following two strategies for identifying the values system operating in a media presentation are particularly useful:

- *Analyze the characters appearing in the production as the embodiment of values.* In media presentations, heroes and heroines personify those qualities that society considers admirable. Heroes generally prevail in media entertainment programming because they embody the values that are esteemed within the culture. For instance, originally Superman was described as committed to "Truth and Justice." But as a consequence of the Cold War era of the 1950s, "The American Way" was added to this declaration of values embodied by Superman.

- These values are often the source of the hero's courage and strength. In westerns, heroes like John Wayne adhered to a strict moral code: never draw first or shoot a man in the back. Although this code sometimes puts the hero at a momentary disadvantage, any violation of these principles would have meant his ultimate downfall.

In contrast, villains generally epitomize those negative values that threaten the worldview of the presentation. Villains are not bound by the moral constraints to which heroes must adhere; they are free to draw first, lie, and cheat. However, these momentary advantages are not powerful enough to topple the moral order of the universe. Villains are inevitably brought to justice for their wrongdoings—and, in a larger sense, for their transgressions against the moral order of the universe (as personified by the hero).

Even nonfiction heroes who appear in the media are celebrated because they embody these cultural values. In reality, however, few people can fulfill these expectations. Public figures fall from grace once their flaws have been exposed by the media—almost as though the public cannot forgive them for being human. (For more discussion, see Chapter 10, American Political Communications.)

Examine the hierarchy of values at the conclusion of the presentation. As the protagonists and villains engage in conflict, the values that they personify are also in opposition:

- Good versus evil
- Justice versus injustice
- Truth versus falsehood
- Love versus hate
- Internal satisfaction versus material acquisitions
- Immediate satisfaction versus delayed gratification

The outcome of the production establishes a hierarchy of values. For instance, the culminating battle scene in action films resolves the conflict between good and evil. As the good guys win and justice prevails, a system of values has been firmly established.

Measures of Success. Media programming furnishes perspective into the ideal of success, as defined by the culture in which the media presentation was produced. Success can be identified through the *kinds* of behavior that are rewarded in media presentations and *how* they are rewarded. Thus, it is possible to construct a composite picture of success in American culture by examining cumulative media messages:

1. *As Validation.* The roots of the American myth of success can be traced to our Puritan tradition. According to the Puritan doctrine of predestination, God foreordained all things, especially the salvation of individual's souls. This doctrine also provided an elaborate rationale and justification for personal achievement. Material success on earth was regarded as a sign that a person was predestined to go to heaven.

   A secular version of Puritanism has translated easily into the American capitalistic definitions of success. A very subtle system of morality justifies the system. Those who succeed, somehow, are deserving; those who fail are unworthy.

2. *As Immortality.* The notion of "upward mobility" suggests a heaven on earth, beyond worldly cares and concerns. Successful people attract public attention and adulation. Fame makes them appear bigger than life; truly successful people leave a legacy that lives on after their deaths.

3. *As Conquest.* Striving for success is often portrayed as a test of personal resolve, requiring discipline, sacrifice, commitment, and sacrifice. In an 1888 instructional book entitled *Road to Success; a Book for Boys and Young Men,* the Reverend Aaron Wanner declares that success is not for the frail: "A weak, sickly body is a great impediment in the way to one's success. It is like a broken, leaky roof, which subjects everything in the house to injury."[32]

4. *As Self-Determination.* Heroes are in control, free to determine their own fate, and in a position to assert their individuality.

5. *As Physical Ideal.* Movie stars are objects of admiration because of their appearance. Moreover, athletes are admired for their athletic prowess.

6. *As a Contest.* Success is a sport, in which people compete against one another. Popular books offer strategies that give individuals the advantages they need to come out on top:
   - *Winning through Intimidation,* Robert Ringer
   - *Nonverbal Communication for Business Success,* Ken Cooper
   - *The Psychology of Effective Living,* Roger C. Bailey

7. *As American Dream.* According to the Horatio Alger myth, anyone can succeed through hard work. If you believe hard enough in

your dream, it will come true. However, this myth also serves as an elaborate defense of the status quo. Those members of minority groups who manage to succeed are offered as proof that the system works for everyone. In the process, the Horatio Alger myth minimizes the effort required for minorities to overcome cultural hurdles. And by extension, those who do not succeed must be slackers.

8. *As the Acquisition of Wealth.* For some, the accumulation of possessions is the ultimate measure of success. Within this orientation, notions of an afterlife are not even considered; existence has been confined to this world. Consequently, life's meaning is reduced to a contest: in the words of the popular bumper sticker, "The one who dies with the most toys wins." Through some sort of consumer transmutation, we become what we purchase. If we *look* successful, we *are* successful.

SUMMARY

Applying the following questions related to *Cultural Context* can provide insight into media messages:

1. Media and Popular Culture
   a. In what ways does the media presentation *reflect* the following?
      1. Cultural attitudes
      2. Values
      3. Behaviors
      4. Preoccupations
      5. Myths
      6. Cultural changes
      7. Attitudes toward groups
   b. In what ways does the media presentation *reinforce* the following?
      1. Cultural attitudes
      2. Values
      3. Behaviors
      4. Preoccupations
      5. Myths
   c. In what ways does the media presentation *shape* the following?
      1. Cultural attitudes
      2. Values
      3. Behaviors

      4. Preoccupations

      5. Myths

2. *Worldview:* What kind of world is depicted in the media presentation?

   a. What culture or cultures populate this world?

      1. What kinds of people populate this world?

      2. What is the ideology of this culture?

   b. What do we know about the people who populate this world?

      1. Are characters presented in a stereotypical manner?

      2. What does this tell us about the cultural stereotype of this group?

   c. Does this world present an optimistic or pessimistic view of life?

      1. Are the characters in the presentation happy?

      2. Do the characters have a *chance* to be happy?

   d. Are people in control of their own destinies?

      1. Is there a supernatural presence in this world?

      2. Are the characters under the influence of other people?

   e. What hierarchy of values is in operation in this worldview?

      1. What embedded values can be found in the production?

      2. What values are embodied in the characters?

      3. What values prevail through the resolution?

      4. What does it mean to be a success in this world?

         a. How does a person succeed in this world?

         b. What kinds of behavior are rewarded in this world?

NOTES

1. Russel B. Nye, "Notes on a Rationale for Popular Culture," in *A Popular Culture Reader,* ed. Jack Nachbar, Deborah Weiser, and John L. Wright (Bowling Green, OH: Bowling Green University Popular Press, 1978), 22.

2. Ibid., 20.

3. Ibid., 23.

4. Michael Brick, "In Colorful Bouts, Hint of Deeper Struggles," *New York Times,* May 10, 2009.

5. Center on Media and Child Health, http://www.education.com/reference/article/how-much-sexual-content-media (updated August 10, 2009).

6. Foster Hirsch, *The Dark Side of the Screen* (Cambridge, MA: Da Capo Press, 2001).

7. Julie Bosman, "Hey, Just Because He's Divorced Doesn't Mean He Can't Sell Things," *New York Times,* August 17, 2006: C-6.

8. David Carr, "Reporters on Film: Drunks and Tarts," *New York Times,* August 14, 2006: C-1.

9. Andrew Jacobs, "An Immigrant Segment by Radio's 'Jersey Guys' Draws Fire," *New York Times,* March 23, 2007: A-20.

10. Alan O'Connor, "Culture and Communication," *Questioning the Media: A Critical Introduction,* ed. John Downing, Ali Mohammadi, and Annabelle Sreberny-Mohammadi (Newbury Park, CA: Sage Publications, 1990), 37.

11. Naomi Wolf, *The Beauty Myth* (New York: William Morrow and Company, Inc., 1991), 156–7.

12. Ibid., 133.

13. Ibid., 167.

14. "Age and Sex Composition, 2010," United States Census Bureau, http://www.census.gov/prod/cen2010/briefs/c2010br-03.pdf.

15. Stacy L. Smith and Mark Choueiti, "Gender Inequality in Cinematic Context? A Look at Females On Screen & Behind the Camera in Top Grossing Films of 2008," Annenberg School for Communication and Journalism, University of Southern California, http://annenberg.usc.edu/Faculty/Communication%20and%20Journalism/~/media/91FF31336D8A48538154CA4F4850635A.ashx.

16. Ibid.

17. Elizabeth Monk-Turner, Mary Heiserman, Crystle Johnson, Vanity Cotton, and Manny Jackson, "The Portrayal of Racial Minorities on Prime Time Television: A Replication of the Mastro and Greenberg Study a Decade Later," *Studies in Popular Culture* 32.2 (Spring 2010), http://pcasacas.org/SiPC/32.2/Monk-Turner_Heiserman_Johnson_Cotton_Jackson.pdf and www.quickfacts.uscensus.gov.

18. George Gerbner and Nancy Signorielli, "Violence Profile 1967 through 1988–89; Enduring Patterns," January 1990.

19. Karen Sternheimer, "Who Is Most Likely to Be a Crime Victim?" *Everyday Sociology* (May 2009), http://nortonbooks.typepad.com/everydaysociology/2009/05/who-is-most-likely-to-be-a-crime-victim.html.

20. Alain de Botton, *Freidrich Nietzsche, The Consolations of Philosophy* (New York: Pantheon Books, 2000), 206.

21. Malcolm W. Browne, "Television Blocks the View," *New York Times,* January 27, 1981: C-2.

22. William B. Helmreich, *The Things They Say behind Your Back: Stereotypes & the Myths behind Them* (New Brunswick, NJ: Transaction, 1983), 44.

23. Associated Press, "Study of Immigrants Links Lighter Skin and Higher Income," *New York Times,* January 28, 2007: A-19.

24. The Hill, http://thehill.com/video/ campaign/258689-gingrich-obama-not-a-real-president.

25. The Opportunity Agenda: Media Research, Media Training, http://opportunityagenda.org/files/field_file/oa_brochure_part_two.pdf.

26. Ibid.

27. David Carr, "The Devil Wears Teflon," *New York Times,* July 10, 2006: C-1.

28. Ibid.

29. Richard Harter Fogle, ed., *The Romantic Movement in American Fiction* (New York: The Odyssey Press, 1966), 3.
30. Walt Whitman, *Leaves of Grass* (New York: The Viking Press, 1959), 26.
31. Milton Rokeach, *Beliefs, Attitudes, and Values: A Theory of Organization and Change* (San Francisco: Jossey-Bass, 1968), 113.
32. Rev. Aaron Wanner, *Road to Success: A Book for Boys and Young Men* (Reading, PA: Daniel Miller, 1888), 12.

5

Structure

In the United States, the concentration of ownership in the media industry has become an extremely troubling trend. In 1981, Ben Bagdikian found that 46 corporations owned or controlled the majority of media outlets in the United States. As of 2013, that number had shrunk to *six* corporations: Time Warner, Walt Disney, Viacom, News Corporation, CBS, and NBC Universal. These corporations control over 90 percent of the media consumed in the United States.[1]

This ownership model fits F. M. Sherer and D. Ross's definition of an *oligopoly:*

> Oligopoly refers to an industry characterized by a few mutually interdependent firms, with relatively similar shares, producing either a homogeneous product (a perfect oligopoly) or heterogeneous products (an imperfect oligopoly). Under such a market structure, the industry leader often sets the price.[2]

As a result, in the Western media system, which is market driven, the latent function behind many programming decisions is *profit.* To illustrate, one of the primary reasons that television executives have embraced the genre of reality shows is because these programs are so inexpensive to produce. These programs do not require hiring professional actors or scriptwriters, which generates extraordinary profits. The popularity of this genre has only added to the glut of profits for the stations and their owners.

IMPACT OF CONSOLIDATION OF MEDIA OWNERSHIP ON CONTENT

The ownership of media production companies in the United States has a significant impact on media content. Although individual media communicators

Table 5.1   Market Value of Top 8 Media Conglomerates

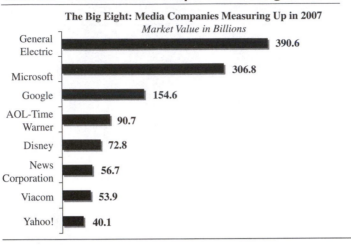

The Big Eight: Media Companies Measuring Up in 2007
Market Value in Billions

Company	Value
General Electric	390.6
Microsoft	306.8
Google	154.6
AOL-Time Warner	90.7
Disney	72.8
News Corporation	56.7
Viacom	53.9
Yahoo!	40.1

or media presentations may present a prosocial ideology, the latent ideology of the corporation is simply to make a profit. Thus, as media literacy consultant Julie Smith observes, "I find it interesting that Unilever owns both Axe and Dove. One aimed at "empowering" women regardless of what we look like . . . the other totally misogynistic."[3]

Media ownership influences content in the following respects:

1. ***Homogeneity of Content.*** Media outlets owned by a mega-corporation have a uniform style, content, and operating philosophy. To illustrate, the medium of radio originally comprised mostly small, independent, locally owned stations. Increasingly, however, small radio stations have been purchased by large conglomerates. These stations have identical formats, playlists, promotions, and jokes, as dictated by the "home office."

   To eliminate the cost of producing their own programming, the parent company of these radio stations often subcontract with national news services. For instance, Metro Networks, a Houston-based company, provides news, sports, weather, and other information to more than 2,300 radio stations, 170 television affiliates, and 700 Web sites, reaching an audience of nearly 100 million people throughout the United States. Metro Networks may serve several stations in one market; in New York, for example, nearly 100 stations subcontract with Metro. Although the news staff at each station rewrites the copy to make it appear distinctive, this practice reduces the diversity of news sources.

   Radio conglomerates also save expenses by purchasing *syndicated* programs. A syndicated program is produced in one location and then sold to stations throughout the country. Thus, if a radio station carries Rush Limbaugh instead of producing a local talk program, they are spared the cost of hiring *three* people: a host, producer, and engineer. Unfortunately, the radio listeners are also denied the opportunity to hear issues being discussed from a local perspective.

Moreover, one conglomerate can dominate an entire region. To illustrate, Clear Channel, Inc., owns all six commercial stations in Minot, North Dakota, the state's fourth-largest city, with a population nearing 37,000.

2. ***Support of Status Quo.*** Because the media are a major industry in the United States, the corporate worldview has become predominant in media-carried content.

The conglomerates that own media companies are beneficiaries of existing political and economic policies. As a result, while media companies may call for some refinements within the existing system, they cannot be counted upon to press for significant changes in the current system. Ben Bagdikian declares, "The lords of the global village have their own political agenda. All resist economic changes that do not support their own financial interests."[4] For example, one avenue for political campaign reform calls for television, as a guardian of the public airwaves, making free airtime available for political ads. Needless to say, the media conglomerates do not support this idea.

3. ***Programming as "Product."*** One of the primary reasons that mega-corporations acquire media companies is for their cash flow potential—which is considerable. As a result, media presentations are thought of simply as products, like shoes or showerheads, to be manufactured and sold.

To illustrate, during the 1950s, local television news was regarded as a public service. Television executives counted on their entertainment division to underwrite the expenses of producing the news. However, by the 1970s, the news operation was expected to break even. Thus, although news programming was not expected to make a profit, news programming should not lose money. Today, however, the news division has emerged as a principal profit center for local television stations. This economic imperative has had a dramatic impact on news content. News stations now select sensational, sentimental, or dramatic stories to attract viewers. As Max Frankel explains,

> News operations] are pressured to find a mass audience with maudlin tales of individual struggle, worshipful portraits of pop celebrities and photogenic scandals that are easily grasped. Anything long or complicated would shrink the audience.[5]

As a result, during the quarterly ratings period known as the "sweeps," local television stations commonly feature week-long "news" stories on provocative topics like wrestling, prostitution, and breast implants in hopes of attracting the largest possible audience.

4. ***Derivative Programming.*** In the Western, market-driven media system, in which the primary *function,* or purpose, is to maximize profit, media companies are reluctant to take artistic risks. Bill Carter discovered, upon interviewing an anonymous media executive,

> The first thing that happens is they throw out the four wilder ideas because they're just too risky. Then they start to tinker with the others. And every change they suggest makes the show more conventional. Then they give you a list for actors and say don't cast anyone not on this list. Then there's a list for directors. And by the time they get the shows, they wonder why they have no original ideas.[6]

In this competitive global economy, it is more difficult to obtain financing from banks. As a result, according to Fabrizio Perretti, a management professor at the Università Bocconi in Italy, film companies are faced with the challenge of competing to make bigger, costlier films while eliminating risk.[7]

In keeping with this conservative philosophy, production studios rely on derivative programming, featuring formulaic plots, sequels and "bankable" stars. Within this context, "new" programming is simply an established genre, with a slight twist. To illustrate, a *New York Times* film review describes *The Heat* (2013) as a "cop-buddy movie with women."[8]

In a column about the upcoming 2013–2014 broadcast television schedule, Maureen Dowd made the following observations about "new" programs:

• So NBC, which some weeks finished last behind Univision, offers us Blair Underwood in *Ironside,* a remake of its old series with Raymond Burr; Minnie Driver in *About a Boy,* a redo of the movie based on Nick Hornby's novel; James Spader in *The Blacklist* as yet another variation on Hannibal Lecter, a suave criminal mastermind strapped to a chair who will only cooperate with the FBI if he works with a young, pretty female agent; and

Jonathan Rhys Meyers in *Dracula,* which doesn't really count as new blood.

- Judd Apatow and Kristen Wiig turned Melissa McCarthy into an outsize star in the movie *Bridesmaids,* so naturally lots of writers raced to produce pilots with plus-size women straining to be funny. Rebel Wilson, the talented, heavyset Aussie actress who played Wiig's obnoxious roommate in *Bridesmaids,* will star in ABC's *Super Fun Night,* about three nerdy girlfriends who aim for madcap Friday nights.

- *Back in the Game* is about a young blonde who joins a beer-guzzling former baseball player in coaching an underdog Little League team. *Bad News Bears* redux. *Resurrection* is about dead relatives popping up on the doorstep—zombies with better skin.

- CBS proffers *Reckless,* described as a sultry legal show set in Charleston, SC, with a comely Yankee litigator clashing over a police scandal with a Southern city attorney "as they struggle to hide their intense attraction." I saw this when the city attorney was a New Orleans cop and it was called *The Big Easy,* starring Ellen Barkin and Dennis Quaid.

- CBS has *Bad Teacher,* based on the 2011 Cameron Diaz movie, and *Friends with Better Lives,* the plot of which sounds just like the 2006 Nicole Holofcener movie, *Friends with Money.*

- Fox has *Enlisted,* a wacky comedy about three brothers in the Army in Florida, which smacks of Bill Murray, Harold Ramis, and John Candy in *Stripes,* even down to what sounds like the same music. J. J. Abrams's *Almost Human* looks like a hand-me-down blend of *RoboCop* and *Blade Runner.*

  Even Fox's freshest ideas are antique: a show about a hunky Ichabod Crane called *Sleepy Hollow* and *24* with Kiefer Sutherland, but this time squeezed into 12 episodes.[9]

In making programming decisions, American media executives often look to foreign programs that already have a proven financial record. Television shows considered for the 2013–2014 broadcast season included programs that originated in Argentina, Australia, Britain, and Israel.

5. *Cross-Promotion.* Cross-promotion is a strategy in which a latent function of media programming is the promotion of other holdings within the corporate empire. As an example, St. Louis television critic Gail Pennington identified the following instances in which local news stories presented on NBC affiliate KSDK in 2004 were actually thinly disguised promotions for other network programs:

Table 5.2   NewsCorp Holdings

Television	Fox Broadcasting Company · Fox Television Stations
TV Stations	WNYW · WWOR · KTTV · KCOP · WFLD · WPWR · KMSP · WFTC · WTXF · WFXT · WTTG · WDCA · KDFW · KDFI · WJBK · KUTP · KSAZ · WUTB · WRBW · WOFL · WOGX · WAGA · KRIV · KTXH · WJW · WTVT · KDVR · KTVI · WITI · WDAF · KSTU · WHBQ · WGHP · WBRC · KTBC
DBS and Cable	FOXTEL · BSkyB · Star · DirecTV · Sky Italia · Fox News Channel · Fox Movie Channel ·FX · FUEL · National Geographic Channel · SPEED Channel · Fox Sports Net · FSN New England (50%) · FSN Ohio · FSN Florida · National Advertising Partners · Fox College Sports · Fox Soccer Channel · Stats, Inc.
Film	20th Century Fox · Fox Searchlight Pictures · Fox Television Studios · Blue Sky Studios
Newspapers	*New York Post · News International · News of the World · The Sun · The Sunday Times · The Times · Daily Telegraph · Fiji Times · Gold Coast Bulletin · Herald Sun · Newsphotos · Newspix · Newstext · NT News · Post-Courier · Sunday Herald Sun · Sunday Mail · Sunday Tasmanian · Sunday Territorian · Sunday Times · The Advertiser · The Australian · The Courier-Mail · The Mercury · The Sunday Telegraph · Weekly Times*
Magazines	*InsideOut · donna hay · SmartSource · The Weekly Standard · TV Guide* (partial)
Books	HarperMorrow Publishers · HarperMorrow · General Books Group · Access · Amistad · Caedmon · Avon · Ecco · Eos · Fourth Estate · HarperAudio · HarperBusiness · HarperCollins · Harper Design International · HarperEntertainment · HarperLargePrint · HarperResource · HarperSanFrancisco · HarperTorch · Perennial · PerfectBound · Quill · Rayo · ReganBooks · William Morrow · William Morrow Cookbooks
Children's Books	Avon · Greenwillow Books · Joanna Cotler Books · Eos · Laura Geringer Books · HarperAudio · HarperCollins Children's Books · HarperFestival · HarperTempest · Katherine Tegen Books · Trophy · Zondervan
HarperCollins UK	HarperCollins Canada · HarperCollins Australia
Other	Los Angeles Kings (NHL, 40% option) · Los Angeles Lakers (NBA, 9.8% option) ·Staples Center (40% owned by Fox/Liberty) · News Interactive · Fox Sports Radio Network · Sky Radio Denmark · Sky Radio Germany · Broadsystem · Classic FM · Festival Records · Fox Interactive · IGN Entertainment · Mushroom Records · MySpace.com · National Rugby League · NDS · News Outdoor · Nursery World · Scout Media

- One story profiled Donald Trump, star of "one of the most successful reality shows on television, *The Apprentice,* airing 'right here on Newschannel 5.'"
- Another story took viewers behind the scenes on *Law & Order: Special Victims Unit,* another NBC series.
- *Cover Story* visited *Saturday Night Live,* marking "30 years of SNL on Newschannel 5."
- A recurring segment called "Monday's Movers and Shakers" featured NBC personalities, such as retiring news anchor Tom Brokaw and *Hardball* host Chris Matthews of MSNBC.[10]

Unfortunately, this promotional strategy may be difficult to detect, unless you are familiar with all of the vast holdings of a media conglomerate. Jeff MacGregor observes,

> To the casual consumer of entertainment, it's almost impossible to discern the linkages between product and promoter. Until recently, for example, *TV Guide* was owned by the News Corporation, Rupert Murdoch's umbrella for his global communications company. News Corp. also owns 20th Century Fox. And the Fox network. Does that account then for the substantial number of decorative cover stories over the last few seasons devoted to *The Simpsons* and *The X-Files*? What about a show like *The Practice,* which was the subject of a cover story last season slugged "the best show you're not watching"? But that's on the ABC network, you say. Yes, it is. But it's produced by the Fox Studio, 20th Century Fox Television.[11]

Table 5.3   NewsCorp Revenue

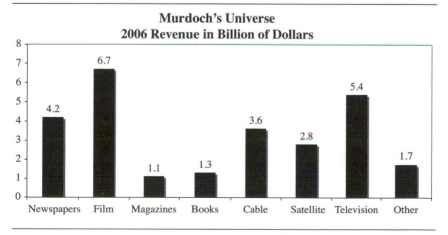

6. **Conflicts of Interest.** These may arise with regard to stories that involve the parent company of a media conglomerate. For example, in 2011, the *New York Times* was criticized for the lack of coverage in its newspaper about the problems that the newspaper has encountered as it added an interactive format to its news operation—including its plan to start charging for access to its Web site and extraordinary technical problems its readers have encountered. In contrast, other newspapers, including *Bloomberg Businessweek* and the *Wall Street Journal,* have published stories about this topic. Moreover, these types of stories that involve other media outlets such as the *London Times, Chicago Tribune,* and *Los Angeles Times* have appeared in the *New York Times.* According to Arthur S. Brisbane, the public editor of the *New York Times,*

> In a way that's visible internally and externally, *The Times* should commit the media team to covering *The Times* itself more aggressively. This would yield stories that readers want to read and blunt criticism that, when it comes to covering itself, *The Times* has a blind spot.[12]

In addition, the executives of these media conglomerates frequently have ties to the political establishment, creating potential conflicts of interest in terms of their coverage. To illustrate, the owner of the *U-T San Diego,* the San Diego, California, daily newspaper, has been criticized for using the newspaper to promote his political and business interests. Columnist David Carr explains,

> Mr. Manchester is anti-big government, anti-tax and anti-gay marriage. And he's in favor of a remade San Diego centered around a new downtown waterfront stadium and arena.
>
> Public agencies that have not gotten the hint have found themselves investigated in the news pages of *The U-T.* A sports columnist who was skeptical of the plans found himself out of a job, and the newspaper has published front-page editorials and wraparound sections to promote political allies who share its agenda.[13]

7. **Ignoring Public Service Responsibilities.** As part of the drive to maximize profits, many media outlets have cut staff, which not only compromises the quality of programming, but can also jeopardize

public health and security. A famous example occurred in 2002, when a train derailed in Minot, North Dakota, leaking thousands of gallons of toxic chemicals into the air. One person died and hundreds were treated for immediate health problems. After the town's emergency alert system failed, local officials and panic-stricken residents tried to call one of these stations, KCJB (910 AM), which was the town's designated local emergency broadcaster, but no one answered. Instead of providing emergency information to the city's residents, the stations continued to play the programmed music that was piped in from out of state. At the time of the accident, none of the city's six commercial radio stations—all owned by Clear Channel Communications—had local staff members available who could have issued warnings to local residents. Professor Eric Klinenberg declared,

> (Clear Channel has) replaced live local talent, deejays, talk show hosts, programmers, with automated programming, oftentimes faked to sound like it's local, even though it's programmed in a remote studio thousands of miles away. That night in Minot, North Dakota, there was no one in any of those six stations. . . . The result is that when the Emergency Alert System failed, there was no way to get the word out.
>
> I think this is a story that Americans need to know, because when we make policy decisions to allow more consolidated media ownership, to allow one company to own six stations, it's my belief, my experience, that we compromise our local security, our national security.[14]

INTERNAL STRUCTURE

The *internal structure* of a media organization consists of the following elements: the *resources* of the production company, the *organizational framework* (i.e., different departments, lines of responsibility), and the *process of decision-making*. These organizational factors have an impact on day-to-day decisions, as well as long-range planning.

Case Study: Television News Operation

To illustrate, consider the organizational structure of a television news operation and its impact on news content.

The Resources of the Station. The resources of a news operation can have a dramatic affect on a station's ability to gather and report the news. Local television stations range from sophisticated operations with $30 million budgets to skeletal one-person news departments. As Max Frankel explains, the size of the staff (writers, reporters, videographers, and editors) drastically affects the depth and quality of news coverage:

> Television news staffs could not possibly show a profit if they rigorously tried to investigate a crime wave or social trend or school performance. A camera-wielding crew of experienced reporters would have to spend days, even weeks, on assignment to do such stories. Most local stations, seeking profit margins of 35 to 50 percent, could never pay for such talent. So they chase squad cars and ambulances and stand "live" before brick walls and try to validate glib judgments about the performance of a mayor, warden, or fire chief. And their anchors merely smile and opine their way through the day's headlines about murder, disease, weather, and sports.[15]

Other big-budget items include subscriptions to national and international news services, satellite transmission, sophisticated mini-cams, and helicopters—all of which can be cut to save expenses.

A typical television station employs a large staff, including writers, reporters, videographers, and editors. (Anthony Brown/Dreamstime.com)

Because of these limited resources, local television news operations sometimes must rely on *video news releases* (VNRs)—reports that are produced to look like news stories but actually promote the interests of a company represented by the public relations firm that mail VNRs to local broadcast stations. Jeff Pooley explains, "VNRs—which *USA Today* once described as 'Hamburger Helper for newscasters'—are a boon to cash-strapped newsrooms, which rarely identify the source of the footage."[16]

In 2011, the FCC fined Fox Television Stations, Inc., $4,000 when station affiliate KMSP-TV of Minneapolis failed to identify airing a General Motors-provided VNR during a news broadcast and fined Comcast for airing two VNRs from General Mills and Allstate.

Video news releases also have been used for political purposes. In 2004, it was discovered that the Bush administration had violated federal law by promoting its Medicare program throughout the United States disguised as television news segments. The VNR contained all of the formulaic elements of a broadcast news story, including a voiceover by a person who signed off, "In Washington, I'm Karen Ryan reporting." However, Karen Ryan was not a journalist; instead, she was an actress whom the public relations firm had hired to produce the VNRs.

Although the audience was expecting to receive an informative report about the Medicare program, they were instead presented with the government's "spin" about the program. Consequently, the Government Accountability Office, an investigative arm of Congress, declared that the video "constitute[s] covert propaganda" because the government was not identified as the source of the story and, as a result, violated the ban on using taxpayer money for propaganda.

The FCC has proposed legislation that would require that television stations disclose the sources of financial support behind a VNR.

The Organization of the Newsroom. As the chief operating officer of the television station, the *general manager* is primarily responsible for the overall operation of the station, including long-term planning, community service, programming, and budgetary considerations. Ordinarily, the general manager is not involved in the day-to-day activities in the newsroom; however, if he or she becomes enamored of a pet project for the news, it usually finds its way onto the air.

The *business manager* is responsible for all financial aspects of the news station. As such, he or she monitors the entire operation from a fiscal point of view, including costs associated with the news broadcast. The recommendations of the business manager on the purchase of news gathering

Table 5.4 The Structure of a Newsroom

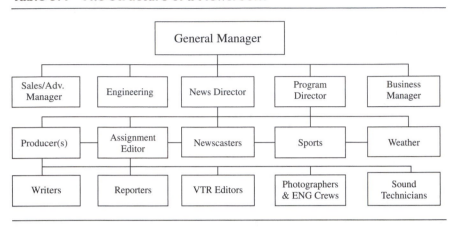

equipment, salaries for writers, reporters, and anchors can have a significant impact on the quality of the newscast.

The *news director* is directly responsible for the station's daily newscasts. However, according to Jim Willis and Diane B. Willis, the news director's mission to produce the news often is compromised by the pressure to maintain strong ratings:

> Often the quality that the news director would like to have in the newscasts is deemed too expensive to produce by owners and upper management. One key reason this is true is that too many upper-level managers tend to look at newsroom expenses as costs rather than investments that will pay dividends later in a quality news product. . . . Often, too, the kind of patience a news director would like to exhibit to give his or her staff a chance to shine is cut short by the demands of upper management and owners to produce first-place newscasts sooner rather than later.
>
> These tensions often cause news directors to leave their position and move on to other markets. The average length of employment of many news directors at any single station is often less than two years.[17]

The decision-making process in the broadcast newsroom involves the following considerations:

- Who is the initial gatekeeper for news stories?

    While the assignment editor is generally the person responsible for assigning stories to reporters, in larger stations the initial gatekeeper may be a person in an entry-level position. This person, who opens the mail and answers the phones, only passes along the information he or she considers newsworthy.

- What are the criteria for the selection of stories?
- Is the process of news selection arbitrary (one person) or consultative?
- Is there an appeal process?
- How is it determined which crews (reporters and camerapeople) are assigned to a story?
- How are deadlines for stories determined?

    Time constraints can have a direct bearing on the quality of news coverage. For example, journalists often rely on particular sources for information based on the "rule of the rolodex"; that is, once they have found a source who is not only a good interview but is also readily available, they often go back to this person again and again.

The decision-making process in the entertainment media industry has become so bureaucratic that it often affects the creative process. According to Larry Doyle, an idea has to clear a panel of executives—nearly an impossible task:

There are many number of logical theories to explain the bureaucratic swarming—Chinese-box conglomeration, network ownership by parts manufacturers; panic . . . but still, it's an amazing thing to see. It is not unusual these days for a television series creator to have to answer to 10 or more executives. . . . "Can we start the story sooner?" "Can we raise the stakes?" "Can we make the lead more rootable?" they ask interchangeably, not moron so much as joylessly correct automaton.[18]

MEDIA AND GOVERNMENT REGULATION

The relationship between a country's media system and its government's regulatory policy influences the quality and diversity of media messages. Each country maintains its own policy with regard to the content and dissemination of information through the channels of mass communication.

    In the United States, the First Amendment to the Constitution declares that "Congress shall make no laws abridging the freedom of speech, or of the press." Over the years, the term has been expanded to include any governmental body, local or federal. The First Amendment was established on the premise that the United States is a marketplace of ideas. All forms of ideas should be expressed, and each individual must be able to make his/her own decision about what is right and appropriate.

The Supreme Court has ruled that five categories of speech are not protected by the First Amendment: *obscenity, false advertising, "fighting words" inciting to riot,* and *defamation.* The challenge, then, is to determine the scope and the limits of these categories.

Legislating restrictions on speech is a complex and delicate matter. For instance, what people consider to be obscene changes over time. The original conception of obscenity referred to material that aroused "impure thoughts." This definition of obscenity is subjective; what is obscene to one person may not be to another.

Obscene material must be judged on the basis of the following criteria:

- "The material (taken as a whole) depicts or describes in a patently offensive manner sexual conduct specified by state or local law." However, the minimum standard of what is "patently offensive" is obscure.
- "An average person, applying contemporary community standards, looking at the work taken as a whole, determines that it appeals to the prurient interest." In this case, a court would apply a local, not a national community standard, which means that a work of art could be considered obscene in Little Rock but protected by the First Amendment in Chicago, Illinois. Thus, a community may pass its own laws declaring material obscene, but it must clearly define what constitutes obscenity.
- "The material taken as a whole lacks serious scientific, political, literary, or artistic value."

A legal precedent has been established (*Pope v. Illinois,* 1987) that a jury must use what a reasonable person under the circumstances would consider has scientific, literary, or artistic value as its guideline.

For material to be declared obscene, it must meet all three criteria. For example, in 1989, the city of Cincinnati charged the Cincinnati Museum of Art with six separate obscenity law violations for displaying a collection of photographs by photographer Robert Mapplethorpe. While the jury found that the photos met the first and second criteria, they ruled that the material did have artistic value, and accordingly, the case was dismissed.

Unlike print media, broadcasting over the airwaves is regulated by the Federal Communications Commission (FCC). The rationale often given for allowing the government to regulate (and license) this form of speech is as follows:

- *Scarcity of the airwaves.*
  Because only a limited number of broadcast frequencies are available, a formal procedure for licensing and use of the airwaves is necessary.
- *Public ownership.*
  The airwaves are owned by the people. Broadcasters therefore are entrusted with using the airwaves, so long as they serve the public interest.
- *Characteristics of broadcast media.*
  The broadcasting media (radio and television) are pervasive. Because broadcast programming comes directly into the home, the public needs protection from misuse.

As a result, broadcast stations have an obligation to serve the public interest. In their study of the historical foundations of the First Amendment, Dwight L. Teeter, Jr., and Don A. Le Duc observe,

> In essence, the [Supreme Court] held that by accepting the privilege of using the limited and valuable public resource of spectrum space, each broadcast licensee also assumed an obligation to exercise this privilege for the benefit of the public; an obligation the FCC had the authority to enforce on behalf of the public.[19]

However, this imperative to serve the public interest is often in conflict with the pressure on stations to generate profits.

In order for stations to operate, they must be awarded a license from the FCC (the duration of a TV license is for five years; a radio license is good for seven years). The criteria for acceptance are as follows:

- *Threshold.* All applicants must meet minimum criteria for citizenship, character, financial, and technical ability.
- *Comparative licensing.* Consideration is given to applicants who can provide the best service, as well as to groups that reflect cultural diversity. When a frequency becomes available, the FCC must hold public hearings to consider applications. However, there is generally an expectancy of renewal, giving the current license holder the advantage. Although the FCC is prohibited from censoring content, they are charged with maintaining the following programming standards:

- ○ *Obscene or indecent programming.* Under current regulations, this type of programming is absolutely prohibited.
- ○ *Personal attack and editorial.* The FCC establishes parameters for public debate on controversial issues and makes a distinction between personal attacks and political debate.

With the emergence of digital technology as a mass medium, cheap, competitive wireless broadband will be critical to the development of the digital economy. Consequently, who holds the rights to use the electromagnetic spectrum has become an essential issue.

Between 2001 and 2010, on behalf of the U.S. government, the Federal Communications Commission (FCC) raised $33 billion by leasing portions of the spectrum to the highest bidder. In 2012, the FCC approved a proposal to reclaim public airwaves now used for broadcast television and auction them off in 2014 to create additional wireless Internet systems, with a portion of the proceeds paid to the broadcasters. Reporter Eduardo Porter explains this plan:

> [The FCC] wants to acquire up to 120 Megahertz of spectrum, with 40 to 80 MHz being the more realistic goal. It will reorganize the spectrum into a big contiguous band—moving TV broadcasters into one compact block—and auction it off to wireless companies that value it much more highly.[20]

Commission officials and Congress have estimated that the process could generate $15 billion in proceeds.[21]

Although this current plan is designed to foster more competition, AT&T and Verizon Wireless, which currently control approximately two-thirds of the cellular communications market, are vying to maintain their dominance of this market, arguing that opening the spectrum to multiple small companies would be inefficient and ultimately would reduce the amount of revenue that the government could realize. In a letter to the FCC written in April 2013, AT&T declared, "The reduced auction revenues would mean less (and potentially no) broadcast spectrum cleared for mobile wireless use and less (or no) surplus available to fund the Spectrum Act's other goals."[22]

The development of new media technologies is redefining the philosophical basis for the regulation of broadcasting content. As an example, cable television (as well as cable radio) can carry considerably more channels than broadcast television. In addition, cable television is a service that the audience purchases; we invite cable into our home, as opposed to the more pervasive nature of traditional broadcast technology. Consequently, Attorney Michael Kahn contends these technological changes affect the regulation of broadcasting content:

> The whole intellectual framework for regulating radio and traditional television is based on radio and television technologies that are more than fifty years old. While the public may own the air, the cable companies own their cables. These days, it's cheaper to operate a local cable station than a local newspaper. As a result, reasons given for limiting the reach of the First Amendment in the regulation of radio and traditional TV don't easily transfer to cable TV. This is all good news for both consumers of news and producers of media, in that the basic First Amendment freedoms should be given more breathing space through cable technology than under the old regulation scheme of the FCC.[23]

Copyright

Copyright refers to the legal right of artists or their publishers to control the use and reproduction of their original works. However, enforcing national copyright laws—especially in an international arena—has been nearly impossible. International piracy of American films and music results in the loss of tens of thousands of jobs both inside and outside the industry and costs billions of dollars in lost wages, lost tax revenue, and diminished overall economic output. A study commissioned by the Motion Picture Association of America found that in 2005, movie companies lost $6.1 billion in revenues due to piracy.[24]

Efforts by the United States to pressure other countries to establish copyright laws has been a delicate matter. However, in 2007, the United States announced that it would impose strict tariffs on Chinese-manufactured goods in retaliation for China's violation of trade agreements.

In the media age, copyright regulations that heretofore had been rather straightforward have become more confusing. Using information that is presented in one medium and presenting it in another can provide layers of complexity that frustrate media communicators. Patricia Aufderheide explains,

> Not understanding your rights can . . . be expensive, and can fatally slow production in a deadline-driven business. But the worst effect is self-censorship—the decision not to use a photo or audio clip because you're not sure if you'd get in trouble with the law. . . . The evolution of

digital platforms and social media, and the reality of rapidly changing business models, not knowing your fair-use rights means not knowing—or even ceding—your free-speech rights under copyright law.[25]

For example, fair use is a legal principle that refers to the amount of information from the copyrighted material of others that can be quoted without permission or payment. Aufderheide cites the example of Prithi, a media communicator who was experienced "self-censorship" because of her confusion about fair use:

> Prithi did a beautiful arts feature on the history of a musical for radio. She never had to worry about all the illustrative music clips she used, because the service has a blanket license. But now she can't podcast it; the license agreement doesn't extend that far.[26]

However, fair use enables individuals to quote the copyrighted material of other people, without permission or payment, if they are "repurposing" it. Aufderheide explains,

> [Prithi] depended on blanket licensing to develop her story. She could have made her decisions according to fair use without making aesthetic sacrifices; she has a great case. Because she hasn't done a fair-use rationale, she's not in a good position to argue for the legality of the podcast. But if her quotations from the musical do fall under fair use (they are used for a different reason than simply having people enjoy the musical, and she uses as much as she needs to make her point), then she can podcast it with comfort.[27]

Net Neutrality

The principle of *Net neutrality* looms as a regulatory issue that will affect the future of the Internet. Net neutrality asserts that all Internet communication should be distributed without prejudice to volume or content. Net neutrality is a principle that guarantees a "level playing field" with regard to access of the digital landscape. Unlike other mass media channels, the Internet offers individual citizens and big companies the same opportunity to access information. Indeed, individuals can even produce and distribute information. A free and open Internet is essential to freedom of speech, innovation, and the exposure to different beliefs and ways of life.

However, major Internet service providers (ISPs) like AT&T, MCI, and Charter contend that they should have the right to "prioritize" the information that is distributed through their networks. The criteria for this multi-tiered system would be based upon commercial considerations. Cable and telephone companies want to sell specialized services that would speed some content to users more quickly for a fee. The highest priority would be for those conducting business directly with these companies.

Civil liberties organizations such as www.savetheInternet.com and the Electronic Frontier Foundation argue that allowing an Internet service provider to favor some content amounts to a violation of free speech and the potential for unfair competitive advantage. Without Net neutrality, an Internet service provider could block or limit data transfer from certain sites.

In December 2010, the FCC passed rules that would create two classes of Internet access: one for fixed-line providers and the other for the wireless Net. These first binding network neutrality rules would prevent fixed-line broadband providers like Comcast and Qwest from blocking access to sites and applications. At the same time, however, wireless companies would have more latitude with regard to limiting access to services and applications. Citing the wireless proposal, Senator Al Franken warned that these rules were effectively sanctioning discrimination on the mobile Net:

> Maybe you like Google Maps. Well, tough. If the FCC passes this weak rule, Verizon will be able to cut off access to the Google Maps app on your phone and force you to use their own mapping program, Verizon Navigator, even if it is not as good. And even if they charge money, when Google Maps is free. If corporations are allowed to prioritize content on the Internet, or they are allowed to block applications you access on your iPhone, there is nothing to prevent those same corporations from censoring political speech.[28]

In November 2011, the FCC filed a revised set of "Open Internet" rules, which maintain that an Internet service provider must treat all traffic on its system equally, without giving priority to any particular type of data or application. However, reporter Nate Anderson observes that these rules are different for wireless providers, in the following respects:

> First, *transparency:* fixed and mobile broadband providers must disclose the network management practices, performance characteristics, and commercial terms of their broadband services.

Second, *no blocking:* fixed broadband providers may not block lawful content, applications, services, or non-harmful devices; mobile broadband providers may not block lawful websites, or block applications that compete with their voice or video telephony services. Third, *no unreasonable discrimination*: fixed broadband providers may not unreasonably discriminate in transmitting lawful network traffic.

Mobile networks still have broad leeway to discriminate and throttle and even block certain apps, though some of the most obviously objectionable activities are forbidden.[29]

When a draft of the rules came out in December 2011, roughly 80 grassroots organizations signed an open letter avowing their disapproval, complaining that the rules "leave wireless users vulnerable to application blocking and discrimination," use "unnecessarily broad definitions," and claiming that specialized services "would create a pay-for-play platform that would destroy today's level playing field."[30]

At the same time, Verizon has challenged the Open Internet Order. In this ongoing saga, in May 2013 the U.S. Supreme Court supported the FCC's defense of Net neutrality. Supreme Court Justice Antonin Scalia commented, "The court must defer to the administering agency's construction of the statute so long as it is permissible."[31]

Beyond the specifics of the Open Internet Rules, the FCC has raised some serious questions about its purview. Wyatt explains,

The FCC, meanwhile, favors a level playing field, but it cannot impose one as long as its authority over broadband is in legal doubt. It has proposed a solution that would reclassify broadband Internet service under the Communications Act from its current designation as an "information service," a lightly regulated designation, to a "telecommunications service," a category that, like telephone service, is subject to stricter regulation. The FCC has said that it does not want to impose strict regulation on Internet service and rates, but seeks only the authority to enforce broadband privacy and guarantee equal access. It also wants to use federal money to subsidize broadband service for rural areas.[32]

In 2011, the U.S. Senate voted to keep an open Internet by preserving the FCC rules that were designed "to prevent Internet service providers from using speed or prioritization of traffic flow to discriminate on behalf of favored content partners."[33]

However, Net neutrality remains an issue that is still a matter of contention. Hogan Lovells, former member of the FCC, declared, "We're in the third inning of net neutrality. From here it's going to leave the FCC and move to the courts with some oversight in Congress."[34]

One solace with regard to the possible abolition of Net neutrality can be found in the principle of *media ping pong,* which holds that when government or corporate entities impose repressive regulations, activists implement new technological strategies that circumvent the regulations. In the case of Net neutrality, activists could simply construct a new Internet that focuses on ideas rather than commerce (perhaps modeled after the Intranet found in many colleges and universities).

SUMMARY

Applying the following questions related to *structure* can provide insight into media messages:

1. What are the ownership patterns within the media industry?
   a. What are the ownership patterns within the particular media system you are examining? (e.g., television, film, radio)
   b. Who owns the production company that has produced the presentation you are examining (e.g., television station, newspaper, film company)?
2. Does the ownership of the media presentation have an impact on its content?
   a. Support of status quo
   b. Homogeneity of content
   c. Programming for profit
   d. Cross-promotion
3. Does government regulation affect the media presentation?
4. What is the internal structure of the media organization responsible for producing the media presentation? How does this internal structure influence content?
   a. What are the resources of the production company?
   b. What is the organizational framework of the production company?
   c. What is the process of decision-making in the production company?

NOTES

1. "Who Owns What," *Columbia Journalism Review,* http://www.cjr.org/re
   -sources/index.php. Web site updated June 26, 2013.
2. Frederic M. Sherer and David Ross, *Industrial Market Structure and Economic Performance,* 3rd ed. (Boston: Houghton Mifflin, 1990).
3. Julie Smith, interview with author, Webster University, July 5, 2013.
4. Ben Bagdikian, *The Media Monopoly,* 5th ed. (Boston: Beacon Press, 1997), 36.
5. Max Frankel, "What's Happened to the Media?" *New York Times Magazine,* March 21, 1999: 38–40.
6. Bill Carter, "Shrinking Network TV Audiences Set Off Alarm and Reassessment," *New York Times,* November 22, 1998.
7. Adam Davidson, "How Does the Film Industry Actually Make Money?" *New York Times Magazine,* June 26, 2012: 16–17.
8. A. O. Scott, "Cop Buddies Packing Extra X Chromosomes," *New York Times,* June 28, 2013.
9. Maureen Dowd, "Serving up Schlock," *New York Times,* May 21, 2013.
10. Gail Pennington, "Newschannel 5: Where the Fluff Comes First," *St. Louis Post-Dispatch,* November 18, 2004: F-1.
11. Jeff MacGregor, "Why It Takes 400 Pages to Tell You What's On," *New York Times,* October 11, 1998.
12. Arthur S. Brisbane, "Business News You Didn't Read Here," *New York Times,* March 5, 2011.
13. David Carr, "Newspaper as Business Pulpit," *New York Times,* June 10, 2012.
14. Eric Klinenberg, interview on *Democracy Now!,* January 26, 2007, www .democracynow.com.
15. Frankel, "What's Happened to the Media?"
16. Jeff Pooley, "Hamburger Helper for Newscasters," *Brill's Content* (December 1998/January 1999): 46.
17. Jim Willis and Diane B. Willis, *New Directions in Media Management* (Boston: Allyn and Bacon, 1993), 198–9.
18. John Files, "Bush's Drug Videos Broke Law, Accountability Office Decides," *New York Times,* January 7, 2005: A-16.
19. Dwight Teeter and Don R. Le Duc, *Law of Mass Communications: Freedom and Control of Print and Broadcast Media,* 8th ed. (Westbury, NY: Foundation Press, 1995).
20. Eduardo Porter, "From Lottery to Oligopoly in Wireless Spectrum," *New York Times,* June 4, 2013.
21. Edward Wyatt, "FCC Backs Proposal to Realign Airwaves," *New York Times,* September 28, 2012.
22. Porter, "From Lottery to Oligopoly in Wireless Spectrum."

23. Michael Kahn, Attorney, Stinson, Mag & Fizzell, interview by author, June 6, 1999, St. Louis, Missouri.

24. Steven McElroy, "Financial Impact of Film Piracy," *New York Times,* September 30, 2006: B-8.

25. Patricia Aufderheide, "How Well Do You Know Fair Use?" *Columbia Journalism Review,* July 26, 2012. http://www.cjr.org/feature/copywrong.php?page=all.

26. Ibid.

27. Ibid.

28. Brian Stelter, "FCC Is Set to Regulate Net Access," *New York Times,* December 20, 2010.

29. Nate Anderson, "U.S. Net Neutrality Rules Finalized, in Effect November 20," in *Law and Disorder: Tech Law and Policy in the Digital Age,* http://arstechnica.com/tech-policy/news/2011/09/us-net-neutrality-rules-final-ized-in-effect-november-20.ars. Italics in original.

30. Sarah Kessler, "New Net Neutrality Rules Become Official," September 23, 2011, ads by Google Comcast® Official Site, http://mashable.com/2011/09/23/net-neutrality-rules-become-official/.

31. Edward Wyatt, "A Ruling Could Support FCC's Net Neutrality Defense," *New York Times,* May 22, 2013.

32. Edward Wyatt, "Google and Verizon Near Deal on Pay Tiers for Web," *New York Times,* August 4, 2010.

33. "Media Literacy Project Applauds Net-Neutrality Vote in Senate," press release, Media Literacy Project, http://medialiteracyproject.org/news/press-room/media-literacy-project-applauds-net-neutrality-vote-senate.

34. Kenneth Corbin, "Net Neutrality 2011: What Storms May Come," *Internet News,* December 30, 2010, www.internetnews.com/government/article.php/3918831.

6

Framework

INTRODUCTION

The introduction often foreshadows what to expect in the course of a media presentation. The opening of a film, television, or radio program acquaints the audience with the primary characters, plot outline, and the worldview of the programming. For instance, the James Bond films typically begin at the "climax" of another adventure. This scene is stripped of all context; we don't know who the villains are or why Bond is after them. But ultimately, as with the upcoming adventure, these details don't matter. The opening sequence conveys messages about the Bond series—specifically, that the spy thrillers are sophisticated, international in scope, and filled with action.

In addition, an introduction often poses a question or raises a mystery to be addressed in the course of the narrative. In entertainment programming such as police dramas, the question is "Who done it?" In news articles, the introduction makes a series of statements that are supported in the body of the report.

Title

The *title* of a media presentation generally encapsulates the essential meaning of the media presentation. Due to the competitive nature of the media industry, newspaper headlines, advertising slogans, political mottos, and song and movie titles are also designed to generate interest in the presentation. Some titles suggest thematic concerns addressed in the presentation; others titillate with promises of sex and violence. Even titles for film sequels, such as *Iron Man III* or *Toy Story IV,* announce that the audience should expect more of the same formulaic characters, action, and plot.

Indeed, the title is so critical that before legendary producer Roger Corman would launch a new film project, he would first conduct market research to find a film title that would catch the interest and imagination of the audience, such as *Naked Paradise* or *Attack of the Crab Monsters* (1957). He then created an entire film around these titles.[1]

Illogical Premise

A premise refers to the initial circumstances, situation, or assumptions that serve as the point of origin in the narrative. A description of premise usually answers the question, "What is this program about?"

According to Samuel Taylor Coleridge, our response to fiction is characterized by a "willing suspension of disbelief" in which the audience accepts the premise of the program, no matter how outlandish. The suspension of disbelief enables us to participate in fantasies and science fiction programs that would otherwise stretch our credulity.

Once this illogical premise has been accepted, the remainder of the narrative progresses in a logical fashion. To illustrate, consider the following premise:

> A scientist in a galaxy far from earth discovers that his planet faces imminent destruction. He does not have the time to save himself or his wife; however, he is able to construct a small rocket for his infant son. The rocket, carrying the boy, lifts off just before the planet explodes.
>
> The rocket finds its way to earth. Significantly, because of the earth's atmosphere, the boy has super powers; he can fly, has super strength and hearing, and never needs a haircut.

Once the audience has accepted the extraordinary premise of *Superman,* the remainder of the narrative proceeds naturally: the boy assumes a human identity, moves to the city, finds a job, and fights crime.

In some cases, the audience accepts, without question, a premise with ideological overtones. For example, the premise of police shows assumes the following: 1) the world is a dangerous place; 2) members of lower classes and African Americans are predators who pose a threat to the dominant culture; 3) the heroes know (without a trial) who is innocent and who is guilty; and 4) what is needed is a strong, undeterred authoritarian presence to remedy these problems. The reactionary political ideology behind this premise, in which civil liberties are sacrificed in the name of law and order, is made to look like an appealing option in this turbulent world.

Advertising frequently relies on an illogical premise to sell products. Once its premise has been accepted, an ad can be very persuasive. For instance, one television commercial begins with a shot of a door with the name "The Ponds Institute" etched on the glass. The door swings open, and audience members suddenly find themselves in the midst of a group of people in lab coats, walking purposefully as they conduct their business. A voice-over announces, "Here at the Ponds Institute, we are concerned with combating the effects of aging on the skin." This scenario instills us with confidence in Ponds beauty products. But upon reflection, several questions arise regarding the premise:

- Exactly where is the Ponds Institute?
- Can you get a degree from the Ponds Institute?
- Is it located near the Sassoon Academy?
- What kind of research is conducted at the Ponds Institute?
- Are the people wearing lab coats actually scientists?
- If the people shown are scientists, what are their areas of specialty?
- What kind of methodology is employed in its research?
- Can we obtain a copy of the results of the research?

Thus, as you begin to watch a film, see an ad, or read the newspaper, examine the underlying assumptions behind the premise of the presentation. At that point, you are in a position to make a conscious decision whether or not to willingly suspend your disbelief.

Plot

"Let me tell you about the movie I just saw."

A plot is a series of actions planned by the artist to build upon one another, with an introduction, body, and conclusion. The foundation of plot is *conflict*. Characters are initially confronted with a dilemma, which is resolved by the end of the story. Thus, plot is driven by action: *characters doing things*.

Explicit Content

One way to approach the study of plot is through an analysis of *explicit* and *implicit* content.

Explicit content refers to the significant events in a story that are displayed through visible action. When asked to describe a media program, the audience selects the essential pieces of explicit information in the story that answer the following question: "What was the program about?" To illustrate, consider the following scenario:

> A man bops another fellow over the head with a brickbat, takes his money, and flees. Later in the program he is caught and carted off to jail.

The audience constructs meaning by selecting the essential pieces of explicit information in the story. In this example, five distinct actions are described: 1) clubbing; 2) theft; 3) flight; 4) apprehension; and 5) incarceration.

In his study of children's comprehension of television content, W. Andrew Collins found that children typically have difficulty remembering explicit details and identifying important scenes:

- Eighth graders recalled 92 percent of the scenes that adults had judged as essential to the plot.
- Fifth graders recalled 84 percent of the scenes that adults had judged as essential to the plot.
- Second graders recalled an average of only 66 percent of the scenes that adults had judged as essential to the plot.[2]

According to Collins, young children's limited grasp of explicit content impairs their ability to interpret media presentations:

> Young children fail to comprehend observed actions and events in an adult-like way because they arrive at different interpretations of the various actors' plans or intentions. . . . Thus, it is possible that second and third graders take away not only a less complete understanding of the program than fifth and eighth graders do, they may also be perceiving the content of the program somewhat *differently* because they retain (and work off of) a different set of cues.[3]

Significantly, the standard against which the children's performance is measured consists of a sample of *adults*. However, there is no guarantee that individuals over the age of 21 can successfully identify all of the essential scenes in a narrative. Although adults are generally more knowledgeable than children, they are not necessarily informed or interested in all topics. In addition, adults are frequently distracted by competing activities; as a result, they are often unable to devote their full attention to a media presentation and may miss essential scenes. Moreover, reaching adulthood does not necessarily guarantee intellectual or emotional maturity.

As mentioned in the discussion on audience reception theory (see Chapter 2), the following factors can affect how an individual interprets media content:

- *Background*
  How much does an individual already know about the subject?
- *Interest Level*
  How interested in the subject is the member of the audience? How attentive is he/she?
- *Predisposition*
  What is the attitude of the audience member toward the subject (positive or negative) going into the conversation?
- *Priorities*
  What issues are of particular concern to the audience member? Why?
- *Demographic Profile*
  - National Origin
  - Gender
  - Race
  - Ethnic Origin
  - Age
  - Education
  - Income
- *Psychological Profile*
  - Self-concept
  - Primary relationships
  - Significant life experiences
  - Ways of relating to others
  - Ways of dealing with emotions
  - Personal aspirations
- *Communications Environment*
  - What is the size of the audience?
  - What are audience members *doing* while they are receiving the information?
- *Stage of Development*
  - Chronological
  - Cognitive
  - Emotional

Implicit Content

Implicit content refers to those elements of plot that remain under the surface:

- What are the *motives* behind characters' decisions and actions? (Motive answers the question *why* the characters behaved as they did.)
- What are the *connections between events* that occur in the plot?
- What are the *connections between the characters* that occur in the plot?
- Are the *consequences* for characters' actions made clear?

To illustrate, let's re-examine the scintillating scene presented earlier in our discussion on explicit content:

A man bops another fellow over the head with a brickbat, takes his money, and flees. Later in the program he is caught and carted off to jail.

In addition to the essential events (i.e., explicit content), a number of questions remain:

- Why did the first man hit the second fellow?
- Was there a prior relationship between the two men?
- Why does the first man run?
- Why is he punished at the end of the story?

W. Andrew Collins's study revealed that children had even greater difficulty identifying *implicit* content than they had deciphering the *explicit* content:

- Eighth graders recalled 77 percent of the implicit items that adults had agreed upon.
- Fifth graders recalled 67 percent of the implicit items that adults had agreed upon.
- Second graders had an overall score of fewer than half (47%) of the implicit items that adults had agreed upon.[4]

These results suggest that young children are developmentally incapable of recognizing relationships between events. Interestingly, the second-grade girls out-performed the boys, "who appear to be performing at about chance level (between 30% and 40%) on this level of inference."

Thus, despite the best intentions of some media communicators to attach a moral to programs, young children may be unclear about the cause-effect relationship of events depicted in the media. And once again, the standard of measurement in the study is the highly subjective comprehension level of adults.

To further complicate the issue, many media programs present a world that is seemingly free of consequence. Heroes in action films routinely violate laws in the name of a higher moral good. High-speed car chases, destruction of property, and assault without just cause would not go unpunished in real life but are somehow justifiable in media programs. To illustrate, at the conclusion of *Die Hard* (1988), Officer John McClane emerges from the shell of a huge building that he has destroyed in his efforts to nab the villains and save their hostages. As the dead and wounded are carted off, McClane is reunited with his wife. They embrace, hail a cab, and, to the sound of Christmas music, head home. In real life, however, McClane would be taken to the police station to explain his role in the affair. But dealing with the consequences would be anticlimactic, and consequently are left out of the film.

MEDIA LITERACY TIPS

Taking Notes on Film/Television Programming

Explicit and Implicit Content

Identifying *explicit content* is an essential first step in the thorough and systematic analysis of media messages. The most effective way to identify the explicit content is to take notes during the presentation. Record relevant scenes and significant bits of dialogue. Making vague generalizations will not suffice. You must refer to specific detail from the narrative to support your position.

Unlike print, which provides a text on which to reflect, this note-taking process is particularly tricky when viewing film or television. You are writing in darkness, recording what just occurred while new events are unfolding. However, as you become more comfortable with this process, you will be prepared to present a clear, defensible analysis of media programming.

Screening a film or television program for analytical purposes requires active involvement on your part. It is important that you take notes, so that you can make sense of the film after the screening.

continued

As you screen a film or TV program, take notes on *explicit content*:

I. Background Information
    A. Title
    B. Year
    C. Director
    D. Actors
    E. Names of significant characters
    F. Other significant information (e.g., studio, producer)

II. Note Significant Scenes
    A. Essential events in these scenes
    B. Significant bits of dialogue

After the screening, review your notes to identify implicit content: Implicit content consists of those elements of plot that remain under the surface

I. What were the motives behind the behaviors of the characters? (Why did the characters behave in the manner that they did?)
II. What were the connections between the significant events in the narrative?
III. Was there any foreshadowing of events?
    A. Significant events that reoccur later in the narrative
    B. Significant dialogue that recurs later in the narrative

IV. What was the relationship between?
    A. The significant events in the narrative
    B. The characters in the narrative

Does this examination of explicit and implicit content provide any perspective into themes or messages in the media presentation? Explain.

Subplots

Narratives often contain secondary stories, called *subplots*. Subplots may initially appear to be unrelated to one another. However, because the characters operate within the same worldview, the subplots may comment on different aspects of the same thematic concerns.

To illustrate, in crime genres (e.g., police dramas, film noir, or detective tales), subplots are integral to the protagonists finding the solution to the mystery presented at the beginning of the narrative. The hero conducts his or her investigation by pursuing various lines of inquiry, which typically are unclear to the audience. Consequently, identifying connections between the subplots can furnish perspective into the themes and messages in the presentation.

GENRE

We have all watched dozens of situation comedies on television. But what exactly *is* a situation comedy? What elements are common to all of these programs? These shared characteristics make up the *genre* of situation comedies.

The word genre itself simply means "order." A genre is a standardized format that is distinctive and easily identifiable. Examples include reality shows, romances, sci-fi, situation comedies, westerns, and the evening news. A genre is not confined to one medium. For instance, at one time or another, westerns have appeared in print, on radio, television, and film.

Formula

Genres are characterized by *formula*; that is, patterns in *premise, structure,* and *plot, characters, setting, and trappings.* Individual programs generally conform to the formula of a genre. As John Cawelti observes, "Individual works are ephemeral, but the formula lingers on, evolving and changing with time, yet still basically recognizable."[5]

A formula acts like a roadmap that helps the audience follow the story. Film critic Neal Gabler explains,

> You show an audience an attractive young man and woman who playfully bicker at the beginning of a movie and it roots for them to wind up together at the end. Or show a bully pushing around a decent fellow and viewers root for the latter to defeat the former. The audience reacts not because it knows the formula—it reacts because the formula knows the audience.[6]

In discussing the formulaic aspects of genre, it might be useful to focus on one genre: the situation comedy (or sitcom). For example, Lawrence E. Mintz describes the sitcom formula as follows: "a half-hour series focused on episodes involving recurring characters within the same premise. (That is, each week we encounter the same people in essentially the same setting.)"[7]

Formulaic Premise

How would you describe a typical sitcom?

A *formulaic premise* refers to an identifiable situation that characterizes a genre. A formulaic premise answers the question, "What is this genre about?" According to journalist Jon Caramancia, sitcoms adhere to the following formulaic premise:

> Here's a traditional sitcom setup: A new person is introduced into a circle that has established relationships and routines, and high jinks ensue. Everyone regards the contagion funnily, moves around him or her to avoid confrontation, and professes not to understand the mannerisms of the intruder, which don't neatly align with How Things Have Always Been Done. Eventually, of course, things line up— sweet, sweet resolution.[8]

However, the formulaic premise that characterizes a particular season particularizes the question of "What is the program about?" to "What is going on in the culture at this time?" Thus, after looking at the premises of the new sitcoms, Ed Martin, television columnist for MediaPost, found that "an awful lot of them are about parents moving in with kids and kids moving in with parents."[9]

As its name suggests, the comedy is generated through everyday situations rather than stand-up monologues. The stories feature the characters coping with everyday life (e.g., Homer Simpson gets a promotion). Sitcom characters do not murder each other. Instead, they tell "white lies" or are guilty of some minor transgression. Contending with these everyday situations enables the characters (and, by extension, the audience) to put life's minor irritations and problems into perspective. The cumulative message behind the sitcom premise is that life is a maze filled with traps. However, these situations are always relatively minor and can be resolved within a 30-minute episode.

Formulaic Structure

A genre generally fits within an identifiable, unvarying *structure,* or organizational pattern. In many genres (including the sitcom), the standard formula is order/chaos/order. The initial order of the story is disrupted almost immediately. The chaotic stage takes up the majority of the program and is the source of much of its humor. By the conclusion of the program, the status quo is finally restored. The cumulative message behind this structure is that problems are all solvable, and justice always prevails.

Formulaic Plot

Only a finite number of general *plots,* or stories, appear within a given genre. For instance, the plots of the popular ABC sitcom *Modern Family* generally fall into the following categories:

- Jealousy issues develop between different members of the families
- Misunderstandings between characters that disrupt the community
- Events affect characters' comfort level, support system, or storyline
- An outsider momentarily changes the dynamic between characters
- Characters reestablish bonds of their relationship through conflict

Although these general plots are predictable, the embellishments, detail, and small nuances *within* these plots keep each episode fresh and interesting.

Many of the plots revolve around misunderstandings between the characters. Communication is clearly valued as a means of both preventing and resolving problems.

Plot complications also occur due to acts of deception. A cumulative message of formulaic plots in sitcoms involves the value of truthfulness. Deception never pays in the world of the sitcom; the characters always get caught.

Another common locus of conflict is excess hubris, or pride. Characters who possess too much pride and ambition betray the members of their community. These characters are not evil, for evil does not exist in the world of the sitcom; they are simply misguided. Due to an inflated sense of self, they make errors in judgment. At the conclusion of the episode, the character's hubris is exposed to the other characters (and to the audience as well).

Another cumulative message found in formulaic sitcom plots is related to *identity.* Know yourself and be satisfied with who you are. Characters who have violated the moral code of sitcoms by trying to be someone they're not suffer the consequences. Ultimately, self-knowledge and personal happiness are more important than achievement and material gain.

A *conventional storyline* is a recurring incident that is characteristic of a particular genre. Examples include the gun duel in a western, the wedding scene in a romance, or the car chase in the action genre. Because conventional storylines appear so frequently in a particular genre, these incidents assume a meaning that is commonly associated with the genre. Consequently, a conventional storyline in a program can be used to convey messages.

For instance, the "*perp walk,*" in which a suspect is shown walking into the police station in the custody of the police, is a conventional storyline in television news. According to journalist Ray Suarez, the perp walk sends the message that the suspect is guilty:

> More than merely a visual cliche, the perp walk has helped to col-
> lapse the distinctions between suspect and criminal. My voice in
> countless narrations said all the right words—"accused" and "alleged"
> and "according to police"—but the pictures said "guilty," "guilty"
> and "guilty." The visuals became part of our nightly melodrama, our
> dispatches from the war zone, flashed to an increasingly suburban
> audience. The suspects, shorn of their presumption of innocence by
> the exigencies of television and the public relations aims of the police,
> could not refuse to participate in the ritual.[10]

Stock Characters

Stock characters appear so frequently in a particular genre that they are instantly recognizable when they appear in a program. For instance, when we watch a western, we are already acquainted with the hero's sidekick; we have met the old coot a thousand times before. Stock characters may be thought of as stereotypes that are associated with a genre rather than a particular race, ethnicity, or gender. Other examples include the honest friend, the talkative old woman, the suave gambler, the simple country boy, the blundering drunkard, the super sleuth, the eccentric scientist, and the folksy TV weatherman.

Sitcom characters must be generally friendly and likable. As veteran TV sitcom producer Carl Reiner observes, "Warm is an important word. You laugh easier when funny things are happening to nice people."[11] In this world, people are basically good. It is permissible for characters to be eccentric and annoying, however, so long as they are not malicious. The principle characters recognize the essential goodness beneath a character's imperfect exterior and accept them because they are a part of their community—at home or at work.

Formulaic Setting

A formulaic setting refers to a standard background against which the action takes place. A limited number of sets are employed in any sitcom.

Most of the activity centers around the interior, with only brief exterior shots used to establish the setting. For instance, the title of the sitcom *The Office* derives from the workplace, which is where nearly all of the action occurs. The setting of the series displays the trappings one would find in a typical office: desks, computers, copy machines, and cubicles. Moreover, specific locations within the setting correspond to particular behaviors. For instance, the water cooler is the place in which gossip is exchanged; the food area is a place in which interactions between characters occurs, and the boss' office is a locale in which differences in status between management and employee become very obvious.

Changes in the formulaic setting can reflect corresponding shifts in the culture. To illustrate:

- In the 1950s, sitcoms like *Leave It to Beaver* took place in the home, reflecting (and reinforcing) the American cultural myth of the conventional family structure.
- In the 1970s, sitcoms like the *Mary Tyler Moore Show* moved to the workplace, reflecting the breakup of the nuclear family.
- In the 1990s, the conventional setting shifted to a public hangout, such as the coffee shop in *Friends*.
- Like the *Mary Tyler Moore Show,* the setting for *30 Rock* (2006–2013) is the office. The sitcom is named after the address of the characters' workplace, reflecting its importance as the hub that connects the diverse characters in the series.

Conventional Trappings

Conventional trappings are props and costumes that appear so often that they become identifiable with a genre. These trappings furnish the audience with cues about people, events, and situations in the presentation. For instance, the white coats and surgical masks worn by the cast of *Grey's Anatomy* signals that these characters are doctors. And the appearance of tents and jeeps in *Iwo Jima* (2006) intimates that the film is part of the war genre.

The trappings of a genre may change over time, creating the mistaken impression that the genre has disappeared. For instance, the western appears to have disappeared as a popular TV genre. However, it can be argued that the police show has emerged as an updated version of the western genre. Although the urban landscape has replaced the frontier, and the car has supplanted the horse, the function, characters, and essential premise remain the same. The lawman still fights crime, even though the outlaws are rustling drugs instead of cattle.

Variations in the Formula

In order to appear distinctive and fresh, *generic programming* (i.e., programming belonging to a particular genre) may feature the following variations in elements of the formula:

Characters. In some generic programs, the main variation is a change in the gender, age, or sexual orientation of the characters. For instance, in 2013, the *Michael J. Fox Show* featured the titled character as the formulaic sitcom dad—except that he, like Fox, has Parkinson's disease. Ed Martin observes,

> Barriers are broken in television when characters you don't normally see in lead roles are put into lead roles and have a little fun with themselves. That will make or break the show, if you think he is having fun.[12]

The formulaic characterization of this sitcom conveys the message that Fox is a conventional sitcom figure in all respects, aside from his illness.

Setting. In the crime show franchise *CSI,* the locale is the only difference between two of the series, as reflected in the titles of two of the series: *CSI: NY* and *CSI: Miami.* The settings give each series it own distinctive flavor.

FUNCTIONS OF GENRES

Genres share common manifest objectives. For instance, the primary function of the situation comedy is to entertain or amuse the audience. But in addition, a genre also may contain shared latent functions. For instance, the sitcom is a morality play that offers instruction to the audience. Garry Marshall (producer of *Happy Days, Laverne and Shirley,* and *Mork and Mindy*) observes, "We tried to be useful. We did shows about mental health, about diabetes, about death, blindness, and epilepsy. Tolerance. That's what we tried to teach. Be nice to each other."[13]

In addition, genres serve a therapeutic function, providing a very healthy release for audiences, putting people in touch with their feelings. In this era in which people (particularly males) are not encouraged to confront their emotions, genres touch a range of primal feelings within the individual. Thus, the horror genre arouses feelings of fear. Comedies make us laugh. Action films tap into feelings of anger. And tragedies give us permission to cry.

EVOLUTION OF A GENRE

Tracing the evolution of a genre can provide considerable perspective into corresponding changes in the culture. To illustrate, 1950s soap operas sometimes alluded to "the other woman" (accompanied by the single, sinister note of an organ). Today, entire programs are dedicated to "the other woman," signaling the culture's more permissive sexual mores, as well as society's preoccupation with sex.

The situation comedy of the 1950s reflected the cultural life of the period. After the disruption of World War II, the United States was preoccupied with a return to normalcy. Consequently, the biggest challenge facing the 1950s sitcom characters was change. For example, in *Leave It to Beaver,* disruptive elements like puberty and girlfriends threatened the sanctity of the Cleaver household. However, each episode concluded with the comforting return to normalcy. Within this context, the 1950s sitcoms featured a zany character who was surrounded by a rational supporting cast. For instance, much of the humor in *I Love Lucy* stemmed from Lucy's efforts to fit into a normal world.

The setting for *I Love Lucy* was the home. Lucy's world consisted of her husband and child and her neighbors, Fred and Ethel Mertz. One of the formulaic plots consisted of Lucy's efforts to break into show business. Husband Ricky Ricardo staunchly refused to allow his wife to realize her dream and, within the context of the show, with good reason. Lucy was deluded; she had no talent and was incapable of functioning on her own. (In actuality, Lucille Ball was an enormously talented comedienne and the star of the show.) But in order to realize her dream, Lucy would willfully disobey her husband. Ricky would inevitably get wind of this deceit and "teach her a lesson." The message was clear: Lucy's place was in the home.

By the 1970s, the formula of the sitcom had shifted, reflecting corresponding changes in the culture. In an era characterized by rapid cultural change, the role of the central figure was to provide stability in what had become an absurd and chaotic world. Thus, the central figures such as Mary Richards (*The Tyler Moore Show*), Alex Rieger (*Taxi*), and Barney Miller (*Barney Miller*) were rational characters surrounded by a zany cast.

Film actress and comedienne Lucille Ball in a scene from the iconic *I Love Lucy.* (Hulton Archive/Getty Images)

Change was now accepted as inevitable. The supporting characters became the source of the humor in these series. The chief concern became how to maintain a sense of balance in the face of change.

Sitcoms such as *All in the Family* dealt with topics of cultural concern, such as racism and homosexuality. Female characters like Mary Tyler Moore succeeded on their own, without the support of a male. Moreover, the family at home had been supplanted by the "family" at work, reflecting the breakup of the family and emergence of the workplace as the center of activity. The crew at *WKRP in Cincinnati* may have bickered among themselves, but they rallied when a member of their community needed support.

By the 1980s, the genre of the situation comedy evolved into a number of different sub-genres, due in part to the narrowcasting of the audience into distinct categories. Rick Mitz identified seven sub-genres within the situation comedy format: 1) domestic sitcoms; 2) kidcoms; 3) couplecoms; 4) scificoms; 5) corncoms; 6) ethnicoms; 7) careercoms; and 8) historycoms.[14]

These sub-genres reflect the cultural concerns, preoccupations, and myths surrounding subcultures in America. These sub-genres adhered to the general formula (premise, structure, and thematic concerns) that defined the sitcom genre. At the same time, however, each sub-genre has a different setting and cast of characters, reflecting its distinct target audience. For instance, a couplecom like *Mad about You* took place in a domestic setting, featuring a young married couple and their friends, and relatives. The plots focused on humorous situations that arose as the couple adapted to married life.

In general, the sitcoms of the 1990s focus on characters' attempts to adapt to the complexities of modern culture. Programs feature an array of people in transition. For instance, in *Frasier,* the main character is faced with a difficult adjustment to a new stage of life. Although he is successful professionally, Frasier is divorced and has moved to a new city. Frasier lives at home with his father and is locked into a state of perennial adolescence. Many of the plots revolve around Frasier's attempts to work out his personal issues with his father and brother and validate himself to them.

As with previous sitcoms, nineties sitcoms operate according to the order/chaos/order structure. At the beginning of an episode, things are calm. Then something occurs that throws them off balance. But although the circumstance, by itself may be harmless (e.g., Frasier getting his dad a birthday gift), the incident takes place within a larger context that reveals why the character is in a state of eternal dissatisfaction (Frasier has never been able to please his father).

Unlike the 1950s sitcoms, this return to order is not so much a resolution of issues as a momentary truce in the long-term effort to contend with the complexities of modern life. In the 1990s sitcom, the characters in the community provide support for one another. But in this complex world of diminished expectations, all they can provide is comfort, rather than solutions.

In the world of the 1990s sitcom, gratification often comes from small pleasures. Indeed, the most popular sitcom of the nineties, *Seinfeld,* was "a show about nothing." One scene from *Everyone Loves Raymond* sums up this worldview: after Raymond's dad eats a delicious piece of chocolate cake made by his wife, he comments, "This cake almost makes it all worthwhile." In a larger sense, the sitcoms of the 1990s served this function for the audience, providing a momentary diversion from the stresses of contemporary culture.

In the wake of the 9/11 tragedy, audiences preferred the comforting worldview of sitcoms. Jeff Zucker, president of NBC entertainment, explained, "After Sept. 11 there was a rush to familiar faces and familiar friends, programs where you knew the characters and cared about them. That's why shows like *Frasier* and *Raymond* and *Friends* have prospered."[15]

The economic recession that began in 2008 was reflected in *Girls* (2012), a sitcom that focused on four main female characters facing unemployment, roommate issues, dwindling finances, and dependence on parental support. Each episode found the characters navigating the uncertain

The cast of the popular television show *Seinfeld.* (Corbis)

path between service work and continuing their educations in hopes of alleviating their circumstances.

CONCLUSION

Because the conclusion of a media presentation is the last segment that an audience is exposed to, it influences how we respond to the narrative as a whole. Consequently, examining the conclusion can be a valuable key to interpreting media messages.

Illogical Conclusion

In *The French Lieutenant's Woman,* novelist John Fowles argues that the conclusion of a narrative must be a logical extension of the initial premise, characters, and worldview, free of further intrusion by the artist:

> You may think novelists always have fixed plans to which they work, so that the future predicted by Chapter One is always inexorably the actuality of Chapter Thirteen. . . . [But] *we wish to create worlds as real as, but other than the world that is.* Or was. This is why we

cannot plan. We know a world is an organism, not a machine. We also know that a genuinely created world must be independent of its creator. . . . It is not only that [the character] has begun to gain an autonomy; I must respect it, and disrespect all my quasi-divine plans for him, if I wish him to be real.[16]

Fowles compares the process of writing a novel to giving birth. After creating the characters, setting, and worldview of the novel, the artist must then let go, allowing the characters to fulfill their destinies. Although this process can be agonizing for the parent/author, Fowles declares, "I let the fight proceed and take no more than a recording part in it. . . ."[17]

In light of Fowles's observations, it is striking that conclusions to popular media presentations are so often false, confused, or simply illogical when considered within the flow of the program.

One explanation can be found in the study of popular culture. In order to attract and maintain an audience, media presentations focus on complex issues, reflecting cultural interests, concerns, and preoccupations. Unfortunately, these complicated issues must be resolved within strict time constraints (e.g., 24 minutes for a sitcom). These conditions often result in conclusions that offer simplistic answers to complex problems. Tide detergent will make you a better mother. Using Axe grooming products makes young men sexually irresistible to women. And Ultra Brite toothpaste will make you irresistible.

Illogical conclusions also respond to the audience's desire for a happy ending. In his study of fairy tales, Bruno Bettelheim observes,

The dominant culture wishes to pretend . . . that the dark side of man does not exist, and professes a belief in an optimistic meliorism. . . . The message that fairy tales get across . . . [is] that a struggle against severe difficulties in life is unavoidable, is an intrinsic part of human existence—but that if one does not shy away, but steadfastly meets unexpected and often unjust hardships, one masters all obstacles and at the end emerges victorious.[18]

Mindful of this demand for a satisfying resolution, media communicators feel compelled to insert illogical endings that, however, make the audience leave the theater with smiles on their faces. The "feel-good movie of the year" is a relatively new cliché found in film reviews, signaling the degree to which this category of films has become valued by audiences, and consequently, film studios.

A third explanation stems from industry considerations. Film studios, Broadway producers, and authors now routinely protect their investments by conducting focus groups before releasing their final product. If the survey results are negative, executives from the film studios (who own the rights to the films) are not hesitant to alter the endings.

For instance, the conclusion of *A Stranger among Us* (1992) was reshot after an unsuccessful preview at Cannes. Producer Howard Rosenman explained, "After our second preview, we knew we had to reshoot. We were losing our target audience (women under 30) because the heroine Emily (played by Melanie Griffith) ended up with the wrong guy. . . . We retested in Pasadena, and the scores went up considerably."[19] However, director Michael Apted (*Thunderheart*) cautions, "Suddenly, you're pandering to the public and treating movies like soap suds, instead of somebody's vision."[20]

The history of Hollywood films is replete with instances in which the endings of films have been altered. Even legendary film director Orson Welles was unable to prevent RKO Studios from reshooting the conclusion of *The Magnificent Ambersons* (1942), giving the film an upbeat (but artificial) ending.

Michael Douglas and Glenn Close in *Fatal Attraction* (1987). (Paramount Pictures/ Photofest)

However, inserting an artificial conclusion often undermines the message of the media presentation. To illustrate, in *Fatal Attraction* (1987), happily married New York lawyer Dan Gallagher (Michael Douglas) has an affair with Alex Forrest (Glenn Close). But after Alex informs Dan that she is pregnant, her behavior becomes so erratic that Dan decides to end the affair. According to scriptwriter James Dearden, *Fatal Attraction* initially was written as a morality tale: "It was a commentary on human responsibility, on the moral consequences of one's actions."[21] Thus, in the original ending, Alex commits suicide, Dan's fingerprints are discovered on the weapon (he had held the knife in a previous scene), and it is insinuated that Dan will be punished for his moral transgression.

However, test audiences responded negatively to this ending. Director Adrian Lyne said, "They would have thrown rocks. . . . (The audience) had grown to hate his woman . . . to the degree that they wanted retribution."[22] As a result, the studio spent $1.3 million to reshoot the ending. In the revised version, Alex is a psychopath who terrorizes Gallagher and his family. This substitute ending reframes the meaning of the film. Dan is no longer responsible for his infidelity, but instead is a victim of an obsessed stalker. Ultimately, it is Dan's wife Beth (Anne Archer) who saves herself, her family, and her marriage by stabbing the deranged Alex. According to Richard Corliss, by killing Alex, Beth not only saves her family, but in essence, forgives Dan's cheating.[23] In the final shot sequence, Dan and Beth stand with their arms around one another (a sign of protection). The camera then pans to a close-up of a family photograph: order has been restored.

Significantly, the test audience was not comfortable with good-guy Gallagher being responsible for the betrayal of his family, and instead was willing to accept the vilification of a sexually aggressive, independent woman. As Professor Jane Ferry declares, "The film's message is clear. Single professional women are psychotic and . . . must be silenced, especially if they seek more than the limited role of wife and mother."[24]

Audiences accustomed to the swift and immediate resolution of entertainment programming are often unprepared to contend with the sustained media coverage of news events. For example, when the Iraq War began in 2003, television coverage was continuous. However, as the situation became prolonged, without apparent end in sight, the public (and, consequently, the networks) began to lose interest in the crisis.

Examining the conclusions of a media presentation can provide insight into possible *latent functions*. To illustrate, the conclusion of the 1955 animated version of George Orwell's *Animal Farm* was markedly different from the ending of the original novel. Written in 1945, the book is an allegory about the struggle between the capitalistic farmers and the proletariat farm animals. At the conclusion of the novel, the farm animals look back and forth at the capitalistic humans and the tyrannical pigs (who represent the totalitarian Soviet Communist regime) and find it "impossible to say which was which." However, in the animated film, the farm animals direct their criticism *only* at the Communist pigs.

Journalist Stonor Saunders has uncovered evidence that after Orwell's death in 1950, the U.S. Central Intelligence Agency (CIA) purchased the film rights to *Animal Farm* and altered the conclusion to make its message more overtly anti-Communist.[25] Thus, this entertainment program assumed a latent propagandistic function, serving as a tool of U.S. foreign policy.

Media Literacy Strategies

Envisioning a conclusion consistent with the logical flow of a narrative can be an effective strategy for identifying its latent messages. A classic example can be found in the highly successful 1950s TV sitcom *The Honeymooners.* The lead character, Ralph Kramden (Jackie Gleason), is a big, blustery bus driver; each week he becomes embroiled in a harebrained scheme so that he can get what "he deserves." However, once the comedic elements have been stripped away, Ralph is a terribly unhappy and selfish person, plagued with *hubris* and a deluded sense of self. When he doesn't get his way, Ralph "playfully" threatens his wife Alice and pal Ed Norton. ("Pow—to the moon!") In order to launch his get-rich-quick scheme, Ralph continually deceives Alice, lying to her or pilfering the household money.

At the end of each episode, the folly of Ralph's excessive ego has been exposed. Ralph parades in front of Alice, looking repentant and trying to find the words to ask for forgiveness. After some hesitation, Alice always relents. The program inevitably concludes with an embrace of reconciliation, with Ralph declaring, "Baby, you're the greatest."

But what would be the *logical conclusion* of an episode of *The Honeymooners*? A key to identifying media messages is: given the initial premise,

---

The HONEYMOONERS

In *The Honeymooners,* Ralph Kramden (Jackie Gleason) bullies his buddy Ed Norton (Art Carney), much to the displeasure of wife Alice (Audrey Meadows). The happy ending at the conclusion of each episode offers a simplistic conclusion that is not consistent with the logical flow of the program.

---

characters, and worldview, how *should* the presentation logically end? The conclusion of *The Honeymooners* may include the following possible scenarios:

- Ralph goes into therapy
- Ralph and Alice see a marriage counselor
- Alice leaves Ralph

Suggesting an ending consistent with the logical flow of *The Honeymooners* raises questions about the cultural attitudes of the period about marriage and relationships.

Is this Ralph's problem solely, or does Alice share in the responsibility? What is Ralph's attitude toward women? And why is Ralph so driven to make "the big score"?

A related line of inquiry is *preferred conclusion*: How do you *want* the story to end? Your response to the narrative reveals a great deal about your personal belief system. In the case of *The Honeymooners,* should one minimize problems to keep a marriage going? Any preferred conclusion to *The Honeymooners* reveals your personal attitudes toward marriage, sex roles, and relationships.

CHARACTER DEVELOPMENT

During the course of a narrative, characters often engage in a process of self-discovery that enables them to succeed at the conclusion. As a result, character development gives an artist the opportunity to make thematic statements. Examining what the primary characters have learned by the conclusion of the story can therefore be a useful method for identifying media messages:

- *Have the major characters changed as a result of the events in the story? How? Why?*
- *What have the characters learned as a result of their experience?*
- *What does this development reveal with regard to themes and messages of the presentation?*

SUMMARY

Framework refers to various structural elements of a production: introduction, plot, genre, and conclusion.

Keys to Interpreting Media Messages: Framework

Applying the following questions related to **Framework** can provide insight into media messages:

A. **Introduction**
  1. *Title*: What does the title of the presentation signify?
  2. *Introduction as Foreshadowing Device*:
     a. What events constitute the introduction of the media presentation?
     b. What does the introduction tell us about the presentation?
     c. Does the introduction foreshadow events and themes in the body of the production?
  3. *Illogical Premise*
     a. Is the premise of the presentation logical?
     b. What are the underlying assumptions behind the premise of the presentation?
     c. What is the impact of this premise on the messages conveyed in the presentation?
     d. Do you accept the underlying premise in the presentation?
     e. If not, are you willing to suspend your disbelief?
B. **Plot**
  1. *Explicit Content:* What are the significant events in the story?
  2. *Implicit Content*
     a. What is the relationship between the significant events in the narrative?
     b. What is the relationship between the characters in the narrative?
     c. What are the characters' motives for their actions?
     d. Are the consequences to specific behaviors defined?
  3. Subplots
     a. Can you identify any subplots in the narrative?
     b. Are there any connections between the subplots that provide insight into the worldview, characters, and themes in the production?
C. **Genre**
  1. Does the presentation belong to any recognizable genre?
  2. Is there a predictable formula for the genre? What insights do these formulas provide into the genre? Into the specific program?
     a. Formulaic Function
     b. Formulaic Premise

      c. Formulaic Structure

      d. Formulaic Plot

          ○ Conventional Storyline

      e. Stock Characters

      f. Setting

      g. Conventional Trappings

   3. What does this genre suggest about:

      a. Cultural attitudes and values?

      b. Cultural preoccupations?

      c. Cultural myths?

      d. Worldview?

   4. Can you trace the evolution of this genre?

      a. Have there been shifts in the genre over time?

      b. What do these shifts in genre reveal about changes in the culture?

D. Conclusion

   1. *Function*

      a. What is the purpose behind the conclusion of the narrative?

      b. Is there a latent function behind the conclusion? Explain.

   2. *Character Development*

      a. Have the major characters changed as a result of the events in the story? How? Why?

      b. What have the characters learned as a result of their experience?

   3. *Illogical Conclusion*

      a. Does the conclusion of the presentation follow logically from the established premise, characters, and worldview?

      b. If not, how should the presentation have ended, given the established premise, characters, and worldview?

      c. How would you have *preferred* for the story to end? Why?

NOTES

1. J. Philip di Franco, ed., *The Movie World of Roger Corman* (New York: Chelsea House Publishers, 1979).
2. W. Andrew Collins, "Children's Comprehension of Television Content," in *Children Communicating,* ed. Ellen Wartella (Beverly Hills, CA: Sage Publications, 1979), 27.
3. Ibid., 28.
4. Ibid., 29.

5. John Cawelti, "Myth, Symbol, and Formula," *Journal of Popular Culture* 8 (Summer 1974): 15.

6. Neal Gabler, "The Nation: The Illusion of Entertainment; Just Like a Movie, but It's Not," *New York Times,* August 4, 2002: D-1.

7. Lawrence E. Mintz, "Situation Comedy," in *TV Genres,* ed. Brian G. Rose (Westport, CT: Greenwood Press, 1985), 119.

8. Jon Caramancia, "Letting Go of Whimsy in Favor of Feeling," *New York Times,* May 13, 2013.

9. Stuart Elliott, "A Season of Families, Vampires and Aliens," *New York Times,* May 19, 2013.

10. Ray Suarez, "But What If the 'Perp' Walks?" *New York Times,* March 13, 1999: A-27.

11. Mintz, "Situation Comedy," 114.

12. Elliott, "A Season of Families, Vampires and Aliens."

13. Mintz, "Situation Comedy," 115.

14. Rick Mitz, *The Great TV Sitcom Book* (New York: R. Marek Publishers, 1980).

15. Bernard Weintraub, "TV's Comforting Laugh Track," *New York Times,* October 31, 2001.

16. John Fowles, *The French Lieutenant's Woman* (Boston: Little, Brown and Company, 1969), 105–6.

17. Ibid., 417.

18. Bruno Bettelheim, *The Uses of Enchantment: The Meaning and Importance of Fairy Tales* (New York: Vintage Books, 1976), 7.

19. Glenn Fowles, "It Ain't Over until It's Happy," reprinted in the *St. Louis Post-Dispatch,* July 7, 1992: D-4.

20. Ibid.

21. Susan Faludi, *Backlash: The Undeclared War against American Women* (New York: Doubleday, 1991), 120.

22. Ajean Harmetz, "*Fatal Attraction* Director Analyzes the Success of His Movie, and Rejoices," *New York Times,* October 5, 1987: C-17.

23. Richard Corliss, "Killer," *Time,* November 16, 1987: 72.

24. Jane Ferry, "Babylonian Babe: Boffo at the Box Office," unpublished paper, October 1997.

25. Laurence Zuckerman, "How the CIA Played Dirty Tricks with Culture," *New York Times,* March 18, 2000.

7

Production Elements

OVERVIEW

Production elements have an impact on the *style* and *quality* of a media presentation. Production values are roughly analogous to grammar in print, in that these elements influence:

- *The ways in which the audience receives the information*
- *The emphasis, or interpretation placed on the information by the media communicator*
- *The reactions of the audience to the information*

The clever mass communicator uses production values to engage the audience in the media experience. To illustrate, in *Paradise Lost,* John Milton uses a literary technique that allows the reader to vicariously participate in Satan's descent into hell. *Read the following passage aloud*:

> Him the Almighty Power Hurl'd headlong flaming from th' Ethereal Sky With hideous ruin and combustion down To bottomless perdition, there to dwell In Adamantine Chains and penal Fire, Who durst defy th' Omnipotent to Arms, Nine times the Space that measures Day and Night To mortal men, he with his horrid crew Lay vanquisht, rowling in the fiery Gulf Confounded though immortal.[1]

By the time that you have finished reading this exhaustive run-on sentence, you are out of breath and have, on some level, experienced Satan's fall from grace.

These stylistic elements operate on an *affective,* or emotional, level that frequently escapes our conscious attention. Referring to visual language,

Rudolph Arnheim observes, "In fact, these purely visual qualities of appearance are the most powerful of all. It is they that reach us most directly and deeply."[2] Production elements can create a mood that reinforces manifest messages or themes in a media presentation. For example, in horror films, the manipulation of lighting, music, and screen space arouse intense feelings of terror in the audience. Further, these stylistic elements may convey independent messages (e.g., the glamour associated with screen violence). (For additional discussion of affective response, see Chapter 2, Process.)

EDITING

The selection and arrangement of information convey messages about the significance of content. Legendary broadcast journalist Walter Cronkite closed his broadcasts with his signature, "And that's the way it is," which suggested that the only events of the day worth considering had been covered during that evening's program.

All media presentations are faced with the challenge of fitting information into the existing time and space constraints of the medium. As an example, the front page of a newspaper includes approximately six stories. In any given day, it is safe to say that a hundred items are important enough to be included on the front page. Editors are faced with the task of deciding which stories to include, as well as the amount of time or space allotted to each story. In addition, editing decisions are often made for pragmatic reasons. For instance, it is not uncommon for newspaper articles to be condensed to make room for additional advertising.

Consequently, a fundamental rule for media practitioners is: "Don't fall in love with your work." The filmmaker who becomes too attached to a project may find it painful to cut the movie to a length that audiences will willingly sit through and the studio will release.

Editing decisions often fall into the following categories:

Inclusion and Omission

Given the time and space limitations, critical decisions involve both what to *include* and what to *omit* from a media presentation. Because these decisions have been reached before the presentation reaches the public, the audience is often unaware of the selection process.

Only a limited number of people in a newsroom actually make the decisions of inclusion and omission that shape our understanding of the world. Newspaper staffs generally designate one person to keep the "daybook" of events that will be covered by the paper that day. To illustrate, for years, daybook editor Tom McElroy has been the person who decided what stories are carried by the Associated Press. Reporter Chris Hedges observes,

> Tom McElroy, 39, an editor at the Associated Press with a silver stud in his left ear and a black bicycle helmet tossed casually on his desk, would not make anyone's list of media heavyweights. But from his small, cluttered cubicle in Rockefeller Center, covered with pages of faxes and news releases, he puts together the Associated daybook. This Press daybook, a schedule of daily events in the city, often determines what gets covered in New York and what does not.
>
> "If an event is not listed on the A.P. daybook it is not worth doing," said Edward Skyler, who works in the public relations department at Bloomberg.[3]

Thus, examining a variety of newspapers or comparing the nightly news with unedited C-SPAN coverage of events is a particularly useful line of inquiry. What has been included? What has been omitted?

Arrangement of Information

Cronkite's signature statement not only promised to present all of the news; he also pledged to give us the news in *order of importance.* The arrangement of information makes a statement about the relative merit and value of content. What appears first is, obviously, most essential. What appears last is of lesser importance.

Sustained Coverage

Given the limited attention span of the public, occasional coverage of an issue signals that the issue is of limited importance. But covering an issue on an ongoing basis conveys the message that it is important and worthy of continued monitoring.

Temporal and Spatial Inferences

Through editing, media communicators establish relationships between people, as well as connections between locations and events in a narrative. For instance, a flashback is an editing technique in which a past event is inserted into the narrative to show the influence of the past on the present.

CBS News anchor Walter Cronkite interviewing President John F. Kennedy on September 2, 1963. (Library of Congress)

Filmmakers also create the impression that events on screen are occurring simultaneously through the editing technique of *cross-cutting*. This technique involves inserting footage from different locations next to each other, which gives the impression that events are occurring at the same moment. For instance, in the classic Russian film *Potemkin* (1925), Soviet filmmaker Sergei M. Eisenstein tells the story of a riot at the battleship *Potemkin.* Eisenstein selected a succession of images (called a *montage*) consisting of soldiers, a woman crying, and a baby carriage bouncing down the steps out of control to underscore the relationship between the authoritarian power of the Cossacks, the suffering of the people, and the devastation of the town.

In like fashion, *spatial inferences* draw connections between occurrences at different sites. For instance, a formulaic establishment shot in television consists of a wide shot of a building. The camera then zooms in, dissolving into an interior scene. The inference is that the interior scene is taking place in the building that was shown in the exterior shot.

Editing can also suggest *causality.* The juxtaposition of scenes can show the consequences of actions (e.g., the villain admitting guilt, followed by a shot of him or her going to jail). Sequencing one shot after another can also dramatize the impact of events on people. In soap

POTEMKIN

Media communicators are able to manipulate time and space as a means of establishing relationships between people, locations, and events. The classic Russian film *Potemkin* (1925) tells the story of a riot at the battleship *Potemkin*. Soviet filmmaker Sergei M. Eisenstein selected a succession of images (called a montage) to comment on the relationship between the authoritarian power of the Cossacks, the suffering of the people, and the devastation of the town.

---

operas, a revelation in the story is frequently followed by reaction shots, which reveal how all of the principal characters are affected by the goings-on.

COLOR

Color is a visual element that has a powerful effect on audiences. Wallace S. Baldinger declares,

> [Color] affects our waking moments, consciously or unconsciously, and also, when we are dreaming, our sleeping moments. It influences—sometimes to a frightening extent—our moods and states of mind, soothing or amusing us, stimulating or revolting us, driving us even to madness.[4]

"I am feeling blue," "He is green with envy," and "This news is red hot" are examples of how colors are associated with, and inspire, particular emotions.

According to Baldinger, colors are associated with universal human emotions:

> Owing to association with certain experiences and objects, we feel that certain hues are "warm" and others "cool." By association with late-afternoon sunshine, fire, or heated iron, on the one hand, and with nightfall, water, ice, snow, on the other, we group yellow, orange, and red together as warm hues and green, blue, and violet together as cool. The artist draws on the ideas which we thus connect with color when he [sic] selects and organizes hues, sometimes even making us feel hot or cold by reaction to them.[5]

In general, the affective properties of colors are as follows:

- *Warm colors, like red, orange, and yellow, tend to make us feel happy, secure, positive, and intensely involved.*
- *Cool colors, like blue or violet, make us feel calm.*
- *Dead colors, like gray or black, make us feel sad, alone, or uncomfortable.*

To illustrate, a group of preschool children from Reggio Emilia, Italy, were asked to describe four pictures of a tiger. These pictures were identical, with one exception: each version was reproduced in a different color. The children described these pictures in very different terms, showing the influence of color on perception:

- *Yellow tone*
  - "It's an enchanted and hot forest, full of sun like an enormous fire."
  - "The tiger is also on fire and ferocious."
- *Blue tone*
  - "It seems to be a dream. The tiger seems to be a fantasy."
  - "It's like a forest at the bottom of the sea. Or else a land far away in the clouds."
- *Green tone*
  - "It's like being immersed in a sea of tall grass. It's the most normal because it's green."
  - "It's a quiet forest. It makes me feel [sleepy]."
  - "You can almost smell the scent of mint."
- *Gray tone*
  - "It's frightening, scary, because it's dark like the night. There isn't even a ray of sun."
  - "It's a magical forest with strange noises. It's like being in a place that doesn't exist, like a ghost town."[6]

However, the precise meaning associated with a particular color depends on several factors:

- *Color contrast* may also evoke particular moods. Warm colors and pleasing color contrasts generate a positive response in the audience. However, contrasting color combinations such as red and purple produce a visual tension that is sensed by the audience.

- Primary colors contain degrees of saturation, or shades that touch a range of emotions. Thus, although blue is generally thought of as a cool color, a light blue feels warm and enveloping.
- The *context* in which a color appears also affects its meaning. For instance, green is often associated with nature and health. However, in *The Wizard of Oz* (1939), the green complexion of the Wicked Witch of the West looks unnatural and evil.
- *Cultural context* can play a role in the meaning of color; colors sometimes assume a special significance within a particular culture. To illustrate, black is associated with mourning in most Western cultures, while other colors express feelings of sadness and loss in Asian cultures. Robert L. Stevenson explains,

Imagine receiving a Christmas present wrapped in black paper or a sympathy card in neon pink. You could make a comparable mistake by offering red roses to a German or Polish acquaintance, yellow or white chrysanthemums to most Europeans, any purple flowers to a Brazilian, or white lilies to a Canadian. All of these are associated with funerals or death in the respective cultures.[7]

Interior designers take these affective properties of color into consideration when they decorate public spaces such as business offices, hospitals, and schools. Restaurants make generous use of the color orange, which has been found to stimulate the appetite.[8] Faber Birren describes the ideal color scheme for schools:

It is good standard practice to use white for all ceilings, both for consistent appearance and to reflect an abundance of shadow-free illumination. . . . Libraries, rest rooms for teachers, school offices . . . could well be in the subdued tones of Pale Gold, Fern Green, Colonial Green, Smoky Blue.

Cafeterias should be in Peach, Coral, Rose, Pumpkin, Flamingo. All of which are cheerful and appetizing.

The gymnasiums, shops, manual training, and domestic arts rooms probably are best in luminous tones of Soft Yellow, Peach, Beige. Locker rooms and dressing rooms in Coral will reflect a flattering light.[9]

Colors often reinforce themes and messages in media presentations. As an example, in *The Wizard of Oz,* the beginning of the film is shot in

The cast members of *The Wizard of Oz* cast dark shadows to lend a sense of foreboding to the scene. (Bettmann/Corbis)

black and white, reflecting Dorothy's rather mundane existence in Kansas. But after her home has been uprooted by a tornado, she opens the door to discover that she has landed in Oz. And what a world! Oz is a warm, enchanting place, thanks in large measure to the introduction of a pastel color scheme. The set is dominated by delicate shades of gold, blue, and green.

This dramatic effect is in marked contrast to a subsequent scene in which Dorothy and her friends enter the forest on their way to meet the Wizard of Oz. This scene is dominated by dark colors, including the sky and costume of the Wicked Witch of the West, reinforcing the dark, foreboding worldview of the forest.

LIGHTING

Media communicators use lighting to convey messages. Those aspects of a page or screen that are in the light attract attention and are therefore considered to be of prime importance, while objects that remain in the dark are considered to be of little consequence.

As a result, lighting frequently is used for dramatic emphasis. A brightly lit photograph evokes feelings of security and happiness, whereas a dark picture filled with shadows stirs feelings of fear and apprehension in the audience. Dim lighting can also trigger a sense of powerlessness and loss of control, as the viewer must struggle to grasp a clear visual understanding of the environment. Flat lighting exposes everything equally, and as a result makes the world of the photo appear dull and monotonous. In contrast, different gradations of light are more lively and suggest an interesting and exciting world.

STANDARD LIGHTING TECHNIQUES

10.2a *Key light*: principal light source—directional spot

10.2b *Back light*: rims top and separates object from background—directional spot

10.2c *Fill light*: slows shadow fall-off—flood or soft (spread) spot

10.2d *Side light*: spotlight coming from the side (usually opposite key) directional

10.2e *Kicker light*: directional spot from back, off to one side, usually from below

Moreover, in a two-dimensional form such as photography, film, or television, lighting casts shadows that are as substantial as any of the "real" objects being depicted. Consequently, shadows can dramatize relationships by literally connecting people or objects. For instance, Alfred Hitchcock's suspense classic *Dial M for Murder* (1954) tells the story of Tony (Ray Milland), who devises an elaborate scheme to murder his wife Margot (Grace Kelly). However, Margo resists this attempt on her life and manages to kill the intruder in self-defense. Tony then frames Margo, so that it appears that Margo had killed the man in an act of premeditated murder. However, with the arrival of Inspector Hubbard (John Williams), Tony's plan begins to unravel. As Tony shows the inspector around the apartment, he opens the door to the kitchen, which has bars across the windows (out of sight of the camera). The light through the window casts a shadow of bars across the doorway, foreshadowing Tony's eventual incarceration.

The *source* of light is another device for dramatic effect and thematic expression. Rudolf Arnheim describes a painting by Rembrandt entitled *Descent from the Cross*:

[T]he (hidden) light . . . brightens the body of Christ, which is being taken down from the cross. The ceremony is performed in a dark world. But as the light falls from below, it heightens the limp body and imparts the majesty of life to the image of death. Thus the light source within the picture tells the story of the New Testament—that is, the story of the divine light transferred to the earth and ennobling it by its presence.[10]

According to David Goen, lighting has its own distinct code of meaning:

Bright Lighting	Dim Lighting
• Innocence	• Death
• Purity	• Evil
• Religious faith	• Lack of communication
• Delicacy	• Pollution
• Delight	• A problem of religious faith
• Joy and goodwill	• Foreshadowing trouble
• Life	• Force and strength
• Discovery	• Something hidden[11]

The *quality* of light—hard or soft—comments on the objects depicted in the picture. Lighting can either flatter characters or produce a glare that accentuates their flaws, depending on the intention of the communicator. Goen explains:

> Soft light creates minimal contrast: It seems to wrap around an object, enveloping and bathing it, obscuring defects and minimizing surface detail. It is light that doesn't seem to come from any particular direction. Soft light can reveal the subtleties of gradation of tone, that is, the transition of light to dark tones.
>
> Hard light creates high contrast: Light that produces sharply defined outlines brings out any texture in the subject and can seem harsh and brutal. . . . High contrast lighting shows a much more limited range of tones. Your shadow under a direct light, such as a bare light bulb or the midday sun, is much more consistent in tone and is a fairly uniform darkness.[12]

Blade Runner (1982) is a futuristic film in which director Ridley Scott employs hard lighting to create a pessimistic world of the future. Due to human beings' abuses of the environment, the climate is dark and gloomy, and it is continually raining. From an aerial view, flames leap up at the camera from some unknown fuel source, conjuring up biblical images of hell. There is no natural source of light in the film, reflecting humanity's unnatural condition. Instead, the street is illuminated by hideous neon signs that only accentuate the imperfections in the faces of the people who inhabit this world. A sense of hopelessness permeates the film, much of it due to the use of lighting.

SHAPE

The primary unit of visual communication is the *dot*. The dot is a reference point that directs the attention of the viewer. The dot is also the beginning of a more complex visual plan; a series of dots, when linked together, form a *line*.

A line suggests a sense of direction. In Western culture, a diagonal line running from the left-hand bottom corner to the right-hand top has an *ascending* quality, suggesting positive feelings of progress and enlightenment. Conversely, a diagonal from left-hand top to right hand bottom has a *descending* quality, producing a sense of pessimism, danger, and failure. This sense of direction is inverted in Eastern cultures.

The meaning of a line may also be influenced by the amount of pressure that the artist applies to the paper. A delicate line can suggest caution, refinement, or hesitancy. A bold line suggests conviction or passion.

A *shape* is created when a line comes back to itself and is distinct from any other shape or space. Each of the three basic shapes has its own distinctive character.

The Circle

The *circle* possesses a mystical quality. Because this shape has direction and is complete, it is associated with endlessness, wholeness, and the cyclical conception of time (e.g., the zodiac and clock faces). In many cultures, the circle is a symbol of the sun, and as a result signifies warmth and life. In Mayan culture, the circle was viewed as a "symbol of perfection" or the "balancing of forces."

In many ancient civilizations, the circle was also a symbol of protection. In antediluvian Babylonian culture, laying a circle of flour around a person's sickbed was a ritual designed to keep demons away. Thus, the circle *separates,* setting objects apart (e.g., a "social circle"). But a circle can also *join* people and things together within its parameters. Stonehenge and Avebury are examples of ancient uses of the circle to mark the boundary of a sacred area. In medieval Europe, magicians used the circle to delineate sacred space:

> The circle is not only intended to keep something out but also to keep something in—the magical energy which the magicians will summon up from within themselves in the course of the ceremony. . . . If it were not for the circle the energy would flow off in all directions and be dissipated. The circle keeps it inside a small area and so concentrates it. The same motive lies behind the circle of people who link their hands at a séance.[13]

According to Eva C. Hangen, the circle image has a universal significance that can be traced through a variety of cultural artifacts:

- *Circle of fire: monastic chastity, magic, inviolability*
- *Wedding ring: continuing devotion and love*
- *Four circles linked to a fifth, larger one: the words of wisdom*
- *In Mexico, two serpents entwined into a ring: time without end*
- *In China, a circle separating two serpents: the two principles claiming the universe.*[14]

Because the circle is smooth, round, and has no edges, it has a friendly, non-threatening quality. As a result, animators use this shape when creating positive characters. The roundness of Homer Simpson, Mickey Mouse, and the Pillsbury Dough Boy gives these cartoon characters a lovable quality, while villains like Mr. Gru (from the animated film *Despicable Me*) and Megamind are both angular.

Shape can also influence the popularity of consumer products. According to reporter Natalie Angier, making products into a round shape—known as the "cute factor"—bolsters their commercial appeal:

Sales of petite, willfully cute cars like the Toyota Prius and the Mini Cooper (have) soared. . . . As though the original Volkswagen Beetle wasn't considered cute enough, the updated edition was made rounder and shinier still. "The new Beetle looks like a smiley face," said Miles Orvell, professor of American studies at Temple University in Philadelphia.[15]

The Square

In contrast to the circle, the *square* is very much of this world. A square is precise, consisting of horizontal and vertical direction. College students asked to describe the square came up with the following properties:

- *Fair*
- *Precise*
- *Dependable*
- *Solid*
- *Stable*
- *Straight*
- *Honest*
- *Dull*
- *Ordinary*
- *Boring*
- *Lacking imagination*

The Triangle

A *triangle* is formed through the connection of lines at 60-degree angles. Paul Martin Lester declares, "Triangles are the most dynamic and active of shapes. As energetic objects, they convey direction, but they can burden a design with the tension they can create."[16] Triangles are therefore associated with motion, conflict, tension, abandonment, and power. The tension between the angles endows this shape with a mysterious power. The ancient Egyptians claimed that the triangular structure of the pyramids preserved the bodies and spirits of the kings buried within their walls. Richard Cavendish explains, "The true pyramid was merely a representation in stone of the sun's rays shining to earth through a gap in the clouds, and by its possession the king could transport himself at will to the celestial kingdom of the sun god."[17]

Similarly, a modern legend claims that the Bermuda Triangle, formed by the southern tip of Florida, Puerto Rico, and Bermuda, is the locus of some "sinister force field." Since 1854, approximately 50 ships have been lost without trace in this area of water.

According to Hangen, the following meanings have been assigned to triangles:

- *In general symbolism: equality, democratic thinking, perfection*
- *In Christian symbolism: the Trinity*
- *When pictured with divergent rays: eternity, the rays indicative of glory and brightness*
- *In art and architecture, in designs with apex pointing upward: heaven*
- *In flower arrangement: triangular form lying on long side: repose; standing on the acute angle: stateliness and power; standing in an inclined position: dynamic force.*[18]

SCALE

Scale refers to the relative size of objects. Scale is a very basic means of conveying messages; the larger an object appears, the more important it is.

Scale can also serve as a thematic device. For example, in the classic film *King Kong* (1933), the relative size of objects on screen serves as a metaphor for the complex relationship between humanity and nature. The scene that introduces King Kong juxtaposes the giant ape with the diminutive heroine, Ann Darrow (Fay Wray). Where Kong (or nature) is powerful, human beings are frail, weak, and ineffectual. Ann is particularly vulnerable, a victim of her own feminine nature (as defined by 1930s American culture).

King Kong shows his size by standing atop New York's Empire State Building during an attack by fighter planes in a scene from the 1933 film *King Kong*. (AP Photo)

After King Kong has been captured, Ann relaxes in her Manhattan apartment with her boyfriend, Robert Armstrong (Carl Denham). Within the sanctity of these walls, which are scaled to the dimensions of its human occupants, Armstrong reassures Ann: "You're safe now, dear. You're with me." But alas, Kong has escaped. At this moment, the huge ape's face appears at her window, reducing the "normal" bedroom to dollhouse proportions. The ape's huge arm sweeps into the room, brushing off Armstrong's feeble defense and snatching the heroine. Civilization is again exposed as a rather thin façade. Nature (including human impulses and needs) looms large in all of us, despite our pretenses of civilization and control.

At the climax of the film, King Kong, now on the run, seeks refuge atop the Empire State Building. In this shot, a tiny Kong clings to the mammoth structure. Once again, scale reflects relative power; Kong (and by extension, nature) has ultimately become a victim of civilization. For the moment, human beings have succeeded in denying their own instincts, passion, and devotion, as embodied in King Kong. The ape gently lays Ann on a ledge before plunging to his death. Fay is left

SCALE *KING KONG*—JUNGLE

In King Kong (1933), relative size served as a metaphor for the complex relationship between humanity and nature.

only with her cultivated, uninspiring boyfriend and some vague, ambiguous emotions.

RELATIVE POSITION

Where a character or object appears on the screen (or page) sends a distinct message to the audience. In Western cultures, objects appearing toward the front attract immediate attention, whereas objects placed in the background are generally considered to be of secondary importance. Moreover, Westerners tend to pay more attention to objects situated on the *right* side of the screen. Herbert Zettl explains:

> In practice, this means that if you have a choice, you should place the more important event on the right side of the screen. In an interview show, for example, if you consider the guest more important than the host, place the guest on screen-right rather than the host. Most prominent hosts, however, do not want to be upstaged, and so they occupy the more conspicuous screen-right position.[19]

Human beings tend to look for balance; that is, an equal distribution around the center. Because of this natural predisposition to order, or *gestalt,* the audience feels unsettled if all the activity is placed on one corner of the screen. Consequently, media communicators who want to generate feelings of suspense among audience members take advantage of this natural predisposition for order, balance, and harmony.

For instance, in the classic romantic film *Camille* (1937), starring Greta Garbo and Robert Taylor, the two lovers are positioned so that their faces are equidistant from the center of the screen. This use of space anticipates the climax of the love scene, when the lovers' lips meet in the exact center of the screen.

Conversely, media communicators convey themes and messages by creating tension through *imbalanced* space. As art educator Albert Henry Munsell has observed,

In *Camille* (1937), Marguerite (Greta Garbo) and Armand (Robert Taylor) are deep in reverie. The two lovers are positioned so that their faces are equally distant from the center of the screen. This use of space establishes a sense of anticipation for when the lovers' lips will meet in the exact center of the screen at the climax of the love scene. (MGM/Photofest)

Any long duration of unbalance, either mental, physical or spiritual is an aggravated form of disease. . . . Yet short periods of unbalance are very stimulating in the effort which they produce to regain balance.[20]

In addition, the space *outside* of the screen is frequently employed in suspense and horror genres for dramatic effect. The space beyond the visual control of the viewer represents the unknown and therefore can be employed to surprise or shock the audience. *Aliens* (1986), directed by James Cameron, takes this principle a step further. In this film, the source of terror is hidden *within* the characters, waiting to emerge at the opportune moment.

Table 7.1   Relative Position—Where the Character or Object Appears on the Screen (or page) Sends Distinct Messages to the Audience

3	6	1
	7	
4	5	2

Media communicators also employ relative position to draw connections between people, objects, or events. To illustrate, in the classic suspense film *Psycho* (1960), director Alfred Hitchcock uses relative position to furnish perspective into the character of Norman Bates (Anthony Perkins). Norman and Marion (Janet Leigh) are in the parlor of the Bates Hotel. Norman has fixed a sandwich for Marion, who is staying overnight at the Bates Motel. She is fleeing after having stolen money from her boss. The shots of Norman talking include stuffed birds in the background. After Marion comments on the stuffed birds, Norman's response lends insight into his tortured soul: "I think we're all in our private traps . . . and none of us can ever get out. We scratch and claw, but only at the air and only at each other and never break out of it." The birds mounted on the wall reinforce the notion that Norman is both a predator and victim of his past.

MOVEMENT

Movement adds a dimension to images that make the world on-screen appear lifelike. As a result, people tend to assume that the events being depicted are real, and consequently believe the messages that are conveyed in the programming. To illustrate, in 1895, during the infancy of film, the Lumière brothers produced a film entitled *Arrival of a Train*. As the title suggests, this celebration of movement consisted of a train pulling into a station at an angle 45 degrees from a stationary camera. Reportedly, audience members fled from the theater, terrified.

The direction of movement conveys distinct messages:

- Movement directed *toward* the audience can either be friendly (e.g., an invitation or sign of intimacy), aggressive, or menacing.
- Movement directed *away* from the audience can signal either abandonment, retreat, avoidance, or resolution.
- Movement directed *upward* often is a positive sign (something going to heaven, or perhaps outer space).
- Movement directed *downward* often is a negative sign (e.g., crashes or fights), or signals defeat.

The exact meaning of the movement is, to some degree, determined by the context in which the motion takes place.

For instance, in David Puttnam's film *The Mission* (1987), an early scene shows a young missionary (Jeremy Irons) struggling to scale a steep mountain in order to reach a South American Indian tribe. His climb up the mountain is contrasted with the falling action of a majestic waterfall. Water cascades from the cliffs above, showering the young missionary as he ascends the mountain. This juxtaposition of movement reinforces thematic concerns that are examined throughout the film: while it is difficult for human beings to control their nature and ascend to heaven, it is all too easy to fall from grace.

The media communicator also must respect the natural *logic* of movement. A car moving from left to right across the screen must continue this directional flow, or *vector,* unless the director deliberately shows the car changing directions. Otherwise, the audience feels disoriented and may dissociate from the action.

Motion involves not only direction but also *rhythm*—that is, the rate or pace at which movement occurs. A slow camera movement or the use of slow motion can be very restful and reassuring. Commonly employed in sporting events and newscasts, slow motion also furnishes the viewer with the opportunity to study detail in a shot in order to understand both *what* happened and *how* it occurred.

In Western culture, left-to-right movements are considered more restful and natural than right-to-left movements, due in part to the way that people are trained to read. Western filmmakers therefore establish a positive and harmonious atmosphere through *left-to-right* movements and employ *right-to-left* movements to intensify feelings of tension and disharmony.[21]

ANGLE

Angle refers to the level at which the camera is shooting in relation to the subject. The choice of angle conveys distinct messages. Shooting up at a person makes the subject appear larger, more important, and powerful, and his or her position or attitude as legitimate. Conversely, shooting down at a subject makes the subject appear small, weak, frightened, or vulnerable.

To illustrate, a successful series of ads for AT&T that began running in 2012 features an adult (Beck Bennett) interviewing children. Rather than looking down at the children from an "adult" perspective, the camera is placed at the eye-level of the children. This camera angle conveys the message that the audience should take these children seriously, and that the adults in the audience should treat them (and their concerns) with consideration.

The choice of angle also can affect the audience's attitude toward the subject. A classic example of this dramatic use of angle is found in Leni Riefenstahl's *Triumph of the Will* (1934), a Nazi propaganda film documenting Adolph Hitler's party convention at Nuremberg. The camera was continually tilted upward at Hitler to create a sense of divine presence and inspire awe in the audience. Indeed, the documentary was so successful in its effort to deify Hitler that the Allies banned the film for several years after the end of the war.

WORD CHOICE

Language is not simply a vehicle for conveying information but actually shapes the audience's understanding. According to linguist Kenneth Burke, language *precedes* thought. That is, ideas, concepts, and things do not exist until there are words to recall, categorize, and talk about them. To illustrate, because Russian meals consist of *breakfast, dinner* (early afternoon), and *sup-*

Leni Riefenstahl filming under the Nazi flag on 1934 Nazi Party Day in Nuremberg. Riefenstahl's use of camera angles made Hitler look powerful and imposing on screen. (Library of Congress)

per, introducing the concept of a "business lunch" in the 1980s was difficult to understand and explain. However, as Russian businesspeople were introduced to the "business lunch" in their travels, they brought the concept back with them. Now, business lunches are part of the Russian lexicon.

As societies evolve, new words are continually being invented. Lexicographer Grant Barrett provides the following examples of terms that are derived from digital culture:

- *MOOC:* an acronym for a massive open online course, an online class that allows students from anywhere to view lectures and receive instruction, usually for free.
- *Nomophobia:* fear of losing or forgetting one's mobile phone, or of being outside of the phone's signal area. From no more (phone|phobia).
- *Pet Shaming:* posting a picture of one's pet to a social media site with a sign in the picture that details some mischief or wrongdoing by the animal.

- *Waitress Mom:* a poor white working mother without a college education. The term first rose to prominence among political demographers and marketers in the 2010 midterm elections. Its usage increased sharply in October around the presidential debates.[22]

In addition, language often assumes new meanings through cultural context. Examples include:

- *Dox:* to find and release all available information about a person or organization, usually for the purpose of exposing their identities or secrets. "Dox" is a longstanding shortening of "documents" or "to document," especially in technology industries. In 2012, the high-profile Reddit user Violentacrez was doxed by Adrian Chen at Gawker to expose questionable behavior.
- *Fracking:* hydraulic fracturing, a method of extracting natural gas or oil from shale formations. Although the word is not new, it became commonplace as the extraction practice grew more widespread, producing an abundance of natural gas but also raising concerns about possible environmental and health risks.
- *Swag:* a stylish and confident demeanor or attitude. A shortening of "swagger." This term has been used in recent years but became huge this summer following its repeated use in pop songs and by large numbers of (mainly) young men. Its popularity has since fallen.[23]

Because the choice of words can change the essential meaning of a concept, the selection of particular words in a media presentation can provide insight into the media communicator's attitude *toward* a subject. To illustrate, the Israeli and Palestinian press use different synonyms to describe the conflict in the Middle East, reflecting their dramatically different points of view:

Israeli Press	Palestinian Press
Disputed Territories	The Occupied Territories
Suicide Bombers	Martyrs
Insurgents	Resistance Fighters
Pinpoint Preventive Operations	Assassination

Word choice can also furnish perspective into shifts in a culture. To illustrate, *culturomics* has emerged as a quantitative methodology that traces the frequency of words appearing in print as an indication of changes in the culture. Columnist David Brooks explains this methodology:

[In 2011,] the folks at Google released a database of 5.2 million books published between 1500 and 2008. You can type a search word into the database and find out how frequently different words were used at different epochs. . . .[24]

Brooks provides the following example of how word choice can disclose changes in a culture:

Daniel Klein of George Mason University has conducted one of the broadest studies with the Google search engine. He found further evidence of the two elements I've mentioned. On the subject of individualization, he found that the word "preferences" was barely used until about 1930, but usage has surged since. On the general subject of demoralization, he finds a long decline of usage in terms like "faith," "wisdom," "ought," "evil" and "prudence," and a sharp rise in what you might call social science terms like "subjectivity," "normative," "psychology" and "information."

Klein adds the third element to our story, which he calls "governmentalization." Words having to do with experts have shown a steady rise. So have phrases like "run the country," "economic justice," "nationalism," "priorities," "right-wing" and "left-wing." The implication is that politics and government have become more prevalent.[25]

Connotative Words

Connotation refers to the meaning associated with a word beyond its *denotative* (dictionary) definition. The meaning of a connotative word is universally understood and agreed upon. For instance, the word "house" simply describes a structure. However, "home" conjures up a much richer picture—a family gathered around the hearth, children playing video games, and the smells of dinner wafting in from the kitchen.

Sometimes the connotative meaning of a word has a cultural context. For example, in the United States, the sun has a positive association; to have a "sunny disposition" is a complement. But in Egypt, which is largely desert, the sun is perceived as cruel. As a result, to be described as "a ray of sunshine" would be an unfavorable comment. Instead, being compared to moonlight would be considered a complement.

Advertising often relies on connotative words to sell their products. Brand names like "Country Time" lemonade call up positive associations from the cultural myth of small-town America as a way to sell the product. (For further discussion, see Chapter 9, Advertising.)

Political consultants often apply positive terminology to describe their causes. For instance, the two camps in the abortion debate are designated as *pro-choice* and *pro-life.*

Euphemisms

Euphemisms are terms that are designed to minimize the reaction of the audience to disturbing media messages. For instance, as described by the public relations offices of hospitals, nobody ever dies; instead patients experience *negative patient-care outcome.*[26]

Public relations firms also rely upon euphemisms as a strategy to promote unpopular policies and programs. As an example, as the gambling industry devised its campaign to legalize casinos throughout the United States, polls revealed that some people considered gambling to be immoral. Consequently, efforts to legalize casinos throughout the United States met with less resistance when the name of the industry was changed from *gambling* to *gaming.*

Advertisers often employ euphemisms to change the public perceptions of products. For instance, the California fruit industry has changed the name of *prunes* (with its dietary connotations) to *dried plums.*

Politicians rely on euphemisms to discuss issues and policies that might be unfavorably received by the public. Thus, rather than using the word "hunger" to describe the 12 percent of Americans (35 million) who could not put food on their table at least part of the year, the Agriculture Department now describe these people as experiencing *very low food security.* (For further discussion, see Chapter 10, American Political Communications.)

Public figures who are caught in scandals commonly use the following euphemistic terms to explain their resignations: "To spend more time with my family," or "To pursue other interests."

However, the choice of euphemisms can convey unintended meaning. To illustrate, *New York Times* columnist Joe Nocera describes the terms commonly used at the IMG (the Intercollegiate Athletics Forum held in 2012):

[T]he kind of meeting where football games are routinely described as "product," television networks are "distribution channels," and rooting for State U. is an example of "brand loyalty." The university presidents, conference commissioners, athletic directors and corporate marketers who attend spend very little time mouthing the usual pieties about how the "student-athlete" comes first. Rather, they gather each year to talk bluntly about making money.[27]

These euphemisms, commonly employed in the world of management, convey the message that college athletics is no longer an amateur enterprise that has an educational benefit for students, but instead is now considered a professional and profitable business.

Jargon

At times, the purpose of word choice is obfuscation—to hide the meaning of a concept. This can be accomplished through the use of *jargon*—specialized language that is unintelligible to everyone outside of the particular field in which the jargon is found.

To illustrate, columnist Stuart Elliott found the following examples of jargon found at the 2013 Association of National Advertisers:

> Examples included "bounce rate," "conversation across multiple entry points," "cross-channel buying experience," "cross-functional breakthrough teams," "customer decision journey," "ecosystem playing field" and "zetabytes." There were also "news release," used as a verb; "return on engagement," as opposed to return on investment; and "stability agents," in counterpoint to change agents.
>
> One speaker acknowledged a potential effect of glib trade talk. "We sometimes hide behind a veil of impenetrable jargon," said Laura Simpson, global director for the McCann Truth Central unit of the McCann Worldgroup.[28]

CONNOTATIVE IMAGE

Some images possess universal associative properties. Images of babies evoke warm feelings associated

Some images engender universal responses. For instance, the photo of a young child evokes a universally warm emotional reaction from the audience. (Paul Hakimata/Dreamstime.com)

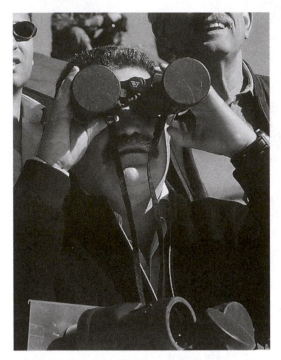

Israel's Defense Minister Amir Peretz is caught looking through binoculars without realizing the plastic lens-caps were left on as he watches during a military drill in the Golan Heights in 2007. (AP Photo/Effi Sharir)

with innocence, life, and love, irrespective of culture, gender, income, or race. Similarly, an image of a rose is an eternal symbol of romantic love. Other images are sure to evoke negative feelings of fear or revulsion.

But *context* can also influence the meaning of images. For instance, fire can symbolize either protection or destruction—the precise connotative meaning becomes clear through the context of the presentation.

In addition, *cultural context* can affect the meaning applied to an image. As an example, long before the swastika became the emblem of the Nazi Party in the 1920s, it was regarded as a positive symbol throughout the world. The word is derived from the Sanskrit word *svastika,* which means "well being and good fortune." Indeed, synagogues in North Africa, Palestine, and Hartford, Connecticut (U.S.) were decorated with swastika mosaics. Buddha's footprints were said to be in the shape of swastikas.

The earliest known swastikas date from 2500 or 3000 BCE in India and in Central Asia. In the early twentieth century, the swastika was a common icon in the United States. As an advertising promotion, Coca-Cola gave away swastika pendants. During World War I, the American 45th Infantry division wore a shoulder patch adorned with an orange swastika. Only after the Nazis adopted this symbol was the swastika associated with evil.

However, photographs may also convey *unintended messages.* A famous example occurred in 2007, when BBC news captured a photo of Israeli Defense Minister Amir Peretz watching military maneuvers of Israeli troops in the Golan Heights. The photograph revealed that Peretz was peering through binoculars that still had lens caps on. This photograph reinforced the popular conception of Peretz (and the Israeli administration) as inept in the handling of the 2006 invasion of Lebanon.

PERFORMANCE

A strong performance can elevate a mediocre film, TV, or radio script into a moving experience. The keys to a good performance are *nonverbal* and *verbal* performance skills.

Nonverbal Performance Skills

Mahima Ranjan Kundu defines nonverbal communication skills as "all the gestures, expressions, postures, etc. that are used in the process of communication."[29] Communications scholars estimate that nonverbal communication comprises 65 percent of all communication between people.[30]

Nonverbal elements such as appearance, costume, facial expression, body type, gestures, and movement play a role in hiring selections, work appraisals, and promotions. Media relations consultant Tripp Frohlichstein provides the following suggestions for people appearing in the media:

- *Eye contact*
  Good eye contact is important in convincing the viewer of your credibility. Wandering eyes may represent deceit, confusion, or

The clear and persuasive nature of nonverbal communication is epitomized in the performance of silent film stars like Charlie Chaplin. His walk, gestures, and facial expressions were a central part of his familiar endearing persona—the Little Tramp. (Library of Congress)

lack of sincerity. When on television, maintain eye contact with the reporter asking the questions. If you are on a talk show, talk primarily to the host and do not look at the camera. If someone else is talking, look at them to show your interest. Even with a print reporter or a radio host, maintain solid eye contact. Some reporters assume that shifty eyes signal shifty thoughts.

- *Gestures*
  Use gestures when appropriate and natural. Since we think in pictures, gestures can help augment points being addressed. . . . Do not use broad sweeping gestures for TV because the camera sees only a limited area. (When standing, keep your hands at your side except when gesturing.)

- *Open face*
  Keep your eyebrows up and smile when appropriate. This helps you better convey your pride, as well as intensity. When the eyebrows are flat, so are your voice and feelings. When your eyebrows are down, so is the interview and you may be perceived as angry or negative.

- *Nodding*
  Don't nod in agreement if the interviewer is reciting a litany of your company's negatives. You may simply be saying, "I'm listening," but this could be perceived by the audience as agreeing with those negatives.

- *Glasses*
  Avoid shiny metal or chrome frames that will catch and reflect the light. Thin tortoise shell frames are best. Neutral shades that blend with your hair and skin tone are recommended. Make sure they fit correctly so you are not always pushing them up on your nose.

- *Mannerisms*

DO	*DON'T*
○ Sit up straight	○ Fold your arms
○ Lean forward	○ Make fists
○ Keep your hands folded in your lap or on the arm of your chair when not talking	○ Dig fingers into arms of chair
○ Keep your head perpendicular to your shoulders to add to your authority	○ Pick cuticles
	○ Tap fingers

- Pay attention to the person who is talking (mentally and visually)

- Keep an open face and smile when appropriate
- Sit with legs together or crossed at the knee

- Fiddle with pencils

- Jiggle legs
- Slouch

- Swivel back and forth on a swivel chair
- Smoke

In addition to the above rules, women have several additional guidelines to observe:

DO
- Sit with legs crossed at the ankles

DON'T
- Cross your legs at all if your skirt is short
- Coyly tilt your head
- Have purse visible
- Play with earrings or hair

- *Costume* and *makeup* are other important ingredients in performance. Frohlichstein includes the following tips for men:
  - Blues, tans, and grays are best
  - Blue or pastel shirts
  - Appear in outfit that explains your profession (doctors, construction, businessmen, etc.)
  - Polished shoes
  - Don't wear black, brown, yellow-reds, red-oranges, or loud, clashing colors (causes bleeding and blurring on home screen)
  - Don't wear sunglasses outside or photogray glasses inside (it makes you look like a criminal)
  - Accept make-up if offered

In addition to the rules cited above, women should observe the following guidelines:

- Wear closed-toe shoes
- Avoid sexy or frilly outfits
- Avoid clunky or glittering jewelry (distracting)
- Red, grays, and blues are acceptable colors for women

- Women shouldn't wear too much lipstick. The same color as tongue looks natural. Women should get a pancake make-up as close to skin tone as possible, cheating toward a slightly darker shade if you can't get an exact match. Test it on the back of your hand. . . . Put on exposed areas, including back of hands.[31]

Nonverbal performance elements play a particularly significant role in television news presentations. A shrug, lifted eyebrow, or frown can provide commentary on the scripted news content.

In a classic study, Dr. Brian Mullen was able to identify a connection between a newscaster's facial expressions and the voting behaviors of audience members. Mullen monitored the nonverbal performances of the network anchormen (with the sound off) during the week prior to the 1984 U.S. presidential election, rating the anchors' facial expressions when they mentioned presidential candidates Ronald Reagan and Walter Mondale.

Mullen next surveyed a cross-section of Americans to determine 1) their choice of presidential candidate, and 2) the television newscaster they watched most often. Mullen discovered the following:

- Peter Jennings of ABC consistently appeared more positive when referring to Ronald Reagan.
- The voters who regularly watched Jennings were more likely than others to vote for Reagan.

Mullen concluded that the results "are consistent with a link between newscasters' facial expressions and viewers' voting behaviors."[32] Mullen hastened to qualify the results of his study. The methodology was admittedly subjective (after all, what *is* a positive expression?). Moreover, it remains unclear whether Jennings actually influenced his audience or merely attracted those viewers *already* predisposed to support Reagan.[33]

However, this study demonstrates that performance does influence the public, even in the "objective" world of broadcast journalism. Undoubtedly, Jennings was unaware that he exhibited positive behaviors when he spoke of Reagan; nevertheless, this nonverbal message was clear to the public. Audiences look to media figures for approval and disapproval on a wide variety of topics. Consequently, media communicators should be aware that even subtle nonverbal expressions have a powerful impact on the public.

Verbal Performance Skills. When used effectively, a performer's delivery and voice quality reinforce media messages. Frohlichstein identifies the following aspects of effective verbal performance:

- *Volume*
  Do not use loudness to make a point—you'll lose warmth. Too soft a voice makes you hard to hear and the listener loses the message. . . . Also, low volume lacks emotional commitment.
- *Tone*
  Tone refers to the quality or character of sound. A deep tone suggests authority, power, and confidence. Frohlichstein observes, "Exercise your voice before doing interviews. Use varying pitch and modulation."
- *Clarity*
  People must understand the words you are saying. "Nuance" can become "new ants."
- *Speed*
  Too fast and listeners can't follow you. Too slow and you become ponderous and boring.
- *Pacing*
  Vary it to keep listener interest.
- *Feelings*
  It is vital that your voice reflects your interest and concern with the topic.[34]

But beyond all of the technical reasons behind an actor's success, there is also an intangible quality to performance. Marilyn Monroe enjoyed a unique relationship with the camera. The camera seemed to look beyond Ms. Monroe's glamour, revealing her vulnerability. Marilyn Monroe did indeed look larger than life on the silver screen, which is one reason why Monroe has retained her following long after her death.

SOUND ELEMENTS

The element of sound can either enhance or alter moods. Sound occurs in three different forms in media productions: *dialogue, music,* and *background sound.*

Dialogue is written material that is intended to *sound* like conversation. However, if you transcribed an actual conversation between a small group of people, you would probably discover that it would be confusing to read. The conversation would be filled with interruptions and times when several people are speaking at once. Further, this transcript would be characterized by interpolations, such as "you know" and "like," which are intended to give the speaker extra time to compose his/her thoughts.

In contrast, scripted dialogue is clear and free of interruptions. An excellent example of effective dialogue can be found in Ted Tally's screenplay of Thomas Harris's novel *Silence of the Lambs* (1991). Consider the first encounter between FBI candidate Clarice Starling and the sophisticated, nefarious Dr. Hannibal "The Cannibal" Lecter:

> DR. LECTER
> *You're so ambitious, aren't you. . . .? You know what you look like to me, with your good bag and your cheap shoes? You look like a rube. A well-scrubbed, hustling rube with a little taste. . . . Good nutrition has given you some length of bone, but you're not more than one generation from poor white trash, are you—Agent Starling. . . ? That accent you've tried so desperately to shed—pure West Virginia. What is your father, dear? Is he a coal miner? Does he stink of the lamp?*

His every word strikes her like a small, precise dart.

> DR. LECTER (cont.)
> *And oh, how quickly the boys found you! All those tedious, sticky fumblings, in the back seats of cars, while you could only dream of getting out. Getting anywhere, yes? Getting all the way to the F . . . B . . . I.*

> CLARICE (shaken)
> *You see a lot, Dr. Lecter. But are you strong enough to point that high-powered perception at yourself? How about it. . . ? Look at yourself and write down the truth. (She slams the tray back at him.) Or maybe you're afraid to.*

> DR. LECTER
> *You're a tough one, aren't you?*

> CLARICE
> *Reasonably so. Yes.*

DR. LECTER

And you'd hate to think you were common. My, wouldn't that sting! Well you're far from common, Clarice Starling. All you have is the fear of it. (pause) Now please excuse me. Good day.

A great deal has occurred in this very brief bit of dialogue. Although Clarice is conducting the interview, it is clear that Dr. Lecter is very much in control. Clarice (and the audience) discover that the doctor is extraordinarily charming, intelligent, and perceptive—dangerous qualities when combined with Lecter's vicious nature.

We also learn about Clarice in this sequence. Dr. Lecter has zeroed in her background and motivation for pursuing a career in the FBI. She feels violated—and with good reason, as Lecter coldheartedly exposes her deepest fears and insecurities. However, Clarice fights back, showing Lecter (and us as well) that she is indeed tough enough to withstand the trials awaiting her in the remainder of the film.

Moreover, a strange, complex relationship forms between Starling and Dr. Lecter during this scene. Clarice is fascinated by Lecter's certainty about the world, his powers of perception, and even the evil that drives him. Lecter has been testing Clarice, and the novice FBI agent has successfully withstood his attempts to intimidate her and destroy her resolve. By the end of the conversation, Lecter acknowledges that Clarice is "far from common." This admission, however, does not prevent him from continuing to play games with Agent Starling, a challenge that she recognizes and accepts.

Thus, a script may contain a great deal of information and complex layers of meaning. Consequently, dialogue that is presented very rapidly can confuse the audience, undermining the intended message.

Music has a subtle yet powerful influence, enhancing our moods and distracting us from our immediate concerns. In that regard, music therapy has emerged as an effective treatment for a variety of physical conditions. Soothing music helps premature babies use oxygen more effectively, gain weight faster, and as a result, leave the hospital more quickly.[35] Stroke patients have also learned to develop their cadence, stride, and foot placement by moving to synchronized music.[36]

Music is also employed as a behavior management approach. Many companies have installed preprogrammed Muzak in the workplace in an effort to improve office productivity.

Music is also employed to accelerate the turnover rate of customers. According to Stephanie Coulter, some restaurants play fast-paced songs at a high volume "to get people agitated so they eat faster, talk more, drink more."[37] One study found that people chew an average of 4.4 bites a minute to fast music, but only 3.88 bites a minute to slow music.[38] Some convenience stores play classical music to dissuade teens from congregating.

Music also serves as a narrative device that conveys subtle messages about the media presentation. For instance, theme music for the NBC evening news simulates the rhythm of teletypes, which heralds the seriousness and legitimacy of the news program. Music is a particularly effective narrative device in foreign films, in which the audience is largely unfamiliar with the language in the film.

The soundtrack of a film or television program is used in conjunction with the visuals, to "punctuate," or emphasize, themes and messages. For example, a very moving scene in Michael Moore's documentary *Fahrenheit 9/11* (2003) shows the aftermath of the attack on the World Trade Center. The debris from the explosion falling to earth was accompanied by the sound of a piano, playing scales, from high to low. This falling motion (which was shown in slow motion), combined with the music, captured the profoundly sorrowful mood of the country in the wake of the tragedy.

A tune, rhythm, or chord can also signal a narrative shift, preparing the audience for a transition between scenes and foreshadowing upcoming events. For instance, the appearance of the theme song in the film *Jaws* (1975) always signaled the approach of the killer shark before he attacked his next victim.

Background sound refers to the noises that normally occur within a setting, such as crowd noise at a baseball game or waves lapping up on the beach. To add a feeling of realism, *sound effects* are frequently added to the audio track of a film and television programming. Sound effects are prerecorded sounds such as doors closing, horses galloping, and spurs jingling that are added to broadcast presentations for dramatic emphasis. Without background sound, a media presentation would be noticeably artificial. The message would be that what we are watching, in fact, is a media presentation and not real life.

Much of the dramatic thrust of martial arts movies is created during the postproduction process, when the action is "sweetened" by the sounds of thumping rugs, tearing sheets, and dropping bags of flour. In addition, the synthesizer has emerged as an important technological innovation that produces a range of sound effects.

The balance *between* these three areas of sound—music, dialogue, and natural sound—also conveys messages. To illustrate, two film versions of the legendary story of Robin Hood featured similar climactic scenes:

Robin's men storm the castle to dethrone Prince John and restore King Richard to the throne of England. In the midst of the fray, Robin meets the villainous Sir Guy of Gisbourne in combat and emerges victorious.

In *The Adventures of Robin Hood* (1938), starring Errol Flynn, Erich Wolfgang Korngold's stirring film score dominates the soundtrack, heightening the romance and epic drama of the duel. In contrast, in *Robin Hood: Prince of Thieves* (1991), starring Kevin Costner, natural sound was the dominant sound element (i.e., the clanging of the swords and the grunting of the two warriors), dramatizing the violence and danger of the battle, as opposed to the romantic feel of the 1939 original.

SUMMARY

Mindful of the principle of economy, the skillful media communicator uses style not merely as ornamentation but as a means of reinforcing messages. Production values subtly affect how the audience responds to media content.

Media communicators often make conscious decisions with regard to the choice of production values such as color lighting and angle. However, at other times they may make an intuitive choice—because it "feels right." In these cases, media communicators are instinctively selecting the color scheme or camera angle that best fits the intended mood of the presentation. Consequently, even if communicators are unwilling (or unable) to articulate the reasons behind their selections, they nevertheless are making decisions based on the affective properties of these production elements.

Consequently, examining production values can be a useful approach to the analysis of media presentations.

NOTES

1. John Milton, *Paradise Lost, Paradise Regained, and Samson Agonistes* (Garden City, NY: Doubleday & Company, 1969), 20.
2. Rudolf Arnheim, *Art and Visual Perception* (Berkeley: University of California Press, 1974), 97.
3. Chris Hedges, "Journalists Really Do Have an Agenda," *New York Times,* January 6, 2001.
4. Wallace S. Baldinger, *The Visual Arts* (New York: Holt, Rinehart, and Winston, 1960), 16.
5. Ibid., 15.

6. George Forman, "Viewer's Guide to 'The Hundred Languages of Children,'" University of Massachusetts–Amherst, 1991, mimeograph.

7. Robert L. Stevenson, *Global Communication in the 21st Century* (New York: Longman Publications, 1994), 63–4.

8. NBC Radio, June 19, 1992.

9. Faber Birren, *Light, Color, and Environment* (New York: Van Nostrand Reinhold Company, 1982), 81–2.

10. Rudolf Arnheim, *Art and Visual Perception: A Psychology of the Creative Eye* (Berkeley: University of California Press, 1974).

11. David Goen, "Attaining Visual Literacy: How Pictures Function as Signs and Symbols" (M.A. thesis, Webster University, 1991), 54–5.

12. Ibid.

13. Richard Cavendish, ed., *Man, Myth, and Magic* (Wichita, KS: McCormick-Armstrong, 1962), s.v. "Circle."

14. Eva C. Hangen, *Symbols: Our Universal Language* (Wichita, KS: McCormick- Armstrong, 1962), 72.

15. Natalie Angier, "The Cute Factor," *New York Times,* January 3, 2006.

16. Paul Martin Lester, *Visual Communication: Images with Messages* (Belmont, CA: Wadsworth Publishing Company, 1995), 44.

17. Cavendish, *Man, Myth, and Magic,* s.v. "Pyramid."

18. Hangen, *Symbols: Our Universal Language,* 113.

19. Herbert Zettl, *Sight, Sound, Motion: Applied Media Aesthetics* (Belmont, CA; Wadsworth, 1990), 112.

20. Albert Henry Munsell, *A Grammar of Color* (New York: Van Nostrand Reinhold Company, 1969), 14.

21. Richard L. Stromgren and Martin F. Norden, *Movies: A Language in Light* (Englewood Cliffs, NJ: Prentice Hall, Inc., 1984), 49.

22. Grant Barrett, "Words of 2012," *New York Times,* December 22, 2012.

23. Ibid.

24. David Brooks, "What Our Words Tell Us," *New York Times,* May 20, 2013.

25. Ibid.

26. Charles Downey, "Word Processing," *St. Louis Post-Dispatch,* October 22, 1994: D-1.

27. Joe Nocera, "Show Me the Money," *New York Times,* December 10, 2012, www.nytimes.com.

28. Stuart Elliott, "A Conference with Dual Constituencies Vows to Improve," *New York Times,* March 17, 2013.

29. Mahima Ranjan Kundu, "Visual Literacy: Teaching Non-Verbal Communication Through Television," *Educational Technology* 16.8 (August 1976): 31.

30. Ibid.

31. Tripp Frohlichstein, *Media Training Handbook* (St. Louis: MediaMasters, 1991), 31–7.

32. Brian Mullen et al., "Newscasters' Facial Expressions and Voting Behavior of Viewers: Can a Smile Elect a President?" *Journal of Personality and Social Psychology* 51.2 (August 1986): 291–5.

33. Ibid.

34. Frohlichstein, *Media Training Handbook,* 31.

35. Bob Condor, "Used to Improve Health, Mind, and Mood, Music Therapy Is Sounding Better All the Time," *Chicago Tribune,* December 28, 1998: B-1.

36. Ibid.

37. *St. Louis Post-Dispatch,* January 5, 1998.

38. Ibid.

WORKSHEET: KEYS TO INTERPRETING MEDIA MESSAGES

These pages may be used as a reference for media literacy analysis.

I. Process
   A. Media Communicator
      1. Who is responsible for creating the media production?
      2. What are the demographic characteristics of the media communicator(s)?
      3. How do these characteristics affect the content and outlook of the media production?
      4. Is there a preferred reading in the presentation that reflects the embedded values of the media communicator?
   B. Function
      1. What is the purpose behind the production?
      2. Does the media communicator want you to think or behave in a particular way as a result of receiving the information?
      3. Does the production contain any of the following?
         a. Latent functions
         b. Multiple functions
         c. Undefined functions
         d. False functions
         e. Competing functions
   C. Comparative Media
      1. What are the medium's distinctive characteristics?
      2. In what ways does the choice of medium affect:
         a. The communication strategy?
         b. The communication style?
         c. The content?
   D. Affective Response
      1. How does the media communicator want you to be feeling at particular points in the plot?
         a. Why does the media communicator want you to be feeling this way?
         b. Is the media communicator successful in eliciting this intended emotional response?
      2. Do your affective responses provide insight into media messages? Explain.
      3. Do your affective responses provide insight into your personal belief system? Explain.

E. Audience
1. For whom is the media presentation produced?
2. Is there more than one intended audience?
3. What values, experiences, and perspectives are shared by the audience?
   - Do these shared values, experiences, or perspectives influence the audience's understanding or interpretation of the presentation?
4. How do the experiences and perspectives of the individual audience member affect his/her interpretation of the presentation?
5. How does the choice of audience influence the strategy, style, and content of the media presentation?
6. Do the strategy, style, and content of the media presentation provide insight into the intended audience(s)?

II. Context
   A. Historical Context
   1. What does the media production tell us about the period in which it was produced?
      a. When was this media production first presented?
      b. How has the media presentation been influenced by the events of the day?
      c. Does the media presentation comment on the events of the day?
   2. Does an understanding of historical events provide insight into the media presentation?
      a. Media Presentations Made during a Particular Historical Period
         1) What events were occurring when the presentation was produced?
         2) How does an understanding of these events furnish perspective into the presentation?
      b. Historical References
         1) Are there historical references in the media production?
         2) How does an understanding of these historical references affect your understanding of the media presentation?
   3. Did the media presentation anticipate or foreshadow any political or historical events? Explain.
   4. Did the presentation play any role in shaping the events of the day? Explain.

5. In the case of entertainment programming, how accurately does it present historical events?
   a. Is the dramatization an accurate portrait of events? Compare the presentation with historically accurate accounts of the event or period.
   b. Are the causes leading to the events in the presentation clear?
   c. What were the consequences of the dramatized events?
6. In the case of a news story, how much historical context has been provided?
7. Where would you find the answers to these unanswered questions?

B. Cultural Context
   1. Media and Popular Culture: In what ways does the media presentation reflect, reinforce, and/or shape cultural:
      a. Attitudes
      b. Values
      c. Behaviors
      d. Preoccupations
      e. Myths
   2. Worldview: What kind of world is depicted in the media presentation?
      a. What culture or cultures populate this world?
         1) What kinds of people populate this world?
         2) What is the ideology of this culture?
      b. What do we know about the people who populate this world?
         1) Are characters presented in a stereotypical manner?
         2) What does this tell us about the cultural stereotype of this group?
      c. Does this world present an optimistic or pessimistic view of life?
         1) Are the characters in the presentation happy?
         2) Do the characters have a chance to be happy?
      d. Are people in control of their own destinies?
         1) Is there a supernatural presence in this world?
         2) Are the characters under the influence of other people?
      e. What hierarchy of values is in operation in this worldview?
         1) What embedded values can be found in the production?
         2) What values are embodied in the characters?
         3) What values prevail through the resolution?
         4) What does it mean to be a success in this world?

a) How does a person succeed in this world?

b) What kinds of behavior are rewarded in this world?

C. Structure

1. What are the ownership patterns within the media industry?

   a. What media ownership patterns exist in the country (or countries) you are examining?

   b. What are the ownership patterns within the particular media system you are examining (e.g., television, film, radio, Internet)?

   c. Who owns the production company that has produced the presentation you are examining (e.g., television station, newspaper, film company)?

2. Does the ownership of the media presentation have an impact on its content?

   a. Support of status quo

   b. Homogeneity of content

   c. Programming for profit

   d. Cross-promotion

3. Does government regulation affect the media presentation?

4. Describe the internal structure of the media organization that is producing the media presentation. How does this internal structure influence content?

   a. What are the resources of the production company?

   b. What is the organizational framework of the production company?

   c. What is the process of decision-making in the production company?

III. Framework

A. Introduction

1. Title: What does the title of the presentation signify?

2. Introduction as foreshadowing device:

   a. What events constitute the introduction of the media presentation?

   b. What does the introduction tell us about the presentation?

   c. Does the introduction foreshadow events and themes in the body of the production?

3. Illogical premise

   a. Is the premise of the presentation logical?

   b. What are the underlying assumptions behind the premise of the presentation?

      c. What is the impact of this premise on the messages conveyed in the presentation?

      d. Do you accept the underlying premise in the presentation?

      e. If not, are you willing to suspend your disbelief?

B. Plot

  1. Explicit content: What are the significant events in the story?

  2. Implicit content

      a. What is the relationship between the significant events in the narrative?

      b. What is the relationship between the characters in the narrative?

      c. What are the characters' motives for their actions?

      d. Are the consequences to specific behaviors defined?

  3. Subplots

      a. Can you identify any subplots in the narrative?

      b. Are there any similarities or connections between the subplots that provide insight into the worldview, characters, and themes in the production?

C. Genre

  1. Does the presentation belong to any recognizable genre?

  2. Is there a predictable formula for the genre? What insights do these formulas provide into the genre? Into the specific program?

      a. Formulaic function

      b. Formulaic premise

      c. Formulaic structure

      d. Formulaic plot

      e. Conventions

         1) Conventional storyline

         2) Setting

         3) Stock characters

         4) Trappings

  3. What does this genre suggest about:

      a. Cultural attitudes and values?

      b. Cultural preoccupations?

      c. Cultural myths?

      d. Worldview?

  4. Can you trace the evolution of this genre?

      a. Have there been shifts in the genre over time?

      b. What do these shifts in genre reveal about changes in the culture?

    D. Conclusion
       1. Character development
         a. Have the major characters changed as a result of the events in the story? How? Why?
         b. What have the characters learned as a result of their experience?
       2. Illogical conclusion
         a. Does the conclusion of the presentation follow logically from the established premise, characters, and worldview?
         b. If not, how *should* the presentation have ended, given the established premise, characters, and worldview?
         c. How would you have *preferred* for the story to end? Why?

IV. Production values: What messages are conveyed by the selection of the following production elements?
    A. The selection of production elements convey messages (e.g., shooting up at a subject legitimizes the subject; shooting down on a subject minimizes the importance of the subject or what he/she says or represents).
       1. What *manifest messages* are conveyed by the following production choices in the media presentation?
       2. What *latent messages* were you able to identify by examining the following production choices in the media presentation?
    B. Production elements
       1. What production choices have been made by the media communicator?
       2. What messages are conveyed by these production choices?
       3. How do these production elements reinforce/convey media messages?
       4. Production elements
         a. Editing
         b. Color
         c. Lighting
         d. Shape
         e. Scale
         f. Relative position
         g. Movement
         h. Point of view
         i. Angle

    j. Connotation
- 1) Words
- 2) Images

    k. Performance

    l. Sound
- 1) Music
- 2) Dialogue
- 3) Background sound

PART 3

MEDIA FORMATS

8

Journalism

PROCESS: FUNCTION

American news programming, as delivered through different channels of mass communications (newspapers, magazines, radio, television, and the Internet), serves a variety of functions:

- *Information.* In the United States, news outlets are essential to the public's ability to make informed decisions. The Society of Professional Journalists' code of ethics declares:

  The public's right to know of events of public importance and interest is the overriding mission of the mass media. The purpose of distributing news and enlightened opinion is to serve the general welfare.
  Journalists who use their professional status as representatives of the public for selfish or other unworthy motives violate a high trust.[1]

Hard news stories furnish readers with a vital connection to the nation and the world.

In addition, news programs keep readers informed about their community. Local news programming, weather forecasts, television listings, and calendars of events help individuals function on an everyday basis. Moreover, birth announcements, weddings, and obituaries keep the reader informed about significant rites of passage that take place within the community.

- *Persuasion.* The press offers a point of view on events and serves as a forum for debate. Journalists take this charge seriously. The *St. Louis*

Post-Dispatch carries an editorial platform authored by Joseph Pulitzer in 1907 that clearly defines this function:

I know that my retirement will make no difference in its cardinal principles, that it will always fight for progress and reform, never tolerate injustice or corruption, always fight demagogues of all parties, never belong to any party, always oppose privileged classes and public plunderers, never lack sympathy with the poor, always remain devoted to the public welfare, never be satisfied with merely printing news, always be drastically independent, never be afraid to attack wrong, whether by predatory plutocracy or predatory poverty.[2]

In principle, the persuasive function is confined to the editorial section of the paper or is accompanied by an identifying graphic on the TV screen. However, journalists can also subtly influence public opinion through such production elements as word choice, editing decisions, and story placement.

- *Entertainment.* Market considerations blur the distinction between news and entertainment. Features, sports, and celebrity gossip frequently appear on the front page of the newspaper, the space traditionally reserved for the most important news of the day. Further, television programs like *Entertainment Tonight* and *NFL Today* employ the conventions of news programs, such as desks, anchorpeople, and video backdrops, further blurring the distinction between news and entertainment.
- *Disclosure.* The U.S. press plays a critical role in detecting injustices and abuses within its political, social, and economic systems. To illustrate, in the 1970s, investigative reporters Bob Woodward and Carl Bernstein of the *Washington Post* uncovered a story of a burglary at the National Democratic Headquarters at the Watergate Hotel, leading to criminal convictions, a presidential resignation, and legislative reforms.

    However, the economic distress facing many newspapers has challenged their ability to continue to conduct these types of investigative pieces. David Jackson, a member of an investigative team, commented, "I couldn't be prouder of the people that are there and the job that they have done. But both as a citizen and a journalist, you have to wonder whether the paper will have the resources moving forward to continue to do that work."[3]

- *Agenda Setting.* Even if a newspaper or TV news program doesn't tell us what to think, it does tell us what to think *about.* Newspapers are not always successful in persuading their audience to adopt their positions on issues like national health care or legalized abortion; however, there is little doubt that media coverage brings these issues to the attention of the public.
- *Profit.* As a market-driven industry, American news operations are geared to produce a profit. The drive to attract an audience influences the selection of news stories that are dramatic and sensational, and have an identifiable cast of characters and a clear narrative structure (with a beginning, middle, and conclusion). As a result, the majority of local TV newscasts—once traffic, weather, and sports are excluded—consists of crime and accident stories.[4] Former presidential press secretary Mike McCurry laments,

> [The press] has lost any sense of nobility about their profession. Just go channel surfing and you see pro wrestling, and you see roller derby, and you see *Hardball* with Chris Matthews and you see *Crossfire*; it's kind of all the same genre. It's false conflict presented as serious discussion.[5]

But significantly, a survey reveals that 62 percent of the American public thinks that the news is too sensationalized, and 76 percent said the press spent too much time reporting on the private lives of public officials.[6] This would suggest that newspapers might be more successful if they were less driven by profit and instead concentrated on their role in providing a public service.

- *Persuasion.* In countries that feature a state-owned media system such as China and North Korea, the media are regarded as an instrument of the government and can be used to shape attitudes and behaviors.

MEDIA COMMUNICATOR

The more familiar you are with the individuals who report and produce news programming, the better prepared you are to interpret the information contained in their stories. In print journalism, the people who write the stories are relatively anonymous. Articles typically are accompanied only by the name of the reporter.

Editorials that appear in the newspaper are unsigned, so you have no way to identify the writer. A brief blurb often accompanies columnists who appear in the newspaper. However, an alarming trend in print journalism is *selective disclosure,* in which only a portion of a contributor's background and affiliations is presented. For example, in 2005, Henry Blodget wrote an op-ed article about the dot-com bubble for the *New York Times* entitled "What Technology Went Where and Why." The article identified the author as a former Wall Street analyst who "writes frequently for *Slate.*"

However, what went unmentioned was that Blodget had been permanently barred from the securities industry and fined $4 million for issuing fraudulent and misleading research reports on Internet stocks, violating federal laws. Clearly, this background information would have furnished significant perspective on the opinions that he expressed in the editorial.

Ironically, due to the overwhelming access to publications in the age of the Internet, identifying journalists has become even more problematic. To illustrate, newstran.com is a Web site that translates over ten thousand newspapers from their original languages into many other languages. By clicking "Peru," a menu of nine newspapers appears, enabling you to select articles from any of the papers, translated from Spanish to the language of your choice. However, identifying the background and point of view of each reporter in these papers—as well as the ideology of each newspaper—is a daunting task, to be sure.

Because of the visual nature of television news, broadcast anchors and reporters are recognizable; indeed, these journalists are often regarded as celebrities. However, it should be noted that essential personnel who influence the content of broadcast news programs—the owners, news directors, producers, writers, and editors—remain anonymous, behind the camera.

One of the most challenging aspects of analyzing news presented on the Internet is becoming familiar with the media communicator. A reporter may be using a pseudonym, may have no expertise in the field, and may bring a distinct ideology to the coverage of an issue. (For more discussion, see Chapter 12, Issues in Media Communications.)

Sources

Because industry pressures demand that reporters cover a wide range of topics within a limited time span, journalists depend on a network of sources with the expertise to assimilate, interpret, and present this complex information. These sources have access to information that would otherwise be unavailable to the journalist.

With news being disseminated at a staggering rate, many organizations post stories without investigating the legitimacy of their sources or the veracity of their information. In 2012, an Iranian paper published an article in which the American satirical publication *The Onion* was cited as a legitimate news site. The fictitious article announced an equally fictitious poll in which 77 percent of white, rural workers would rather have a beer with former Iranian president Mahmoud Ahmadinejad than with U.S. president Barack Obama.[7]

Assembling a *demographic profile* of these journalistic sources can help to put their contributions into perspective. Factors that should be considered when identifying sources include *gender, age, economic bracket, educational background,* and *professional background.* Other important factors to consider include:

- *Affiliation.* The organization with which the source is affiliated can provide insight into the political orientation of a source. For instance, an article may identify a source as a member of the Heritage Foundation, "a conservative think tank." But what does this mean? Who funds this organization? And what is its mission?
- *Motive.* Understanding *why* a source has agreed to appear in the newspaper is critical to putting his/her contributions into perspective. The media often rely on a few sources who appear repeatedly in different venues. To illustrate, on September 30, 2012, the Republican governor of New Jersey, Chris Christie, appeared on all three network Sunday morning talk shows: *Meet the Press* (NBC), *Face the Nation* (CBS), and *This Week with George Stephanopoulos.*
- In addition, a news presentation sometimes relies heavily on contributions from one particular source. In these instances, the audience would be well served by asking the following questions:
  - Why is the source volunteering this information?
  - What is the anticipated outcome of this contribution?
  - Does this information reflect a personal or professional bias on the part of the source?

Finally, considering the *reporter's* motive for using a particular source can be informative. According to *Los Angeles Times* staffer David Shaw, reporters sometimes speak through sources by selecting experts who corroborate their own points of view: "Reporters often call a source because they want a quotation to illustrate a particular point, and they are sure to get exactly what they want if they call a source whose attitudes they already know."[8]

At other times, reporters select sources simply because the sources are *available*. Daniel Okrent, the public editor of the *New York Times,* explains,

> Bad reporters find experts by calling up university press relations officials or brokerage research departments and saying, in effect, "Gimme an expert"; some academic publicity machines send out rosters, complete with phone numbers, e-mail addresses and areas of expertise, so that the lazy journalist doesn't even have to make that first call.[9]

- *Areas of Expertise.* It is also valuable to consider the nature of the source's expertise. It is not unusual for sources to give their opinions on topics outside their areas of specialization.

At times, a reporter's over-reliance on sources undermines the integrity of news coverage. According to *New York Times* columnist Tom Wicker, a source can punish reporters in a number of ways, including "lost access, complaints to editors and publishers, social penalties, leaks to competitors, [and] a variety of responses no one wants."[10] Wendell Rawls, Jr., assistant managing editor of the *Atlanta Journal and Constitution,* admits, "Yes, there are times when I feel uncomfortable reporting facts that I imagine will cause a source some pain. I deal with it by calling up the source and telling him [sic] what I'm going to do. I don't let the source get ambushed."[11]

Anonymous Sources

Identifying sources is often complicated by the issue of anonymity. Using unnamed sources gives reporters wider access to inside information by allowing informed individuals to talk without fear of recrimination. As an example, during the Watergate investigation, *Washington Post* reporters Woodward and Bernstein relied on a confidential source within the Nixon administration (codenamed "Deepthroat") to obtain vital inside information that otherwise would not have been available. (Thirty years later, it was revealed that "Deepthroat" was Mark Felt, the number-two man at the FBI at the time.)

Anonymous sources can go "off the record" in several ways:

- The most common use of anonymous sources occurs when the source remains confidential, but the reporter is free to publish the information.

Reporters Bob Woodward (right) and Carl Bernstein, whose reporting of the Watergate case won a Pulitzer Prize, sit in the newsroom of *The Washington Post* on May 7, 1973. (AP Photo)

- Sources may provide *deep background*—that is, provide the context that puts a story into a broader perspective and points the reporter in a particular direction. As a result, the source is not directly acknowledged in the story.
- Both the source and the information remain confidential. However, the reporter is free to seek corroboration elsewhere.

However, the use of anonymous sources makes it impossible for the reader to ascertain the credibility, affiliation, and motive of the person furnishing the information. Martin A. Lee and Norman Solomon explain,

If the unnamed source is a whistleblower speaking accurately and truthfully about his or her boss or agency, the information can be considered a "leak," and in all likelihood the reporter will be serving the public interest. If, on the other hand, the unnamed source is the voice of a government agency and there's no legitimate reason for the source to be unnamed, the information can be considered a "plant," and in all likelihood the reporter will be serving the interest of the agency, not the public.[12]

But even if the motive is unclear, what is certain, according to Robert Booth, is that "all unauthorized disclosures are committed by people who ultimately wish to influence outcomes, events and opinions."[13]

An example of the damage of unspecified motives occurred during the run-up to the war in Iraq. The *New York Times* made extensive use of anonymous sources, who declared that Iraq possessed weapons of mass destruction. However, after the invasion, no one was able to locate the storehouse of weapons. Further, it was disclosed that these anonymous sources were Iraqis who stood to personally benefit from a U.S. invasion. As a result, in 2004, the *New York Times* published a public apology for failing to shed light on the motives of their sources:

> Accounts of Iraqi defectors were not always weighed against their strong desire to have Saddam Hussein ousted. . . . The most prominent of the anti-Saddam campaigners, Ahmad Chalabi, has been named as an occasional source in *Times* articles since at least 1991, and has introduced reporters to other exiles. He became a favorite of hard-liners within the Bush administration and a paid broker of information from Iraqi exiles.[14]

The *New York Times* then revised its policy with regard to the use of anonymous sources:

- The policy requires that at least one editor know the identity of every source.
- Anonymous sources cannot be used when on-the-record sources are readily available.
- They must have direct knowledge of the information they are imparting.
- They cannot use the cloak of anonymity for personal or partisan attack.
- They cannot be used for trivial comment or to make an unremarkable comment seem more important than it is.[15]

Some news organizations subscribe to a policy in which they state the *motive* behind a source choosing to remain anonymous. As an example, in 2012, an article in the *New York Times* discussed a decision by CNN to incorporate the personal journal of Christopher Stevens, U.S. Ambassador to Libya, into its story about the attack on the American consulate in Benghazi, which resulted in the death of Stevens and three other diplomats. The article included the following explanation by a CNN employee of why he or she had decided to remain anonymous:

> "It was a murky call," a senior CNN executive said. He spoke on condition of anonymity because the network was limiting public response to comments made by Mark Whitaker, the managing editor of CNN Worldwide, on Monday morning.[16]

Every country has its own regulations with regard to the protection of sources. In the United States, every state except Wyoming offers a measure of protection for confidential sources. However, many journalists and civil libertarians advocate the establishment of a national "shield law." Law professor Geoffrey R. Stone declares,

> Congress should expeditiously enact a federal journalist-source privilege law, which would protect journalists from compelled disclosure of their sources' confidential communications in the same way psychiatrists and lawyers are protected. . . . A strong and effective journalist-source privilege is essential to a robust and independent press and to a well-functioning democratic society. It is in society's interest to encourage those who possess information of significant public value to convey it to the public, but without a journalist-source privilege, such communication will often be chilled because sources fear retribution, embarrassment or just plain getting "involved." As we have seen over the past several years . . . the absence of a journalist-source privilege leads to confusion, uncertainty and injustice. At the hands of unrestrained federal prosecutors, journalists have taken a serious battering.[17]

Public Figures

In the United States, people can be subjected to media scrutiny as "public figures" if they have met the following criteria:

- Voluntarily stepped into the spotlight
- Assumed an important role in the resolution of important public issues
- Had an impact on a public issue
- Become a public figure through means other than simply media attention[18]

In the past, public figures could expect some semblance of privacy, even if they were the objects of media attention. But in the age of modern media, newsmakers must assume that all public functions are being recorded, regardless of locale. Videos recorded on cell phones give people glimpses into "backstage activities"—areas of privacy previously hidden from public view.

Unfortunately, unscrupulous journalists abuse this journalistic license, intruding into the personal affairs of celebrities. In 1997, the intrusion of the press resulted in the death of Princess Diana of Great Britain, who was killed in a high-speed automobile crash after being pursued by paparazzi. And more recently, actress Tori Spelling (who was pregnant at the time) was in a car accident in 2011 after being chased by paparazzi while trying to take her kids to school.

Other countries have their own policies regarding press coverage of public figures. For instance, in France, where public figures are primarily defined as government officials, the litmus test for press coverage of public figures is whether a disclosure would affect policy. Thus, when former French president François Mitterrand was asked by a journalist during his presidency whether it was true that he had a daughter outside his marriage, he replied: "Yes, it's true. And so what? It's none of the public's business."[19]

Moreover, concerns about litigation can affect press coverage of celebrities. French libel laws are so protective of private lives that the least intrusion in print or broadcasting can lead to legal action and heavy fines.

Disclosure vs. Privacy

A related issue involves the challenge of protecting national security in an open society. In the United States, citizens have a right to information that affects the public. But at the same time, airing this information can potentially jeopardize security measures that require secrecy. During the first four and a half years of the Obama administration, six current and former government officials were indicted in leak-related cases—twice the number brought under all previous administrations combined.

In 2013, federal investigators seized two months of reporters' and editors' phone records at the Associated Press. The extensive network of subscribers to this news service includes newspapers and television and radio stations throughout the United States. In addition, records were seized from home phones and cell phones. This action by the Justice Department was in response to the 2012 publication of information about the CIA's disruption of a Yemen-based terrorist plot to bomb an airliner. The Obama administration argued that this public disclosure jeopardized the safety of the CIA "mole" who had uncovered the plot, as well as future operations. According to Justice Department spokesman William Miller, the established procedure in such cases is as follows:

We must notify the media organization in advance unless doing so would pose a substantial threat to the integrity of the investigation. Because we value the freedom of the press we are always careful and deliberative in seeking to strike the right balance between the public interest in the free flow of information and the public interest in the fair and effective administration of our criminal laws.[20]

However, in a letter to Attorney General Eric H. Holder, Jr., Gary Pruitt, the president and chief executive of the Associated Press, called the seizure a "serious interference with AP's constitutional rights to gather and report the news."[21]

After the story broke in May 2013, President Obama discussed the AP case as an example of the ongoing tension in democratic societies between the protection of national security information and the people's right to know:

We must enforce consequences for those who break the law and breach their commitment to protect classified information. But a free press is also essential for our democracy. That's who we are. And I am troubled by the possibility that leak investigations may chill the investigative journalism that holds government accountable.[22]

President Obama then initiated a review of the current policy and practices, directing Holder to identify ways to tighten the rules pertaining to when prosecutors may seek information that could disclose reporters' sources.

In July, Holder announced new guidelines that would limit the conditions under which journalists' records could be obtained and would make it more difficult for prosecutors to obtain a journalist's records from telephone companies without advance notice. The notifications would give the news organizations a chance to contest the request in court. Holder explained,

The Department of Justice is firmly committed to ensuring our nation's security, and protecting the American people, while at the same time safeguarding the freedom of the press. These revised guidelines will help ensure the proper balance is struck when pursuing investigations into unauthorized disclosures.[23]

In addition, the Justice Department's report recommended that ways other than criminal investigations should be found to deal with leaks of classified information. White House spokesman Matt Lehrich explained,

There are circumstances in which leaks are better addressed through administrative means, such as withdrawal of security clearances or imposition of other sanctions. The president agrees with the Justice Department's recommendation, and has directed his team to explore how the administration could more effectively use alternatives in appropriate cases.[24]

But in addition, columnist Bill Keller advocates the establishment of a National Shield Law, characterized by the following features:

Before compelling a journalist to testify or surrender records, the government would be obliged to meet the journalist's lawyers in front of a judge. The prosecutors would have to make a good case that they had no other way to find the leak, that they would not cast their net so widely as to intrude on other reporting operations, and that identifying the leak was more important than the public value of the story. It's not clear whether a shield law would have thwarted the government's surveillance of the AP or Rosen. But it would have taken away the prosecutors' power to decide unilaterally.[25]

Point of View: The Illusion of Objectivity in the Press

A key to the interpretation of news programming is dispelling the myth of the objectivity of the press. Identifying the point of view of a story, program, or news operation (e.g., MSNBC or Fox News) will enable you to put the news report into perspective.

The American press adheres to the principles of accuracy and objectivity. The Society of Professional Journalists' code of ethics declares,

Good faith with the public is the foundation of all worthy journalism.

1. *Truth is our ultimate goal.*
2. *Objectivity in reporting the news is another goal which serves as the mark of an experienced professional. It is a standard of performance toward which we strive. We honor those who achieve it.*

However, this code assumes that: 1) an absolute truth exists; and 2) journalists are in a position to present this ideal truth without personal bias or distortion.

We live in a complex, subjective world in which the truth may be difficult to identify. As legendary newspaper commentator Walter Lippmann has observed, news only approaches truth in cases of quantifiable information, such as the temperature, sports scores, and election results. But even in these cases, information can be far from absolute. For instance, a weather report can only accurately measure the specific place where the temperature is being calibrated. Variables such as the amount of green space in the region verses densely constructed areas that retain heat can cause a fluctuation of several degrees in temperature within a 30-mile radius.

However, readers often confuse fact with truth. To illustrate, in July 2012, the following headline appeared in the *New York Times*: "Syria Moves Some Chemical Weapons, U.S. Says."[26] But although it is a *fact* that American officials made this comment, the statement is not necessarily *true*.

Because there is no universal agreement on truth, faithfulness to the ideal of objectivity becomes an impossibility. Ben Bagdikian declares, "Objectivity contradicts the essentially subjective nature of journalism. Every basic step in the journalistic process involves a value-laden decision."[27]

Ironically, both liberals and conservatives have accused the press of biased reporting against their political activities. According to Ted J. Smith, both sides are correct:

Critics on the left . . . attack journalists for being insufficiently critical of mainstream policies, leaders, and institutions, for excluding minority views, and for unreflective repetition of the assumptions and values of capitalist economics and bourgeois democracy. Supported by numerous academic studies, there can be little doubt about the basic validity of this claim.

Among conservatives, belief in the liberal bias of the media is almost an article of faith. . . . Conservatives base their case on the claims that journalists, especially in the prestigious national media, are liberal in their political views, and that those views are reflected in coverage.[28]

An important consideration in a discussion of objectivity concerns the issue of *intention*: Are reporters surreptitiously trying to sway readers to their point of view?

Ultimately, the question of intention is *irrelevant*. Journalists make daily decisions that, regardless of intention, suggest a particular point of view. For instance, in reporting a story, the perspective that is reported first is regarded as the legitimate position.

Indeed, some scholars find this notion of objectivity in the press to be not only *unrealistic* but *undesirable*. Author Mark Hertsgaard argues that American journalists have become trapped by a modern ethic of objectivity, forcing the press to forego its responsibility as opinion leaders. According to this ideal of objectivity, journalists can only report stories when: 1) an event has occurred, or 2) an outside agent has brought up an issue. As a result, American journalists are limited to reporting the official positions of those in authority. Hertsgaard observes,

> How could the public be expected to develop an opinion on a given issue unless that issue was posed for their consideration? In the American system, that was the responsibility of the press. Yet the modern ethic of objectivity precluded such journalism. . . .
>
> In accordance with their avoidance of partisanship, many journalists seemed to regard strenuous challenging of the government as an improper violation of the rules of objectivity. Honest adversarial journalism they equated with, and often dismissed as, "advocacy" journalism.[29]

In principle, the information that appears in the front section of a newspaper is devoted to "objective" news reporting. But acknowledging the subjectivity of this principle, the *New York Times* has published a "Readers' Guide" that delineates "[o]ther journalistic forms that provide additional perspective on events." These additional "journalistic forms" that appear in the news section include:

- **Reporter's Notebook:** A writer's collection of several anecdotes or brief reports, often supplementing coverage of a major news event like a summit meeting or an important trial. The items provide glimpses behind the scenes that flesh out the reader's sense of a major story.
- **Memo:** A reflective article, often with an informal or conversational tone, offering a look behind the scenes at issues or political

developments. The article (with a title like "Political Memo," "White House Memo," or "Memo from London") may draw connections among several events, or tell the reader who or what shaped them.

- **Journal:** A sharply drawn feature article focusing on a place or event (and labeled with the place name, whether foreign, national, or regional). A journal article is closely observed and stylishly written, often light or humorous in tone. It is intended to give the reader a vivid sense of a place and time.

- **News Analysis:** A close examination of the ramifications of an important news situation. It includes thorough reporting, but also draws heavily on the expertise of the writer. The article helps the reader understand underlying causes or possible consequences of a news event, but does not reflect the writer's personal opinion.

- **Appraisal:** A broad evaluation, generally by a critic or a specialized writer, of the career and work of a major figure who has died. The article often accompanies the obituary.

- **Review:** A specialized critic's appraisal of works of creativity— movies, books, restaurants, fashion collections. Unlike other feature writers, critics are expected to render opinions in their areas of expertise.

- **News-Page Column:** A writer's regularly scheduled essay, offering original insight and perspective on the news. The column often has a distinctive point of view and makes a case for it with reporting. (Columns in the newspaper are displayed with the writer's name and the column's title inset into the text.)

The news sections also present a number of regular feature articles that carry labels indicating the topics—for example, the Saturday Profile in the foreign pages and Market Place in Business Day.[30]

The emergence of cable news channels Fox News and MSNBC has ushered in a new era of American journalism. Despite the claim of Fox News to be "Fair and Balanced," the principle of objectivity has been replaced by a transparently ideological news system. Freed from this illusion, the audience can then filter the news through this perspective, knowing that the coverage is approaching the subject from a particular ideological position.

Rather than objectivity, a more realistic and constructive set of journalistic principles with which to assess news programming has emerged, consisting of *transparency, perspective, judgment, and fairness*:

- *Transparency.* Being clear about the point of view of the publication, the reporter's perspective, and the background and motive of sources enables audience members to filter the information and make up their own minds about the topic.
- *Perspective.* In a world in which events often appear unconnected and consequences only appear over time, journalists have a responsibility to put these events into meaningful perspective. At the same time, however, the audience has the responsibility to challenge these assertions to make sure that journalists handle this charge responsibly.
- *Judgment.* Journalism is as much an art as it is a craft; that is, in the many individual cases that come across an editor's desk, the situations are complex. As a result, editors and reporters rely upon *news judgment* in deciding what stories to include and omit, as well as how to treat subjects. However, at times, there may be disagreement, even among veteran journalists, about how to treat a story.
- *Fairness.* Understanding that it is difficult to uncover an absolute truth, journalists have a responsibility to represent all sides of an issue. Byron Calame, public editor of the *New York Times,* explains,

Getting both sides of a story and sorting them out for readers is the basic job of newspaper reporters and editors. This is a key to creating a newspaper that is fair—both to readers and to the people and institutions that are the subjects of stories. Seeking comment from those written about, especially when they are put in an unfavorable light, is a particularly important aspect of fair coverage. It helps ensure that readers get the most complete and accurate view possible of a newsworthy development.[31]

Once journalists recognize that their decisions convey messages that influence the reader, they will be more conscious of the ramifications of the choices they make. And once audience members realize that objectivity is an unobtainable ideal, they will be in a better position to factor the point of view of the content into their interpretation of the story.

Homogeneity in the Newsroom

The typical newsroom is predominantly young, male, and white. This lack of diversity can influence the selection and treatment of stories that appear in their news presentations. This is not to suggest that these staff members are necessarily vicious bigots. However, because people are limited by their own experience, they may be guilty of a *benign* racism, sexism, or classism, in which they are oblivious to information or wording that would be offensive to minorities.

To illustrate, on a "CNN Headlines News Program" broadcast in 2006, CNN host Glenn Beck interviewed Keith Ellison. Ellison is a U.S. citizen, born and raised in Detroit, Michigan, who had just become the first Muslim ever elected to Congress. In this interview, Beck made clear his bias against people who hold Muslim religious beliefs:

GLENN BECK: I, I will tell you. May I? May we have five minutes here where we're just politically incorrect and I play the cards face up on the table?

KEITH ELLISON: Go there.

GLENN BECK: Ok. No offense, and I know Muslims, I like Muslims, I've been to mosques. I really don't believe that Islam is a religion of evil. I think it's been hijacked, quite frankly. With that being said, you are a Democrat. You are saying let's cut and run and I have to tell you, I have been nervous about this interview with you, because what I feel like saying is sir, prove to me that you are not working with our enemies and I don't—I know you're not. I'm not accusing you of being an enemy, but that's the way I feel and I think a lot of Americans are feeling that way.

KEITH ELLISON: Well, let me tell you the people of the 5th Congressional District know that I have a deep love and affection for my country. There's no one who is more patriotic than I am. And so, I don't need to prove, to prove my patriotic stripes.[32]

Although Beck could easily dismiss this media stereotype of Muslims as harmless, he would surely take the matter more seriously if the characterization disparaged his own racial/ethnic group.

More diversity among decision-makers would avert this type of problem. Tim McGuire, managing editor of the *Minneapolis Star Tribune,* declares, "It's time we stop and listen to minority voices that have an understanding and perspective white editors and reporters don't have."[33]

At a Poynter Institute conference entitled "Redefining the News: Reaching New Audiences through Diversity," professionals and scholars made four recommendations designed to infuse a diversity of viewpoints in the newspaper:

- *Develop story ideas within the community*
- *Cultivate sources from a variety of backgrounds and perspectives*
- *Redesign news beats*
- *Reshape newsroom culture*

However, a 2011 report from the American Society of News Editors found that the percentage of both women and people of color (African Americans and Latinos, etc.) who write for sports news outlets continued its third straight year of decline. The percentage of sports editors who are female or African American was less than 10 percent for 2010. This seems particularly incongruous, given that in 2009, almost 70 percent of players in the NFL were African American.[34] As Seymour Topping, director of editorial development for New York Times Co. Regional Newspapers, declares, "We must forge ahead even more strongly to reach the . . . goals of accurately representing the diversity in American society."[35]

COMPARATIVE MEDIA

Innovations in media technology have created a range of channels through which the news is delivered, including print newspapers, radio, television, the Internet, and mobile devices. Significantly, A 2012 survey found that 67 percent of the participants had accessed newspaper content via computers, smartphones, and tablets in the previous week.[36] Further, Americans spend about the same amount of time keeping up on the news (just over an hour a day) as they did a decade ago.[37]

However, the selection of different media results in the audience getting a different *kind* of news. Watching the news on television provides insight into the events as they unfold, while print journalism furnishes valuable perspective into these events. Consequently, the best course of action is a *balanced media diet,* consulting different media to get a broader understanding of news events.

Print

As a product of the American economic system (as well as a significant player), the journalism industry experienced a state of economic crisis between 2008 and 2010. During this period, newspaper circulation decreased by more than 10 percent. The industry sold about 44 million copies a day—fewer than at any time since the 1940s. Many papers folded, leaving vast regions without newspapers with roots in their communities. Further, large media conglomerates like the Tribune Company, which operates the *Chicago Tribune,* the *Los Angeles Times,* and six other daily papers, filed for bankruptcy protection.[38] Staff positions declined to fewer than 40,000 employees, the lowest level since 1978.[39]

Newspapers face stiff competition from other media. In 2012, *New York Times* columnist David Carr reported,

There has been a sharp decline in the proportion of Americans who got news yesterday only from a traditional news platform—from 40 percent then to 33 percent currently.[40]

However, local and community news remain big attractions for newspapers. Publishers who cater to small/medium markets saw their circulation increase in 2011 by using this strategy.[41] Daily newspapers have increased their sales of Sunday editions by focusing on local events and engaging their readers.

The availability of newspapers online has helped keep young adults interested in news. During the first quarter of 2012, daily visitors to newspaper Web sites increased by 10 percent among the 18-to-24 age group. Twenty-four percent said they read only print newspapers, while 48 percent only read digital versions of newspapers. Thirty-four percent of this age category read both print and digital newspapers.[42]

Radio

U.S. commercial radio news also is on the decline. In Philadelphia, for example, the number of AM radio stations featuring news coverage has shrunk from five to two over the past quarter century.[43]

However, because the medium of radio lends itself to discussions about politics and sports, the format of talk radio is thriving. Talk-radio hosts are broadcast by more than 1,200 radio stations, plus the Internet, satellite radio, and television. Combined, they reach more than 100 million Americans weekly—about a third of the nation. It must be noted that the function of this format is not *information* but *persuasion.*

Television

Although nearly half of the population spends at least 30 minutes a day getting its news from TV, the number of people who regularly watch nightly network news has declined by 23 percent—half the total recorded in 1993.[44]

In response, many local broadcast stations have instituted austerity measures that have affected the quality of their newscasts. According to the Pew Research Center, the decline in viewership has been accompanied by cutbacks in the reporting ranks of television networks. Local news broadcasts are characterized by shorter stories and reduced coverage of politics and government, along with increased reliance on three main topics— weather, traffic, and sports.[45] Amy Mitchell, the report's main author, wrote, "This adds up to a news industry that is more undermanned and unprepared to uncover stories, dig deep into emerging ones or to question information put into its hands."[46] Indeed, 31 percent of survey respondents said they "have stopped tuning to a (local) news outlet because it no longer provided them with the news they were accustomed to getting."[47]

Digital Media

As of 2012, more U.S. residents obtained news online than through other traditional formats. Sixty-one percent indicated that they received at least some of their news information online.[48]

Mobile phones and tablets are largely responsible for the surge in digital news consumption; young people largely turn to social media as a primary source of news information. A 2011 Knight Foundation Study reveals that among digital media options (i.e., social media, Internet, and mobile digital media platforms), 56 percent of high school students use social networks as a daily source for news and information—23 percent higher than Internet portals. Indeed, the median age of an adult newspaper mobile user is 17 years younger than the print reader.[49]

Significantly, people in their forties are even more likely to turn to their computer for news than younger adults, with 58 percent online at least three days a week.[50]

The Internet offers a choice of media within one newscast. The audience can use print, video, graphics, and audio, thereby receiving different dimensions of a news story within one medium. Moreover, in line with the digital communications model, the audience exercises increasing control over media content. Individuals can research Internet sites to find stories on topics of their choosing.

IMPACT OF DIGITAL MEDIA ON JOURNALISM PRACTICES

In the world of digital journalism, reporters rush to "scoop" their competition. Consequently, the number of sources required to verify a story has been reduced from two sources to one—sometimes with disastrous results.

Another significant feature of digital media is that the audience has unprecedented control. Individuals can decide what features (e.g., video or photos) they want or hit a "hot link" to learn more about particular aspects of a story. Howard Kurtz observes, "The good news is that the average consumer can . . . choose from sources he [sic] trusts and enjoys rather than being spoon-fed by a handful of big corporations."[51]

Interactive media has had an enormous impact on the standards and practices of journalism. As an example, digital journalism works according to a "virtual" deadline, in which readers have continual access to up-to-the-minute news. As a result, instead of requiring two sources to confirm the accuracy of a story, editors have reduced this procedure to *one* source—sometimes with disastrous results:

- Reporting on the school massacre in Newtown, Connecticut, the *New York Times* named the wrong person as the gunman online, and, even the next day in print, it made serious errors about how Adam Lanza entered Sandy Hook Elementary School, about his weapons, and about his mother's role at the school. The story also identified Ryan Lanza as the gunman instead of his brother Adam.
- Reporting on the unfolding Boston bomb massacre, CNN's John King falsely reported that a "dark-skinned male" had been arrested in connection with the crime.

Citizen Journalism

Digital technology has also led to the establishment of the *citizen journalism* movement, an audience-driven source of news production and distribution that circumvents the traditional gatekeepers of news and information such as newspapers, radio, and television news programming. Citizen journalism fulfills an essential role of societal watchdog, calling attention to important information that is under-reported by the mainstream media, as well as putting this information into meaningful perspective.

Digital media technology is particularly well suited for the complex and dangerous reporting climate in authoritarian countries in which traditional news operations do not have access to information. Journalistic "correspondents" are citizens who, equipped with cell phones, report on events that are not covered by the mainstream press. Indeed, many mainstream journalists now look to independent or freelance fact-checkers online who live tweet or blog as politicians make public appearances.

Wired magazine and NewAssignment.Net have spearheaded a collaborative approach called *crowdsourcing,* in which members of the public, serving as citizen correspondents, contribute their knowledge and research to coverage of one story. For instance, in June 2012, when Iranian citizens took to the streets to protest President Mahmoud Ahmadinejad's re-election, the government limited the access of the mainstream international press, giving rise to a collaborative style of news gathering—a combination of the few reports by mainstream journalists, accompanied by videos, photographs, tweets, and blogs from citizen journalists.

The day after the election the *Huffington Post* posted a blog containing aggregated news on the Iranian election. Within a week, the blog—with several updates an hour during the day—had received more than 100,000 comments and five million page views. As Bill Mitchell, a senior leader at the Poynter Institute, observes, "Instead of limiting ourselves to full-blown articles to be written by a journalist (professional or otherwise), the idea is to look closely at stories as they unfold and ask: is there a piece of this story I'm in a particularly good position to enhance or advance?"[52]

However, at this stage, citizen journalism currently faces some shortcomings that compromise its status as a serious form of journalism. First, because few bloggers find full-time job opportunities, little original reporting is produced. A survey of the top 10 blogs found that only 13 percent of the posts involved on these sites had original reporting, such as reviewing documents or interviews.[53]

In addition, consistent standards and practices for citizen journalism haven't yet been established. Although some blogs are well researched and fair in their coverage of issues, others are merely personal reflections. Citations and references are frequently not cited. In addition, there is no way to verify information on authors, including their background, credentials, and possible motives for contributing. Finally, because of the intense competition, citizen journalists may feel pressured to sensationalize their entries to attract an audience.

However, the process of establishing standards of accuracy, thoroughness, fairness, reliability, ethics, and transparency are currently underway.

Richard Edelman, CEO of the public relations giant of the same name, observes, "Bloggers do not need to disclose their sources, but they should attribute specific content to a company or another blogger if used verbatim."[54] At the 2006 Yearly Kos Convention of bloggers, Jennifer Palmieri, former deputy White House press secretary under President Bill Clinton, held a "pundit project training" in which she told bloggers how to present themselves in television interviews—what to wear, how to sit, and what to say.[55]

In addition, new resources are being developed to help formalize this field, such as the Technorati Web site, which tracks what is being discussed in the blogosphere, including French, German, Italian, Korean, Chinese, Japanese, and English sites.

AUDIENCE

Although the newspaper audience is physically removed from the writer, research provides a clear portrait of the regular newspaper reader. Newspapers have developed series of metrics that inform the editors about the interests and habits of their audience. Alan Murray, who oversees online news at the *Wall Street Journal,* observes,

> How can you say you don't care what your customers think? We care a lot about what our readers think. But our readers also care a lot about our editorial judgment. So we're always trying to balance the two.[56]

Although newspapers are readily available for the general public, newspapers have emerged as an elite medium. The typical audience member is older, well educated, and earns a relatively high income. These demographic characteristics cut across racial and gender lines. Older, well-educated, and affluent African Americans read newspapers even more faithfully than their white counterparts. Further, working women are more likely to read newspapers than women who do not work outside of the home.[57]

Over the past decade, readership has fallen in all age groups. However, young people are particularly indifferent to the print medium. Among people 30 and younger, the percentage has dropped by 20 percent.[58] Young people often regard newspapers as:

- An "old people's habit . . . something you see old people do while waiting for a bus"

- Speaking for the status quo and against societal change
- A cold and impersonal medium
- A "middle-aged medium" (produced by older adults for an older audience)[59]

Significantly, role modeling can be a factor in determining newspaper consumption patterns among young people. College students are far more likely to read the paper if their parents routinely read the newspaper. In fact, students are likely to read the paper at the same time of day and in the same location as their parents.[60] This would suggest that one way for parents to encourage their offspring to read the newspaper is simply to read the paper themselves.

People tend to read the newspaper for the following reasons:

- Immediacy and thoroughness of print journalism
- Local awareness and utility
- Habit
- Entertainment
- Social extension or gossip[61]

Although almost all readers (92%) skim through the entire newspaper, people generally read only about one-fifth of the paper. However, newspapers serve as a reference at various times of the day; over 50 percent of readers turn to a newspaper two or more times in a given 24-hour period, consulting the paper for information such as sales or movie schedules.[62]

One advantage still held by the newspaper over fast-paced outlets such as radio, TV, and the Internet is that a majority of people find it relaxing to read the newspaper.[63]

Content preferences among readers remain remarkably stable over time. People read the paper according to an established order (e.g., the sports section first, then the front page). Although some sections of the newspaper may be of interest to a relatively small number of people, those readers maintain a fierce loyalty to that section.

STRUCTURE

In the United States, news outlets generally are privately owned, and a major function (or purpose) is *profit*. As a result, the corporate worldview has become predominant in media-carried content. Ben Bagdikian observes,

> No sacred cow has been so protected and has left more generous residues in the news than the American corporation. . . . [At the same time],

large classes of people are ignored in the news, are reported as exotic fads, or appear only at their worst—minorities, blue-collar workers, the lower middle class, the poor. They become publicized mainly when they are in spectacular accidents, go on strike, or are arrested. . . . But since World War I hardly a mainstream American news medium has failed to grant its most favored treatment to corporate life.[64]

Economic factors have an enormous impact on the content of news programming. Approximately 60 percent of newspaper space is devoted to advertising. (See Figure 8.1.) Another 16 percent of space is devoted to public relations-oriented content, including public relations releases, story memos, or suggestions that come from corporations.[65]

Moreover, there is very little original investigative reporting in today's news programming, due to economic constraints. As a result, according to journalist Donald Barlett, news magazines like *Time* can no longer focus on investigative reports:

I think the budgetary aspect of this also includes devoting the kind of space that our work requires, that *Time* magazine no longer has, quite

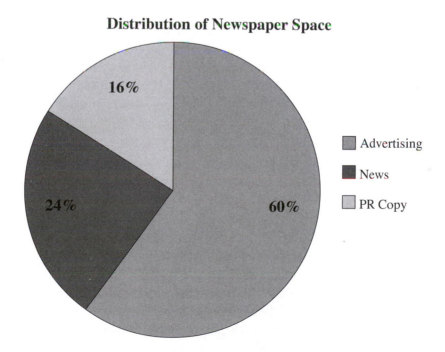

Distribution of Newspaper Space

Advertising

News

PR Copy

16%

24%

60%

Figure 8.1   Newspaper Space

frankly. If you look at the magazine today, the long stories that we wrote could not appear today.[66]

Moreover, while more material is being generated than ever before, very little original work is being produced. The Project for Excellence in Journalism examined how a variety of news outlets in the United States, including newspapers, television, radio, and the Internet, covered a single day's worth of news and discovered that there was enormous repetition and amplification of just two dozen stories. As a result, although "Google News" offered access to 14,000 stories within two clicks, they were actually accounts of just 24 news events.[67]

Instead, news organizations increasingly cover *staged events,* such as speeches and ribbon cuttings. These ceremonies have little news value, primarily serving the interests of the sponsoring organizations. These allocations leave little room for actual news content in the newspaper.

- *Homogenization of News Content*
  While there are more news outlets than ever before, there are actually *fewer* voices.

The following economic developments have contributed to the *homogenization of news content*:

1. *One-newspaper cities.* In 1940, 57 percent of cities in the United States carried two or more newspapers. But by 2011, that number had dropped to 2 percent.[68] This trend toward one-newspaper cities reduces the range of perspectives available to readers. During the time of multi-newspaper cities, the papers frequently offered opposing editorial positions—one was liberal, the other conservative. As a result, the readers were exposed to a range of political perspectives. Today, many one-city papers compensate by offering both liberal and conservative perspectives on the op-ed page of the remaining paper; however, this approach means that *neither* side has much of a forum for commentary.

2. *Newspaper chains.* A newspaper chain is a large company that owns newspapers in different locations throughout the country. In the United States, newspaper chains dominate the journalistic landscape. One-third of the top 100 American newspapers by circulation are owned by one of four companies: Gannett, Tribune Company, NewsCorp, or McClatchy. This amounts to a daily circulation of 8,682,000 daily newspapers.[69]

   Newspapers that have made the transition from an independent company to part of a chain of newspapers have seen an increase in advertising, accompanied by a decrease in news content. In addition, editorial policies either reflect the ideology of corporate ownership or become bland to avoid controversy. According to Ben Bagdikian, newspaper chains tend to hire less-qualified journalists to curb expenses.[70]

3. *Conglomeratization of alternative newspapers.* Alternative papers often began as "underground" publications that covered local politics, avant-garde arts activities, and alternative lifestyles. However, many of these publications have been absorbed by chains of weekly newspapers. As an example, Voice Media Group, based in Denver, Colorado, publishes alternative newspapers in Denver, Los Angeles, New York, Houston, Dallas, Minneapolis, St. Louis, and Miami. These shifts in ownership often are accompanied by changes in content, featuring an emphasis on entertainment coverage and less political coverage and social commentary. As a result, the St. Louis newspaper, the *Riverfront Times,* is not permitted to endorse political candidates. The rationale is that the corporation has no stake in the local communities, and that an endorsement might alienate readers.

4. *Reliance on syndicated stories.* Syndication is an arrangement in which individual papers throughout the country purchase the rights to carry a popular columnist. In addition to the prospect of attracting fans of the columnist, syndication saves the expenses incurred by hiring a fulltime columnist. But in the process, the audience loses a voice that can furnish a local perspective on important issues and events. Moreover, syndicated stories are generally picked up long after they have originally appeared, losing their timeliness. As an example, *New York Times* columnist Maureen Dowd's commentary regularly appears in that publication on Saturdays, and in the *St. Louis Post-Dispatch* on the following Wednesday. Dowd's column, which comments on the events of the day, often loses its original meaning and value when it appears four days later.

- *Influence of Advertising on News Content*
Advertisers, who account for 75 percent of newspapers' revenue, can influence news content, in several ways:
   - *Favorable treatment in the press.* According to columnist Russell Baker, the news coverage of advertising clients often is markedly sympathetic:

      During Robert Sam Anson's brief tenure as editor of *Los Angeles* magazine, the business side committed to a fifteen-page supplement, to be written by the editorial side and called

"The Mercedes Golf Special." Mercedes didn't promise to take any ads, but it was hoped that the car maker would think kindly of the magazine for future issues.[71]

- *Self-censorship.* Occasionally, editors either suppress or rewrite a story without being asked, for fear of offending advertisers. For instance, newspapers and magazines are leery of writing about the health hazards of cigarettes, concerned with the possibility of losing the advertising revenue from the tobacco industry. Baker provides the following example:

> The tobacco companies' hefty advertising in many a magazine seems in inverse proportion to the publications' willingness to criticize it. Over at the American Cancer Society, media director Susan Islam says that women's magazines tend to cover some concerns adequately, but not lung cancer: "Many more women die of lung cancer, yet there have hardly been any articles on it."[72]

- ** Merging of editorial content and advertising.* Ads sometimes appear in the form of editorial content, as *advertorials.* Advertorials blur the distinction between ads and editorial content. Very little effort is made to distinguish these advertorials from other stories featured in newspapers or magazines. The disclaimer "advertisement" is often buried in the ad, placed away from the visual field. At other times, the ad simply includes the name of the product in small print.

  For example, hospitals advertise on television and in newspapers, establishing "partnerships" with local news outlets. Reporter Blythe Bernhard provides insight into these "partnerships":

> Hospitals sponsor health segments that are aired during the evening news. In some cases, large hospitals produce their own stories and send them directly to TV stations. And in newspapers and on media websites, advertisements can take on the look of news articles.[73]

In response, the Association of Health Care Journalists and the Society of Professional Journalists has released guidelines declaring that newsrooms should not favor sponsoring hospitals on story topics or sources and should prohibit news staff from appearing in sponsored programming or ads.

- ** Advertisers prescribing content.* At times, advertisers assume a direct role in the editing of *editorial content* (editorial content refers to news content: everything in the newspaper that is not paid space). In 2009, some news editors at the *Dallas Morning News* began reporting directly to the general manager in charge of advertising sales.[74]

- * *Conflicts of interest.* As part of the corporate community, newspaper owners are susceptible to conflicts of interests that compromise the paper's coverage of people and issues. On occasion, the owners of these wealthy and influential news organizations have intervened directly in editorial decisions. To illustrate, in 2012, Gregory J. Osberg, chief executive and publisher of the Philadelphia Media Network (which publishes the *Inquirer,* the *Daily News,* and Philly.com) informed his staff that he would be overseeing all articles related to the newspapers' impending sale; if any articles ran without his approval, the editors would be fired.[75] The controversy centered around the proposed sale of the newspapers to a group of investors comprised of powerful members of the Democratic party, including a former mayor, governor, and the owner of a local sports team and . . . a power player in South Jersey politics. The following decisions favored these prospective buyers:
  - ◦ The *Inquirer* killed an article about a real estate developer who had put together a competing bid to buy the company.
  - ◦ A post on the *Daily News's* PhillyClout blog that mentioned other potential buyers was removed.
  - ◦ Reporters were asked by management not to mention the $2.9 million tax credit the company had received for relocating within the city limits of Philadelphia.[76]

FRAMEWORK

Introduction

The introduction of a news story can provide insight into the point of view and underlying messages of a story.

Premise

The *premise* can furnish perspective into the unwritten assumptions behind an article. For instance, in June 2013, an article by Peter Nicholas and Adam Entous appeared in the *Wall Street Journal* entitled "Obama Confidantes Get Key Security Jobs" discussed two nominations by the president to fill national security positions: Susan Rice (National Security Advisor) and Samantha Power (UN Ambassador).

The lead paragraph of the article begins as follows:

President Barack Obama further tightened his control of U.S. foreign policy Wednesday by tapping a pair of trusted advisers for key national-security roles.[77]

An analysis of the article reveals the following assumptions:

- That the story is about Obama, rather than about foreign policy.
- The story doesn't mention the foreign policy implications of these appointments, but instead discusses the appointments as a personal matter.
- That these appointments constitute a power play, giving Obama more control.

Print Headlines

Readers receive their initial impressions about a newspaper or magazine story through headlines. However, headlines are rarely composed by the reporter who wrote the story. Instead, this task is delegated to a local copy-writer who may not understand the intent, or even the main point, of the story.

A primary function of a headline is to *inform* the reader about the principal thrust of the story. Consequently, the headlines that appear in newspapers may vary widely. Studying various headlines that cover the same story can also inform the reader of the point of view of a news organization. After U.S. helicopters based in Iraq killed eight people in Syria in 2008, CNN ran the following headline on its online news site:

"Syria Accuses U.S. in Deadly Attack."[78]

However, Fox News ran a different headline for the same story:

"U.S. Official Says It Is Unclear If Attack Killed Al Queda Target."[79]

The CNN headline focused on the assignation of blame for the American attack on Syria. In contrast, the Fox News headline bypasses the moral question of blame, and instead focuses on *why* the attack transpired. Moreover, raising the possibility that an American enemy had been the target of the attack suggests that the attack was warranted. Neither headline is a lie, but the choice of a headline for the same story can demonstrate ideologies of the news provider.

In addition, a headline also must *attract attention* by being provocative, if not sensational. Unfortunately, these competing functions can work at cross-purposes, altering the meaning of the story—sometimes with humorous results. Consider the following headlines:

"Safety Experts Say School Bus Passengers Should Be Belted";

"Typhoon Rips through Cemetery; Hundreds Dead"; and

"Iraqi Head Seeks Arms."[80]

Moreover, some headlines are misleading because they are overly simplistic. For instance, in 2007, the following headline appeared in the *New York Times*:

"Pakistan Sends Tribal Leaders to Salvage Truce Broken by Taliban."

However, the story behind the headline was actually more complex. Taliban leaders in the North Waziristan area of Pakistan did call off the peace deal, but only after President Pervez Musharraf deployed troops to several checkpoints in the region in violation of a truce signed by the two parties. The military had agreed to pull back to its barracks and take down checkpoints in exchange for a suspension of hostilities from the militants.

At times, headlines can actually *conceal* meaning. To illustrate, a 2006 story in the *New York Times* reporting on the presidential election in Venezuela carried the following headline:

"Venezuelans Give Chavez a Mandate to Tighten His Grip."[81]

This headline seemed to suggest that recent events gave former Venezuelan president Hugo Chavez dictatorial control. But in reality, this "mandate" was an *election,* which Chavez won with over 60 percent of the Venezuelan voters.

However, headlines also may inadvertently *disclose* latent meanings in an article. A classic example can be found in a story that appeared in the *St. Louis Post-Dispatch* in 1991 about William Kennedy Smith, who was charged with rape in Florida. Significantly, the headline, "Trial Starts in Kennedy Rape Case," was inaccurate; the name of the alleged perpetrator was not Kennedy but *Smith.* Nevertheless, the headline did furnish perspective into the real story—the ongoing saga of the Kennedys, a family that remains the object of national fascination. Moreover, the headline helps explain why a rape case in Florida would make the front-page news in Missouri.[82]

Television and radio news programs often employ promotional slogans designed to attract an audience. In the process, these slogans are designed to shape the audiences' perception of the programming. For instance, Fox News uses the slogan "Fair and Balanced," which promotes its perspective as objective. But as discussed earlier, the *latent* function of Fox News is to promote a conservative political agenda.

Front Page/Cover

The front page of newspapers now includes stories that were formerly placed in other sections of the paper—sports, business, human interest, and entertainment news. In addition, many newspapers now place "teasers" highlighting features in the rest of the paper as a way to entice people to purchase the newspaper. Indeed, these headlines and photos are placed above the fold (in the upper half of the newspaper), so that they are visible in the newspaper dispensers found in convenience stores and at street corners. Several newspapers have taken this trend a step further by eliminating news stories *entirely* from the front page of their early Sunday editions and filling the page with teasers. Finally, in some newspapers, such as the *Ladue (Missouri) News,* the front page has been given over to advertising; customers pay to have a photo and article appear on the front page of the publication. This trend has also been adopted by online editions of newspapers. As an example, in the digital version of the *New York Times,* the front page first appears with a large "pop-up" ad at the top of the page.

The Introductory Paragraph. In print journalism, the most essential information is positioned in the first paragraph of the story. This *inverted pyramid style* of American journalism dates back to the nineteenth century, and the invention of the telegraph. Concerned that the telegraph lines would go down at any moment, editors insisted that reporters send the most important information across the wires first. Background information and details were then included later in the story. The pyramid structure also enables editors to make room for late-breaking stories or additional advertisements at the last minute by cutting the least essential information from the end of the story. Readers should therefore expect to find the answers to the following questions in the first paragraph: *who, what, when, how,* and *why.*

The body of the story is designed to elaborate on the information presented in the lead paragraph. At times, however, the first paragraph is an incomplete or even inaccurate summary of the body of the story. For example, in 2009, Stephanie Clifford authored an article in the *New York Times* entitled "A Look Ahead at the Money in the Communications Industry." The lead paragraph announced a slight decline in spending for communications-related activities in 2009—but a positive report within the context of past and future spending:

> In 2009, communications spending is likely to show a 1 percent decline for the year, the first notable decline in at least four decades. In five years, advertising spending in magazines will finally have rebounded after five years of decline—but at $9.8 billion, it will still be nowhere near the $12.9 billion it was in 2008. And by 2013, the video game market will be almost the size of the shrinking newspaper industry.[83]

However, buried in paragraph 10 is a statement about a more sustained and problematic contraction in the media industry, accompanied by a decline in revenues:

> James P. Rutherfurd, executive vice president and managing director of private equity firm Veronis Suhler Stevenson, said, "Even assuming an economic recovery over the next five years, newspapers, consumer magazines, TV and radio are shrinking and will not, in that period of time, get back to what they saw before."[84]

Consequently, when reading newspaper articles, it is important to verify whether the lead paragraph indeed encapsulates the major thrust of the article.

Plot: Explicit Content

Framing Techniques

The following techniques, intentionally or unintentionally, affect the point of view of a story by "framing" the way in which a story is to be interpreted:

1. *Presentation of opinion as fact* is a framing technique in which reporters inject opinion, disguised as fact, into a story. To illustrate,

in October 2012, First Lady Michelle Obama appeared on Nick-elodeon, a cable station directed at young people, to promote her "Let's Move" program (an initiative designed to reduce the rate of obesity among America's youth). The Romney campaign declined an invitation for its candidate to appear on the program, saying that it didn't fit into the campaign schedule. In his coverage of this incident, reporter Tim Graham of foxnews.com contributed a passage in which opinion is inserted into this standard news story:

> It's doubtful that the Romney campaign feared liberal tilt among the kids. It's much more likely that they were pressed for time, or this appearance simply isn't the best use of their time with just 26 days to go until Election Day.[85]

The story is not presented as an opinion or editorial piece; rather, it is presented as a standard news story.

2. *Vague authority* refers to instances in which reporters cite un-documented or generalized groups to support a particular point of view. For instance, in an article about Israeli politicians' positions on Palestinian policy, *New York Times* reporter Jodi Rudoren commented,

> Many in Israel saw Mr. Barak's statements less as a serious new policy initiative and more as an attempt to distinguish himself politically from the rest of the cabinet amid increasing talk of elections being called for in early next year rather than as sched-uled in October 2012.[86]

3. *One person cross-section* is a framing technique in which one person is used as a symbol of a larger group—which may not be the case. To illustrate, in 2011, National Public Radio (NPR) broadcast a report on the immediate aftermath of the devastating earthquake and tsunami that not only killed over 10,000 people but also damaged a major nuclear facility, which has long-term ramifications for the health of the population. NPR approached this story by focusing on one survivor as an example of the situation facing the population as a whole. Reporter Rob Gifford begins the story as follows:

> GIFFORD: When the huge earthquake struck at precisely 2:46 on Friday afternoon, Yumi Takano was in her home, about a mile

from the sea. The house stood firm in the quake, but Mrs. Takano knew immediately what she had to do.

Ms. YUMI TAKANO: (Foreign language spoken)

GIFFORD: I ran, she says. I grabbed my neighbor and ran. We jumped into the car, and we were out of there within 15 minutes.

Anyone who waited longer was swept away as 26 minutes after the earthquake, a wall of water moving faster than a racehorse did what no earthquake could, and demolished the whole suburb of Arahama.

Ms. MIYUKI ARIMATSU: (Foreign language spoken)

GIFFORD: We've lost everything. The house, the car, everything, says Miyuki Arimatsu. . . .

Mr. MAKATO ITO: (Foreign language spoken)

GIFFORD: Sixty-four-year-old Makato Ito has lost seven members of his extended family. He wanders in a daze around the evacuation centers of Sendai, looking for them.[87]

4. *The designated spokesperson* occurs when the press arbitrarily appoints a spokesperson to assume a position of authority and leadership in relation to a particular issue or event. This person may indeed be a leader of an organization or an "expert" (e.g., university professor). But whether these designated spokespeople actually enjoy the support of a broad constituency is open to question.

5. *The slanted sample.* Sampling the public for its response to issues and events is a very common journalistic approach. However, this sample may be chosen in an arbitrary fashion and therefore is not representative of the public at large. For instance, in an article that appeared in the *St. Louis Post-Dispatch* entitled "Waking Up a Sleepy City," six young people were selected to discuss the future of St. Louis. The article began as follows:

The *Post-Dispatch* recently gathered together six young adults who are native to St. Louis. They have faced and are facing choices about where to live and work. They exemplify the kind of talented, young adults that American cities are trying to attract.[88]

The story was accompanied by a photograph of the six young men and women—all white. The *Post-Dispatch* received numerous letters to the editor commenting on the slanted sample of the article and the messages that it conveyed, including the following comment from Alvin A. Reid:

> Once again, "Imagine St. Louis" has decided to discuss the future of St. Louis without the input of any African-Americans. Six young people interviewed, six photos on cover, two on the inside and no black people . . . insulting. It's disgusting. Since the subject is "The Brain Drain" I guess I am to assume:
>
> A. Black people don't leave St. Louis for greener pastures, or visit other metropolitan areas, so thus they could not have an opinion.
> B. Black people have no brains.
> C. You couldn't find any African-Americans to interview.
> D. You didn't try to find any African-Americans to interview. (This is the answer that I believe to be true.)
>
> I ask the editors of this page, "If a black person were visiting St. Louis from San Francisco, Washington, or another metropolitan area, what would they think after seeing 'Imagine St. Louis'?"[89]

6. *The "not available" ploy.* Investigative pieces that include the statement that "the subject was unavailable for comment" implies that the subject was uncooperative, ducking the reporter, and had something to hide. This statement often neglects to clarify the circumstances:
   - Whether the person was in town
   - When the person was contacted (i.e., day or evening)
   - Where a person was contacted (i.e., at home or at work)
   - How often the reporter attempted to reach the person
   - The time frame in which the reporter attempted to contact the subject (e.g., over a three-day period)

Fortunately, some newspapers now provide the context behind the subject's inaccessibility (e.g., "repeated attempts to reach the subject over a three day period were unsuccessful").

7. *The passive catch-phrase.* Sentences can be written in either the *active* or *passive* voice. In the active voice, the subject is explicitly responsible for the action (e.g., Bob threw the ball). But in the passive voice, the subject is the *receiver* of the action (e.g., The ball was thrown to Bob). The passive voice is particularly useful in describing

an action in which the actor is unknown. To illustrate, in the sentence, "The door had been closed before we arrived," it is unclear who closed the door.

The passive voice frequently is used to deflect responsibility, since it is unstated *who* has initiated the action. Further, this use of the passive voice creates the impression that an opinion is common knowledge or generally accepted. As an example, in his coverage of the 2010 elections in Myanmar (formerly called Burma), *New York Times* reporter Mark McDonald wrote, "A new Constitution was passed in 2008 in a referendum that *was widely assailed* as a sham."[90] This wording makes it possible for the reporter to express sentiments critical of the authorities without putting the individuals who made the statements in personal jeopardy. But at the same time, this framing technique could call into question the authenticity of the subject, as well as his/her comments.

8. *Selective quotes.* Reporters can influence the meaning of a story by deciding *when* to use quotes, *whose* quotes to include, and *which parts* of the person's interview to extract into a quote. Quotes can be manipulated in the following ways:
   - Including only those statements that support a particular point of view
   - Taking quotes out of context to magnify or distort their meaning
   - Juxtaposing separate statements together to form an entirely new meaning
   - Including grammatical or syntactical errors to make a person appear unprepared, uneducated, or foolish
   - Cleaning up a quote to make a subject appear more knowledgeable and authoritative

9. *Inaccurate paraphrase.* Instead of quoting a subject, reporters sometimes paraphrase what their subjects said. However, a reporter's paraphrase may not always be an accurate summary of the statement of the subject. For instance, in her review of Al Gore's book *Earth in the Balance,* Michiko Kakutani observes,

> Mr. Gore writes of undergoing a midlife crisis around the same time. He says that in 1989, having just turned 40, lost a presidential campaign and seen his son, Albert, nearly die in an automobile accident, he became "impatient with my own tendency to put a finger to the political winds and proceed cautiously."[91]

However, an editorial in the Internet newspaper the *Daily Howler* pointed out that Gore never used the term "midlife crisis":

> The diagnosis is that of the thoroughly unlicensed professional therapist, Dr. Kakutani. . . . And since we can assume that Gore is aware of the term, the truth about this is really quite simple: in this book, Gore deliberately chose not to write of "undergoing a midlife crisis." In fact, he seems to describe a different sort of experience—he talks in this same section about "an outer manifestation of an inner crisis that is, for want of a better term, spiritual."
>
> Well, Kakutani had a "better term" in mind, and she put it in Gore's mouth—"midlife crisis." It played well with her theme that Gore is a bit strange, and consumed with "New Age psychobabble." What do you do if you want to say that, and your subject won't cooperate by using such terms? Simple—you paraphrase! You put the desired words in his mouth—and tell readers that that's what he "said."
>
> Welcome to the world of paraphrase, where inventive journalists find clever ways to get hopefuls to "say" things they like. The power of paraphrase is the power to spin, and the press corps tends to use power freely.[92]

10. *Statements taken out of context.* Statements often derive their meaning through context. Taken alone, humorous or ironic statements often have the *opposite* meaning than is actually intended by the speaker. To illustrate, in May 2013, Rachel Maddow presented a segment on her program about new technologies that enable thieves to launder money. She begins her explanation by using herself as an example to illustrate how the technology works: "So say, hypothetically that I, Rachel Maddow, am a profoundly successful crack dealer."

   But after this introduction, Maddow provides a concrete description of "her" activities that, if taken out of context, would be a confession implicating her in a crime:

   > I have made a million dollars, and I have it wadded up in five dollar bills. . . . But if I want to buy something in keeping with my self-image, like a Ferrari . . . I have to get the money out of my living

room. . . . I can't take it to the bank. . . . I need a safe place to put my dirty money.[93]

11. *Extraneous inclusion* is a reportorial technique in which information is added to a story that, on the surface, appears to be immaterial to the story. However, this extraneous information can influence readers' attitudes about the story. To illustrate, in 2006, 72 professors, administrators, and graduate students at Georgetown University protested the administrative appointment of former Under Secretary of Defense Douglas J. Feith to a faculty position in its School of Foreign Service; some even accused Feith of war crimes in connection with his role in the Iraq conflict.

An article discussing the negative reaction of the faculty appeared in the *International Herald Tribune.* The article, written by Jason DeParle, included the following passage:

> Professors in the school were widely opposed. . . . One is Susan Terrio, who has appointments in anthropology and French *and whose resume lists several writings about French chocolate makers. (From Master Chocolatiers Today: Bayonne and the Basque Coast.)* She complained that Mr. Feith's appointment was *"presented as a fait accompli."* (Emphasis added)[94]

The extraneous information about Terrio implies that the professor (and, by extension, all of the professors) protesting Feith's appointment were silly, effete academics who were not competent to judge Feith's qualifications for the teaching appointment.

12. *Putting a word in quotations.* Putting a word in quotations questions the accuracy of the statement. To illustrate, in a review of the TV special "Kids Pick the President" that appeared on the children's cable channel Nickelodeon in 2012, Fox News writer Tim Graham described the program as a "news" special.[95] His selective use of quotation marks insinuated that the results of a survey conducted on the program that favored President Obama was not credible and reflected a hidden agenda.

13. *Biased interviewing strategies.* A reporter can slant a story through the type of questions he/she poses to subjects:
   ○ *Compliance as assertion*
     Reporters come to an interview prepared with a point of view (and a quote) to include in an article and are only asking for the

consent of the subject. In this case, reporters may phrase a question, "Would you agree that. . .?," "Would you say that. . . ?," or "So what you are saying is. . . ."

o *Leading or loaded questions*

This type of question is loaded in such a way that 1) the question reveals the point of view of the reporter, and 2) the wording colors the response to the question. In a 2007 broadcast of *60 Minutes,* Katie Couric made her opinions obvious when questioning Democratic Primary candidate John Edwards about his decision to stay in the race despite his wife's cancer:

> Some people watching this would say, I would put my family first always, and my job second. Even those who may be very empathetic to what you all are facing might question your ability to run the country at the same time you're dealing with a major health crisis in your family. . . . Can you understand their concern, though, Senator Edwards, that gosh, at a time when we're living in a world that is so complicated and so dangerous that the president cannot be distracted by, rightly so, caring about his wife's situation?[96]

Any response to a question phrased like this (even a denial) legitimizes the position of the reporter.

o *"Gotcha" questions*

Reporters' questions take the form of a pop quiz, the ostensible goal being to test the credibility of the subject, as well as the veracity of a subject's claims. For instance, before the 2000 U.S. presidential election, a Boston television reporter asked George W. Bush to name the leaders of a series of foreign countries. He could not.

But whether or not Bush could provide the names of foreign leaders is not a true indication of whether he has a comprehensive understanding of foreign policy. Instead, it is a technique that attracts public attention to the reporter and his/her news program.

o *Hypothetical question*

Questions beginning with phrases such as "What would happen if. . . ?" put the subject in a speculative position that is then presented as fact. In addition, hypothetical questions frequently catch the interviewee off guard, so that he/she may offer an opinion that is not thoroughly considered.

○ *Either/or choices*

In this persuasive technique, reporters offer a limited range of responses to their interviewees. Like students taking a multiple choice exam, subjects may then feel compelled to select the best answer among the choices offered, even though it may not actually be the "best" answer. However, as media consultant Tripp Frohlichstein observes,

> There are five different responses to an "either/or" question. If the choices are "a" or "b," you can respond with:
>
> 1. "a"
> 2. "b"
> 3. both "a" and "b"
> 4. neither "a" nor "b"
> 5. "c" (an alternative not given by the reporter).[97]

Television offers an additional set of *visual framing techniques* that enable TV journalists to influence the opinions of the audience. For example, documentary filmmaker Robert Greenwald has identified the following visual framing techniques that were employed during coverage of the Iraq War by Fox News:

- *Nonverbals.* Former Fox reporter Jon Du Pre describes the practice of giving "a wink and a nod" to signal approval of a story.
- *Ad-libs.* Making a comment after a story enables the reporters to cross the line from a news report to a commentary. Du Pre maintains that during the 2004 presidential campaign, Fox news reporters made a series of "ad-libs" that castigated Democrats, such as "North Korea loves John Kerry," and Kerry got an "attaboy" and a "pat on the back" from the North Koreans.[98]

Implicit Content

As mentioned earlier in the chapter, television is a medium that is better equipped to focus on *explicit* content (i.e., events) than print. However, newspaper accounts are better suited to examine the *implicit* content (i.e., causes, connections, and consequences) *behind* events or issues. However, even in a newspaper article, the complex factors contributing to an event (e.g., the situation in the Mideast) may be difficult to include in the limited space allotted for the article. Moreover, a news story may only represent

---

MEDIA LITERACY TIPS: IMPLICIT CONTENT

One approach to journalistic analysis borrows from the concepts of explicit and implicit content outlined by W. Andrew Collins (discussed in Chapter 6).

We live in a complex world, in which events occurring in one part of the world reverberate in other regions—sometimes years after the initial incident. One such example is climate change; the greenhouse gases released in the air have contributed to a gradual climate change that affects all nations—regardless of their direct culpability in the matter. The five journalistic questions that that defined the parameters of journalism during the second half of the twentieth century—who, when, where, why, and how—fit roughly into Collins' notion of *explicit content*: identifying the significant events in a story. However, reporting should focus on the *implicit information* as well:

- *Motive*: Why did this event occur?
- What are the *connections between events?*
- What are the *connections between people?*
- What are the consequences to the events?
    - Immediate consequences?
    - Long-term consequences?

---

an installment in a far larger story, which is still in the process of unfolding. As writer Ben Hecht once observed, trying to determine what is going on in the world by reading newspapers is like trying to tell time by watching the second hand of a clock.[99] Thus, while newspapers provide information on the day's events—the *who, what, when, where,* and *how* questions that are the hallmarks of journalism—they may not have the space to consider the broader *why* question. Moreover, the consequences of an event may not be readily apparent. For instance, it will be many years before the ramifications of global warming become fully evident.

PRODUCTION ELEMENTS

Journalists find themselves in something of a dilemma with regard to the use of production elements. For instance, repeating one word throughout a story (e.g., "he said, she said") is considered bland and uninteresting writing. On the other hand, synonyms (e.g., he *argued,* she *declared*) possess connotative meanings that can make an article appear biased. In like fashion, on any given day, there may be 15 stories that arguably belong on the front page. However, because of space limitations, the editors must select six stories, which signals the relative importance of news stories. At other times, however, journalists convey messages to the reader through production elements such as placement of stories, word choice, and connotative images. But regardless of the intention of the media communicator, production elements convey (or reinforce) messages. Consequently, examining production elements is a valuable way to identify media messages.

Editing

When preparing a story, a journalist assembles an abundance of information that must be condensed into a clear, coherent, and concise presentation, free of grammatical errors, stylistically consistent, and accurate with respect to facts and citations. A reporter makes a number of editing decisions that can convey subtle messages, including:

1. *Which stories to include and omit.*

   Certain stories are given attention in the press, while other stories are ignored. These editing decisions are often very subjective, reflecting the priorities and values of the newspaper staff.

   To illustrate, in July 2013, the trial of George Zimmerman, who was arrested for the death of Trayvon Martin, dominated the airwaves. CNN carried the trial throughout the day, and cable stations such as MSNBC devoted their evening programming to discussing that day's developments.

   A number of other events also occurred during this period. Edward Snowden released classified information regarding the U.S. government's surveillance of American civilians and then avoided arrest, seeking safe haven abroad. In addition, the democratically elected government in Egypt was toppled by the Egyptian military, followed by massive demonstrations in the streets.

   But neither of these stories received the media attention comparable to the Trayvon Martin story. As Frohlichstein observes, "News is whatever the editor says it is."[100]

   The question arises, then: Why would the editors select one particular story (e.g., the Trayvon Martin story) as the most "important" news story? The immediate impact of a story on the community is a major factor in the amount of coverage a story receives.

To illustrate, in the wake of a terrorism alert issued by the White House in 2004, it was found that the further a publication was situated from the New York and Washington areas, where the risk was said to be greatest, the less coverage the threats received. For three days following the alert, the *Washington Post* and the *New York Times* each carried at least two front-page articles—and nearly two full pages or more inside the paper. In contrast, the *Austin American-Statesman* (Texas) carried only one front-page article about the warnings from the *New York Times* News Service or the Associated Press.

According to managing editor Fred Zipp, "If the warning had been that Al Qaeda is going to attack the tower on the University of Texas campus or a University of Texas football game, then we would have been . . . aggressive." Philip Taubman, the Washington bureau chief of the *New York Times,* adds, "For *The New York Times* and *Washington Post,* this is personal. Our readers live in these communities. Many of our staff members live in these communities."[101]

But in addition to the immediate impact of a story on the community, other criteria that determine how much attention a particular story will receive in the media include:

- *The long-term impact of a story on the community.* The significance of the Trayvon Martin murder trial extended beyond the ruling on George Zimmerman's guilt or innocence and touched on a range of social issues, including:
  - *Race and racism,* complicated by the minority standing of Zimmerman.
  - *The gun law controversy.* In Florida it is lawful for a citizen to "stand his or her ground" and kill someone in self-defense.
- *The entertainment sensibility.* The televised trial contained many of the dramatic elements that lend themselves to popular television programming: an identifiable cast of characters, narrative structure (order/chaos/order), and a mystery ("who done it") that would be revealed at the end of the "program."
- The televised event contained elements of popular genres that attract large audiences: reality shows, trial/justice shows (à la *Judge Judy*), and crime dramas.

Each year *Project Censored* publishes its list of the top 10 underreported news stories of the year. A panel of distinguished media professionals and scholars collaborate to "seek, identify, and publicize stories on important issues that have been overlooked or underreported by the news media."[102]

The 10 most under-reported stories for 2010–2011 include the following topics:

1. More U.S. Soldiers Committed Suicide Than Died in Combat
2. U.S. Military Manipulates the Social Media
3. Obama Authorizes International Assassination Campaign
4. Global Food Crisis Expands
5. Private Prison Companies Fund Anti-Immigrant Legislation
6. Google Spying?
7. U.S. Army and Psychology's Largest Experiment Ever
8. The Fairytale of Clean and Safe Nuclear Power
9. Government Sponsored Technologies for Weather Modification
10. Real Unemployment: One Out of Five in U.S.[103]

Project Censored also identifies the top 10 "junk food news" stories—the most *over-reported* news stories. The following stories received much more coverage than they deserved:

1. Olympic Medalist Michael Phelps Hits a Bong
2. Jessica Simpson Gains Weight
3. First Lady Michelle Obama's Fashion Sense
4. The Brangelina Twins
5. Lindsay Lohan Dating a Woman
6. The Presidential First Puppy
7. Heidi Montag "Marries" Spencer Pratt
8. Barry Bonds Steroid Trial
9. Jamie-Lynn Spears Gives Birth
10. The Woes of Amy Winehouse[104]

2. *The order in which stories are presented.*

The arrangement of news content is an indication of its importance. Former *New York Times* managing editor John Geddes explains,

> Remember, journalism is about telling me what's important and telling me what's important in the order of its importance. It's always a compared-to-what. Something happened on Day One, when nothing's going on in the world, it may merit one column of coverage. The same thing happening on a very busy day may merit an inch of coverage.[105]

On a practical level, most of us start to read a section of a paper at the beginning. As a result, an article placed on page five is not as likely to be read as a story appearing on page two. *Chicago Tribune* managing editor Dick Siccone adds,

> One of the most important things a paper does is give readers guidance about what is the most meaningful. The stories which are most desirable for readers appear in consecutive order . . . page one, page two, page three. [Placement] signals to readers exactly what they most need to read.[106]

Thus, stories that appear first in broadcast news programs are considered most important. In like fashion, newspaper articles that are closest to the front page are regarded as most significant.

As an example, on December 15, 2012, the front page of the *New York Times* was dominated by the headline announcing the horrific mass murder of 28 people (including 20 elementary school children) in Newtown, Connecticut. On the same day, on the bottom of page *nine,* the *New York Times* ran a story with the following headline: "Man Stabs 22 Children in China." The story was eerily parallel to the front-page story. However, the placement of the stories conveys a message about the ethnocentric American society: the massacre in China was not considered as important to American readers as the tragedy that occurred in U.S. territory.

Indeed, the placement of stories can influence public attitudes for government policies and decisions. In 2004, the editors of the *New York Times* conducted a self-study on the paper's coverage of the Iraq War and concluded that its placement of stories supported the Bush administration's case for going to war in Iraq. The report notes, "Articles (making) dire claims about Iraq tended to get prominent display, while follow-up articles that called the original ones into question were sometimes buried in the back pages. In some cases, there was no follow-up at all."[107] Significantly, the *New York Times* continued this practice long after this self-study was released. On January 28, 2007, a story about an antiwar protest in Washington, D.C., that attracted hundreds of thousands of people from around the country was buried on page 20 of the paper, whereas an article about tennis player Serena Williams occupied page 1.

3. *What information to include (and omit) in a story.*

Decisions about what to include and what to omit in a particular story shape an audience's understanding of a news event. Again, these editing decisions can indicate prevailing attitudes and policies, as reflected by the mainstream media. As an example, in 2013, a news story alleged that IRS personnel had "targeted" conservative Tea Party groups that had sought tax-exempt status. Subsequent news stories raised questions about the White House assembling an "enemies list" of political opponents.

However, weeks after this story was made public and made part of the national political agenda, it was discovered that "liberal" political groups also had been the subject of targeted research.

On June 27, 2013, National Public Radio ran a story that, according to the IRS Inspector, "progressive" political organizations were also on the IRS "Be On the Lookout" list for special attention. Yet, later on the *same* day, NPR news continued to air the original version of the story, again neglecting to mention that progressive groups had also been "targeted." This selective editing has an impact on the message, framing this story as part of an ideological conflict rather than a report about an error in judgment by members of a government bureaucracy.

The composition of a story also may be affected by time and space constraints. Newspaper editors face a daily challenge of fitting the information into the allotted time or space. Geddes explains,

> The four (basic news) sections—on, say, a Wednesday—run about 200 columns. The day, in terms of space, begins about 11 o'clock when one of our senior editors goes to each of the individual desks and asks, what do you have? Do you need any space? Is there anything of note? That is brought to me or whoever's doing space that day at about 11:30. And we try to pass judgment. Is this meritorious? How do we stand with our budget? Do I have five long stories for which space is being requested for tomorrow? Is that too much for the reader? Is there an option to hold for another day, or is there news that's forcing this to run right now? We balance all those things. And then we give that request for space to our colleagues in production. They take the news requirements and the advertising requirements, combine them to make up the whole paper.[108]

In television news, stories are rarely longer than two minutes in length. Thus, when examining a news story, it is appropriate to ask the following questions:

- What essential information is included in the story?
- What is the reporter's justification for including the information contained in the story?
- What essential information is missing?

- What additional information would be valuable for understanding the story?

4. *Depth of coverage.*

How much attention is devoted to a story is another indication of the importance the editors place on the topic. Brief mention of a subject suggests that the issue is of minimal importance, whereas in-depth treatment informs the audience that the public should treat the subject seriously. Geddes explains, "We're trying to capture what's important today in a given space. And we're trying to relay that to readers using the relative size of the story and the coverage as an indicator of importance."[109]

5. *The amount of emphasis devoted to particular aspects of a story.*

Reporters provide more detailed explanation of those elements of a story that they deem to be important. For instance, stories about candidates vying for their party's nomination for president of the United States often dwell on the amount of money that they have raised, as opposed to their positions on issues.

6. *Sustained coverage.*

The frequency with which a story appears over time keeps certain issues in the public's consciousness. But in addition, sustained coverage signals that the editors consider the story to be of importance. In contrast, sporadic coverage sends the message that an issue is relatively unimportant.

To illustrate, in 2005, ABC News devoted a total of only 18 minutes of airtime to the genocide taking place in Darfur, Sudan. At the same time, NBC had only five minutes of coverage during all of its evening newscasts, and CBS only three minutes—about a minute of coverage for every 100,000 deaths in that country. At the same time, the incarceration of Martha Stewart was the subject of an average of 130 minutes of coverage by the three networks during their nightly newscasts.[110]

Moreover, examining story placement over an extended period of time can be an effective line of inquiry. When stories first appear, they are given prominent positions in news programming—on the front page in newspapers or among the first stories in television news. However, the final chapter of a news story often occurs long after public interest in the issue has waned, appearing on the back pages (or at the end of the broadcast news program). For instance, in 2008, the organization ACORN was accused by conservative Republicans of conducting fraudulent voter registration drives in poor neighborhoods. The story received so much media attention that the

U.S. Census Bureau and the IRS severed their contracts with the organization, Congress suspended its funding, and private donations dried up. In 2010, the organization was forced to file for bankruptcy. However, in 2009, the story of a report by the nonpartisan Congressional Research Service exonerating Acorn of all guilt appeared on page A-15 of the *New York Times*.

This pattern encourages media communicators to adopt a "front page/back page" strategy, in which they initially deny all charges even if they are guilty, knowing that if enough time elapses before the truth comes out, the story will receive minimal media attention.

7. *Whose perspectives are presented, and in what order?*

In order to maintain a balance, reporters should include all sides to a story—although this doesn't always happen. Even when all sides are presented, the viewpoint presented first is often considered to be the more legitimate, established point of view.

Scale

Print

The size of a headline sends a signal about the importance of the story. Seventy-two-point headlines traditionally have announced momentous news events, such as the outbreak of World War II and the Japanese surrender in 1945. The size of the headline draws the reader's attention and signals that all other news of the day is of little importance compared to this story.

Examining the size of headlines provides clues about the importance attached to a story. But in addition, large headlines convey a latent message about the sensationalization of news in the current era, as part of a larger effort to attract readers and maximize profits.

Scale is an area of analysis that can follow several lines of inquiry:

- Comparing the size of headlines in a newspaper on a given day as indication of the value that the editors place on the stories.
- Comparing the size of the headlines devoted to the same story *in different newspapers* as indication of the value different news operations attach to the story.
- Identifying the headlines of past stories as indication of the importance attached to certain types of stories over time.

Relative Position

The arrangement of stories *within* a single page affects the audience's perception of news content. Stories on the top half of the page are accorded greater importance by the reader than stories appearing near the bottom.

Readers often regard the composition of a newspaper page as a collection of separate stories. However, editors often consider the relationship between the stories when laying out the stories. As Dick Siccone observes, "Some days you make statements, some days you don't."[111]

In addition, *gestalt analysis* is an approach in which we are seeing the page as a whole, drawing connections between events in order to identify cultural preoccupations and concerns. Gestalt refers to a psychological principle with regard to humans' *predisposition to order.* People naturally look for patterns as a way to make sense of their environment.

As an example, in 2011, *New York Times* reader Tricia Zimic wrote to its public editor, Arthur S. Brisbane, to express her concern about the juxtaposition of images that appeared in its January 4 edition:

> The unfortunate placement of the color advertisement next to the black and white photos of the devastating personal stories of loss and survival following the earthquake in Haiti was disturbing and shocking. While I understand that *The Times* is under financial pressure and that such advertising is necessary, this demonstrates poor judgment and a lack of sensitivity, and suggests that nobody is looking at the big picture.
> Tricia Zimic, Maplewood, N.J.[112]

As Ms Zimic's letter points out, the placement of these photographs conveys some disturbing messages. The juxtaposed photographs comment on the gulf between the rich and poor. Class distinctions exist—even on a newspaper page. More than any specific destination, the ad promises "escape" from one's cares. Moreover, money buys a measure of control to people's lives. But Haitians cannot escape their misfortune, or worse, the misfortune of their children.

As Ms. Zimic points out, this placement demonstrates "poor judgment and a lack of sensitivity, and suggests that nobody is looking at the big picture." The reasons behind this placement are revealing. The *New York Times* is a business that minimizes staff while maximizing duties, resulting in these kinds of mistakes. As a result, staff members strive to be "objective" observers who are unmoved by what they see and produce. This leads to callousness, in which the staff doesn't consider the implications of what they are writing and arranging on the page—the "big picture."

Moreover, this experience at the *New York Times* is a microcosm of society's studied indifference as a defense mechanism to contend with the suffering and injustice that appears all around us.

Word Choice

Examining the word choice in an article can provide perspective into the journalist's point of view. For example, in 2011, *New York Times* reporter Eric Lipton wrote an article about Florida Congressman John L. Mica's support for the Sun Rail commuter rail project. The reporter's choice of words in the article conveys the message that this project was an example of wasteful spending and procedural disregard:

> Representative John L. Mica, a Florida Republican and chairman of the House Transportation and Infrastructure Committee, has spent years *badgering* federal agencies, *bullying* state officials, *blocking* Amtrak naysayers and trying to *bypass federal restrictions* to build support and *squash opposition* to the commuter line. (Italics added)[113]

One useful line of inquiry involves breaking down a sentence according to its grammatical parts of speech.

- *Nouns*: Words that describe a person, place, or thing.

  Journalists are presented with a range of choices in the selection of nouns. Journalists make frequent use of *synonyms*: that is, nouns that have distinct, associative meanings that are clear to the audience. Columnist John Leo explains, "'Actress-model' and 'onetime beauty queen' really mean 'bimbo,' whereas 'womanizer' means 'lecher.'"[114]

  The *Dictionary of Cautionary Words and Phrases,* compiled by a group of professional journalists, includes the following connotative nouns and their connotative meanings:
  - "Community" implies a monolithic culture in which people act, think and vote in the same way. Do not use, as in Asian, Hispanic, black or gay community. Be more specific as to what the group is: e.g., Black residents in a north side neighborhood.
  - Avoid gender enders. For instance: actress, comedienne, heroine, poetess and starlet. Instead, use gender-neutral terms such as actor, comedian, executor, hero, poet and star.

- ○ Use "leader" with caution. Be more specific: Black politician, black activist. Implies person has approval of an entire group of people.
- ○ "Man" may be used when both men and women are involved and a more clearly defined term is not available. Frequently the best choice is a substitute, such as "humanity," "a person" or "an individual."[115]

- *Adjectives*: Complements to nouns, providing additional information about a person, place, or thing (e.g., a *tall* person).

  To illustrate, in an article posted on Al Jazeera English, the English-language counterpart to Al Jazeera Arabic TV, columnist Judea Pearl points out how an adjective expressed the station's point of view toward the conflict in the Middle East: "For example, the phrase 'war on terror' is invariably preceded by the contemptuous prefix 'so-called.'"[116]

- *Verbs* describe action.

  The choice of verbs in a media presentation can have a drastic impact on the meaning. Again, a word can have numerous synonyms that describe a range of different actions. One way to discover the connotation of a particular verb is to substitute synonyms and see how the meaning changes. To illustrate, consider the following sentence: Johnny *walked* home. Now substitute the synonyms *walking, strolling, staggering,* or *rushing* someplace. Consulting with a thesaurus provides you with a list of words that have roughly the same denotative meaning but contain other connotative, or associative meanings as well.

  For instance, in an article describing a speech that President Obama delivered to the United Nations, reporter Helene Cooper employed strong verbs as a way of expressing a sense of determination on the part of the president on the issue of freedom of speech:

  > In a 30-minute address, he *vowed* to protect the enduring ability of Americans to say what they think. He *promised* that the United States "will do what we must to prevent Iran from obtaining a nuclear weapon." And he *asserted* that the flare-up of violence over a video that ridicules the Prophet Muhammad will not set off a retreat from his support of the Arab democracy movement.[117]

Adverbs describe *how* something is done (e.g., quickly, carelessly). Consequently, the adverbs in the articles can comment on the actions of newsmakers. To illustrate, a check of *Newsweek's* Twitter feed reveals the editor's political leanings through their word choices:

- Does the GOP *really* think a repeat of George W. Bush's mistakes is what the American people want? (Twitter feed, September 13, 2012)
- Did Romney's *ill-timed* assault on President Obama over Libyan attacks go too far? (Twitter feed, September 12, 2012)
- Mitt Romney is *likely* to run the dirtiest campaign we've seen in a long, long time. (Twitter feed, September 11, 2012)

Connotative Images

Photographs can add a particular emphasis to a story or, in some cases, convey entirely separate messages. But although we tend to believe what we see in the newspaper or on the television screen, it must be remembered that photographs present only a *version* of reality. Photojournalist Howard Chapnick explains,

> Over the years, I have seen many examples of journalistic distortion by pictures taken out of context, by the use of prejudicial rhetoric in captioning of photographs, and by editors making composites of two separate news photographs and publishing it as one image. There are dozens of ways to alter reality if journalistic integrity is absent.[118]

In many cases, the photographs that appear in the newspaper are *file photos* that may have been taken long before the event being covered. Frequently, the public relations department of a company furnishes photographs of the subject if a story involves one of their employees.

Further, the framing of a picture establishes arbitrary boundaries that can affect our perceptions of reality. For instance, a photographer can establish relationships that do not exist by isolating two figures in a crowd. Tabloids take this principle a step through *imagistic layering,* in which two images are positioned next to one another to create a new meaning. And now, thanks to digital technology, objects in photographs can be seamlessly manipulated or eliminated altogether. (For more discussion of photographs, see Chapter 2.)

Graphics

Both broadcast and print journalism rely on graphics in order to cater to the skimming habits of their readership and attract readers. However, this

---

MEDIA LITERACY TIPS: PHOTOGRAPHS

The following questions are useful in considering the role of *photographs* within the context of print journalism articles:

- *What is the function of the photo?*
- *How do you feel as a result of looking at the photograph? (What is your affective response?)*
- *Is this a posed or spontaneous shot? What does this reveal?*
- *What is the relationship between the print article and the photograph?*
- *What messages are conveyed by the photo?*

---

format is frequently more flashy than informative. For instance, the graphics for Fox News Alert originally conveyed the message that what was to follow was important. But now, the graphic is used indiscriminately—simply to call for the attention of the audience.

NOTES

1. *The Quill,* November/December 1991.
2. *St. Louis Post-Dispatch,* platform from the newspaper's Web site.
3. David Carr, "A Scandal in Chicago That Justifies Investigative Journalism," *New York Times,* December 15, 2008.
4. Will Lester, "Growth of Online News Readers Levels Off," Associated Press/Associated Press Online, July 30, 2006.
5. Samer Farha, "TVSpy," in *Shoptalk,* September 24, 1998, shoptalk@listserv.syr.edu.
6. Roper Center, http://newseum.org.
7. "Iran News Agency Falls for Onion Spoof," *Sky News,* September 29, 2012, http://uk.news.yahoo.com/iran-news-agency-falls-onion-spoof-021016965.html.
8. Martin A. Lee and Norman Solomon, *Unreliable Sources: A Guide to Detecting Bias in the News Media* (Secaucus, NJ: Carol Publishing Group, 1990), 17.
9. Daniel Okrent, "Analysts Say Experts Are Hazardous to Your Newspaper," *New York Times,* October 31, 2004: D-2.
10. Lee and Solomon, *Unreliable Sources,* 17.
11. Martin Gottlieb, "Dangerous Liaisons," *Columbia Journalism Review* (July/August 1989): 26.

12. Lee and Solomon, *Unreliable Sources,* 17.
13. Robert Booth, "Full Disclosure on Leaks," *New York Times,* October 22, 2003.
14. The Editors, "The Times and Iraq," *New York Times,* May 26, 2004.
15. Clark Hoyt, "The Public Editor: Culling the Anonymous Sources," *New York Times,* June 8, 2008.
16. Bill Carter, "Amid Criticism, CNN Defends Reporting on Ambassador's Journal," *New York Times,* September 25, 2012.
17. Geoffrey R. Stone, "Half a Shield Is Better Than None," *New York Times,* February 21, 2007.
18. William E. Francois, *Mass Media Law and Regulation,* 2nd ed. (Des Moines, OH: Drake University School of Journalism, 1978), 137–8.
19. Elaine Sciolino, "Questions Raised about a Code of Silence," *New York Times,* May 16, 2011.
20. Charlie Savage and Leslie Kaufman, "Phone Records of Journalists Seized by U.S.," *New York Times,* May 13, 2013.
21. Ibid.
22. Mark Lander, "Obama, in Nod to Press, Orders Review of Inquiries," *New York Times,* May 23, 2013.
23. Charlie Savage, "Holder Tightens Rules on Getting Reporters' Data," *New York Times,* July 12, 2013.
24. Ibid.
25. Bill Keller, "Secrets and Leaks," *New York Times,* June 2, 2013.
26. Eric Schmitt, "Syria Moves Some Chemical Weapons, U.S. Says," *New York Times,* July 13, 2012.
27. Ben Bagdikian, *The Media Monopoly,* 3rd ed. (Boston: Beacon Press, 1990), 63.
28. Ted J. Smith III, "The Watchdog's Bite," *The American Enterprise* (January/February 1990): 63–4.
29. Mark Hertsgaard, *On Bended Knee* (New York: Farrar Straus Giroux, 1988), 334.
30. Reader's Guide, *New York Times.*
31. Byron Calame, "Listening to Both Sides, in the Pursuit of Fairness," *New York Times,* November 5, 2006: D-12.
32. Democracy Now!, November 13, 2006, www.democracynow.org.
33. Charles L. Klotzer, "There," *St. Louis Journalism Review* (October 1991): 2.
34. Conference on "Redefining the News: Reaching New Audiences through Diversity," the Poynter Institute for Media Studies, St. Petersburg, Florida, October 1992.
35. Kevin Blackstone, Wake Forest University School of Law, Spring 2012, "The Whitening of Sports Media and the Coloring of Black Athletes' Images."
36. Pat Widder, "Minorities' Newsroom Presence Edges Higher," *Chicago Tribune,* April 1, 1993: Business Sec., 3.

37. Marina Hendricks, "Young Audience Engagement with Newspaper Sites Also Rising," Newspaper Association of America, April 25, 2012, http://www.naa.org/News-and-Media/Press-Center/Archives/2012/Newspaper-Websites.

38. Will Lester, "Growth of Online News Readers Levels Off," Associated Press Online, July 30, 2006, www.ap.org.

39. David Swensen and Michael Schmidt, "News You Can Endow," *New York Times,* January 28, 2009.

40. Brian Stelter, "Local TV News Is Following Print's Path, Study Says," *New York Times,* March 18, 2013.

41. David Carr, "Tired Cries of Bias Don't Help Romney," *New York Times,* September 30, 2012.

42. Cheryl Sadowski, "Newspapers Show Sunday Readership Increases," Newspaper Association of America, November 14, 2011, www.naa.org.

43. Hendricks, "Young Audience Engagement with Newspaper Sites Also Rising."

44. Howard Kurtz, "The Big News: Shrinking Reportage," *The Washington Post,* March 13, 2006: C-1.

45. Lester, "Growth of Online News Readers Levels Off."

46. "Network News: Durability and Decline," the State of the News Media, 2011, *Pew Research Center's Project for Excellence in Journalism,* http://stateofthemedia.org/2011/network-essay.

47. Ibid.

48. Research Excerpt: News/Pew Research Center's Internet & American Life Project, September 29, 2011, http://www.thearf.org/focalpoint/research_excerpt.php/0762458fc2338e5f0d0938c6a07ff779e46691d4.

49. Pew Research Center for the People and the Press, http://www.people-press.org/2010/09/12/section-2online-and-digital-news/.

50. "Across Platforms, 7 in 10 Adults Access Content from Newspaper Media Each Week," SenseMaker Report Newspaper Association of America (NAA), March 25, 2013, http://www.naa.org/en/Trends-and-Numbers/Readership.aspx.

51. Ibid.

52. Kurtz, "The Big News: Shrinking Reportage."

53. Pew Research Center for the People and the Press, http://www.people-press.org/2010/09/12/section-2online-and-digital-news/.

54. Simon Owens, "Original Reporting Featured in 13% of Posts in Technorati Top 10 Blogs; Techcrunch Contains Highest Ratio," *Bloggasm,* February 6, 2009, http://bloggasm.com/13-of-posts-in-technorati-top-10-blogs-involve-original-reporting-techcrunch-contains-highest-ratio.

55. Adam Nagourney, "Gathering Highlights Power of the Blog," *New York Times,* June 10, 2006: A-10.

56. Ibid.

57. Jeremy W. Peters, "Some Newspapers, Tracking Readers Online, Shift Coverage," *New York Times,* September 5, 2010.

58. "Why Newspapers?," http://www.naa.org/info/whynewspapers/1.html.
59. The Pew Research Center's Project for Excellence in Journalism: The State of the News Media 2012, http://stateofthemedia.org/2012/newspapers-building-digital-revenues-proves-painfully-slow/newspapers-by-the-numbers.
60. Lee and Solomon, *Unreliable Sources*, 122.
61. Gerald C. Stone, *Examining Newspapers* (Newbury Park, CA: Sage Publications 1987), 109.
62. "Why Newspapers?" http://www.naa.org/info/whynewspapers/1.html.
63. Leo Jeffres, *Mass Media Processes and Effects* (Prospect Heights, IL: Waveland Press, Inc., 1986), 123–4.
64. Lester, "Growth of Online News Readers Levels Off."
65. Ben Bagdikian, *The Media Monopoly,* 3rd ed. (Boston: Beacon Press, 1990), 18.
66. Roper Center, http://newseum.org.
67. Democracy Now!, September 23, 2007, www.democracynow.org.
68. Katharine Q. Seelye, "Study Finds More News Media Outlets, Covering Less News," *New York Times,* March 13, 2006.
69. Mickey Huff and Project Censored, *Censored 2012: The Top Censored Stories and Media Analysis of 2010–2011* (New York: Seven Stories Press, 2011), 11.
70. Alliance for Audited Media, http://www.auditedmedia.com.
71. Bagdikian, *The Media Monopoly,* 66.
72. Russell Baker, "The Great Media Meltdown," *New York Times,* September 19, 1999.
73. Blythe Bernhard, "TV-Hospital News Raises Questions about Ethics," *St. Louis Post-Dispatch,* March 31, 2011.
74. Richard Perez-Pena, "Some Dallas Editors Will Report to Ad Sales," *New York Times,* December 4, 2009.
75. Amy Chozick and David Carr, "Interference Seen in Philadelphia Papers," *New York Times,* February 15, 2012.
76. Ibid.
77. Peter Nicholas and Adam Entous, "Obama Confidantes Get Key Security Jobs," *Wall Street Journal,* June 5, 2013, online.wsj.com/.../SB1000142412 7887324798904578526691341334060.
78. "Syria Accuses U.S. in Deadly Attack," CNN, October 26, 2008, http://www.cnn.com/2008/WORLD/meast/10/26/syria.iraq/.
79. "U.S. Official Says It Is Unclear If Attack Killed Al Queda Target," Fox News, October 28, 2008, http://www.foxnews.com/story/0,2933,444199,00.html.
80. Michael Hartley, "Silly Newspaper Headlines," http://www.mvhs.net/~salvo/texts/sillyhead.html.
81. Simon Romero, "Venezuelans Give Chávez a Mandate to Tighten His Grip," *New York Times,* December 5, 2006.
82. "Trial Starts in Kennedy Rape Case," *St. Louis Post-Dispatch,* December 3, 1991: A-1.

83. Stephanie Clifford, "A Look Ahead at the Money in the Communications Industry," *New York Times,* August 4, 2009.

84. Ibid.

85. Tim Graham, "Linda Ellerbee, *Washington Post* Take Cheap Shot at Romney after He Turns Down Nick News Invite," Fox News, October 11, 2012, foxnews.com.

86. Jodi Rudoren, "Israeli Officials Offer Opposite Views on Palestinian Stalemate," *New York Times,* September 25, 2012.

87. Rob Gifford, "Japan Struggles to Cope with Disaster's Magnitude," National Public Radio, *Morning Edition,* March 14, 2011.

88. Greg Jonsson, "Waking Up a Sleepy City," *St. Louis Post-Dispatch,* March 11, 2001.

89. Alvin A. Reid, Letters to the Editor, *St. Louis Post-Dispatch,* March 11, 2001.

90. Mark McDonald, "Leader of Junta Confirms Myanmar Is Planning 2010 Elections," *New York Times,* January 5, 2010.

91. Michiko Kakutani, "Review, *Earth in the Balance,*" *New York Times,* November 22, 1999.

92. *Daily Howler,* December 8, 1999.

93. *Rachel Maddow Show,* May 28, 2013, www.nbcnews.com/id/26315908. wwwrachelmaddow.com.

94. Jason DeParle, "Out of the Frying Pan, into the Freezing Cold," *International Herald Tribune,* May 26, 2006: 5.

95. Graham, "Linda Ellerbee, *Washington Post* Take Cheap Shot at Romney after He Turns Down Nick News Invite."

96. *60 Minutes,* CBS Television, March 25, 2007, Season 39, Episode 27.

97. Tripp Frohlichstein, *Media Training Handbook* (St. Louis: MediaMasters, 1991), 54–6.

98. *Outfoxed,* Robert Greenwald, director, Carolina Productions, 2004.

99. Ben Schott, "The Year in Questions," *New York Times,* December 31, 2006: D-9.

100. Tripp Frohlichstein, interview by author, July 21, 1992.

101. Leonard Downie, "Threats and Responses: The News Media," *New York Times,* August 5, 2004. www.nytimes.com.

102. Peter Phillips and Project Censored, *Censored 2007* (New York: Seven Stories Press, 2007), www.projectcensored.org/the-top-25-index/.

103. Ibid., http://projectcensored.org.

104. Ibid., http://projectcensored.org.

105. Byron Calame, "All the News That Fits the Allocated Space," *New York Times,* January 29, 2006.

106. Dick Siccone, managing editor, *Chicago Tribune,* interview by author, April 28, 1992.

107. The Editors, "The Times and Iraq," *New York Times,* May 26, 2004.

108. Calame, "All the News That Fits the Allocated Space."

109. Ibid.

110. Ibid.

111. Dick Siccone, interview.

112. Arthur S. Brisbane, "A Necessary Clash of News and Advertising," *New York Times,* January 22, 2011.

113. Eric Lipton, "A Congressman's Pet Project; a Railroad's Boon," *New York Times,* June 27, 2011.

114. John Leo, "Reading between the Hyphens," *U.S. News & World Report,* May 21, 1990: 23.

115. Multicultural Management Program Fellows, *Dictionary of Cautionary Words and Phrases: An Excerpt from the Newspaper Content Analysis Compiled by 1989 Multicultural Management Program Fellows* (Columbia, MO: University of Missouri School of Journalism), 1989.

116. Judea Pearl, "Another Perspective, or Jihad TV?" *New York Times,* January 17, 2007.

117. Helene Cooper, "Obama Tells UN New Democracies Need Free Speech," *New York Times,* September 26, 2012.

118. Howard Chapnick, "Markets & Careers," *Popular Photography* (August 1982): 42.

9

Advertising

OVERVIEW

The average American is immersed in advertising:

- In 2012, U.S. ad spending reached a record $139 billion.[1]
- 41 percent of a prime time hour is now filled by commercials.[2]
- By the age of 65, the average American has seen two million TV commercials.[3]
- American children are exposed to over 40,000 ads per year.[4]
- When *Dateline NBC* recently asked children to choose between a banana and a rock with a Scooby-Doo sticker on it for breakfast, nearly all chose the rock.[5]

The United States has arrived at the stage of *ubiquitous advertising,* in which all conceivable public space is dedicated to advertising, including checkout lines, gas pumps, ATM machines, and urinals. *Place-based video screens* show advertisements in public spaces, such as gas stations and doctor's offices. Advertisers also reach consumers in nontraditional ways, including podcasts, blogs, video games, e-mail messages, cell phones, and video on demand.

Some disagreement exists about the effectiveness of advertising messages. Studies show that 9 out of 10 people can't remember the product or company featured in the last commercial they watched, even if it was less than five minutes ago.[6] However, advertising pioneer Tony Schwartz makes an important distinction between *memory* and *recall* in advertising:

Researchers narrowly focus their questions on a subject's recollection of commercial content, which they consider the essence of what makes a message effective. . . . [However,] if we make a deep attachment to the product in the commercial, there is no need to depend on their remembering the name of the product. Seeing the product in the store should evoke the association attached to the product in the commercial.[7]

Thus, although you may not remember specific information about an advertisement, the ad will help the product appear familiar to you when you are wandering down the grocery store aisle.

PROCESS

Function

American consumers rely on advertising for a range of goods and services. We scan the papers for bargains, entertainment information, holiday gift ideas, and trends in fashion. Public service spots warn us about dangers in society (e.g., "Say no to drugs") and encourage us to be better citizens by giving to various charities.

Advertising performs a variety of *manifest functions:*

- Informing the public about a product.
- Attracting the attention of the consumer to the product.
- Motivating the consumer to action.
- Stimulating markets.
- Supporting the business community.

In addition, advertising serves a number of *latent* functions:

- *Persuasion.* Advertising cannot convince you to purchase something that you truly don't want: if you don't like coconut, no ad will convince you that you do. However, impulse displays located by the checkout counters in stores stimulate a desire for items that you may fancy but are not thinking about at that moment. And in cases in which the customer is already shopping for a product, ads are designed to steer the consumer to their particular brand.

    Nevertheless, advertisers try to convince you that you don't merely want a product but, in fact, *need* it. Indeed, advertising copy is often phrased in the form of an *imperative,* or command (e.g., "Buy it today!").
- *Establishing and maintaining a lasting relationship between the consumer and a company.* Advertisers strive to establish a *parasocial*

relationship with the audience, making the consumer feel known, appreciated, and special. The Campbell-Mithun-Esty advertising agency observes, "We must come into our customers' homes and lives as understanding friends and remain as welcome guests because of the honesty and good grace with which we present ourselves."[8] Although ads are presented through the channels of mass media, they often assume an interpersonal tone. It should, therefore, not come as a surprise that the personal pronoun "you" is the most frequent word used in advertising. For instance, a radio spot for Hampton Inn includes the following claim:

At Hampton Inn, we know how you feel. . . . Hampton Inn—we're with you all the way.

Because Hampton Inn knows you so well, it can provide for all of your lodging needs.

In addition, many ads try to establish and maintain a longstanding relationship between a company and its customers. As a result, the word "trust" is another frequently used word in advertising. Consequently, by the age of two, children have developed a loyalty to specific brands.[9] The company, therefore, can ask for (and expect) consumer loyalty in return, in the form of purchases.

- *Shaping attitudes.* Before advertisers can influence specific consumer behaviors, they are often faced with the more fundamental problem of shaping *attitudes.* Thus, the Campbell-Mithun-Esty advertising agency sees its primary task as creating "desired attitudes" among consumers: "What attitudes must we establish or change? What habits do we want formed? Do we want that person to know something new has happened, or become aware of additional product uses, or sample our product, or change a negative attitude or misconception?"[10]

    As a result, some ad campaigns begin by creating a positive image for the company rather than selling a product. Thus, television ads for oil companies describe how they clean up the environment and search for new solutions to energy problems.

    When encountering one of theses "public relations" advertisements, it is appropriate to ask *why* the company has chosen to solicit the goodwill of the public. For instance, ad campaigns by oil companies are designed to enhance the credibility of the industry in the face of catastrophic environmental disasters caused by oil companies.

- *Fostering consumer culture.* Beyond the promotion of a particular brand, advertisers encourage audience members to think of themselves in terms of their consumer behavior. This conditioning begins early. Some stores carry miniature carts for children, complete with a sign, "Shopper in Training." Further, the premise of a popular board game called "Mall Madness" is a trip to the mall, complete with no-limit credit cards.

  Indeed, an individual's sense of identity is defined by his or her choice of products. Consumers declare their membership in a group by wearing clothing with corporate logos. Ironically, by wearing designer labels or sweatshirts with commercials logos, consumers transform themselves into walking billboards, advertising these products.

- *Establishing standards of behavior and lifestyle.* Advertising is in the business of establishing standards of behavior—how to look, where to go, and what to do with our time. Further, advertising has assumed a major role in the delineation of taste. A marketing executive for Pepsi-Cola once offered the opinion that his competitor, Diet Coke, had made a conscious decision to keep the taste of its product indistinct: although nobody initially *liked* Diet Coke, no one *disliked* the product either. Then, through clever promotion ("Just for the taste of it"), consumers learned that it was stylish to drink Diet Coke. Eventually, the consumer developed a taste for the soft drink.

  In addition, ads have been incorporated into our lifestyles. "Just Do It" (Nike) and "Got Milk?" (U.S. Dairy Farmers and Milk Processors) are examples of ad slogans that have become a part of the common vernacular.

- *Breeding dissatisfaction with self.* In order to motivate people to purchase products, advertisers strive to convince them that their product will lead to personal improvements or solve a particular problem. But from another perspective, this strategy is designed to convince consumers that the product will remedy some personal inadequacy. In order to sell their products, ads continually tell women that they are overweight, need cosmetic "support" to look better, or simply are too old. Women are constantly asked to compare themselves to the models and actresses who appear in advertising. This barrage of messages can have a harmful effect on the self-image of young girls and women.

- *Entertainment.* Advertising was one of the first public communications formats to recognize that any message, if presented in an entertaining fashion, will interest the public. For instance, one of the prime attractions of the Super Bowl is the ceremonial unveiling of new commercials.

However, advertising must not be so entertaining that it distracts the audience from its primary function of selling a product. To illustrate, the legendary radio comedians Bob and Ray were hired for a Piel's beer ad campaign. Their skits were so funny, however, that they were fired; people loved the ads but could not remember what product they were promoting. In contrast, annoying ads are successful—not because people *like* the ads but because they are *memorable.*

- *As principal message.* Instead of simply supporting programming, in some cases, the programs *themselves* are advertisements. The Home Shopping Network attracts large numbers of viewers who enjoy the promotion of the products. Only slightly less subtle is MTV. In addition to the sponsors of MTV programming, the entertainment content *itself* is advertising—music videos originated as marketing material that promoted artists' concerts and CDs and provided exposure for recording artists.

Some articles on the Internet that appear to have an informational or entertainment function are actually designed to generate advertising profits through a strategy called *search engine optimization.* In order to research a topic, search engines scan the digital domain to find key words. Thus, if you are investigating the moons of Jupiter, the search engine locates sites that contain the key words "moons" and "Jupiter." Internet ad companies place articles on the Internet with the purpose of generating "hits" on key words and links. The more hits that a site receives, the higher it appears on the Google search list—its list of recommended sites— thereby "optimizing" the chances that a person conducting a computer search will find them.

Reporter David Segal describes the process of search engine optimization (SEO):

If you own a Web site, for instance, about Chinese cooking, your site's Google ranking will improve as other sites link to it. The more links to your site, especially those from other Chinese cooking-related sites, the higher your ranking. In a way, what Google is measuring is your site's popularity by polling the best-informed online fans of Chinese cooking and counting their links to your site as votes of approval.[11]

Thus, it is important to consider the *function* behind the appearance of the article on the Internet. Although the manifest function of search engine optimization may be information or entertainment, the latent function is *profit*. It is important to remember that commercial search engines like Google are designed to generate revenue—not serve as your local library.

However, only 38 percent of searchers are aware of a distinction between paid and unpaid results among search returns.[12] Danny Sullivan, the editor of *Search Engine Watch*, declares, "Anybody who looks for something on any search engine and thinks the results are the best or most impartial results, or that they came back completely organically is totally mistaken."[13]

Process: Media Communicator

Identifying the media communicator is an important step in the analysis of advertisements. To illustrate, ads directed at children often feature actors and models who are a bit older than the target audience members, and as a result, serve as role models. The thought process of young audience members works according to the following syllogism: l) the kids in the ad are cool and popular; 2) these kids use the product; 3) I want to be like them; 4) I'll purchase the product. Teenagers in the audience accepted these messages from their "peers," little realizing that the jargon was written by adults, whose interests, values, and motives differ markedly from their target market.

Adults make the same mistake of thinking that the performers in ads are the actual media communicators. Thus, an ad in which Washington Redskins Quarterback Robert Griffin III endorses a deodorant operates according to the same syllogism: l) RG3 is cool and popular; 2) RG3 uses the product; 3) I want to be like RG3; 4) I'll purchase the product.

In a practice known as *affiliate marketing,* shoppers who post product links that drive Web traffic and sales to retailers are often paid by social media shopping sites. A variation of this strategy is *social shopping,* in which a prominent socialite or stylish magazine editor posts links to his/her favorite fashions from online retailers. If the consumer makes a purchase, the site gets a commission.[14]

Performers in advertisements fall into the following categories:

Actors

Casting directors screen candidates carefully to find actors who will be most convincing in the role. Hooper White advises advertising executives,

You should furnish the casting director with a complete written description of the actor you have in mind. Is he or she hard nosed or easygoing, aggressive or passive, funny or serious, quiet or loud? Don't limit the written description to physical details. Be sure to discuss, in writing, the *entire characterization*. You will find that this forces you to clearly identify the character, thereby helping the casting director to find the right actor.[15]

Characters

Because the audience has known characters like the Marlboro Man, Mr. Whipple, Madge the manicurist, and Juan Valdez for decades, they are regarded as real people who can be trusted to tell the truth about the benefits of the product. As a result, Carlos Sanchez, the actor who has portrayed Juan Valdez since 1969, is an international celebrity:

> When Juan Valdez walks the streets of Manhattan or Paris, a poncho over his shoulder, delighted passers-by point, yell greetings and ask for autographs. He is thronged. "It's astonishing the power of publicity," said. . . Carlos Sanchez. "My Colombian friends see how the American people receive me, taking photos, and they say it is crazy."[16]

Celebrities

Enlisting celebrities to endorse products is a very successful advertising strategy. In an extension of this approach, some celebrities now promote their own lines of products. It must be noted, however, that these performers are paid hefty fees to endorse these brands, whether or not they actually *use* them. Further, celebrity ads sometimes elevate these spokespeople to positions of undue authority; however, celebrity status does not necessarily qualify an entertainer to recommend the type of hay fever medicine you should use or who to support for president.

Models

Advertisements frequently use models who display the desired "look" admired by the target audience. These models also embody a cultural ideal, which in many cases is not only unrealistic, but *unhealthy*. The female models in fashion and cosmetics ads are, on average, between 13 and 19 pounds underweight, which, according to the American Psychiatric Association, falls within the range of anorexia.[17]

Icons

Icons like the Aflac Duck, Martin the Gecko (for Geico Auto Insurance), and the Keebler Elves are designed to embody the corporate image of its client. These cartoon characters are likable and memorable, and project qualities that can be associated with the product. However, these fictitious characters have no connection whatsoever with the quality of the product or the policies of the company. In 2001, a sex discrimination lawsuit was filed against Metlife, a life insurance corporation that licensed the Peanuts character Snoopy as its corporate icon. There is no small irony in this love-able symbol representing a company that has been anything but endearing to its workers.

Just Folks

Testimonials from "average people" lend authenticity and credibility to an ad. The more amateur their performance, the more the audience identifies with them and believes their testimony. This "real people" approach should not be confused with a strategy in which actors *portray* average consumers.

CEOs

A variation on this strategy involves using actual company personnel to sell the product. As a rule, CEOs are not polished pitchmen; however, con-sumers enjoy seeing the corporate heads of companies as "regular guys" who believe in their product.

Attention-Getters

Every local television station carries commercials by outrageous pitchmen who attract attention by screaming, rollerskating, dressing up in ape suits, or by offering "crazy, crazy low prices." Of course, it is not unreasonable to ask: Why would anyone *want* to buy a product from a person who is either that crazy or that annoying?

Product as Character

Ad agencies strive to establish a product identity that resonates with the public. John Ferrill, executive vice president and creative director of Young and Rubicam, explains,

> Every product has a personality. Whether the clients have consciously thought about it or not, people perceive a brand in a certain way. Jello-O is a member of the family; it's friendly, it's fun. Anacin is very businesslike; it gets the job done, but it does it in a very straight, unglamorous, matter-of-fact kind of way. I could name almost any product and you'd have some impressions on . . . really what it is. The brand personality is the description of a product stated as though that product were a person.
>
> If you're trying to write a statement for Oil of Olay, you might characterize the brand as "feminine." You might say she is mysterious, possibly foreign in origin. She understands beauty secrets and the needs of women. She is an authoritative friend.[18]

Process: Comparative Media

The most direct means of convincing a consumer to purchase your product is for potential customers to sample the product, so that they can actually feel, smell, see, and taste the product for themselves. However, in order to promote a product to a mass audience, advertisers must use other senses. For instance, beer ads must use visuals to suggest the taste and texture of the beverage. To illustrate, a Coors Light Beer ad takes place in a packed football stadium, where the capacity crowd clearly is suffering in stifling heat. Suddenly, the gate opens, and the Coors Light Beer Silver Bullet train enters the field, transforming the hot climate into a frosty winter world. The visuals of snow and ice call to mind the cold, crisp taste of Coors Light Beer.

Every medium has its own distinctive characteristics that determine its ability to promote particular types of products to specific audiences. Jay Schulberg of the Ogilvy and Mather Advertising Agency explains,

> [T]he media can do different things. TV can create awareness more quickly with a larger percentage of the population at a lower cost. To do that in print becomes prohibitively expensive; it's almost impossible. However, print can inform better.

If one has a complicated message, or where the consumer is spending a lot of money for a product, such as a VCR or a television set, people want information, and you can get a lot more into print than you can get into a 30-second spot. So where TV may create the awareness, say, for a car, people want to read about what the car has, in my view.[19]

Advertisers consider the following factors when deciding which medium is most suitable for promoting their products:

- *Which medium is best suited to convey the advertising message?*
- *Which medium is the target audience most likely to use?*
- *Which medium will display the product most attractively?*
- *Factoring in the costs and benefits associated with each medium, how can clients make the most efficient use of their advertising budgets?*

Table 9.1   Comparative Media

Newspapers

Advantages	Disadvantages
Geographic Market Selectivity	Lack of Permanence
Flexibility—Ease of Ad Insertion	Poor Printing Quality
Editorial Support	Limited Demographic Orientation
Broad Coverage	Wasted Circulation
Considerable Reader Interest	High Cost for National Advertisers
	Ad Can Be Buried

Magazines

Advantages	Disadvantages
Demographic Market Selectivity	Lack of Flexibility in Last-Minute Changes
Long-Life Ad Capability	Limited Availability
Good Quality Print Production	High Cost—Especially for Color
Editorial Support	Limited Local Ad Opportunities
Reader Interest	Ad Can Be Buried
Upscale Audience/Prestige	

Radio

Advantages	Disadvantages
Geographic and Demographic Market Selectivity	Lack of Permanence
	Perishability

Universal Accessibility	Clutter
Relatively Inexpensive	Lack of Visual Support
Personal Nature of Radio	Limited Impact—Background Medium
Pace Determined by Advertiser	
Local Appeal	
Portability	
Costs for Ads Have Remained Stable	
Growth of the Radio Audience	
Flexible Format	

- Time can be bought on short notice
- Changes can be made on short notice

Television

Advantages	Disadvantages
Visualization of Product	Perishable Ad Message Unless Repeated
Geographic Market Selectivity	Relatively Expensive
Significant Market Penetration	Clutter-Messages Lost in Group of Ads
Can Deliver Huge Audiences	Not Terribly Selective Medium
Legitimacy of Medium	Limited Time for Presentation
	Relatively Inflexible Format

- Ad slots often bought up well in advance of presentation

Internet

Advantages	Disadvantages
Flexibility-Ability to Update	Ad can be immediately deleted
Ads Can Blend in with Editorial Text	Can Get Lost in Clutter
Can Use Multiple Media to Convey Information	Expensive to Maintain Site
Ad More Effective Outreach to Potential Costumers	Difficult for Consumer to Locate the Ad—Lack of Comprehensive
Ability to Track Consumer's Other Purchases	Web Index
Ability to Track Effectiveness of Ads	
Ability to Target Audience-Microcasting	

Print

Print ads generally are very carefully crafted. In contrast with a 30-second television spot, a print ad is the equivalent of one frame. Consequently, the production elements (e.g., color, angle, and lighting) have been carefully coordinated to reinforce the advertising message.

The medium of print is unmatched in its ability to convey detailed information about a product. In addition, the tangible nature of print allows consumers to refer back to ads when they want specific information.

Moreover, readers tend to associate print ads with the publication in which they are published; consequently, ads placed in prestigious periodicals are accorded commensurate respect.

Print ads can blend in with editorial content. In fashion magazines it is often difficult to distinguish between an article and an ad promoting a particular line of apparel.

Radio

It is impossible for a radio commercial to display the features of a brand; however, advertisers can take advantage of the imaginative possibilities of the medium to sell the product. In a radio ad for Volkswagen, the narrator poses the following question: "How do I help you visualize the Volkswagen Jetta?," followed by a sequence of classical music selections that suggest gracefulness, performance, and being "at one" with the automobile. The narrator concludes by inviting the audience to "imagine the difference between mere transportation and pure driving pleasure."

Like print ads, radio commercials can blend in with the regular programming. To illustrate, an ad for Southwest Airlines uses an *integration ad strategy* that promotes products conversationally to take advantage of this characteristic:

> The D.J. . . . . discussed the South by Southwest music festival, a popular annual event held in Austin, and conclude[d], "You know, the best way to get down to Austin for South by Southwest is Southwest Airlines. They have tons of flights. It's the way I travel."[20]

Radio ads often feature catchy jingles, as well as sophisticated recording techniques and performances. Indeed, former ad composer Barry Manilow was able to parlay his understanding of jingles (simple melodies and snappy lyrics) into a successful career as a pop recording artist.

Radio messages must be simplified and the presentation concise. The advertiser must condense as much information into the abbreviated time allotted, at the same time making sure that the information is presented clearly enough to be easily followed. The radio advertiser is limited to one minute, or approximately 200 to 300 words; in contrast, the print advertiser can use as many as 1,000 words to promote a product.[21] Because the pace is determined by the advertiser, the message is irretrievably lost if the audience is inattentive. But at the same time, since members of the audience are often engaged in competing activities, they may be particularly susceptible to subtle advertising messages.

Television

Television remains the most prestigious advertising medium. Merely by appearing on the airwaves, products (and companies) assume a measure of legitimacy. No matter how goofy they act, local pitchmen enjoy minor celebrity status in their communities simply by appearing in front of the camera.

Television commercials combine visuals, sound, and narrative information to convey their advertising messages. Arthur Bellaire advises,

> The video and the corresponding audio should relate. Don't be demonstrating one sales feature while talking about another. . . . While the audio should be relevant to the video, don't waste words by describing what is obvious in the picture. Rather, see that the words interpret the picture and thereby advance the thought. Rely on the video to carry more than half the weight. Being a visual medium, television is more effective at showing than telling. Avoid static scenes. Provide for camera movement and changes of scenes.[22]

Television offers the following advantages in the promotion of products:

- *Demonstration.* Television is supreme in its ability to show how a product is used.
- *Dramatization.* Advertisers find that ads are effective when they "activate" the product by showing it being used by people. Beyond simply demonstrating how a product is used, television ads present a scenario in which the product makes a significant impact on the lives of the characters.
- *Performance.* More than any other medium, television is particularly adept at presenting people who are consuming and enjoying

the product. A convincing performance can make a difference in persuading its audience to purchase the product.

- *Affective Appeal.* The combination of music and pictures can touch the emotions of the viewer.

However, fewer people are watching traditional advertising on television; 2012 Nielsen ratings revealed that ABC was down 7 percent among the audience preferred by most advertisers, viewers between the ages of 18 and 49; CBS was down 18 percent; and Fox Broadcasting was down 26 percent.[23]

Innovations in media technology have added to the challenges facing TV advertisers. Although advertisers spend over $70 billion a year on television commercials, 54 percent of people who own DVRs skip the ads altogether.[24]

According to Kelly Kahl, the chief scheduler for CBS, television networks have to recalculate the meaning of success with "people adjusting to new ways of watching television."[25] Consequently, advertisers have developed the following strategies to keep people tuned in to television ads:

- One-second ad spots, called "blinks," that don't give listeners time to change the station before the message is delivered.
- Ambiguous commercials in which the product being advertised is unclear. This "mystery" keeps people in suspense (and watching).
- Personalized ad messages that appeal to the specific interests and needs of the audience.
- High production quality, so that the entertainment value of the spots is, in some cases, superior to the programming.

Increasingly, advertisers have become reliant on *product placement,* a technique in which products are embedded into the narrative itself. In a typical product placement arrangement, an agency signs a client for a retainer and places the product in various media presentations, as many times as is appropriate and possible. Product placements in media presentations have become a primary source of ad revenue, generating $8.25 million in 2012. That amount is expected to double by 2016.[26] As Ray Warren, managing director at OMD USA, declares, "If there's going to be a can of soda on a table, it might as well be our client's can of soda."[27]

Is product placement an effective promotional vehicle? In 1982, the producers of the film *E.T.* approached Hershey, the makers of M&M candies, proposing a deal in which, in return for a fee, the candy would appear in the

Pierce Brosnan and Michelle Yeoh on a BMW motorcycle in a scene from the James Bond film *Tomorrow Never Dies* (1997). The film incorporated product placement advertising for BMW, Omega watches, and even Visa credit cards. (Keith Hamshere/AFP/Getty Images)

film; the company declined. Instead, E.T.'s young earthling companion Elliott used the Reese's Pieces to mark a trail for the alien to follow. Within a month of the premiere of the film, sales for the candy jumped by 65 percent.[28]

The number of product placements in media presentations is staggering. To illustrate, *Transformers: Dark of the Moon* (2011) incorporated 71 identifiable brands and products into the film.[29]

In the early days of product placement, the product was shown being used by characters in the story, as when Marty McFly (Michael J. Fox) drank a Pepsi in the 1985 film *Back to the Future*. Over time, however, a more subtle form of product placement has emerged, in which products are cleverly embedded into the narrative. In this approach, called *product integration,* products become central to the narrative, which sends the message that the brand is essential to the characters (and to the audience as well).

In some cases, the entire storyline is conceived with product placement in mind. For example, in a 2009 episode of the reality show *Celebrity Apprentice,* the contestants were asked to write a jingle for Chicken of the Sea brand tuna. ITVX's Q-Ratio, a research methodology that considers how often a product is on the screen, how it is woven into the story of the program, and if characters hold it or speak about it, predicted that 85 percent of the audience would recall Chicken of the Sea after the show.[30]

Product placement has also become central to character development in the narrative. For instance, in the TV drama *Falcon Beach,* different General Motors vehicles (i.e., Pontiacs, Cadillacs, and Buicks) were matched with the character most closely mirroring the consumer profile of the brand. Thus, Paige (Jennifer Kydd), the lead female character, was depicted driving a sleek Pontiac Solstice, while her mother (Allison Hossack) drove a reliable, sturdy (yet stylish) Cadillac SRX.

Using products as props or part of the set legitimizes the product and is therefore a very subtle form of persuasion. For instance, in the NBC drama series *Friday Night Lights,* the characters regularly met for dinner at an Applebee's restaurant.

However, some writers and producers complain that the imperative to slip product promotion into a script can undermine the integrity of the story. Scott Miller, a story producer on the reality show *American Dream Derby,* was required to get Diet Dr. Pepper into every episode, regardless of what was happening on-screen:

> These were moments when people were crying, or two cast members were screaming at each other, or two allies were sneaking off to strategize, and there were several times when it was: "Let me stop and make sure everyone has a can of Diet Dr. Pepper." I'd literally be below the frame line, handing a can of Diet Dr. Pepper to someone who didn't have one. First and foremost, I want to tell a good story. I'm not necessarily there to help make a commercial.[31]

In response, a collective of show business unions, including the Writers Guild of America–West, the Writers Guild of America–East, and the Screen Actors Guild, denounced the practice of "stealth advertising" and called for a code of conduct to govern this practice. The group issued a position paper saying,

> We are being told to write the lines that sell this merchandise, and to deftly disguise the sale as story. Our writers are being told to perform the function of ad copywriter, but to disguise this as storytelling.[32]

Other product placement strategies include:

- *Product Placements for Target Audiences.* In this practice, brands are placed in presentations intended for the group most likely to purchase the product. For instance, the children's film *Madagascar 3:*

Europe's Most Wanted (2012) provided product placement for the following brands: Airbus, Ducati, New York Nicks, HP, and Duane Reade, among others.

- *Product placements appear in different media.*
  - *Books.* In 2005, HarperCollins Publishers released a children's book entitled *Cashmere If You Can.* The plot of the book follows the adventures of Wawa Hohhot and her family of Mongolian cashmere goats who live on the roof of Saks's Midtown Manhattan store. A Saks Fifth Avenue marketing executive came up with the idea, and the department store chain owns the text copyright.
  - *Popular Music.* In the top 20 songs of 2005, Mercedes-Benz was mentioned 100 times, Nike 63, Cadillac 62, Bentley 51, and Rolls-Royce 46.[33]
- Some genres are particularly suitable for product placements:
  - The reality genre lends itself to product placements, in part because the sets must include branded products as part of its "real" look. In 2011, of the top 10 primetime shows with the most product placement, 9 of them were unscripted, or "reality," shows.[34]
  - Product placements are beginning to appear in newscasts. Stations have arranged for their anchors to sip McDonald's iced coffees during the morning shows, which producers claim appear to be "softer news" than afternoon news programs.
- Certain products are more likely to be marketed through product placement than others. For instance, in 2011, the following products were the most frequently placed brands in films:
  - Apple products appeared in 17 (or 42.5 percent) of the 40 films that were number one at the U.S. box office in 2011, showing up nearly twice as often as the nearest brand.[35] Indeed, in the Chinese film *I Know What Women Want,* every third scene contained an Apple product.[36]
  - Nike, Chevrolet, and Ford each appeared in 24 percent of the top films.
  - Sony, Dell, Land Rover, and Glock appeared in at least 15 percent of the top films.[37]

Digital Media

In 2011, online ad spending grew by 23 percent, to $32.03 billion. It is anticipated that in the next few years, digital media will supplant print as the dominant advertising channel.[38] Already, online research has surpassed print media as the source that consumers make use of when they are preparing to make a purchase.[39]

Moreover, television and Web technology are converging, so that the old television set is being transformed into an "entertainment appliance" that can be used for online purchases. The screen has been converted to a virtual display window, with the left-hand side reserved for continuous advertising. If you fancy a pair of shoes that an actor or actress is wearing in a situation comedy, you will be able to click on the image and order the item.

Although a customized banner, or pop-up ad, automatically appears on the computer screen when the user hits a particular site, the click-through rates on these are extremely low—perhaps because the advertising function is so obvious. However, the fluid nature of interactive media masks the advertising function. In the technique of *native advertising,* an advertisement that appears in an online version of an established publication like *Atlantic Monthly* is indistinguishable from the form and format of an editorial Web site. A variation of this approach is *sponsored content,* in which commercials are styled like program content—some even featuring the hosts of shows that appear on the channels.

Advertising links also may be embedded in editorial copy, without being labeled accordingly, so that individuals seeking additional information on a topic instead find themselves transported to the Web site of an advertiser, who has an advertising fee. Eric Effron provides the following example:

> nytimes.com offers a link to barnsandnoble.com next to its online book reviews, and *The New York Times* gets a piece of the action if anyone buys a book via that route. Because it's *The Times,* we can be fairly sure that reviews aren't skewed to help sales. But it has to be noted that *The Times* now has a financial interest in that book being reviewed that it didn't have before. And it's not coincidental that . . . while most of the newspaper's past articles are available online for just one year and can only be retrieved by paying a fee, *The Times* has made 19 years of book reviews available for free (with the Barnes & Noble "buy option," of course).[40]

Advertisers have adopted new advertising tactics that take advantage of the characteristics of digital media. *Viral marketing* is a technique that is analogous to the spreading of viruses throughout the environment.

KISSmetrics, a blog about analytics, marketing, and testing, provides the following definition of viral marketing:

> [The use of] pre-existing social networks and other technologies to produce increases in brand awareness or to achieve other marketing objectives (such as product sales) through self-replicating viral processes. . . . It can be delivered by word of mouth or enhanced by the network effects of the Internet and mobile networks.[41]

It has been estimated that a successful viral campaign can have 500 to 1000 times more impact than a traditional ad campaign.[42]

Affective Response

Despite working within a very limited format (e.g., a 15-second TV spot), ads can evoke intense emotional reactions among members of the audience.

Ads featuring puppies and babies are guaranteed to produce a warm reaction. The advertiser hopes that the consumer will transfer these positive feelings to the product. Humorous ads work on a similar principle. Laughter is a positive emotional response; we are grateful to people who make us laugh. Arthur Bijur, president of the Freeman Advertising Agency, explains,

> If you can share a smile with someone, you've made a friend. Humor works because it warms people up and relaxes them. Humor creates connection, opens a window to get a message in and makes people feel good about your brand.[43]

Indeed, a study by the USC Marshall School of Business found that consumers can form an emotional bond with a brand that is so strong that purchasing a competitor's product can result in separation anxiety.[44]

Advertisers recognize that products are purchased for psychological as well as product satisfaction. Through psychographic research, advertisers have become particularly adept at identifying the fears, anxieties, and areas of insecurity of their target audience, and then sending the audience personalized messages that first trigger insecurities, and then present their product as the solution to the "problem." For example, a Michelin tire advertising campaign featuring the slogan "Because so much is riding on your tires" is directed at young parents. The ad, which includes a picture of a cute infant sitting on one of the company's products, is designed to generate a response from the target audience capitalizing on parents' protective instincts.

Many ads strive to accentuate the *emotional benefits* of a product. Thus, the phone company is not merely selling a communications system but furnishes the means by which you can "reach out and touch someone" you love. This approach may be used even when the product does not have a logical emotional benefit. As an example, the setting of a Christmas radio spot for Kretchmeyer hams is a holiday dinner at which a young man offers a moving toast: "There is no place I'd rather be right now than with my family." The ad thus positions the product as an essential part of a family holiday celebration. But even if this scenario was genuine, the ham can claim no more responsibility for the emotional richness of the moment than the silverware or canned peas.

An ad strategy that builds on this emotional principle involves creating a problem and then positioning the product as its solution. Thus, a classic ad campaign for Wisk laundry detergent first creates a source of anxiety—"Ring around the Collar"—and then offers the product as its solution.

Ads may be directed at one of the following intrinsic *psychological motivations:*

- *Love*

  Ads often present products as tangible symbols of love, affirming the depth, sincerity, and permanence of your affection.

  Some ads position their product as an essential ingredient in the courtship ritual. Using the right product will make you more attractive and desirable ("Making close comfortable"—Norelco shavers). Giving the proper present can win a person's heart. And some products even promise improved performance in lovemaking ("Make it last a little longer"—Big Red gum).

  These ads call attention to the pleasure that you'll bring your loved one through a thoughtful purchase. But at the same time, this approach is a subtle appeal to the ego of the purchaser; imagine how grateful your partner will be upon receiving the gift, and how wonderful you are for having given it.

  Love between family members is another very powerful psychological motivation. One McDonald's television commercial begins with a young man walking wistfully through a children's playground. He stops at a McDonald's and orders a breakfast to go: "I'm having breakfast with my daughter," he explains to the young woman at the counter. The next scene shows the young man at the hospital, gazing fondly at his newborn child. The ad suggests that daddy's Egg McMuffin has played a significant role in this deeply personal moment. But however illogical, this very powerful latent message about the connection between father and daughter reinforces the manifest pitch for McDonald's.

- *Need for Approval*

  A persistent latent message in advertising is that people can satisfy their intrinsic need for acceptance through their consumer behavior. One particularly effective version of this appeal is based on the complex relationship between children and their parents. For instance, a television recruitment ad for the U.S. Marines begins with a young, rugged-looking young man returning home from boot camp. He is met at the train by his younger brother. The marine immediately asks whether his dad is still angry with him for having enlisted in the marines. Behind this rugged facade, the soldier is still a little boy seeking his father's approval.

  The scene then shifts to the marine entering his old house. He is dressed in full military regalia. His father looks at him from across the room. Silence. Suddenly, Dad moves toward his son and embraces him. This reconciliation scene touches young males in the audience who may be sorting out their own complex feelings toward their fathers. The underlying message is that by joining the Marine Corps, a young man can find the resolution to this fundamental need for acceptance.

- *Guilt*

  American culture can be characterized as exceedingly guilt-ridden. We feel remorse for any number of real and imagined transgressions. Advertisers capitalize on these irrational feelings to promote products. For instance, the ad campaign for Michelin tires discussed earlier ("Because so much is riding on your tires") depicts an infant surrounded (and protected) by the product. The latent message is that parents who care about their children purchase Michelin tires. However, this affective appeal does not hold up under rational scrutiny: Is the choice of brands critical to being a good parent? (Why not buy new Goodyear tires, for instance?) Does buying Michelin tires automatically make you a good parent? And if you're a responsible parent, shouldn't you worry about the other features of the car as well (e.g., the fuel line or transmission), as well as other drivers and *their* tires? The list could go on and on.

MEDIA LITERACY TIPS: GUILT-PROVOKING ADS

When confronted by *guilt-provoking ads,* ask the following questions:

- *Why am I feeling guilty?*
- *How will purchasing the product assuage my guilt?*
- *Is the choice of brand important?*
- *Could an advertiser exploit these feelings of guilt to sell me other products?*

- *Nostalgia for Significant Moments*

  This category of ads associates a product with significant moments that touch people's lives. For instance, a television ad campaign for Volkswagen celebrates the sights and sounds of the 1960s. Its scenes are composed of artifacts from the era, including peace signs, long-haired youth, and popular music. Anne Finucane, chief marketing officer at Bank of America in Boston, observes, "The bus is a symbol of the values you grew up with, the values that made you successful and the values you want to pass on to your children."[45]

  Other ads associate products with Christmas, Fourth of July, and Thanksgiving, in hopes that this sentimental attachment to these holidays will boost product sales. Taking this promotional tack to the extreme, the business community has even *invented* holidays such as Grandparent's Day to stimulate sales.

- *Fixation with Death*

From birth, people are fascinated with their own mortality. H. G. Eysnck explains,

> Freud postulates that the organism has an innate tendency to revert to its initial state. This instinct, which would lead to self-destruction, has to be diverted outward by the developing organism. . . . The death instinct represents one of the two major classes or drives and motives, which—for psychoanalysts—comprise all motivational processes.[46]

This primal attraction to death helps to explain why individuals climb mountains or stand up in moving convertibles. As winter fosters our appreciation of spring, death gives meaning to life.

Several ad strategies are manifestations of this love/hate relationship with death:

- *Denial of Death*
  This ad strategy promotes products as a safeguard against death. Castleguard Security system reminds us that, in an impermanent world, "Give the most valuable gift of all . . . the gift of security." Advertisements for diamonds are even more blatant, selling immortality in the form of their product. A diamond insures that love will be permanent, and that the fortunate couple will live happily ever after.
- *Loss of Control*
  Death represents the ultimate loss of control. BBDO advertising offers the following insight into how the Gillette deodorant campaign, "Never Let Them See You Sweat," capitalizes on our primal need to maintain control in our lives:

  > The "Product" stance is that it "goes on dry, stays dry." But this did not differentiate this superior performing product until the "You" attitude was added: Control, Aspiration. The resulting theme line, "Never Let Them See You Sweat," and the campaign featuring rising young entertainers, has helped revitalize the brand.[47]

- *Abandonment*
  A classic TV commercial promoting the Prudential Insurance Agency focuses on the testimony of a grieving widow. She has been abandoned by her husband and now must contend with the emptiness of her life. "We thought it would never happen to us," she laments, realizing that she is not only alone but impoverished as well. In this case, the insurance represents both financial and emotional comfort and security.
- *Longing for the Past*
  An ad for Tyson chicken reminds us, "So for over 50 years, we've made sure that Tyson's chicken is the leanest and meatiest that they can be." This ad establishes a tradition that makes us feel rooted and safe. At the same time, this return to the past provides us with a sense of confidence in the future.
- *Fear of Failure*
  In American culture, failure is regarded as a form of death-in-life. To illustrate, AT&T produced a series of "Slice of Death" ads, featuring

testimonials by businesspeople who have been let down by their current phone system. Thornton C. Lockwood observes,

> The problem the agency chose to dramatize . . . was phone failure and the problems that creates for business people; loss of credibility with clients, lost sales, demoralized workers, management confusion, and ultimately, even business failure.[48]

Significantly, the first test storyboard scenario was even more overt: a malfunctioning (and malevolent) telephone swallows a young woman who is taking phone orders at a restaurant.

- *Fear of the Unknown*
  An ad for the Travelers contains a photo with religious overtones: a skyscape with streaks of light shining through the clouds. The headline reads,

> Financial Serenity
> The Strength to Leap
> Beyond the World of Worry.

Armed with the protection afforded by the Travelers (with its slogan, "You're better off under the Umbrella"), the audience is prepared to meet whatever challenges lie ahead.

However, affective appeals like those cited above offer only superficial, antiseptic emotional experiences that ultimately trivialize genuine emotional experiences. We are spared the complications and consequences that are a part of any genuine emotional experience. Instead, our involvement need only last for 30 seconds; then we can move on.

Audience

The American Marketing Association offers a rather curious definition of advertising: "A paid form of a *non-personal* presentation and promotion of ideas, goods, or service by an identified sponsor aimed at a particular target market and audience" (emphasis added).[49]

However, it can be argued that in many respects, advertising is an extraordinarily *personal* form of mass communications. After all, the success of an ad depends upon advertisers' ability to identify and then persuade one person. Indeed, John O'Toole, chairman of the Foote, Cone &

Belding advertising agency, regards advertising as a form of *interpersonal* communication. He observes, "When the chord is struck in one, the vibrations reverberate in millions."[50]

Audience Identification

Advertisers commit enormous resources to market research that enables them to become familiar with their audience. Advertisers can track your activity on the Internet, gathering precise information about your background, interests, and financial position. Web sites commonly install *cookies*, a piece of software that plants small, traceable files on the computers of the people who visit their site. This *meta information* (i.e., information about the information) enables advertisers to track activity on the Internet, so that they can gather precise information about the individual consumer.

In addition, advertisers can purchase personal information about you that has been gathered by companies such as Facebook. Reporter Somini Sengupta provides information on four companies that in 2012 were under investigation by the Federal Trade Commission with regard to their collection and use of commercial data:

> Acxiom . . . aggregates data from a variety of sources, including financial services companies, court records and federal government documents; Datalogix, which claims to have a database on the spending habits of more than 100 million Americans in categories like fine jewelry, cough medicine and college tuition; and Epsilon, which also collects transaction data from retailers. . . . BlueKai, based in Cupertino, Calif., creates tracking cookies for brands to monitor customers who visit their Web sites. That [sic] data can be used to show an advertisement when those users log on to Facebook.[51]

Marketing specialists assess both *demographic* and *psychographic* information. Demographic research refers to the study of human populations. Demographic categories such as age, gender, income, education, occupation, race, religion, and family size influence consumer buying patterns. For example, geographic location can affect the choice of color in the purchase of automobiles; black is the predominant automobile color on the East Coast of the United States, while white and lighter shades of cars are preferred on the West Coast.

Psychographic research identifies the attitudes, values, and lifestyles shared by groups falling within these demographic categories. Psychographic research enables advertisers to anticipate the consumption patterns of particular subgroups. To illustrate, Otto Kleppner predicts that you will encounter the following stages of consumerism after completing college:

- *Young single.* You have moved into your own apartment and begun to make your own buying decisions. A high proportion of your income is spent on clothes, personal care, recreation, and entertainment.
- *Young marrieds, no children.* In general, you become more home-oriented. For all but a small proportion of these households, the wife works, providing a higher standard of living for the household. Most consumer buying decisions begin to be made by the female.
- *Young marrieds, children under six.* At this stage, the couple becomes tied down. If the wife quits her job, the family income goes down—although in most cases, the wife continues to work. A move to a larger apartment or house is required.
- *Young marrieds, children over six.* Your children have entered school. At this point, the wife has more freedom for activities outside of the home. The children begin to influence purchasing decisions.
- *Older marrieds with children.* Your expenses increase for education, weddings, etc. You begin to engage in more activities away from home. For instance, you begin to travel more frequently.
- *Older marrieds, no children.* Your children have left home. Smaller living quarters are now required. Your consumption patterns no longer need to consider the children.
- *Older singles.* At this stage you have become widows, widowers, divorcees, and unmarried men or women. You experience a dramatic change in lifestyle as your income is reduced.[52]

These lifestyle patterns have a direct bearing on consumer behaviors. For instance, automobile purchases are most numerous among young married couples with no children, as well as young married couples with children over six. And because young marrieds with small children are generally less mobile than other groups, they are the most promising prospects for television purchases.

Advertising messages are then customized to meet your specific interests, buying habits, and financial capacity. Thus, when you log onto Amazon, your page looks different from every other page in the world. And further, if you change your relationship status on Facebook, you'll start to see ads for antidepressants or weight loss products. Sengupta explains,

Targeted advertising bears important implications for consumers. It could mean seeing advertisements based not just on what they "like" on Facebook, but on what they eat for breakfast, whether they buy khakis or jeans and whether they are more likely to give their wives roses or tulips on their wedding anniversary. It means that even things people don't reveal on Facebook may be discovered from their online and offline proclivities.[53]

A variety of *programmatic buying technologies* have the capacity to instantaneously identify what their users searched for on the Web and then immediately supply an advertisement that takes their personal interests into consideration. Reporter Tanzina Vega explains,

> Programmatic buying includes a number of different technologies and strategies, but it essentially allows advertisers to bid, often in real time, on ad space largely based on the value they have assigned to the consumer on the other side of the screen. Say, for example, that Nike wants to sell running gear to a particular consumer who has a high likelihood of buying shoes based on the data it has collected, including the type of Web sites that consumer typically visits. Because the ad-buying is done through computer trading, the price for that space can change rapidly.[54]

One such process is called "real-time bidding." Reporter Natasha Singer observes,

> Think of these systems as a sort of Nasdaq stock market, only trading in audiences for online ads. Millions of bids flood in every second. And those bids—essentially what your eyeballs are worth to advertisers—could determine whether you see an ad for, say, a new Lexus or a used Ford, for sneakers or a popcorn maker.[55]

Digital technology can identify an individual's interests by detecting what people are viewing online and how much time they spend with an article or subject. Using an approach known as *behavioral targeting,* advertisers are able to target audiences based on their interests rather than on their general media consumption. Reporter Miguel Helft notes,

> Google will then use that information to show people ads that are relevant to their interests, regardless of what sites they are visiting.

An expectant mother may see an ad about baby products not only on a parenting site but also, for example, on a sports or fashion site that uses AdSense or on YouTube, which is owned by Google.[56]

Thus, if you visit the Sears Web page to purchase camping equipment, Sears will upload not merely any purchases but also other sites that you have browsed through, such as cowboy boots. The next time that you visit Sears on the Web, the homepage will be personalized, notifying you about any boot sales. And later, you may receive an e-mail reminding you about a relative's birthday and making suggestions for an appropriate gift. Moreover, you may then begin to receive unsolicited e-mails from other companies about sales for boots—as a result of real-time bidding.

Furthermore, digital software now exists that assembles personal information and, using algorithms, can accurately predict your future purchases. As a result, after you have made a purchase, you may be flooded with e-mails promoting other products that may be of interest to you.

In 2012, Facebook launched a *retargeting campaign* that goes into the "virtual file" of sites you had visited long ago and brings the information to your attention at a later time, when you might be more receptive to its message. Sengupta explains,

A travel Web site could track what its customers were looking at— hotels in New York, for instance—and show those customers an ad once they logged on to Facebook. The tracking is done by a piece of code embedded in the travel company's site. For marketers, more data could mean getting closer to the ultimate goal of advertising: sending the right message to the right consumer at the right time.[57]

Multiple Audiences

Advertising may be directed simultaneously at both a manifest and latent audience. To illustrate, ads that appear in women's magazines such as *Cosmopolitan* or *Vogue* are often surprisingly alluring and seductive, given that the target audience consists primarily of heterosexual women. One way to account for this sexually titillating advertising is that the latent audience actually consists of *males*. Women readers project themselves into the role of the model and then respond to the ads from a male perspective ("How would Bernie like me in this outfit?"). This explanation has some rather disturbing implications. For although magazines directed at a female audience ostensibly promote

An understanding of historical events can enrich the interpretation of an advertisement. As an example, this 2010 ad for Dove liquid dish detergent is nonsensical—the photo shows baby ducklings and otters were bathed in the detergent. This curious use of the product only makes sense within the context of the events surrounding the release of the ad. April 2010 marked the date of the oil rig disaster in the Gulf of Mexico, which was ruinous to the environment. Dove, which is normally used to clean dishes, was therefore promoted as a product that could clean the wildlife that had been doused in oil.

female empowerment, this advertising strategy suggests that women still depend upon male approval in U.S. culture.

HISTORICAL CONTEXT

An advertisement derives much of its significance from the events of the day. Consequently, an ad can provide valuable insight into the period in which it was produced. To illustrate, after the terrorist attack of 9/11, Calvin Klein altered its campaign from a sexy appeal to a more "poignant" approach—snippets of film, in home-video style, of family moments, shot in retro black and white, set to the 1960's Burt Bacharach song "What the World Needs Now Is Love."

Conversely, an understanding of historical events can enrich the interpretation of an advertisement. To illustrate, a 2002 ad for Clorox bleach that appeared in the Midwestern United States only makes sense once the audience is aware of the historical context of the ad. In 2002, the Mississippi and Missouri rivers flooded, polluting the water supply of the entire region. Under these extraordinary conditions, a tiny amount of bleach can purify the water supply. Consequently, the ad consisted of a photo of Clorox bleach, with the headline, "In an emergency, think of this as 38,000 gallons of drinking water."

CULTURAL CONTEXT

Advertising and Popular Culture

Advertisements can serve as a text that reflects, reinforces, and shapes cultural attitudes and values. To illustrate, journalist John Leo argues that the latent messages embedded in a Newport cigarette ad campaign contain "coded scenes of sexual aggression" toward women:

The photos always show outdoorsy yuppies horsing around. But amid all this jollity there is a strong undercurrent of sexual hostility, usually directed at women. Many depict women who seem to be off-balance and menaced, or at least the target of berserk male energy. Women are about to be clanged by a pair of cymbals, carried off on a pole, pulled along in a horse collar, or slam-dunked in the face by a basketball-wielding male.[58]

Journalist Bob Herbert makes a connection between the misogynistic messages found in advertising and attitudes that can lead to acts of violence against women:

A girl or woman is sexually assaulted every couple of minutes or so in the U.S. The number of seriously battered wives and girlfriends is far beyond the ability of any agency to count. We're all implicated in this carnage because the relentless violence against women and girls is linked at its core to the wider society's casual willingness to dehumanize women and girls, to see them first and foremost as sexual vessels—objects—and never, ever as the equals of men.[59]

Advertising can also disclose areas of cultural interest and concern. In that respect, ads can furnish perspective into the following *cultural preoccupations:*

- *Sex*
  American advertisements reflect our culture's ambivalent, adolescent preoccupation with sex. What are some of the cumulative messages about sex in American advertising?
  - *Sex is a cultural obsession*
    The sheer quantity of sexually oriented ads suggest that sex is a national fixation. All products (from perfume to automobiles) have sexual implications. Sex is always on our minds.
  - *Sex is dirty*
    American ads encourage a voyeuristic approach to sex. The audience peeks at models on the printed page or screen, which provides much of the sexual tension in the ads. Female models are posed in a posture of innocence, seemingly unaware that they are objects of desire. If they look at us boldly, they fall into the category of "bad girls."

American ads convey the message that sex is dirty and must be repressed. In contrast, European advertisements generally are much more explicit than their American counterparts. Nudity is not uncommon, either in print and television ads.

○ *Appearance is everything*
You are only as sexy as you look. We do not accept imperfections, either in our sex objects or, by extension, in ourselves. Consumer items, then, assume a magical quality, transforming people into desirable, sexy creatures.

○ *Sex is confined to a narrow stage of life*
Sex is a youth-oriented activity. In advertising, sex ends with marriage. Advertising rarely depicts older adults in sexually suggestive situations.

○ *Sex is objectified*
Many ads show only certain parts of females' bodies, reinforcing the notion that women are sexual objects. In like fashion, sex is not presented as an aspect of a larger relationship but an end in itself.

○ *Sex is a contact sport*
Sex is a contest, in which people compete for the attention of others. That's why we need all the commodities we can muster. Sex has very little to do with one's partner but instead is an ego-centered performance, undertaken for the approval and admiration of others.

○ *Sex is a consumer item*
The sexual style of ads has become its substance: products are sexy. In the ultimate depersonalization of sex, we are asked to believe that the products advertised in a seductive fashion, like cars, have sexual properties.

• *Aging*
Americans' preoccupation with youth is reflected in advertising. Ads for a range of products reinforce the ideal of youth by featuring models who are young, healthy, and fit. Julia Smillie observes, "Constant exposure to images of youth create an impression that youthfulness is the norm and that in order to be accepted, [the consumer] must strive to stay young."[60]

An ad for New Age hair color promises that the product will "restore our hair to its natural color," inferring that aging is an unnatural process. An ad for Shiseido skin cream establishes age as an enemy: "The fragile skin around your eyes. This is where time strikes first." Advertising for cosmetics, plastic surgery, exercise equipment, and hair replacement plans make the very ambitious promise of restoring youth. The headline for an Oil of Olay ad declares, "I don't plan to grow old gracefully, I intend to fight it every step of the way."

In an ad for "Just for Men Hair Coloring," a group of men and women are gathered together. However, one of the men, who has grey hair, has been ostracized from the group. His entire figure is washed out and devoid of color. Thus, gray is equated with being dull and boring, dreary, and unattractive. The ad then instructs the man to "get back in the game" by getting rid of grey hair. Once he has committed to using the product, color is restored to his image—and to his life.

- *Cleanliness*
American advertising often plays on our cultural insecurities about cleanliness. Asked where this antibacterial fetishism comes from, Dr. Jeffrey S. Duchin replies, "A lot of it is not based on science. It is based on our national psyche and what we value—purity and cleanliness."[61]

Over the years, ad campaigns for Listerine mouthwash have been directed at a range of anxieties related to halitosis (i.e., bad breath):
  - *"Could I be happy with him in spite of **THAT**?"* (1923)
  - *"It brought him untold misery; yet only he himself was to blame."* (1924)
  - *"Often a bridesmaid but never a bride."* (1924)
  - *"Why had he changed so in his attentions?"* (1924)
  - *"Their first conversation betrayed the fact that she was not fastidious."* (1925)[62]

Cultural Myths

American ads frequently tap into cultural myths, including the following:

- *Progress.* According to this cultural myth, new is better. Change is good for its own sake. Advertisers persuade customers that this year's models are superior to last year's. Advertisers create new markets by denigrating the old model, breaking last year's promise of quality and durability.

- *Appeal to mythic past.* At the same time, a nostalgic appeal to our mythic past establishes confidence in the product. For example, the highly successful Motel 6 ad campaign positions the hotel chain as a throwback to simpler times. Spokesperson Tom Bodett is a latter day Will Rogers who offers country wisdom and hospitality in a depersonalized corporate world. With country fiddle music playing in the background, Bodett assures us, "We'll leave the light on for ya."
- *Individualism.* Americans like to see themselves as rugged individualists, in the mold of John Wayne and Clint Eastwood. However, a delicate balance exists between *individualism* and *conformity.* People who are *too* different become cultural rejects (nerds, geeks, etc.). The trick to rugged individualism, then, is to stand out by being the epitome of style. The Marlboro man simply leads the pack of conformists.

  Moreover, advertising conveys the message that the way to assert one's individuality in contemporary society is through consumer behavior. Ironically, then, our range of individual expression has been reduced to the creative selection of products.

Cultural Change

Ads may also function as a barometer of cultural change. For example, the topic of divorce is a social phenomenon in American culture that has long been considered taboo in advertising. However, Allen P. Adamson, managing director of marketing company Landor Associates, declares, "Divorce is so common that I don't think people view it as sad and depressing anymore. It's on every movie, every TV show. There aren't any more *Leave It to Beaver* families around."[63] To illustrate, a 2006 television commercial for the Ford Freestyle legitimizes the ever-growing number of family members affected by divorce:

> The Ford commercial shows two parents, two children and a dog spending a weekend shopping, driving and hanging out at the beach—but at the end of the day, the father is dropped off at his apartment. "Thanks for inviting me this weekend," he says while hugging his children. "Sure," responds his apparent ex-wife, perched behind the wheel of the Ford Freestyle. The commercial ends with the father waving as the car drives away.[64]

Worldview

What kind of world is portrayed through advertising?

In many ads, what is really being sold is the *worldview* of the commercial. When you buy a designer shirt or sunglasses, you are purchasing far more than the product; you are admitted into the upscale and trendy world depicted in the ad campaigns. Jennifer Steinhauer observes,

> In most Nine West ads, it is hard to make out the shoes or bag for sale. But the women are young and sexy and never far from a great-looking guy and a romantic setting. A shopper is meant to believe that if she buys the whole package—clothes, tables, sheets and bras—she will join the elite club of those living out the brand's lifestyle in its ads.[65]

Thus, an effective line of inquiry consists of mentally airbrushing the product out of the advertisement and identifying the worldview of the ad. For instance, visualize a beer commercial in which young people are cavorting on the beach. Now, imagine the scene without the cooler of beer. What remains is a delightful social occasion, replete with music, celebration, and romance. But by placing product in the center of the activity, the ad conveys the message that the beer is central to this good time—indeed, you can't really have a party without someone bringing a keg.

Beyond the promotion of specific products, ads convey the following cumulative messages about the worldview of advertising:

- *A material world.* The worldview of ads is reduced to what we can see, feel, touch—and buy. In the here-and-now world of advertising, style has become substance. People discover meaning through the acquisition of consumer goods. To illustrate, during the Christmas season, a billboard was posted in the Westfarms Mall in Hartford Connecticut that announced, "This holiday season let's all take a moment to wish for peace on Earth." However, as part of the advertisement, the words "for peace on Earth" were crossed out, replaced with the wish "that you'll be one of the lucky winners to get all your Visa purchases for free."[66]

Product as Identity

In the world of advertising, products serve as symbols of the consumer's identity; you can "show the world who you are" by driving a particular automobile.

Thus, identity has become a disposable commodity. We can become anyone we want on the basis of how we look and what lifestyle we adopt.

Often, what is being advertised is the model in the ad, who personifies cultural ideals. Even if you can't be the model in the ad, you can vicariously assume the *appearance* of the model by purchasing the product.

- *An uncomplicated world.* This world offers simple solutions to complex problems: all issues can be resolved by purchasing the right product. Moreover, the world of advertising is populated by uncomplicated people who find fulfillment through laundry detergents and car wax.
- *World of immediate gratification.* According to cultural historian David Shi, Americans suffer from "acceleration syndrome," in which they have become increasingly impatient:

Waiting has become an intolerable circumstance. We get on an elevator and immediately rush to close the door button for fear of waiting 10 seconds. . . . Technology has helped create products designed to save time: fax machines, express checkout lines, speed dialing, remote controls, overnight mail delivery, e-mail. But in saving time, these products are making us even more impatient.[67]

This sense of urgency is reflected in the worldview of advertising. In commercials, people cannot postpone their gratification for more than 30 seconds. In one McDonald's ad campaign, the merits of the product are sung to the tune "Temptation," enticing us to rush to McDonald's. To rewrite an old adage, "Nothing worth having is worth waiting for."

- *A self-absorbed world.* In this narcissistic world, satisfaction does not stem from helping others but, instead, from helping *yourself* to as many products as you can afford. Why should I buy L'Oréal hair coloring? "Because I'm worth it." Why spend your money at McDonald's? Because "You deserve a break today." A Christmas radio spot for the Cheese Place asks, "Don't we owe ourselves a little self-indulgence? So why not be a little selfish before the gift giving begins?"[68]
- *A competitive world.* Advertising creates a competitive environment, in which consumers are asked to compare themselves to the models who appear in the ads. This barrage of messages can have a dramatic impact on the self-image of young girls and women.

Ironically, even models who have become our standards of female beauty cannot measure up to this ideal. Through digital imaging (a computer manipulation technique), fashion photographers have eliminated models' wrinkles and imperfections. Thus, an image of actress Michelle Pfeiffer in *Esquire Magazine* required extensive retouching—costing over $1,300—before the photograph was considered suitable. A work order for the job included the following directions: "Soften eye-lines, soften smile line, trim chin, remove neck lines, add blush to cheek, add hair on top of head. . . ."[69]

If an icon of beauty like Michelle Pfeiffer cannot live up to her *own* manufactured image, what chance is there for other women in the general population?

- *A class-segmented world.* The world of advertising is divided into two groups: the haves and the have-nots. Advertisers for Nike and Reebok have built a market for expensive basketball shoes by convincing teenagers that these items are the keys to status. Consequently, many young consumers feel pressured to keep up with this fashion trend, despite the inflated cost of the shoe.

- *An optimistic world.* Ultimately, the worldview of advertising is optimistic, in that even the most troublesome problems can be resolved through the acquisition of consumer goods. Ads show happy people celebrating their good fortune; we too can "discover the possibilities" of life and assume control of our own destinies through prudent consumerism. However, as Stephanie Coontz warns,

The flip side of the urge to have it all is the fear of settling for too little. . . . Some individuals turn even leisure into a form of relentless work as they strive to avoid "missing out" on opportunities. Others are terrified by the possibility of "premature" commitment: The sense that all choice is good and more choice is better is a profoundly destabilizing one for interpersonal relationships.[70]

Images of Success

In an attempt to present products in their most positive light, ads associate their products with success. To illustrate, a classic ad campaign, "Where you're going it's Michelob," positions the beer as a metaphor of success in American culture.

In the television version of this ad, a variety of people are headed toward a state of being called "Michelob." The first sequence follows two

---

MEDIA LITERACY TIPS: WORLDVIEW

Questions to ask with regard to *worldview* in advertising include:

- *What kind of world is being depicted in the ad?*
- *What kind of lifestyle is promoted in the ad?*
  Consumers may actually be attracted to the lifestyle depicted in the ad, of which the product is only a small part.
- *What is the role of the product within the worldview of the ad?*
  Imagine the ad without the product to see whether that consumer item is indeed an essential part of that world.
- *If you did not know what product was being promoted, what would you think was being advertised?*
  Consumers who are interested in the primary product may also be compelled to purchase the other consumer items depicted in the ad.

---

characters ascending a mountain (accompanied by a jingle that begins, "You're on your way to the top"). These upwardly mobile characters overcome odds to assume complete control of their environment. The commercial is choreographed in such a way that all of the characters (mountain climbers, business people, a truck driver, a young couple hustling to meet one another, and people at a barbecue) appear active and purposeful. These fast-paced commercials are characterized by a series of quick cuts, signaling that the Michelob lifestyle is exciting and glamorous.

Michelob is equated with self-knowledge, certainty, confidence, and a sense of direction. The music reminds us:

> Where you're going it's Michelob.
> And along the way you know just where you are and where you're going.
> You've always known it.

These characters are all young, beautiful, and physically fit—there is not a beer belly in the crowd. The main figures are always in the middle of the frame, the center of attention. Everyone is watching (and admiring) them. And because the use of the personal pronoun "you" projects the audience into the advertisement, we are by extension watching people adoring us.

The culmination of the characters' quest ("Where they're going") is the earthly equivalent of heaven—success, or at least a frosty Michelob.

Michelob is a just reward for hard work and an acknowledgement of achievement. Thus, as a metaphor for success, Michelob offers an easy solution to complex problems. Even if you are a total failure, you can maintain the *illusion* of success by drinking a Michelob.

The world of advertising is dominated by mainstream culture. Increasingly, however, as advertisers recognize that subcultures represent a substantial revenue stream, many ads now target these subcultures. A Wendy's ad campaign depicted various "fringe" groups like hippies, who foolishly wanted such unsavory food as alfalfa sprouts. This caricature had the trappings of the 1960s hippie—the long hair, mannerisms, and language—but was devoid of the political and social ideology of the counterculture.

Hierarchy of Values

Advertising often associates products with traditional values such as family, Christmas spirit, and patriotism. For instance, some ads equate consumerism with American democracy. For instance, an ad for the Jeep Patriot announces that the vehicle is "outfitted, military-style, as tribute to our brave men and women who have served in this country's armed forces." Presumably, then, the purchase of a Jeep is a patriotic act. However, this appeal to sell products only cheapens the actual values it pretends to espouse. Freedom has been reduced to the freedom to *buy*.

MEDIA LITERACY TIPS: IDEOLOGY & STEREOTYPES IN ADVERTISEMENTS

As you analyze ads, ask the following questions with regard to *ideology* and *stereotype*:

- *To what groups (or subgroups) do the characters belong?*
- *In what settings are they presented?*
  - *Are they the primary or secondary characters?*
  - *Are they at home or at work?*
- *What kinds of products do they promote?*
- *What do the stereotypes reveal about cultural attitudes toward these groups?*

MEDIA LITERACY TIPS: HIERARCHY OF VALUES

Questions to ask in regard to *values hierarchy* include:

- *What manifest values are being used in the promotion?*
- *What connection does the product have with these values?*
- *What latent values seem to be most prized in the advertisement?*

Social Marketing

Social marketing refers to the use of advertising techniques to promote prosocial behavior. To illustrate, one study found that smoking rates declined by 50 percent among 12- to 14-year-olds who were exposed to antismoking media messages, compared with those who didn't view the ads.[71] In Florida, an antismoking ad campaign directed at middle school students resulted in a 54 percent decrease in tobacco use over a two-year period, and a comparable ad campaign targeting high school students resulted in a 24 percent decline in smoking.[72]

By examining media presentations as a cultural text, social marketers can identify the attitudes and concerns of the audience, and then present media messages that influence its intended audience. To illustrate, an examination of popular media programming found that messages dealing with *appearance* can be far more influential with a young audience than *health* messages. Twelve-year-olds don't internalize messages about the likelihood of cancer 60 years from now; however, they do respond to ads in which a member of the opposite sex is turned off because the smoker's breath stinks.[73]

STRUCTURE

Ownership Patterns

In the market-driven American media system, programming is often subordinate to advertising. As an ABC network executive explains, "The network is paying affiliates to carry commercials, not programs. What we are is a distribution system for Procter & Gamble."[74] During radio's golden era of the 1930s, the stars took second billing to the sponsors in many shows, indicating the importance of advertising. Examples included *The Kraft Music Hall (Starring Bing Crosby)* and *The Pepsodent Program (Starring*

Bob Hope). This practice changed only after advertisers realized the power of a name performer to attract an audience.

Significantly, sponsors are once again producing original programming, obtaining final control over all aspects of programming. Toy manufacturers Mattel and Hasbro developed movie versions of Hot Wheels, G.I. Joe, Bionicle toys, Super Soaker squirt guns, and My Little Pony to promote their products. The companies have veto power over the script and the writers. Jim Wagner, senior vice president for entertainment marketing at Mattel, explained, "We need the entertainment to create a brand for us that's long term."[75]

Surprisingly, companies prefer to advertise their products in programs characterized by bland content. As Edward S. Herman and Noam Chomsky explain,

> Advertisers want . . . to avoid programs with serious complexities and disturbing controversies that interfere with the "buying mood." They seek programs that will lightly entertain and thus fit in with the spirit of the primary purpose of program purchases—the dissemination of a selling message.[76]

Moreover, many media outlets support the status quo, fearful of alienating their advertisers. Ronald K. L. Collins cites instances of *self-censorship,* in which reporters have been called off of stories involving advertisers by their editors: "In a confidential survey of 42 real estate editors by the *Washington Journalism Review,* nearly half said publishers and senior editors had prohibited critical coverage of the industry for fear of offending advertisers."[77]

Advertising and Government Regulation

In 1914, the Federal Trade Commission (FTC) was created by the U.S. Congress. The commission is headed by five commissioners appointed by the president. In 1938, the FTC was given the authority to protect consumers from unfair and deceptive advertising. If there is an illegal activity, both the company and the advertising agency may be held responsible.

According to Lee Peeler, associate director of the FTC, advertisements must comply with three basic rules: 1) an ad cannot be deceptive—that is, mislead consumers to their detriment; 2) objective claims must be supported with competent studies; and 3) advertisers are responsible for the reasonable implications of their ads to consumers. Peeler explains, "If an advertiser says 'I didn't really mean to convey that,' well, that doesn't get them off the hook. All of advertising law is based on what consumers take from the ad."[78]

Although Congress has not provided a comprehensive definition of the term "deceptive," the FTC considers the following criteria in determining whether an advertisement is deceptive:

- The nature of the misstatements (i.e., is it likely to deceive someone?)
- The nature of the audience targeted by the ad (e.g., children, senior citizens)
- The significance of the ad to the consumer's decision to purchase the product (i.e., is it likely to play a material role in the decision to buy?)

If a company is found guilty of using deceptive advertising, it may choose to comply voluntarily with the recommendations of the FTC. In this case, a consent order may be filed with the court, in which the company agrees to halt the ad without technically admitting guilt. Another option is to seek a "thorough" (i.e., formal) litigation. The FTC also may simply notify the public that an offense has occurred. Finally, in some cases the FTC may require corrective advertising, whereby the advertiser must for a reasonable amount of time include corrective statements in their advertisements.

In 2009, the FTC obtained 18 administrative orders, 77 court orders amounting to more than $342.2 million in consumer redress, and 23 court judgments for civil penalties in an amount more than $10 million. It also filed 87 new complaints in federal district court and 27 new administrative actions.[79]

The question remains, however: If regulatory policies and enforcement procedures have been in force for more than half a century with regard to deceptive advertising, why do misleading ads continue to appear in the media?

One reason is that the U.S. Federal Trade Commission (FTC) can only respond to formal complaints by consumers.

Moreover, each advertising claim is carefully and cleverly constructed and, as a result, requires scrupulous research. Reporter Natasha Singer observes,

Michael R. Taylor, the Food and Drug Administration's deputy commissioner for foods, declares, as soon as it proves that one claim is misleading, savvy market-types may dream up another. "Going after them one by one with the legal and resource restraints we work under is a little like playing Whac-A-Mole, with one hand tied behind your back."[80]

In addition, due to its limited staff, the FTC is simply overwhelmed by the number of complaints that are made by the public, resulting in a tremendous backlog of cases. As a result, most of the cases of misleading advertising are never brought to the attention of the FTC. Michael Kahn explains,

> More than 90 percent (of allegedly misleading ads) are never brought to anybody's attention. The FTC is a woefully understaffed organization, not set up to handle a large volume of complaints. They are reduced to looking for the worst examples, the ones they can win. For every one they target, there are probably a hundred others out there.[81]

As an example, in 2010 complaints were filed with the Federal Trade Commission that Pom Wonderful, a company that produced pomegranate juice, had insufficient evidence to support claims that its juice reduced the risks of heart disease, prostate cancer, and impotence. Two years after the complaint was filed, the commission finally ruled that Pom Wonderful had insufficient evidence to support their claims.

Moreover, many ads are not misleading in a legal sense, but instead induce the public to buy a product by appealing to the emotions or associating the product with cultural values, attitudes, behaviors, preoccupations, and myths. For example, an ad that depicts a successful (and beautiful) couple driving an expensive automobile is presenting an alluring cultural fantasy that seems harmless and is reinforced throughout entertainment media. Joseph R. Baca, director of the office of compliance at the FDA's Center for Food Safety and Applied Nutrition says, "The thing is, a lot of claims we see out there are puffery. But they don't get to the point where we can call them fake or misleading."[82] But unless consumers apply critical thinking skills to the messages in ads, they can influence the ways that we think about our world and ourselves.

FRAMEWORK: INTRODUCTION

In advertising, the introduction is intended to attract the consumer's attention, lead the consumer into the rest of the ad, and encompass the essence of the product.

Beyond mere identification, a *brand name* creates an immediate impression and establishes the character of a product. For example, "Hamburger Helper" creates a positive, distinctive image, whereas "Cheap Cereal Filler Meat Supplement" puts a less rosy spin on this type of product. Product names like Mr. Clean Magic Eraser are intentionally exotic or mysterious, conveying the message that the product is unexpected, new, and fresh.

Selecting brand names has become more complicated in a global market. Some words may be difficult to recall in a foreign language or suffer from an unflattering translation. For instance, the literal Spanish translation for the Chevrolet Nova is "No go." Worse yet, the name "Coca-Cola" in Chinese was first rendered as "Ke-kou-ke-la," which means "Bite the wax tadpole," or "female horse stuffed with wax," depending on the dialect. Coke was fortunate to find a close phonetic equivalent in Chinese, "ko-kou-ko-le," which is loosely translated as "happiness in the mouth."

As a result, the strongest trademarks are often *neologisms*—words that have been invented for products. The look and sound of these neologisms are designed to encompass the essence of the product. For instance, when Amtrak unveiled its new high-speed train, the *Acela Express,* to serve the Northeastern United States, Amtrak president George D. Warrington explained that this neologism called to mind a new travel experience for the railroad:

> Acela is more than just a name for Amtrak's new high speed trains, Acela is a brand representing a whole new way of doing business. A combination of acceleration and excellence, Acela means high speed and high quality—we are changing the journey for every customer on every train with faster trip times, comfortable amenities and highly personalized service.[83]

At times, a brand name is designed to send a false impression about the product. For instance, "Hostess Cupcakes Lite" claims to contain one-third fewer calories than its regular brand. However, a close examination of the label reveals that the "lite" cupcakes are actually one-third *smaller* than the original version. One can easily imagine a "superlite" concept, with 50 percent fewer calories, in which the package contains *one* cupcake.

A catchy *slogan* is also integral to the success of an ad. Five times as many people read the headline than the copy in the body of the ad. Memorable slogans are clever, rhythmical, and alliterative, and manage to capture the intended character, or spirit of the product.

For instance, Nike's slogan is a very sophisticated and effective motto, even though the name of the product (Nike) is never mentioned. The slogan lauds athletic effort and tells us that we can succeed despite the odds (or excuses). Buoyed by this pep talk, we are prepared to achieve our goals. Ultimately, the slogan is a not-so-subtle imperative to buy the product: "Just do it."

As with brand names, advertising slogans may assume unanticipated meanings in different cultures. For instance, when Kentucky Fried Chicken first advertised in China, it did not realize that its slogan, "Finger-lickin' good," was translated to "Eat your fingers off"—not a very appetizing prospect.

Labels can influence consumers' perception of a product. For instance, in one study, college students estimated that a 60-piece package of mixed nuts, labeled *Medium*, weighed 64.03 grams; however, students speculated that the *same* package, which was labeled *Small*, was nearly 2 percent smaller (51.78 grams).[84]

Finally, consumers are drawn to distinctive *packaging*, as though the *product* was unique. For instance, Classico pasta sauces are packaged in a mason jar, which suggests that the product is homemade. Thomas Hine explains,

[The ornate Classico jar] encourages people to taste the sauce not as the common commodity it has become but rather as an expression of a place, with its own culture and distinctive ingredients. It makes people feel they are not simply opening a jar of sauce but doing something just a little more special.[85]

Hine points out that the Classico package also provides a sense of membership and identity for the consumer:

It's flattering to the buyer: "We know you've traveled, and we know you don't buy industrial tomato sauce, that you're a more discriminating buyer and are willing to pay a price of about 40 to 50 percent more than Ragu."[86]

Indeed, some old products are repackaged for a new or emerging market. For instance, in 2007, R. J. Reynolds introduced a new line of Camel cigarettes for women, in which the only differences were the name of the brand and the package. Stuart Elliott explains,

Camel No. 9 has a name that evokes women's fragrances like Chanel No. 19, as well as a song about romance, "Love Potion No. 9." Camel No. 9 signals its intended buyers with subtler cues like its colors, a hot-pink fuchsia and a minty-green teal; its slogan, "Light and luscious"; and the flowers that surround the packs in magazine ads.[87]

Because companies repackage products to meet the emerging needs of its customers, packaging can also provide insight into cultural changes. For instance, Campbell's "Soup for One" was developed in response to the increasing number of people who live alone, as well as those whose hectic schedules prevent them from sitting down for the traditional family meal.

Illogical Premise

Ads that appear perfectly reasonable on the surface actually may be based on an illogical premise. The ad campaign "Newport Lights—Alive with Pleasure" provides an excellent example. Given the medical evidence about the health hazards of smoking (which by law must be cited in the ads), this claim could hardly be more absurd.

FRAMEWORK: EXPLICIT CONTENT

When a product is unique, clearly superior to its competition, or of public benefit, the advertiser's task is easy. However, if a product is indistinguishable from other brands on the market, the advertiser must devise strategies that make the product appear alluring and distinctive. This task is even more of a challenge when a product is harmful to the public, such as alcohol or cigarettes.

Some ads present an *incomplete* or *distorted* message in order to present a brand in the best possible light. To illustrate, the FDA issued a statement that advertisements for COX-2 drugs Celebrex and Bextra are misleading by failing to disclose the side effects of the drugs. The FDA cited five print and television ads for making "unsubstantiated effectiveness claims."

The following inconsistencies, fallacies, and incongruities may appear in advertisements:

- *The big promise* is a claim that is far beyond the capabilities of the product. As an example, Axe has emerged as the top-selling deodorant

---

MEDIA LITERACY TIPS: THE BIG PROMISE

When examining ads, consider the following questions with regard to the *Big Promise:*

- *What promises does the ad make with regard to the product?*
- *Which promises can the product reasonably keep?*
- *Which promises are beyond the capabilities of the product?*

in less than four years by promising to help men attract women. One ad on the Axe Web site begins with a shot of an empty beach. Suddenly, a mob of bikini-clad women charge madly toward a man who has applied Axe deodorant. The ad slogan suggests a cause/effect relationship between applying the deodorant and attracting women: "Spray More. Get More. The Axe Effect."

- *Hyperbole.* In a country of seemingly limitless resources, Americans magnify events and locations for emphasis and dramatic effect. The American storytelling tradition is replete with tales that rely upon exaggeration or absurd overstatement. Examples can be found in such tales as George Washington's coin toss across the Delaware River and the legend of Davy Crockett, who, according to the tale, "Killed him a bear when he was only three."

  This literary device also capitalizes on the American competitive spirit. Everything we do (or own) must be the best. However, these advertising claims (e.g., "Milwaukee's finest beer") are merely a statement of opinion.

- *Simile* is a literary device that involves a direct comparison between two things. Such comparisons generally are introduced by *like* or *as.* According to William Lutz, similes are employed "whenever advertisers want you to stop thinking about the product and start thinking about something bigger, better, or more attractive than the product."[88] For instance, a wine that claims "It's like taking a trip to France" is designed induce the consumer into romantic reverie about Paris instead of thinking about the taste of the wine.

- *Parity statements* refer to ads that are worded in a way that suggests that a product is unique, when what the ad is *actually* stating is that the product is indistinguishable from its competition. As an example, Rick Berkoff points out that the Personna Double II slogan ("There is no finer razor made. Period.") could be rephrased as follows: "Personna Double II: It's no better than its competition. Period."[89]

- *Extraneous inclusion* occurs when superfluous information appears in an ad that creates an impression about a product that is not true. For instance, the FTC filed a claim against Winston Cigarettes for an ad campaign in which the company claimed that its product had "no additives." Lee Peeler explained, "The ads left the implication that no additives made Winston safer than other cigarettes, and that's not true."[90] The terms of the settlement required that the ads include the disclaimer, "No additives in our tobacco does NOT mean a safer cigarette."

- *Syllogism* is a subtle line of reasoning that seems true but is actually false or deceptive. For example, a magazine ad for California Almonds displays the following copy:
  - Roasted almonds are tasty
  - Roasted almonds are healthy
  - So, "whenever the urge to snack comes out, make sure California Almonds are in."

The logic of the coy shifts from promoting the *product* (almonds) to a particular *brand* (California Almonds). The question to be asked, then, is: Even if you believe the first part of this syllogism, couldn't you then buy another brand of almonds?

- *Unfinished statements* make implied claims that advertisers are unable to stand behind. Instead, they leave it to the consumer to complete the statement. Lutz provides the following examples:
  - Batteries that "last *up to* twice as long."
  - Twice as long as what?
  - "You can be sure if it's Westinghouse."
  - Just exactly what we can be sure of is never explained.
  - "Magnavox gives you more."
  - This slogan never details what you get more of.[91]
- *Qualifier words* contradict the essential meaning of the concept being expressed. Some qualifier words that create the illusion of quality in fact negate this claim. For instance, the term "chocolate flavored" candy suggests that you are eating chocolate, when in reality you are ingesting artificial ingredients that simulate the taste of chocolate. In print ads, qualifier words are often placed away from the visual flow or appear in the same color as the background to minimize its impact. And in television commercials, phrases such as "some restrictions apply" are either quickly flashed on the TV screen or uttered with inhuman rapidity by the announcer, insinuating that this information is inconsequential.

  Lutz has identified a series of qualifier words commonly found in advertisements:
  - *Help*

  The next time you see an ad for a cold medicine that promises that it "helps relieve cold symptoms fast," don't rush out to buy it. Ask yourself what this claim is really saying. . . . "Help" only means to aid or assist, nothing more. It does not mean to conquer, stop, eliminate, end, solve, heal, cure, or anything else. But once the ad says "help," it can say just about anything after that because "help" qualifies everything coming after it. The trick is that . . . you forget the word "help" and concentrate only on the dramatic claim. You read into the ad a message that the ad does not contain. More importantly, the advertiser is not responsible for the claim that you read into the ad, even though the advertiser wrote the ad so you would read that claim into it.[92]

○ *Virtually*

Lutz warns that claims like "virtually spotless" are deceptive. "After all, what does 'virtually' mean? It means 'in essence or effect, although not in fact.'" Look at that definition again. "Virtually" means *not in fact.* It does *not* mean "almost" or "just about the same as," or anything else.[93]

○ *New and Improved*

An advertiser can present a product as "new" if there has been a "material functional change" in the item. In the same way, a product advertised as "improved" suggests that it has been "made better." However, ads frequently make such claims for products that feature only slight modifications (e.g., changing the shape of a stick deodorant).

MEDIA LITERACY TIPS: EXPLICIT CONTENT

A Consumer Guide to Advertising invites the public to consider the following questions in regard to the *explicit content* of ads:

- *Can the advertiser support its claims?*
  Be wary of any claims, and search for independent confirmation, particularly for large purchases like automobiles and appliances.
- *After watching the ad, do you really know what the product is or does?*
  As amusing as some ads can be, do they provide us with anything more than a brand name? What about price, value, size, shape, and nutritional content? A wise consumer . . . focuses on all of the information needed to make an informed choice.
- *What's not in the ad?*
  Sometimes the most important information is not even mentioned in the ad. It could be that the 15- or 30-second spot is just too tight to fit everything in, but it could also be a deliberate evasion or half-truth on the part of the advertiser. . . . [K]now what you're getting before [making a purchase].

Implicit Content

Nowhere is consequence portrayed as more direct and immediate than in the world of advertising. The relationship between significant events in the narrative is clear. Ads dramatize how products fulfill needs and solve personal problems. Ads show smiling, satisfied consumers who have benefited from the purchase of the product.

However, the long-term consequences to consumers generally go unmentioned in these ads. For instance, the calories and cholesterol contained in fast food over time make American children the most obese in the world. Credit card holders, who accrue a massive debt, do not realize that they eventually have to pay for their purchases (with hefty interest charges).

Genre

Advertisements often are modeled after established genres in order to be instantly recognizable. For instance, some TV infomercials for health products and self-motivation materials mirror the format of the talk show, complete with host, desk, audience, and a "guest" who hawks the product.

At the same time, advertising can be considered a genre of its own, with a distinct structure, plot, and characters.

Formulaic Structure

Advertisements generally operate within the format of order/chaos/order:

- *A problem is quickly introduced that throws the character's world into chaos.*
- *The product is presented as a means of solving the problem.*
- *Order is restored through use of the product. This conclusion is geared to inspire the consumer to action.*

As mentioned earlier, some ad campaigns first *create* a problem and then offer a solution—in the form of their product. Thus, in the classic Wisk ad campaign discussed earlier, "Ring around the Collar" was not an area of tremendous concern until the ad brought this situation to the attention of the public.

Print ads offer a variation of this formula—the initial problem is left entirely to our imaginations, with the visuals emphasizing the restoration of order. Thus, in ads for beauty products, the audience is asked to believe that the product has transformed an ordinary-looking woman into the attractive model depicted in the ad.

Formulaic Plot

In television commercials, the product is generally central to the narrative, the latent message being that the product will play an integral role in our lives as well.

One type of ad campaign features a formulaic repetition of the plot. All of the ads adhere to the same basic plot line; only the nuances of the story (such as the setting or characters) differ. For instance, the Charmin toilet paper ad campaign, featuring Mr. Whipple, always replays the same basic plot:

> Several women pause while grocery shopping to squeeze the Charmin, commenting that they cannot resist the temptation because Charmin is so "squeezably soft." Mr. Whipple appears and, warning the ladies not to squeeze the Charmin, confiscates the goods. However, to Mr. Whipple's embarrassment, the ladies point out that he, too, is fondling the toilet paper—a testament to the irresistible softness of Charmin.

Between 1964 and 1985, Charmin's agency, D'Arcy Masius Benton & Bowles Communications, produced over 500 Mr. Whipple spots—all with the same formulaic plot. This approach was so successful that Mr. Whipple was brought out of retirement in 1999 for another round of commercials, in which he explained that he "couldn't retire" because he had to tell the public about Charmin.

Characters

In order to compensate for the limited time and space in which to present their message, advertising relies on stock characters such as the Harried Housewife, the Out-of-It Husband, and the Sex Siren. These stereotypes evoke instant recognition by the audience by drawing upon a common cultural understanding and consensus.

Ads commonly use costumes, props, and sets to send subtle cues about the characters. For instance, ads that feature actors who are wearing white lab coats convey the message that the advice of these "medical experts" should be heeded.

MEDIA LITERACY TIPS: ADVERTISING CONVENTIONS

The following questions are useful in considering the role of *advertising conventions:*

- *What conventions are used in the ad?*
- *How are these conventions used in the ad?*
- *What messages are these conventions designed to convey?*
- *How are these conventions used to promote the product?*

FRAMEWORK: CONCLUSION

Advertisements do not always follow logically from their initial premise. As discussed earlier, ads frequently conclude with a *Big Promise:* the product will bring you happiness or success. For example, in a Head and Shoulders ad, a young man finds romantic fulfillment after washing his hair. At the very least, advertising exaggerates the importance of a product. For instance, the ads in which a couple jump in the air to celebrate their purchase of a Toyota would appear to be something of an overreaction.

PRODUCTION ELEMENTS

In advertising, as with all media formats, style reinforces messages. The originality of a production suggests that the product is unique as well and encourages the audience to see (and think about) the product in a new way. Production elements can also create a mood that affects how we react to the product. And in some cases, style may make a product look better than it is.

Editing

Copywriters for print advertising strive to keep their messages brief, concise, and simple. According to John Caples, ad copywriters write to the level of a sixth-grade student.[94] At the same time, an effective copywriter "creat[es] a word picture that makes crystal-clear the specific advantage of every feature."[95] Variety in sentence structure avoids monotony and creates a fresh, energetic mood that will carry over to the product. Caples observes that short sentences "put speed and excitement into your ad" and move the audience to action, while long sentences can furnish useful explanations about the product.[96]

In television ads, editing can condense a vast amount of information into a limited time frame. Directors are faced with the challenge of cutting up to 16,000 feet of raw footage to 45 feet for a 30-second ad. Because each second becomes critical, an enormous amount of attention is devoted to the selection and arrangement of images.

For instance, in a 30-second ad selling Kodak camera equipment, a series of photographs encompass the entire lifetime of a woman.

Moreover, the soundtrack and picture are commonly speeded up by as much as 25 percent. Dr. James MacLachlan contends that this technique, which generally goes unnoticed by the audience, increases the unaided recall of the content by as much as 40 percent.[97]

The "MTV" style of quick cuts is also geared to attract and maintain the attention of the audience. This editing technique generates a sense of excitement, sending the latent message that the product is exciting as well. In addition, this style is considered avant-garde, which indirectly comments on the "hippness" of the product.

Color

The selection of bright colors and dramatic color contrasts attracts the attention of the consumer—which is the principle goal of an advertisement. But in addition, the choice of colors sends other subtle messages about the product. Otto Kleppner observes,

> Color talks its own psychological language: To make a drink look cool, there will be plenty of blue in the background; to make a room look warm (for heating advertisements), there will be plenty of red in the background; springtime suggests light colors, and autumn the dark tones. Thus a clue to the choice of the dominating color may often be found in the mood in which the product is being shown.[98]

The choice of colors may also be tied to the psychographic profile of the target audience. John Lyons points out that commercials targeting young girls are often shot through pink and green filters to create a warm, romantic, and traditionally "feminine" tone that subtly influences young girls' response to the product.[99]

Scale

The magnification of images can be a very deceptive ad technique. For example, extreme close-ups make small products look big. As a result, toys that look impressive and durable on screen may in fact be small and flimsy.

Relative Position

The layout of an advertisement can dictate the response of the audience to the product. In Western cultures, a person glancing at an ad is most likely to focus initially on the upper-right-hand portion of the page.

Advertising directors often employ the technique of *structured motion,* in which the layout leads the audience through an ad in a predetermined way. Otto Kleppner explains,

> The art is to attract attention at the head of the page, and by having optical stepping-stones leading from there to the end, hold the ad together and lead the reader through the copy. Flow may also be helped by the line of direction of the artwork, sweeping across the page. It may be helped by *gaze motion,* that is, having the people in the picture look toward or, perhaps with other elements of the ad, lead the eye to the center of attention.[100]

To illustrate, every summer TV ads for Lipton's iced tea appear in which beautiful young people frolic around a swimming pool. Just as our eyes are drawn to these alluring male and female bodies, these images dissolve and are replaced by shots of the product and the brand label.

Ads frequently position their products as the center of the world of the commercial, suggesting that it is an essential part of the situation presented in the advertisement. As mentioned earlier, in beer ads, the product is placed in the middle of the activity. Consequently, these ads convey the message that beer not only accompanies a good time, but it is impossible to have fun without a provision of beer.

Ads often depict situations in which the person modeling the product is the center of attention—presumably due to the product that is being advertised. The advertiser encourages the audience to identify with this principal figure, so that the audience vicariously receives approval by using the product.

MEDIA LITERACY TIPS: EFFECTIVE AD LAYOUTS

Otto Kleppner outlines the following criteria for effective ad layouts:

- *Is it arresting?*
- *Is it clear?*
- *Is it orderly?*
- *Is the most important idea given the most important attention?*
- *Does it invite reading?*
- *If the trademark is needed to identify the product, is it sufficiently visible?*
- *Does the layout leave the desired impression about the product?*[101]

Movement

In television commercials, movement draws the attention of the consumer to specific features of the product. Slow motion enables the audience to scrutinize the product demonstration, adding to the dramatic emphasis of the ad.

Motion can also set the *tone* for the promotion. Motion can lend a dynamic feel to the presentation, giving the impression that the product is exciting and glamorous. Many advertisers now favor the "shaky camera technique," in which the camera jumps around, much like in an amateur home video. In contrast to the slick style found in conventional TV spots, this style produces a genuine, "just folks" impression. Thornton C. Lockwood found that the shaky camera technique employed in an AT&T "business reality" ad campaign "underscored the stress and discomfort the characters experienced" by not using AT&T.[102]

The *direction* of the movement also conveys messages. For instance, in a television spot for *Sports Illustrated,* a sports nut leans toward the camera to tell us about "a great deal" if we subscribe to the magazine. This movement suggests a familiarity and confidentiality with the audience designed to inspire trust.

Word Choice

Connotative Words

Many of the most common and persuasive words used in advertising fall into the following categories:

- *Commencement* words suggest immediacy, importance, and a sense of urgency:
  - *Introducing*
  - *Announcing*
  - *Now*
  - *Suddenly*
- *Convenience* words appeal to the consumers' interest in products that promise to make their lives easier:
  - *Easy*
  - *Quick*
- *Transformational* words are declarations about the degree to which the product will change your life:
  - *Sensational*
  - *Startling*
  - *Amazing*
  - *Remarkable*
  - *Miracles*
  - *Magic*
  - *Revolutionary*
  - *Improvement*
- *Directives* instruct the consumer what to do:
  - *Hurry*
  - *Compare*
- *Customer advantage* words offer consumers feelings of control, vision, wisdom, and superiority:
  - *Bargain*
  - *Offer*
  - *Free*
  - *Sale*

But upon close inspection, connotative words can convey a *false* impression. For instance, processed foods with healthy sounding names such as Lean Cuisine and Healthy Choice frozen dinners send messages about the health benefits of the product. But according to *Guiding Stars,* a system that rates the nutritional value of food on a scale of zero to three stars, these brands received *no* stars.[103]

Code words

Code words are terms that have a particular significance for the target audience. For instance, Audi, an import luxury sedan, has been a longtime

---

MEDIA LITERACY TIPS: CONNOTATIVE WORDS

A Consumer Guide to Advertising cautions the public about the following *connotative words* commonly found in promotional campaigns for food products:

Natural
If you think this product is automatically as good for you as fresh broccoli, think again. Read the label: on one box of cake mix "natural" included modified food starches, mono- and diglycerides, gum arabic, etc. (The one exception is meat and poultry labels, where natural means "minimally processed.")

Dietetic
This usually means low in sodium and does not necessarily mean reduced calories.

Light or Lite
Could mean anything, and may mean nothing. Don't assume that it's lower in calories unless it's on a meat label.

No sugar
Yes, but it could have sugar substitutes such as corn sweeteners. Watch for the words "containing glucose, sucrose, fructose, and dextrose."

No artificial ingredients
What's artificial to you may not be artificial to a food manufacturer! There are no laws that prevent ingredients such as "hydrolyzed vegetable protein" (which involves chemicals) from being included in products listed as containing "no artificial ingredients."[104]

---

sponsor of NBC radio's *Wall Street Report.* "Audiwatch" spokesperson Amy O'Connor urged her audience to "put Audi on our *shortlist.*" This corporate code word (meaning a select group that has survived an elimination process) is both familiar and appealing to the upscale audience Audi is trying to attract. Indeed, identifying these code words can be a useful method of discovering the intended audience for advertisements.

Connotative Image

What kinds of images are most prevalent in advertising?

The public is fascinated by pictures of *people*—particularly young, attractive women and babies—and animals. Images that emphasize the *rewards* of a product are also common. For instance, real estate ads often show customers either learning about the sale of their home or walking into their new house.

A Consumer Guide to Advertising suggests that the public consider whether the visual images in an ad correspond with the words:

> By playing with . . . visuals, the text can be absolutely accurate, but the image in the mind's eye may suggest something very different. . . . Be suspicious. Don't rely on visual images alone to provide you with accurate information. Listen carefully to the words, read the labels and then decide if this product or service is for you.[105]

Advertisers who have ignored the *cultural context* of a connotative image often suffer disastrous results. In one famous example, Nike Air Jordan Basketball shoes sent to stores throughout the Middle East were inscribed with the word "Air" on the heel of each shoe. Unfortunately, the stylized script was nearly identical to the configuration of the Arabic script for "Allah." Offended by what they considered a sign of disrespect to the Muslim religion, the Council on American-Islamic Relations threatened to organize a boycott among the world's one billion Muslims. Nike subsequently apologized for this unintended slight and pulled the shoes from distribution.

Sound

Music serves a variety of functions in advertising. Music establishes a tone (e.g., solemn, dramatic, whimsical, elegant) that instructs the audience on the appropriate response to the advertising message. In addition, music can generate feelings of excitement, joy, and pleasure, which advertisers hope will be transferred to the product. Moreover, the rhythm and repetition of melodies can trigger the consumer's recall of a product at a later point.

Music can make an ad not merely *palatable* but *enjoyable.* In fact, the 1970s jingle "I'd Like to Buy the World a Coke" went on to become a popular hit single. The entertainment value of the music makes it more likely that the audience will hear the commercial message.

Advertisers customize the soundtrack of an ad to its target audience. For instance, after Ford Motor Company's marketing research discovered that pickup truck buyers are likely to be country music fans,[106] Ford truck ads often featured a country music soundtrack to attract its intended market.

Using popular songs enables advertisers to transfer the popularity of a hit tune to their product. A related approach involves using a popular tune, but inserting new lyrics with a commercial message. For instance, a classic Toyota commercial substituted the following lyrics for the Monkees' signature hit "(We're the) Monkees":

Hey hey, we're Toyota
Toyotathon time of the year
Savings are better than ever,
Come on down today.

In some cases, advertisers hire "sound alike" artists to add to the original flavor of the spot. However, this strategy can backfire; in 1989, Bette Midler was awarded $400,000 in a suit against the New York advertising agency of Young and Rubicam for using one of her former backup singers to imitate Midler's rendition of "Do You Want to Dance" in a Ford Mercury commercial.[107]

The cost of purchasing the rights to popular commercial songs can be prohibitive—up to $250,000 for a one-year license.[108] Using *original* music and lyrics can also be an expensive undertaking, but a song that has been especially commissioned for the ad is sure to complement the messages presented through dialogue, voiceover, and visuals. In addition, an original jingle sends a message about the uniqueness of the product.

Older songs in the public domain can serve as an inexpensive way to set the tone for locally produced ads. Because the copyright law has lapsed, this music is free. These "generic" songs can be found in most local libraries. However, because this music appears so frequently in commercials, there is no hope of any product identification with the music.

Background sound dramatizes the commercial message by simulating the sounds commonly associated with the product. For instance, the sound of a can opening, a carbonated beverage being poured into a glass, and people talking and laughing can contribute to the verisimilitude of a beer ad. When ads are produced in a studio, the media communicator uses *sound effects* to recreate the noises that the audience would expect as part of the environment of the ad. However, finding sound effects that capture the more elusive qualities of the product can present a challenge for the audio engineer. For instance, discussing the production of an ad for G.E. Halogen Headlights, White explains,

When the G.E. Halogen Headlight was first turned on in the graphic picture, we highlighted it with a burst of white sound (an effect quite peculiar to a synthesizer). This burst was followed with a synthetic french horn statement, which became the musical logo for the head-light. This horn statement was reiterated three times as the G.E. headlight was mentioned in the voice track.[109]

CASE STUDY

Janis Valdes, a faculty member in the Department of Communications and Journalism at Webster University, conducted the following media analysis of a print advertisement for Viagra, using selected keys to interpreting media messages:

A media literacy analysis of a Viagra print ad using the keys of con-text, framework, and production values provides insight into American popular culture's preoccupation with youth and fulfillment of the romantic ideal. Within this context, the Viagra ad is a modern fairy tale—Cinderella or perhaps Sleeping Beauty is more to the point: a mature couple restored to youthful vigor and living happily ever after, thanks to the magical powers of Viagra.

Although demographics reveal that seniors are a growing majority in the U.S., media messages bombard us with youth-worship. Americans' obsession with aging has created an enormous market for the fountain of youth in all its guises: face lifts, tummy tucks, wrinkle creams, flashy sports cars, and all manner of remedies to increase energy, memory, and sexual function. This cultural context sets the stage for Pfizer Pharmaceuticals to introduce Viagra in December 1997.

A full-page ad in the March 1999 issue of *Condé Nast Traveler* features a handsome, gray-templed man in a well-cut dark suit danc-ing with a slender, silver-haired woman who is dressed in a gold dress and jacket ensemble. The couple is dancing in what, on close inspection, appears to be the foyer of a European castle. The couple's elegant appearance, combined with the setting, create an ambiance of affluence and privilege.

The background is in soft focus, bathed in a golden light that sug-gests sunset and romance. The dancers themselves represent a very traditional notion of a romantic couple. The man is considerably taller than the woman, so that he occupies the upper, or dominant space in the photo. His strength is evident as he easily dips his partner with just one arm, his other hand free. The woman's foot and head are slightly blurred with motion, capturing the spontaneity of the moment. Her husband is literally "sweeping her off her feet" in this romantic place. A woman discreetly descending the stairs in the center left of the background provides an audience for this rendezvous, shifting it to a public setting, which hearkens back to the notion of a ball. Here the romantic ideal has been extended to include those over the age of 25. Nowhere do we find a trace of the unpleasant realities that aging often brings. In fact, the only hint of the couple's maturity is their hair color. In this world, age brings wealth and prestige, the freedom to do as one pleases, and power—the power to buy back one's potency, in pill form if need be. The phrase "Let the dance begin" may spark memories for a generation raised on romantic tunes like "Dancing in the Dark," "I Could Have Danced All Night," and "Shall We Dance?" "The dance" can be interpreted as a metaphor for sex, couched in delicate terms to avoid offending the intended older audience. But the big promise of the ad is that Viagra will restore not just the sex but the romance to the relationship.

The image of the spontaneous and glamorous couple in the ad trades on the romantic ideals the audience was raised on and the fairy tale ending we'd all like to believe in. In keeping with the romantic illusion of the ad, no patient information is included in the text. The inclusion of hard facts about sexual dysfunction and possible side effects would spoil the romantic mood. Ultimately, the ad is not selling a pharmaceutical product, but the most sought-after commodity of all—a return to the romance of youth.[110]

NOTES

1. Marketing Charts Staff, "U.S. Ad Spending Grew by 3% in 2012," MailChimp for Agencies, March 12, 2013, http://www.marketingcharts.com/wp/televi-sion/us-ad-spend-up-3-in-2012-27707/.
2. Marketing Charts Staff, "Primetime TV Hour Includes 41% Commercials," MailChimp for Agencies, June 12, 2009, http://www.marketingcharts.com/television/primetime-tv-hour-includes-41-commercials-9434/.
3. Frank Baker, "Media Use Statistics," Media Literacy Clearinghouse, http://www.frankwbaker.com.
4. "Ad Nauseum," *Mother Jones* 32.1 (January/February 2007).

5. Ibid.

6. Ed Papazian, ed., *TV Dimensions '93* (New York: Media Dynamics, 1993), 343.

7. Tony Schwartz, *The Responsive Chord* (Garden City, NY: Anchor Books, 1973), 69–71.

8. Charles H. Patti and Sandra E. Moriarty, *The Making of Effective Advertising* (Englewood Cliffs, NJ: Prentice-Hall), 63.

9. Baker, "Media Use Statistics."

10. Patti and Moriarty, *The Making of Effective Advertising*, 62.

11. David Segal, "Riding the Hashtag in Social Media Marketing," *New York Times*, November 2, 2013.

12. Ibid.

13. Tom Zeller, Jr., "Gaming the Search Engine, in a Political Season," *New York Times*, November 6, 2006: C-3.

14. Eric Wilson, "Social Shopping: Everybody Wants In," *New York Times*, March 22, 2012.

15. Hooper White, *How to Produce an Effective TV Commercial* (Chicago: Crain Books, 1981), 139.

16. Tim Johnson, "A Man Known Everywhere Except Home: Colombian Coffee Has a Face, and It's Still Juan Valdez," *The Denver Post*, August 15, 1999: M-12.

17. *Adbusters Quarterly* (Summer 1993): 30.

18. Philip Burton and Scott Purvis, *Which Ad Pulled Best?* (Chicago, IL: NTC Publishing, 1988), 41.

19. Ibid., 31.

20. Andrew Adam Newman, "In Dallas, Commercial Radio without Commercials," *New York Times*, April 23, 2007: C-2.

21. John Caples, *How to Make Your Advertising Make Money* (Englewood Cliffs, NJ: Prentice Hall, 1983), 311.

22. Otto Kleppner, *Advertising Procedure*, 6th ed. (Englewood Cliffs, NJ: Prentice-Hall, 1976), 429–34.

23. Bill Carter, "DVR Use One Factor in Networks' Low Ratings," *New York Times*, December 2, 2012.

24. Eliot Van Buskirk, "Many DVR Users Watch Ads Anyway; Even Fast-Forwarders Are Exposed," *Wired*, November 2, 2009, http://www.wired.com/business/2009/11/many-dvr-users-watch-ads-anyway-even-fast-forwarders-are-exposed/.

25. Ibid.

26. Abe Sauer, "Announcing the 2012 Brandcameo Product Placement Award Winners," *Brandchannel*, February 13, 2012, http://www.brandchannel.com/home/post/2012/02/13/2012-brandcameo-product-placement-awards-021312.aspx.

27. CNBC, "Primetime Shows with the Most Product Placement," http://www.cnbc.com/id/45884892/page/11.

28. "How Sweet It Is," *Time,* July 26, 1982: 39.
29. CNBC, "Primetime Shows with the Most Product Placement."
30. Shelly Freierman, "Most Wanted: Popular Demand Products on TV," *New York Times,* April 17, 2006.
31. Sharon Waxman, "Hollywood Unions Object to Product Placement on TV," *New York Times,* November 14, 2005.
32. Ibid.
33. Sauer, "Announcing the 2012 Brandcameo Product Placement Award Winners."
34. CNBC, "Primetime Shows with the Most Product Placement."
35. Rosie Baker, "Apple Dominates Film Product Placement," *Marketing Week,* February 25, 2011, http://www.marketingweek.co.uk.
36. Ibid.
37. Ibid.
38. "Advertising Spending Online Expected to Surpass Print This Year," *Los Angeles Times,* January 20, 2012, http://latimesblogs.latimes.com/technology/2012/01/advertising-spending-online-expected-to-surpass-print-this-year.html.
39. Audrey Watters, "Pew Study Finds 58% of Americans Research Online First before Buying," *Readwrite,* September 29, 2010, http://readwrite.com/2010/09/29/pew_study_finds_58_of_americans_research_online_fi#awesm=~oq6X7OCO28rGL1.
40. Eric Effron, "The Big Blur," *Brill's Content,* February 1999: 44–5.
41. KISSmetrics, a Blog about Analytics, Marketing and Testing, "The Viral Marketing Cheat Sheet," http://blog.kissmetrics.com/viral-marketing-cheatsheet.
42. Ibid.
43. Bernice Kanner, "Silliness Sells," *St. Louis Post-Dispatch,* February 2, 1997: E-1.
44. C. Whan Park and Deborah MacInnis, "Brand Attachment and Brand Attitude Strength: Conceptual and Empirical Differentiation of Two Critical Brand Equity Drivers," Marshall School of Business, University of Southern California, November 11, 2010. Choong@marshall.usc.edu, http://www.marshall.usc.edu/assets/135/22824.pdf.
45. Stuart Elliott, "The '60s as the Good Old Days," *New York Times,* December 10, 2007.
46. H. G. Eysenck, ed., *Encyclopedia of Psychology* (New York: Herder and Herder, 1972), 247.
47. Patti and Moriarty, *The Making of Effective Advertising,* 55.
48. Thornton K. Lockwood, "Behind the Emotion in 'Slice of Death' Advertising," *Business Marketing* (September 1988): 88.
49. Everette Dennis and John Merrill, *Media Debates* (New York: Longman, 1991), 182.

50. Patti and Moriaty, *The Making of Effective Advertising,* 20.
51. Somini Sengupta, "What You Didn't Post, Facebook May Still Know," *New York Times,* March 25, 2013.
52. Otto Kleppner, *Advertising Procedure,* 6th ed. (Englewood Cliffs, NJ: Prentice-Hall, Inc., 1976), 300.
53. Sengupta, "What You Didn't Post, Facebook May Still Know."
54. Tanzina Vega, "The New Algorithm of Web Marketing," *New York Times,* November 15, 2012.
55. Natasha Singer, "Your Online Attention, Bought in an Instant," *New York Times,* November 17, 2012.
56. Miguel Helft, "Google to Offer Ads Based on Interests," *New York Times,* March 11, 2009.
57. Sengupta, "What You Didn't Post, Facebook May Still Know."
58. John Leo, "Hostility among the Ice Cubes," *U.S. News & World Report,* July 15, 1991: 18.
59. Bob Hebert, "Why Aren't We Shocked?" *New York Times,* October 16, 2006.
60. Julia Smillie, interview by author, March 16, 1992, St. Louis, Missouri.
61. Gina Kolata, "Extreme Hygiene; Kill All the Bacteria!" *New York Times,* January 7, 2001: D-1.
62. Edgar R. Jones, *Those Were the Good Old Days: A Happy Look at American Advertising* (New York: Simon and Schuster, 1959), 349–53.
63. Julie Bosman, "Hey, Just Because He's Divorced Doesn't Mean He Can't Sell Things," *New York Times,* August 17, 2006: C-6.
64. Ibid.
65. Jennifer Steinhauer, "That's Not a Skim Latte. It's a Way of Life," *New York Times,* March 21, 1999.
66. Thomas B. Goodkind, "Ultimate Offensive Advertising," the Connecticut Media Literacy Project, November 2000, http://www.medialit.uconn.edu.
67. Diane Toops, "Beyond Instant Gratification," HighBeam Research, May 1, 2001, www.highbeam.com/doc/1G1-75834057.html.
68. KWMU, 90.7 FM, St. Louis, Missouri, December 20, 1991.
69. F. Jacobson and Laurie Ann Mazur, *Marketing Madness* (Boulder, CO: Westview Press, 1993), 198.
70. Stephanie Coontz, *The Way We Never Were* (New York: Basic Books, 1992), 176–7.
71. Richard A. Knox, "On Teen Smoking, Ads Work Both Ways," *Boston Globe,* March 1, 2000: B-1.
72. Martin Merzer and Lesley Clark, "Fewer Teens Smoking since State Began Tough Campaign," *Miami Herald,* March 2, 2000: A-1.
73. Art Silverblatt and Sally Howald, unpublished study, Webster University (2005), St. Louis, Missouri.

74. R. Collins, *Dictating Content* (Washington, DC: Center for the Study of Commercialism, 1992), 77.
75. Evelyn Nussenbaum, "Coming Soon to a Theater Near You: The Moviemercial," *New York Times,* September 21, 2003.
76. Edward Herman and Noam Chomsky, *Manufacturing Consent* (New York: Pantheon Books, 1988), 17–18.
77. R. Collins, *Dictating Content: How Advertising Pressure Can Corrupt a Free Press,* 25.
78. Leslie Savan, "Truth in Advertising?" *Brill's Content* (March 2000): 62.
79. Federal Trade Commission, http://www.ftc.gov/ftc/oed/fmo/budgetsummary11.pdf.
80. Natasha Singer, "Foods with Benefits, or So They Say," *New York Times,* May 14, 2011.
81. Michael Kahn, Attorney, Stinson, Mag & Fizzell, interview by author, June 6, 1999, St. Louis, Missouri.
82. Andrew Martin, "The Package May Say Healthy, but This Grocer Begs to Differ," *New York Times,* November 6, 2006: A-1.
83. "Amtrak Rolls Out 'Acela' Service, High-Speed Trains for Northeast," press release, March 9, 1999, http://www.amtrak.com/news/pr/atk9936.html.
84. Alex Mindlin, "Portions and the Power of Suggestion," *New York Times,* November 7, 2010.
85. Thomas Hine, *The Total Package* (Boston: Little, Brown and Company, 1995).
86. Ibid.
87. Stuart Elliott, "A New Camel Brand Is Dressed to the Nines," *New York Times,* February 15, 2007.
88. William Lutz, *Doublespeak* (New York: Harper and Row, 1989), 92.
89. Rick Berkoff, "Can You Separate the Sizzle from the Steak?" in *Mass Media Issues,* ed. by George Rodman (Chicago: SRA, 1981), 149.
90. Savan, "Truth in Advertising?"
91. Lutz, *Doublespeak,* 95.
92. Ibid., 86.
93. Ibid., 90.
94. Lee E. Norrgard, *A Consumer Guide to Advertising,* 10–11.
95. Caples, *How to Make Your Advertising Make Money,* 370.
96. Ibid., 184.
97. Ibid., 87.
98. White, *How to Produce on Effective TV Commercial,* 118.
99. Kleppner, *Advertising Procedure,* 374.
100. John Lyons, *Guts: Advertising from the Inside Out* (New York: AMACOM Books, 1987), 292.
101. Kleppner, *Advertising Procedure,* 371–2.
102. Ibid., 374.

103. Martin, "The Package May Say Healthy, but This Grocer Begs to Differ."
104. Lockwood, *"Behind the Emotion in* 'Slice of Death' Advertising," 86.
105. Norrgard, *A Consumer Guide to Advertising,* 13.
106. David Huron, "Music in Advertising: An Analytic Paradigm," *The Musical Quarterly* (Fall 1989): 567.
107. Chris Dickinson, "Sell-Outs? Maybe So; Best Sellers? Absolutely," *St. Louis Post-Dispatch,* December 8, 1996: D-3.
108. Steve Gordon Law, "Negotiating a License for Use of Music in a National Television Campaign," http://stevegordonlaw.com/article_aslj_fall01.htm.
109. White, *How to Produce on Effective TV Commercial,* 182–3.
110. Janis Valdes, "Viagra: Let the Dance Begin," Webster University, unpublished paper, April 2, 2000.

10

American Political Communications

The mass media have not merely altered the delivery system of information, but in fact have transformed the American political process. Successful political candidates must be able to use the channels of mass communication to present themselves and their positions to the voters.

IMPACT OF MEDIA ON THE POLITICAL PROCESS

The media have influenced the American political process in the following ways.

Candidate Selection

In the media age, candidates must come across as dynamic, charismatic, trustworthy, competent, and likable. John F. Kennedy was the first politician whose political career was bolstered by the image he projected on television. And in 2007, Senator Barack Obama's announcement of his intention to run for president was received with the excitement generally accorded a rock star. Newton Minow, a Chicago lawyer who served in the Kennedy administration, declared, "This is the sort of thing you get once in a generation. This is a connection between what the voters need and what the voters want. This is the first time I've felt it since Jack Kennedy."[1]

Campaign Finance

Campaign finances affect a candidate's ability to get his/her messages across to the voters. As a result, the escalating expenses required to orchestrate a successful media campaign necessitates that political candidates have access to vast amounts of money.

In 2012, the candidates running for president of the United States spent a combined *one billion* dollars. A large percentage of these funds was used to produce media presentations and buy advertising space or time (depending on the medium). Indeed, the president raised $88 million between October 18 and Election Day on November 6. Fully *half* of the Obama campaign's spending during that time—$83 million—went just to television advertising.[2]

Because current finance regulations "only" made *$65 million* available to each candidate for the 2012 election for president of the United States, all major candidates rejected this option, instead relying on private donations to fund their campaigns.

Once in office, politicians must continue to raise money for future campaigns. As a result, elected officials are forced to devote more of their time to fundraising than to performing their legislative duties.

The ability to raise enough funds to run a campaign has become a major consideration in determining the viability of a candidate. Indeed, the fundraising totals of the candidates are tracked closely by the press, with the candidate who attracted the most money designated as the frontrunner. When Jonathan Tasini ran for the Senate in the 2006 Democratic primary, television network Channel One refused to allow him to participate in the televised debates because he hadn't raised a set amount of funds ($500,000)—even though polls indicated that 13 percent of the voters supported Tasini.[3]

Campaign finance can be particularly discouraging for darkhorse candidates, who must compete with contenders who have access to ample financial resources. In 2008, former Iowa governor Tom Vilsack dropped out of the presidential primary, citing the pressures of fundraising—and his inability to keep up with the campaign fundraising of his competitors—as the chief reason for his withdrawal: "Effort and hard work are not enough. It's about the money, and with states moving (their primaries and caucuses) up on the calendar, the premium on money became higher."[4]

In return for their donations, special interest groups expect favorable treatment from the candidate whom they have supported financially once he/she is in office. This pressure sometimes forces politicians to take positions that they otherwise wouldn't adopt. To illustrate, in 2012, the U.S. Senate rejected attempts to end oil subsidies, despite record profits by the oil industry and overwhelming public support (74% of the American public would be in favor of ending the oil subsidies). Fifty-one senators, who received $5 million apiece in campaign contributions from the oil industry, voted against the oil subsidies. But the 47 Senators

Table 10.1   Contributions of Special Interest Groups to Campaigns

The Top 20 PAC Contributors to Federal Candidates, 2005–2006

DEMS | REPUBS | ALL PAC Name	Total Amount	Democrat%	Republican%
National Assn of Realtors	$3,756,005	49%	51%
National Beer Wholesalers Assn	$2,946,500	31%	69%
National Assn of Home Builders	$2,900,000	26%	73%
National Auto Dealers Assn	$2,821,600	30%	70%
Operating Engineers Union	$2,784,435	78%	21%
Intl Brotherhood of Electrical Workers	$2,782,875	97%	3%
American Bankers Assn	$2,747,299	36%	64%
Laborers Union	$2,680,650	85%	15%
American Assn for Justice	$2,558,000	96%	3%
Credit Union National Assn	$2,412,853	45%	54%
AT&T Inc	$2,341,683	34%	66%
Carpenters & Joiners Union	$2,293,923	74%	25%
United Parcel Service	$2,239,128	32%	67%
United Auto Workers	$2,220,350	99%	1%
American Federation of Teachers	$2,110,948	99%	1%
Teamsters Union	$2,081,100	91%	8%
American Federation of St/Cnty/Munic Employees	$2,048,683	98%	1%
American Medical Assn	$2,011,634	31%	69%
Plumbers/Pipefitters Union	$1,950,100	91%	9%
International Assn of Fire Fighters	$1,872,105	72%	27%

who voted to retain the government subsidies to the oil industry received nearly $25 million each in campaign contributions from the oil industry. Ironically, earlier in the year, these Republicans legislators had threatened a shutdown of the government over the issue of reducing the budget deficit.[5]

Lobbyists, representing special interests, make every effort to influence the decisions of legislators. Lobbyists are often former government officials who use their connections to gain access to politicians. Although these representatives of special interests are only authorized to provide information to politicians, in some cases these special interests play a direct role in the drafting of legislation—a right not afforded to average citizens like you and me. Reporters Eric Lipton and Ben Protess provide the following example from 2012:

> Bank lobbyists are not leaving it to lawmakers to draft legislation that softens financial regulations. Instead, the lobbyists are helping to write it themselves.
>
> One bill that sailed through the House Financial Services Committee this month—over the objections of the Treasury Department—was essentially Citigroup's, according to e-mails reviewed by *The New York Times.* The bill would exempt broad swathes of trades from new regulation.
>
> In a sign of Wall Street's resurgent influence in Washington, Citigroup's recommendations were reflected in more than 70 lines of the House committee's 85-line bill. Two crucial paragraphs, prepared by Citigroup in conjunction with other Wall Street banks, were copied nearly word for word. (Lawmakers changed two words to make them plural.)[6]

In addition, the Federal Election Campaign Act of 1971 (FECA) permits corporations, labor unions, and religious organizations to support political candidates through the formation of *PACs,* or political action committees—a "separate segregated fund" within a company or as a self-sustaining, though related, organization. In 2010, the U.S. Supreme Court overturned sections of the Campaign Reform Act of 2002, making it legal for corporations and unions to spend from their general treasuries to finance independent expenditures related to campaigns. As a result, these "Super PACS" raised $74,554,388.[7]

Individual donors also exercise an enormous influence on politicians. For instance, during the 2012 presidential campaign, Sheldon Adelson, owner of an international gambling empire, contributed more than $70 million to Mitt Romney's presidential campaign.[8] These large donors, who represent a very narrow segment of American society, share a common political agenda. Bob Herbert observes,

> I doubt that many people are aware of just how elite and homogeneous the donor class is. It's a tiny group—just one-quarter of 1 percent of the population—and it is not representative of the rest of the nation. But its money buys plenty of access. These major donors share a common political agenda. They on balance oppose national health insurance, additional anti-poverty spending and reductions in defense spending, but back gay rights and free trade. They are fairly evenly divided on environmental protection and affirmative action.[9]

Given the financial pressures of the political system, it is nearly impossible for politicians to avoid financial entanglements that compromise the performance of their duties. Because political candidates are required by law to disclose the sources of their contributions, it can be extremely worthwhile to scrutinize these records, focusing on the following information:

- How much money have individuals donated to the candidate?
- What industries do they represent?
- Is there any record of the politician's policy positions and voting records in the individual's expressed issues of interest?

The Rise of the Media Consultant

The primary responsibility of the media consultant is to coordinate political ads and unpaid media coverage. However, the media consultant has branched out into all phases of a campaign, including the formulation of campaign strategies.

Media consultants wield an astonishing amount of power. Where candidates used to solicit the support of the party machine, they now scramble for the services of top media consultants. Candidates often defer to the judgment of the consultant—not only on media strategy but on political issues as well. To illustrate, in a 2006 *New York Times* article in which media consultants offered campaign tips to former New York mayor and presidential hopeful Rudolph Giuliani, Paul Begala, Democratic strategist and former aide to President Bill Clinton, was blunt: surrender on abortion.

You can't switch on everything. So surrender to the far right on one issue: abortion. But the only way to do it is whole hog. Use your trump card: 9/11. Tell them the death you saw that day gave you a greater appreciation for the sanctity of life. You're Saul on the road to Damascus. Praise the Lord and pass the delegates.[10]

Media consultants are advertising specialists who borrow heavily from traditional advertising techniques to "sell" their candidates to the public. Media consultants often employ focus groups that gauge the public response to the most minute detail of a politician's appearance. Dana Wilkie explains,

Sunglasses . . . make a candidate appear less credible. Facial hair suggests insecurity. Rarely do you see a major candidate with bad teeth—which may suggest a lack of discipline. And when candidates sweep loose strands across balding patches, this leaves the impression that they try to dodge issues.[11]

Media consultants coach politicians on phrasing, intonations, facial expression, eye contact, and body language, often relying on "electronic response" mechanisms to measure viewers' reactions to politicians' nonverbal cues.[12]

But media consultant Bob Goodman laments,

You can't put a candidate completely in a new package. You can take his [sic] polyester off and put him in a decent-looking suit. You have him blowdry his hair. You can teach him how to keep his eye on the camera. You can try to inspire certain attributes. But you don't have the complete freedom that you do when you're dealing with a bar of soap.[13]

Moreover, media consultant Vincent Breglio complained that "[s]ome candidates just won't listen, they won't do what they're told." He explained that "the extent to which a candidate is manageable" is a prime consideration in the selection of his clients—an alarming criterion for a national leader.[14]

Top media consulting firms command a fee of over $1 million for a single political campaign. Some critics regard political consultants as mercenaries who hire themselves out to the highest bidder. Indeed, consultants must maintain an impressive win-loss record in order to command top fees. As a result, consultants are often reluctant to take chances on worthy candidates who might benefit most from their assistance. Media consultant Sanford L. Weiner admits,

> We would all like to think we have only worked for candidates we believed in, and who represented our own individual political thinking. . . . Unfortunately, as with any profession, economics enter the picture. We have all from time to time, represented clients whom we didn't particularly love, but who could help us pay the overhead.[15]

However, some consultants operate out of a set of core principles, and as a result, offer their services to candidates affiliated with one political party (Republican or Democrat) or work with darkhorse candidates they respect.

The Evolution of Ideological Media

The evolution of ideological media operations like MSNBC (liberal) and Fox (conservative) has given political parties an arena in which to present their perspectives. These television networks, along with other ideological platforms like Rush Limbaugh and other radio talk shows, function in a manner not unlike state media systems in totalitarian countries. These stations reflect the old-time party line, as commentators echo the official talking points of the state.

To illustrate, in the course of the 2012 presidential election, Fox News commentators used the identical talking points as the "spin" put out by the Romney campaign. This ideological echo was satirized brilliantly by Stephen Colbert in an analysis of Romney's facial expression during the third debate.

As Colbert pointed out, the expressed goal of the Romney campaign team was to present the Republican candidate as a "plausible commander in chief" during the debate. He then presented video clips of Fox News reporters parroting this term:

- Bret Hume: "Mitt Romney had a job tonight, and that was to come across as a plausible commander in chief."
- Bret Raefer: "Romney certainly needing to show that he's a, you know, a plausible president."
- A female journalist, on location in Boca Raton, Florida: "Romney did what he needed to do, which was to present himself as a plausible commander in chief."[16]

The audiences of these ideological cable stations see the world differently from one another:

- Just 19 percent of Fox viewers think that increasing government spending would help the economy, while 79 percent think increasing the debt in the process would hurt the economy. MSNBC viewers lean the other way, with 55 percent saying more spending would help and 43 percent saying the debt would hurt the economy.
- MSNBC viewers are more likely to be willing to pay more taxes and to support higher taxes on the rich and Wall Street. Fox viewers are more likely to think the poor should pay more.
- On matters of national security, Fox viewers are more likely to be concerned about a terrorist attack.[17]

The Influence of the Polls

During the 2012 campaign, Nate Silver of FiveThirtyEight published polls forecasting the presidential election that were remarkably accurate. These polls averaged the many daily political polls.

But despite their influence, polls may not be an accurate and comprehensive barometer of public opinion, for several reasons:

- Only the *results* of polls are generally made public, so that the context of the polling sample is omitted. For example, an important consideration in the assessment of polls is the probability that the sample of respondents will actually vote.
  - Polls that use the *general population* as its sample are the least reliable.
  - Polls that use a sample of *registered voters* are considered more accurate; however, about 10 percent who say they're registered really are not.[18]
  - The most accurate sample consists of *likely voters*.

In addition, some demographic groups are not being adequately represented in polls because of the way in which interviews are conducted. Robert Groves explains,

The data are pretty clear that you miss people who live alone, especially younger people who are more likely to be out in the evenings. You tend to over-sample people with young children because they are home. You also tend to over-interview the elderly population because they are at home and are often willing to be polled. You get the unemployed. It's an odd distribution.[19]

- The sample selected for the poll may also reflect a *cultural bias.* For instance, most national polls in the United States are conducted only in English.[20] As a result, the opinions of the Spanish-speaking population are underrepresented.
- Moreover, a poll only captures the *mood of the moment* when it was conducted. Consequently, as new events and information shape public opinion, poll results may be subject to drastic swings. According to Temple University professor John Allen Paulos, polls are just snapshots: "Polls are like weather vanes. They work at the moment, but no one relies on them to say what the weather is going to be like next week."[21]
- Polls often overlook the *depth of conviction* on the part of the voters—in other words, how strongly those polled feel about the issue or candidate they favor.
- Jennifer LaFleur explains,

One figure that can have an even larger outcome on the outcome of a poll is the proportion of undecided people who, come election day, actually may decide. To compensate for this factor, pollsters may force these folks into making a decision by asking them a second question such as, "If you had to decide right now, who would you pick?" The people that make a decision when forced are called "leaners."[22]

Thus, if a poll sample is made up of a number of "leaners," the level of support may be much weaker than a group with definite views.

- The *wording* of the poll also has an impact on its results. To illustrate, in 2013, the Pew Research Center conducted a poll about U.S. government surveillance. One question asked, "Do you favor the government collecting metadata from communications in the United States?" Only 21 percent of the subjects responded yes to this question.

However, when the poll later rephrased the question as, "Do you favor the government collecting metadata from communications in the United

States *as part of anti-terrorism efforts?*," support for the same activity by these subjects increased by 17 points—to 38 percent approval.[23]

A more insidious version of this tactic is the "push poll," which, under the guise of an opinion poll, is used to shape public opinion. David Broder explains:

> Here's how it works: Your phone rings and someone from the "Acme Survey Center," or some other such vague name, says, "I'm taking a survey of voters. In the contest between Gwendolyn Jones and David Broder for the congressional seat in our district, would you favor Jones or Broder or are you undecided?"
>
> If your answer is either Broder or undecided, the "interviewer" then says something like this: "If I told you that Broder's hobby is driving a high-powered sports car at dangerous speeds through residential neighborhoods and seeing how many pet cats and dogs he can run over, would that make a difference in your vote?" After another question or two, the interview closes with a repeat of the ballot question—Jones or Broder or undecided.[24]

To illustrate, in 2012 the Faith and Freedom Coalition conducted the following survey:

1. How do you rate Barack Obama's overall performance as president thus far?
    a. Excellent
    b. Good
    c. Fair
    d. Abysmal
    e. Undecided
    f. I consider him an enemy of liberty and the values that built our great nation
2. Fidel Castro hailed the passage of Obama's health care as a "miracle." Do you think that he is honestly concerned with the well-being of Americans, or is it more likely that Castro sees Obamacare as the fastest, surest way to bring Socialism or worse to America?
3. How much danger do you think liberty is in right now as a result of President Obama's policies, actions, and agenda for America's future?
    a. More serious than the threats we faced in World War II from Nazi Germany and the Japanese because the attack on liberty today is from our own government.

    b. More serious than the threat we faced from the Soviet Union during the Cold War.

    c. More serious than the American Civil War.

    d. All of the above.

    e. Serious but not as serious as the threats listed above.

    f. President Obama is not an enemy of liberty.[25]

- Technology can also play a role in poll results. For instance, polls conducted during the 2008 and, to some extent, the 2012 presidential elections were only directed at landlines; households with cell phones were not contacted. Because younger people tended to use cell phones, this demographic was under-represented in these election polls.

Media and the Balance of Power

The media has greatly enhanced the power of the executive branch of government. Presidents are now able to circumvent the Congress and appeal directly to the American people through the media. Chris Matthews, former press secretary to Senate Majority Leader Tip O'Neill and currently a TV host of the news program *Hardball* (MSNBC), observes, "It is amazing how the monarchy translates so well into the television age and legislatures do not."[26]

Obsolete Political Processes

In this media age, a number of features of the American political system have been rendered obsolete:

- *The Primary System.* The primary system for nominating party candidates was devised in a less sophisticated media era, when politicians could only gain access to voters by traveling around the country and declaring their positions on issues of regional interests and concern. This was also the only means by which the local citizens could hear what candidates had to say.

  But today, thanks to extensive media coverage, state primaries receive national exposure. As a result, candidates can no longer regionalize their messages but are forced to repeat the same menu of positions on national issues at each stop. Consequently, candidates

---

MEDIA LITERACY TIPS: INTERPRETING PUBLIC OPINION POLLS

When faced with the results of public opinion polls, ask the following questions:

- *How old is the poll?*
  The closer to Election Day, the better.
- *What was the size of the sample?*
  The larger the size of the sample, the better.
- *Who was polled?*
- *Who sponsored the poll?*
  Polls paid for by news organizations use safeguards not used by parties in the quick polls that candidates and parties use to guide strategy.[27]
- *Is the poll state or national?*
  State polls, usually a few days older, tell you if a presidential candidate is within striking distance of your state's electoral votes. But national polls can detect last-minute trends.[28]
- *What is the margin of error in the poll?*
  Because polls ask a sample of the population, the numbers can only approximate the tabulation of the entire target population. Statisticians are able to compute a reasonable "margin of error" for each poll, based on its sample size and methodology. If a poll has a three percentage-point margin of error, the totals are likely to fall within plus or minus three percentage points—a six-point swing. In this case, if a poll reports that a Republican candidate is ahead by two percentage points, the Republican could be ahead by as much as five percentage points, or behind by one percentage point.

---

resort to attack ads and peppy slogans to give their campaigns a fresh and dynamic appearance.

In addition, because of the national focus on state primaries, the initial contest in New Hampshire assumes an exaggerated importance. The winners of this primary actually receive very few delegates (Democratic: 18 out of 2,145 delegates needed for nomination; Republican: 23 out of 1,105 delegates needed for nomination). However, the winners of these contests are anointed as the frontrunners by the media. Austin Ranney declares,

The benefits of this early position are many. The frontrunners, no matter how behind they started, rise rapidly in the public opinion polls, and they find it much easier to raise money and enlist volunteers. Their opponents sink in the polls, find it harder to attract money and workers, and often drop out or "discontinue active campaigning."[29]

- *Electoral College.* Surprisingly, candidates are not elected by a direct vote of citizens in the United States. Instead, elections work according to the electoral college system, in which voters choose a slate of electors, who then select the president and vice president. These electors are not obligated to vote for the slate chosen by their states' voters. Consequently, in the case of a closely contested nomination process during the party's convention (see below), the slate may be released from its "official" selection.

  The electoral college system was devised at a time when collecting and tabulating votes throughout the nation would have been unwieldy. Trans`portation Secretary Ray LaHood, R–IL, declares, "[The Electoral College] is merely a relic of times past, running counter to the democratic process."[30] However, the media age offers the opportunity for a quick and precise national tabulation of votes.

- *Political Conventions.* Historically, political conventions were gatherings in which a political party's slate of candidates was selected. However, in the modern political arena, these decisions have been reached long before the convention. Instead, the convention has become strictly a media event, filled with scripted speeches, video sound bites, and rehearsed celebrations, and designed to generate momentum for the upcoming campaign.

PROCESS: FUNCTION

The relationship between the media and politicians in America is a complex mix of conflict and cooperation, support and opposition. For purposes of discussion, it is useful to make the following distinction:

- *The media's coverage of politics*
- *The use of the media by politicians*

These *competing functions* are reflected in the often contradictory, adversarial nature of political communications.

I. *The Media's Coverage of Politics*

The media rely upon politicians for daily programming content. Anything that a significant political figure does is considered newsworthy. The media's coverage of politics include the following *functions,* or purposes:

- *The media inform the public about the political life of the nation*

    The American media educates the public about political affairs and can establish a political agenda for the nation.

- *The media help establish what issues are of importance*

    The cliché commonly employed to characterize the agenda-setting function is that "even if the media don't tell you what to think, they tell you what to think *about*." That is, the coverage devoted to a topic conveys a message about the importance of the topic. To illustrate, in August 2013—more than three years before the next U.S. presidential election—the *New York Times* assigned a fulltime reporter to cover Hillary Clinton, who at that time had not announced her intention to run for office. Professor Brendan Nyhan commented,

> I haven't been sure there is enough news to sustain a full-time reporter's time, and a dedicated beat creates the incentive to make news. A full-time Clinton beat at *The Times* could help cement the perception that she is the inevitable Democratic nominee and effectively serve to pre-anoint her.[31]

- *The media influence public attitudes toward politicians and issues*

    Because of the influence of the channels of mass communication, politicians strive to cultivate the goodwill of the media. When James Buchanan was elected president in 1857, he went to great lengths to reconcile his differences with James Gordon Bennett, editor of the influential newspaper the *New York Herald.* A few weeks after his inauguration, Buchanan wrote to Bennett's wife, acknowledging her congratulations:

> I am glad to learn that Mr. Bennett has promised you "to stick by my administration through thick and thin." Thus far he has given it a powerful support with occasional aberrations, for which I am always prepared and do not complain. He is an independent man and will do just what he pleases—though I know there is an undercurrent of good will towards me in his nature and he is disposed to treat me fairly. The *Herald* in his hands is a powerful instrument and it would be vain for me to deny that I desire its

music should be encouraging and not hostile. Mr. Buchanan makes his mark when he strikes and his blows fall so fast and heavy it is difficult to sustain them. . . . It is my desire as well as my interest to be on the best of terms with him. . . .[32]

- *The media serve as a societal watchdog*

  The media maintain an independence from the government, helping make the government accountable to the people. As a result, the investigative efforts of reporters have contributed to the deposing of leaders, policy changes, and reforms in government.

II. *The Use of the Media by Politicians*

Politicians initially depend upon the media to gain access to their constituents and get their message across. Because the media add legitimacy to people and issues, early media attention is critical to a successful political campaign. Consequently, one of the first steps in a political campaign is to court the media, hoping to receive "free" coverage (i.e., media attention beyond purchased advertising).

Moreover, ongoing media coverage keeps politicians in the public eye and positions them for possible future political races. Indeed, a number of former office holders, including Newt Gingrich, Sarah Palin, and Mike Huckabee, have become members of the media, taking jobs as analysts on cable television news programs.

But even though they appreciate the value of the press, all politicians have been misquoted and their privacy invaded. Consequently, politicians and their staffs devise strategies that will enable them to get advantageous press coverage.

For instance, politicians in positions of power subtly encourage positive media coverage by rewarding those reporters who have composed stories that are considered favorable to the administration. For instance, at a 2009 press conference President Obama called on reporters for questions, following a list of names that had been preselected to ask questions. The White House had decided in advance who would be allowed to question the president and who would not.[33]

Conversely, politicians can *withhold* access if they are displeased with the way that a reporter (or his/her news agency) covers a story. To illustrate, in 2013, Maine governor Paul LePage announced the establishment of a "blackout policy" for newspapers that "oppose[d]" his administration, in which members of LePage's administration would no longer comment on stories published by the *Portland Press Herald,* the *Kennebec Journal,* and the *Morning Sentinel.* This blackout followed the newspapers' publication of stories focusing on how actions of LePage's top environmental regulator departments benefited his former lobbying clients in private industry.[34]

This new policy came to light when a *Press Herald* reporter asked spokesperson Adrianne Bennett to comment on a story about Medicaid expansion. Bennett told the reporter she would not speak to the newspaper about the issue. "Not to the *Portland Press Herald,*" she said.[35] As reporter Andrew Malcolm observes, "It is difficult for a reporter to function as a 'watchdog' for politicians, when he or she must always be careful that their reporting does not eventually deny them access to the politicians they are trying to cover."[36]

Politicians will also use the media as a scapegoat, taking advantage of the public's antipathy for the press to blame media coverage for their own mistakes or unpopular activities. As an example, during the 2012 Republican presidential primary election, Republican candidate Ron Paul was involved in an incident during a campaign stop at a diner in which a woman complained that Paul did not spend enough time talking to the members of the audience. Journalist Michael Barbaro, who witnessed the incident, reported,

> Paul told [CNN reporter Dana] Bash that it was the news media's fault that he could not talk to more voters at the diner, because a gaggle of cameras had formed around the candidate in the narrow restaurant, restricting his movements. "You the media did this to her," Mr. Paul said of the woman in the diner. "She should have been furious with you. [But] the woman . . . even approached Mr. Paul's S.U.V. as he prepared to drive off and began shouting at him through the closed car door to return to the diner and meet her and her mother. . . . [Later, the campaign staff] offered a more detailed explanation of what had happened inside the diner, saying that the candidate had left early because more than 100 members of the news media had "created a mob-like atmosphere" that was unsafe.[37]

In addition, savvy politicians have learned to exploit the competition between journalists to pressure reporters into writing favorable stories. Dan Rather recalls that during his tenure as White House reporter, exclusive interviews with President Nixon were offered only to reporters who had written stories sympathetic to the administration.[38] And in the incident involving Ron Paul described above, Paul staffers "abruptly cut off a brief interview with the CNN reporter Dana Bash when she asked about his ability to connect with voters in New Hampshire . . . [and] proceeded to do a previously scheduled interview with Fox News, a CNN rival.[39]

However, when reporters find themselves bullied by politicians, they can take advantage of the side of this relationship—the fact that politicians depend upon the press. To illustrate, during the George W. Bush administration, reporters began a "silent treatment" during a presidential press conference, forcing spokesperson Ari Fleischer to address an issue that he had been avoiding. Reporter Mark Halperin explains,

The other day, something remarkable happened in the White House press room during spokesman Ari Fleischer's briefing: restraint.

The issue on every reporter's mind was the same. Did the president really mean it when he said that the Democrat-controlled Senate was "not interested in the security of the American people?" . . . Mr. Fleischer arrived knowing he would be grilled on the president's comments. And he faced a difficult choice: repudiate his boss's words or stand by a statement that seemed at odds with the message of bipartisan cooperation the president had tried to convey.

Of course, Mr. Fleischer also knew he had a way out if his carefully calibrated answer was not well received. When press secretaries get into trouble with the questions of one reporter, they turn to other reporters who, eager to get in their own questions or to secure an on-camera moment, raise their hands, shout, and do whatever else is required to steal the floor. Another question is asked, the moment is forgotten and the press secretary gallops free.

For many years, White House reporters have often undermined themselves and their cause by interrupting a colleague who may be closing in on the truth or, at least, on a nonanswer for the public record. . . . But now, just maybe, this era is coming to an end.

The reporter who took part in this landmark moment was Ron Fournier, of The Associated Press, who was invited by Mr. Fleischer to ask the first question. Mr. Fournier inquired about the president's intentions. "Did he misspeak," Mr. Fournier asked, "or does he really believe that Democrats are not interested in the security of the American people?"

Anticipating the issue, Mr. Fleischer gave an answer that some in Washington would call a nonresponsive response. I'm certain there were reporters in the room who thought they could ask the question in a clever way that would have compelled Mr. Fleischer to go beyond his talking points. But instead of interrupting Mr. Fournier and giving Mr. Fleischer a way out, they sat in silence.

Mr. Fournier continued, going back and forth with Mr. Fleischer, with four more versions of the same question. In the end, Mr. Fleischer never really answered directly whether Mr. Bush stood by those controversial words or not. But a point had been made.[40]

Although it is unwise to make generalizations, it is safe to say that all politicians try to control the messages presented to the public through *message management.* Although previous administrations employed communications consultants during election campaigns, the Reagan administration was the first to adopt this approach *after* the election. The Reagan communications team looked at all news stories from the following perspective: Does this information support (or threaten) the goals of the administration? David Gergen, director of communications under both Reagan and Clinton, observes,

For one of the first times I'm aware of, (the Reagan administration) molded a communications strategy around a legislative strategy. We very carefully thought through what were the legislative goals we were trying to achieve, and then formulated a communications strategy which supported them.[41]

This approach to government/media relations consists of the following principles:

- *Plan ahead.* Each Friday, the Reagan communications team discussed upcoming events from a communications perspective. As one participant commented, the central questions were, "What are we going to do today to enhance the image of the President," and "What do we want the press to cover today, and how?"[42]
- *Stay on the offensive.* The Reagan administration made a point of controlling the agenda. The communications team would prepare its message with an eye on its potential effect on the audience. Immediately following a presidential decision, press conference, or significant news event, the Reagan communications team would circulate

among the press to present the administration's interpretation, or *spin,* on the story in order to manage how information was presented, reported, and received by the public.

When faced with events that could be damaging to the administration, the communications team would focus on the management of information during a crisis. This *damage control* strategy was designed to minimize potentially harmful stories relying on the following principles:

- *Respond promptly.* The Reagan team was poised to implement strategies that downplayed negative aspects of the story.
- *Manage the flow of information.* Recognizing that the news media depends on government as a primary news source, the Reagan team made available information that it wanted conveyed and simply withheld information that it was not prepared to discuss. As veteran newscaster Sam Donaldson has observed, "So our options are, do nothing or do it their way."[43]
- *Limit access.* Controlling access to the president reduced the chances that the administration would lose control of its agenda. It was vital, however, that Reagan maintain the *image* of accessibility. Thus, the president was often in view of the cameras, but conveniently out of earshot (for example, boarding noisy helicopters).
- *Speak in one voice.* Once a position was decided upon, it was important that all administration officials present a unified, consistent message. This communications model required that the Reagan team remain discreet and loyal and helps account for the Reagan administration's obsession with leaks to the press by members of the administration.
- *Make it easy on the press.* The Reagan team manipulated media coverage by providing the media with prepackaged information (which, of course, presented the administration's perspective on events). The working assumption was that the press was inherently lazy and would accept the administration's version of news if it made their jobs easier. As Deputy Chief of Staff Michael Deaver explained, "If you didn't have anything, they'd go *find* something."[44]

Thus, the Reagan communications team staged events such as press conferences, speeches, and conventions, which were then covered as news.

- *Use the medium to the administration's advantage.* The Reagan communications team exploited the visual nature of television to present its point of view. According to CBS producer Richard Cohen, Michael Deaver virtually served as executive producer for the television networks, setting up visually compelling backdrops and action-oriented events that the networks found irresistible. Hertsgaard explains,

> Rather than resist the networks' desire for saturation coverage of the President, the Reagan propaganda apparatus would cater to it. The networks wanted visuals of the President? Fine. But they would be visuals carefully designed to promote the Reagan agenda.[45]

- *Mislead when necessary.* The Reagan team engaged in a "disinformation" strategy, in which it deliberately released false information to achieve political goals. For instance, in 1986, the press discovered administration memos confirming that the Reagan administration had released disinformation about Moammar Gadhafi in order to destabilize the Libyan government. In a classic example of disinformation, White House officials admitted to the disinformation campaign but minimized its significance:

> We think for domestic consumption there will be no problems. It's Gadhafi. After all, whatever it takes to get rid of him is all right with us—that's the feeling, we think, in the country. On the foreign scene it will cause problems, though. We're constantly talking about the Soviets doing disinformation. It's going to cause difficulties for us.[46]

Latent Functions

Occasionally, American media have crossed the boundary of objective reporting and *actively* supported the government's political agenda. In 1961, the *New York Times* learned of the impending Bay of Pigs invasion two days before it was scheduled to begin. After President Kennedy personally appealed to the paper not to print the story, the *Times* complied. After the abject failure of the mission, Kennedy later joked that he wished that the *Times* had ignored his request, so that he would have abandoned the mission.[47]

Another latent function involves the government using the media as a vehicle to test policies. U.S. administration officials routinely send out "trial balloons"—leaking information to the public through the media as a way of testing public response before policy decisions are reached.

To illustrate, in 2008, the *New York Times* revealed that the Pentagon had recruited more than 75 retired military officers to appear on TV outlets and in newspapers as "military analysts" who portrayed Iraq as an urgent threat prior to the outbreak of the Iraq war. Internal Pentagon documents repeatedly referred to these military analysts as "message force multipliers" or "surrogates" who could be counted on to deliver administration themes and messages to millions of Americans in the guise of their own opinions. The analysts were given classified Pentagon briefings, provided with Pentagon-approved talking points, and given free trips to Iraq and other sites paid for by the Pentagon.[48] (For more discussion of propaganda, see the "Function" section of Chapter 2.)

Dual Functions

According to Kathleen Hall Jamieson, these two functions—the media's coverage of politicians vs. politicians' manipulation of the media—sometimes merge, much to the detriment of the public.

> "[P]aid TV," consisting primarily of thirty-second political spots, is becoming increasingly newslike, and in the process further fusing the line between news and ads. And candidate speeches, press conferences, one-on-one interviews, and debate answers are increasingly tailored with a view toward getting adlike news coverage.[49]

PROCESS: MEDIA COMMUNICATOR

Media exposure has magnified the importance of the *character* of the political leaders. Former Boston mayor Kevin White explains, "What you need in office is a man who can cope with situations as they arise, situations that no one ever thought of."[50] In that regard, political scientist James David Barber links style to performance—the way in which the president will perform his/her duties. Within this context, Barber devised a formula for predicting presidential performance based upon distinct character types. Barber identified four character patterns, based upon levels of *activity* (Activity/Passivity) and *enjoyment* (Positive/Negative affect):

- The *Active/Positive* personality is distinguished by an industrious nature, combined with the enjoyment of this level of activity. This pattern, typified by Thomas Jefferson, indicates a high level of self-esteem, success in relating to one's environment, and achievement orientation.
- The *Active/Negative* character, exemplified by John Adams, combines intense effort with a relatively low emotional reward. The Active/Negative figure is compulsive, and his/her goal is to obtain and maintain power. As a result, an Active/Negative president such as Lyndon Johnson, Richard Nixon, or George W. Bush brought an inherently rigid approach to the presidency, resulting in escalation of policies long after the issues (e.g., Watergate, Viet Nam) should have been resolved.
- A *Passive/Positive* president, such as James Madison, is a compliant figure who combines a low self-esteem with a "superficial optimism."[51] Because this personality type is primarily looking for acceptance, he or she is unlikely to take an aggressive approach to the implementation of policy.
- The *Passive/Negative* figure, personified by George Washington, "does little in politics and enjoys it less."[52] Withdrawn by nature and possessing a low sense of self-esteem, this personality type regards politics as a civic duty, often serving his term of office with reluctance.

Significantly, Roger Streitmatter has found a correlation between a president's character type and how he has been treated by the media. "Robust" presidents (those who fell within Barber's Active/Positive character delineation) received at least 50 percent more newspaper coverage than presidents exhibiting less attractive character traits. Active/Positive presidents also received 87 percent more "personal news coverage" focusing on their daily activities and family.[53]

As a result, the emerging role of the media suggests a modification of Barber's theory. Style is no longer a reflection of character, but instead is a carefully cultivated *media image* designed to appeal to the American public and, as Streitmatter suggests, attract favorable media coverage as well. Thus, media consultants stage events for their clients that make their candidates appear active and dynamic, such as visiting schools, hospitals, and factories. As presidential archivist Timothy Naftali observes, "Presidencies are constructed; there are whole teams of people who spend the day trying to make the president, Republican or Democrat, decisive or forward looking."[54]

Furthermore, a candidate now must be able to withstand the relentless *scrutiny of the press*. After initially promoting a candidate, the media almost immediately begin to delve into the private lives of these same politicians. When Senator Barack Obama was first considering whether to run for president in 2006, a major consideration was whether he was willing to subject himself—and his family—to the scrutiny of the press. Columnist Jeff Zeleny prophesied, "The next phase of his political development will inevitably draw intense and less flattering scrutiny."[55] For Obama, this phase began almost immediately; 125 newspapers throughout the country published a story that 17 years before, as a student at Harvard Law School in the late 1980s, Obama had accumulated $375 in fines for outstanding parking tickets. (He paid the fine in 2007.)

Point of View

The political information that we receive has been filtered through the channels of mass communications. As a result, determining the point of view of the media communicator has become a vital consideration in the American political process.

Despite its lofty goals of objectivity, the press often brings a distinct point of view to its political coverage. For instance, Senator John McCain, who twice has run for president of the United States, is an engaging man whose personal story, as a survivor of a North Vietnamese prisoner of war camp, is truly heroic. Several reporters who were assigned to cover McCain have admitted that they allowed their feelings for the senator to affect their coverage of the Arizona senator. After covering McCain in the 2000 Republican presidential primary election, Jacob Weisberg, a reporter for *Slate* magazine, acknowledged, "When I set out to spend a few days with McCain last week, I promised my editor that I wouldn't join in this collective swoon. That proved impossible."[56] And in a *Time Magazine* article, Nancy Gibbs and John F. Dickerson admitted that reporters were protective of McCain, withholding information that could have been damaging to the candidate:

A presidential candidate is not supposed to talk at length and on the record about the rules he broke or the strippers he dated, or the time he arrived so drunk that he fell through the screen door of the young lady he was wooing. The candor tells you more than the content, and reporters sometimes just decide to take him off the record because they don't want to see him flame out and burn up a great story.[57]

COMPARATIVE MEDIA

Television has had an enormous impact on the content of political communications. Cable news is cited as the main source of campaign news by 36 percent of Americans, followed by local TV news, network TV news, the Internet, and local newspapers.[58]

However, complex facts are difficult to digest on television and must therefore be simplified. Political speeches now cater to the 30-second sound bite—a brief, catchy, and memorable phrase that can be carried on television news. Who can forget "Read my lips," John Kerry the "flip-flopper," or Mitt Romney's "47 percent"? As a result, media consultant Jane Squier Bruns warns that it may be a mistake to look to television for the answers to complex questions: "If you want to find [in-depth] information, you need to turn to print and other unpaid media coverage. Otherwise, you are making your choices on the wrong basis."[59]

In addition, the number of issues in a televised presentation must be kept to a minimum. Rosser Reeves, a pioneer in political advertising, recalls working with Dwight Eisenhower on his campaign:

> I attended a speech given by General Eisenhower, and he was all over the lot. I counted twenty-seven issues . . . and nobody remembered what he had said. We selected three campaign issues to feature in our campaign ads. I wanted one, but the Republican National Committee insisted on three.[60]

Furthermore, television images often overwhelm verbal messages. Television reporter Leslie Stahl relates a story that illustrates this point. In 1984, Stahl filed a news report for CBS in which she discussed President Ronald Reagan's use of television:

> How does Ronald Reagan use television? Brilliantly. . . . Mr. Reagan tries to counter the memory of an unpopular issue with a carefully chosen backdrop that actually contradicts the president's policy. Look at the handicapped Olympics, or the opening ceremony of an old-age home. No hint that he tried to cut the budgets for the disabled and for federally subsidized housing for the elderly. . . .[61]

This script was accompanied by visuals of Reagan in action: "The president basking in a sea of flag-waving supporters, beaming beneath red-white-and blue balloons floating skyward . . . getting the Olympic torch from a runner, greeting wheelchair athletes at the handicapped Olympics, greeting senior citizens at their housing project. . . ."[62]

Stahl recalls that she "worried" about the response from the White House and was astonished when a Reagan official called to congratulate her. He explained,

> We're in the middle of a campaign and you gave us four and a half minutes of great pictures of Ronald Reagan. And that's all the American people see. . . . They won't listen to you if you're contradicting great pictures. They don't hear what you are saying if the pictures are saying something different.[63]

Ironically, Stahl fell victim to the central message of her story: It's not what you say. It's what you show. And despite what the public may experience on a day-to-day basis, they believe the images that politicians present.

However, as a visual medium, television occasionally shows unscripted moments. For instance, in the first presidential debate of 2012, many stations employed the split screen, which revealed the reactions of a candidate while his opponent was speaking. During the debate, Barack Obama appeared tired and listless, contributing to the general consensus that he had "lost" the debate.

Digital media has become a significant influence on Americans' understanding of the political process. A 2012 survey conducted by the Pew Research Center's Project for Excellence in Journalism found an 11 percent increase over the course of the year in the number of people who considered the Internet their principal source of campaign information,[64] largely due to the expanded role of social network sites (SNS) in the current political landscape:

- 36 percent of SNS users say the sites are "very important" or "somewhat important" to them in keeping up with political news.
- 26 percent of SNS users say the sites are "very important" or "somewhat important" to them in recruiting people to get involved in political issues that matter to them.
- 25 percent of SNS users say the sites are "very important" or "somewhat important" to them for debating or discussing political issues with others.
- 16 percent of SNS users say they have changed their views about a political issue after discussing it or reading posts about it on the sites.[65]

Moreover, people between the ages of 18 and 29 and African Americans are two demographic groups that feel that the social media are particularly important for political activities.[66]

Increasingly, candidates have turned to the Internet as a means of connecting with the voters. According to the Pew Research Center's Project for Excellence in Journalism, Barack Obama's reelection in 2012 can be partly attributed to his outperforming his opponent in the use of social media:

- The Obama campaign posted nearly four times as much content as the Romney campaign and was active on nearly twice as many platforms. Obama's digital content also engendered more response from the public—twice the number of shares, views and comments of his posts.
- Obama also had twice the number of Twitter re-tweets and YouTube comments, likes or views as Romney, and nearly 80 percent more Facebook "likes."
- The Democratic National Convention inspired an extraordinary amount of Twitter conversation since the very first day—more than 9.5 million tweets sent about the events in Charlotte. Indeed, the final day of the convention generated approximately 4 million tweets— approximately equal to the total number from the entire Republican National Convention.[67]

Politicians now use the Internet as a principal fundraising source. Howard Dean was the first national politician to use the Internet as a fundraising vehicle, raising over $25 million in online donations during the 2004 election. During President Barack Obama's campaign of 2008, more emphasis was placed on online fundraising through digital resources. The campaign holds the record for most funds raised digitally—$403 million in 2008 and $504 million in 2012, with the average donation being $53.[68]

But at the same time, the Internet has emerged as a source of unintended information that can affect the outcome of elections. Because of the constant media coverage, politicians occasionally let down their guards and make statements that cost them voter support. But in this digital media environment, public figures must assume that, at any public event, they are being recorded.

To illustrate, during the 2012 U.S. presidential election, Republican candidate Mitt Romney attended a fundraiser in which, surrounded by supporters, he felt comfortable sharing some of his private thoughts, including the following remark:

> There are 47 percent of the people who will vote for the president no matter what . . . who are dependent upon government, who believe that they are victims. . . . These are people who pay no income tax . . . and so my job is not to worry about those people. I'll never convince them that they should take personal responsibility and care for their lives.[69]

In this instance, a waiter recorded Romney's talk on his cell phone. These comments created a backlash on the Internet that sabotaged Romney's campaign.

Unfortunately, this level of media scrutiny limits the pool of potential candidates. It is safe to say that very few people would feel comfortable permitting the press to comb through their past. Indeed, if experience forms character, it can be argued that youthful indiscretions are an important part of growing up. To borrow a line from Groucho Marx, would you vote for anyone whose lives were so devoid of experience that he/she could survive this level of media inquiry? Moreover, this media scrutiny magnifies the human flaws of these candidates and undermines public confidence in politicians. (For more discussion, see Chapter 8, Journalism.)

With the growing reliance on political Web sites for information, some states have begun to develop a set of standards for online campaigning that will promote transparent messages. For instance, in 2010 California convened a bipartisan Fair Political Practices Commission that would develop rules governing online political ads and messaging, in the same way it governs print or broadcast ads. The commission's Subcommittee on Internet Political Activity issued a report with recommendations calling for disclosure statements to appear on Internet ads, including who pays for ads, official campaign Facebook pages, and other online political activities.[70]

But as with any channel of communication, the Internet can be used to mislead voters. One example is the use of "link bombs" to discredit candidates. This occurs when opponents engineer a flood of Web links and cross-links to unfavorable content. As a result, negative articles about the candidate are posted at the top of the search rankings. For example, after 2012 Republican presidential candidate Mitt Romney's remarks about having "binders full of qualified women" during the presidential debate, searches from the words "completely wrong" in Google led to images of candidate Romney.[71]

Affective Response

Media messages that are directed at the emotions can influence voters' attitudes toward issues and politicians, as well as their voting behaviors. The inauguration and the State of the Union Address are rituals designed to inspire feelings of awe and respect for government. At the same time, political campaigns tap into a wellspring of *negative* emotions, such as anger, frustration, and dissatisfaction, to marshal support against their opponents.

Only a few campaign spots outline a specific position on issues. Instead, most of the spots focus on emotionally laden themes—that is, how individuals respond to the issues. Renowned media consultant Tony Schwartz claims that the most effective political campaigns are directed at emotions. Schwartz uses the "deep sell," first identifying voters' feelings about the candidates and the issues and then crafting messages that tap into these pre-existing emotions. In this sense, political ads do not introduce new ideas as much as they evoke an intended response from an emotional base.[72]

Campaign ads may be directed at the following *positive* emotions:

- *Patriotic* ads reinforce our faith in our way of life and inspire a sense of pride in who we are.
- *Reassurance appeals* promote a sense of confidence about the present. As media consultant Roger Ailes observed, "The candidate who makes the public most secure will win."[73]
- Ads for candidates are often designed to inspire *hope* in the audience.

However, other political ads are directed at a range of *primal fears* and *insecurities:*

- *Mistrust of politicians.* One constant political theme is based on the notion that whoever is in office is corrupt, and that only outsiders can reform the system.

- *Fear of calamity.* An ad for Hillary Clinton during the 2012 Democratic primary campaign featured a scenario in which the red emergency phone rang in the middle of the night. The audience was never informed about the exact nature of the calamity. What was important was the steady hand of the person (an actress playing Ms. Clinton) answering the phone and responding to the crisis.

- *Fear of change.* This approach exploits an individual's general anxiety about the future. This approach frequently is employed when one of the candidates is the incumbent. Reporter David D. Kirkpatrick describes a 2006 congressional election, a campaign spot for Representative Heather A. Wilson (R) that emphasized the risks involved in making a change to her opponent, Patricia Madrid:

> In the spot, images of fire mutate momentarily into floating fragments of text before dissolving again into flames: "North Korea conducts nuclear tests. Reductions in military spending. The murder of any American anywhere on earth." As a picture of the North Korean dictator, Kim Jong Il, gives way to an unflattering photo of Ms. Madrid, a narrator asks: "Can we trust her? With so much at stake? Does she have the experience we need? In a world like this, is she the one who will keep our families safe? Patricia Madrid. Don't take the risk."[74]

The message essentially was that even if the voter wasn't satisfied with Wilson's overall performance, at least she was a known quantity.

A variation on this theme raises questions about presidential succession in cases in which a vice-presidential candidate is not highly regarded. For instance, a 1968 Democratic spot focused on Richard Nixon's running mate simply featured the graphic, "Agnew for President," accompanied by uproarious laughter. At the conclusion, a voice-over commented, "This would be funny if it wasn't so serious."

- *Fear of differences.* During the 2013 presidential campaign, a number of apparently unrelated stories involving President Barack Obama appeared in the media:
  - Obama is Muslim
  - Obama is not a U.S. citizen
  - Obama is a Socialist

- ◦ Obama is "not American"
- ◦ Obama is gay

Although the specifics of these stories differed, the cumulative message was *Obama is a foreigner.* People who are perceived as different—even when they belong to the same culture—are regarded as outsiders. Thus, as *New York Times* reporter Nicholas Kristof explains, many Americans associate white skin with being *American,* while people who look different are perceived as *foreign:*

> One study found that although people realize that [Chinese American actress] Lucy Liu is American and that Kate Winslet is British, their minds automatically process an Asian face as foreign and a white face as American—hence this title in an academic journal: "Is Kate Winslet More American Than Lucy Liu?"[75]

It must be noted that this is a common human response—even among segments of the population who themselves are targets of racial discrimination, such as Latinos and Asian Americans. Kristof continues,

> Some scholars link racial attitudes to a benefit in evolutionary times from an ability to form snap judgments about who is a likely friend and foe. There may have been an evolutionary advantage in recognizing instantaneously whether a stranger was from one's own tribe or from an enemy tribe. There's some evidence that the amygdala, a center in the brain for emotions, flashes a threat warning when it perceives people who look "different.". . .
>
> It's not that any of them actually believed Mr. Obama to be foreign. But the implicit association test measured the way the unconscious mind works, and in following instructions to sort images rapidly, the mind balked at accepting a black candidate as fully American.[76]

Thus, during the 2008 presidential campaign, researchers found that subjects subconsciously considered candidate Barack Obama to be *less American* than either Hillary Clinton or John McCain. Indeed, respondents perceived Obama as less American than former British Prime Minister Tony Blair.[77] As a *New York Times* editorial declared, "It is inconceivable that this campaign to portray Mr. Obama as the insidious 'other' would have been conducted against a white president."[78]

MEDIA LITERACY TIPS: AFFECTIVE CAMPAIGN STRATEGIES

Anthony Pratkanis makes the following recommendations for critical analysis of *affective campaign strategies:*

- *Keep track of your emotions while viewing the ad.*
- *Ask yourself, "Why am I feeling (this way) now?"*
- *If you feel yourself getting manipulated this way, turn off the ad.*[79]

Process: Audience

In general, political media programming only influences voters about candidates and issues if their allegiances are weak. On the other hand, partisan voters do not turn to the media for answers, but rather to support their preexisting point of view. Consequently, all of the money and energy of political campaigns is directed at those few voters who have not yet made up their minds. Media consultant Jane Squier Bruns explains,

> You have a spectrum across the scale of potential voters and you whittle it down . . . and you finally get to the point where you know you have to reach this tiny little group in the middle. These are the undecideds who will or will not vote for your candidate—depending on what happens. And that's who the message has to go to.[80]

Significantly, 64 percent of the public prefers to get political news from sources that have no particular political point of view, while just 26 percent prefer news from sources that share their political views. Majorities of most news audiences say they want news with no political point of view, including 70 percent of the *Colbert* and *Daily Show* viewers, *Economist* readers, NPR listeners, and readers of the *New Yorker* and similar magazines.[81]

Today, audience identification has assumed a predominant role in the process of political communications. Tracking polls and focus groups have become an essential means of gauging voter sentiment. As the campaign progresses, tracking polls are conducted more frequently—often on a daily basis by the end of the campaign. Bruns notes,

> They're taking [the voter's] temperature all the time. Initial polls . . . measure where the voters are, what they're thinking. . . . Their

messages are very specifically targeted . . . they know through the polling where they've got to reach voters. . . . . This is not a shotgun approach. We are talking about very, very specific targeting. It's easy to do it mathematically.[82]

Political consultants also conduct psychographic research to anticipate how the voters will respond to particular political appeals. Montague Kern explains, "Buttons and dials are used to test immediate nonverbal responses to televised candidate presentations."[83] "Perception analyzers" measure how focus groups respond to a speech—line by line. Respected columnist William Raspberry observed,

Imagine having your speech writers assemble a scientifically selected cross section of likely voters and try out various concepts, formulations and jokes for their effects on one group or another. You could then tailor your remarks to fit any occasion. . . .

The perception analyzer isn't the only tool in the kit by a long shot. The people who do polls and focus groups and fine-tuned surveys have gotten so good they can divide the electorate into the tiniest of issue-based pieces. Their exquisite science has given us "wedge" issues—those issues with the peculiar ability to find and exploit our political fault lines.[84]

This research enables political consultants to devise communication strategies that appeal to their target audience. Politicians also tailor the style and content of their messages to their target audience.

Further, politicians now are able to bypass the established media gatekeepers, such as newspapers and television stations, and take their messages directly to the electorate via digital devices. (See discussion of "Digital Media Communications Model," Chapter 2.) As columnist Frank Bruni notes,

[The journalist's] role and relevance are arguably even more imperiled by politicians' ability, in this newly wired world of ours, to go around us and present themselves in packages that we can't simultaneously unwrap. To get a message out, they don't have to beseech a network's indulgence. They don't have to rely on a newspaper's attention. [Video presentations produced by politicians and released on YouTube] are reflections and harbingers of an era in which YouTube is the public square, and the fourth estate is a borderline obsolescent one.

The . . . videos, all different but related, simply ratchet up the effort to marginalize naysaying reporters and neutralize skeptical reporting. And as Chris Lehane, a Democratic political strategist, pointed out to me, they take a page from corporate America, whose chieftains have used that same format, as opposed to news conferences or interviews, to distribute sensitive communiqués. Lehane mentioned, for example, the 2007 video in which David Neeleman, then the C.E.O. of JetBlue, explained the airline's brand-quaking operations meltdown.

But corporations answer only to shareholders and customers. Politicians answer to all of us, and have a scarier kind of power, easily abused. So we must see them in environments that aren't necessarily tailored to their advantage. We must be able to poke and meddle. It may not be a pretty sight, and we journalists may not be doing it in a pretty way, but eliminate that and you wind up with something even less pretty: Bachmann, robotically composed, telling you that she's quitting for purely high-minded reasons, with the vigor of the republic foremost in her heart.[85]

CULTURAL CONTEXT

Politics and Popular Culture

Politics has traditionally been the domain of "elitist" programming such as the newspaper, or traditional television panel programs such as *Meet the Press* and *Face the Nation.* However, beginning in 1968, with Richard Nixon's appearance on the popular TV program *Laugh In,* popular media programming has emerged as an effective means for a political candidate to reach the electorate.

In 2012, President Barack Obama aimed to secure the next term of his presidency with visits to the *MTV Forum, The Late Show with David Letterman, The View, The Daily Show,* and *Late Night with Jimmy Fallon.* In contrast, Republican candidate Mitt Romney avoided entertainment television, turning down multiple offers from late-night hosts.[86]

Popular media programming has emerged as a principal source of political news. In a 2009 survey, 21 percent of people aged 18 to 29 cited *The Daily Show* and *Saturday Night Live* as places where they regularly learned presidential campaign news. In contrast, 23 percent of the young people mentioned ABC, CBS, or NBC's nightly news broadcasts as a source.[87]

Comedy has the potential to have an important role in framing the way we think about civic life. The success of a joke depends on a set of shared assumptions between the comic and audience; if the audience is confused about the context of the joke or disagrees with its premise, it will not get a laugh. Thus, political humor can be indicative of cultural attitudes toward politicians and issues. A study released by the Center for Media and Public Affairs (CMPA) found that late-night comedians Jay Leno, David Letterman, Jimmy Fallon, and Craig Ferguson featured jokes about Republican presidential candidate Mitt Romney more than twice as frequently as jokes about Barack Obama. The study, which was conducted from August 27 to October 3, 2012, found that Romney was the target of 148 jokes, while Obama was the object of 62 jokes during that period.[88] Moreover, popular media programming can promote participation in the political process. Prior to the 2012 presidential election, MTV created an online game called "Fantasy Election '12." The roots of this virtual effort lay in fantasy sports teams and strove to get young people involved in the political process. Although the game promoted healthy competition among players and awarded prizes based on specific criteria, the ultimate goal of it was to get young people registered to vote.[89]

Popular media programming can even influence specific legislation. Both the Obama administration and New York City mayor Michael Bloomberg credited Jon Stewart, host of *The Daily Show,* with playing a major role in the passage of a bill committing federal funds to provide health care for the 9/11 "first responders" (i.e., police and firefighters) after a filibuster by Republican senators on December 10 threatened passage of the bill. Stewart devoted one entire show to this issue, in an example of what Professor Robert J. Thompson calls "advocacy satire."[90]

Political Communications and Cultural Myths

Many political ads capitalize upon our cultural self-image; not what we are, necessarily, but how we see ourselves—who we would *like* to be.

- *Mythic past.* Ads featuring a nostalgic look backward at mythic America have an enormous appeal, particularly during times of cultural stress. This appeal is designed to project the legacy of the past onto the future. Politicians talk about the values of small-town America. Ideals like freedom, hope, goodness, are central to this world of possibilities and prospects.

- *The American dream.* These ads offer the promise of opportunity for the individual, in which success comes to the deserving through hard work and faith in the system. Moreover, during the election cycle, voters are empowered; our elected officials ask for *our* support.
- *The romantic ideal.* Political spots offer a worldview filled with the promise of a better future. Reagan's famous "Morning in America" ads maintained that America's best days are ahead.

  It is not surprising that the public has not been receptive to political messages asking us to sacrifice. Michael Dukakis's 1988 admission that he would have to make "tough" choices in budget allocations was countered by George H. W. Bush's more optimistic (and popular) message of *plenty:* we can have it all.
- *The mythic frontier.* The mythic frontier emerged in America in the nineteenth century, as the settlers spread west. According to Frederick Jackson Turner, the mythic frontier is characterized by "restless energy, individualism, self-reliance, the bounteousness and exuberance which comes with freedom."[91] This myth has been used to support a range of political positions. To illustrate, the aftermath of the 2012 mass slaying in Newtown, Connecticut, generated a public dialogue about gun legislation. Opponents justified their position by calling up the frontier myth, in which guns protected families from invaders.

Stereotypes

Due in part to their brevity, political ads often rely on stereotypes. As discussed in Chapter 5, stereotypes are a shortcut that generally presents an oversimplified and distorted depiction of a group of people.

Conventions such as business suits signify legitimacy, competence, and seriousness. Less formal attire, such as shirtsleeves, indicates a common bond with the people and a sympathy with their circumstances. To illustrate, when holding a rally in the White House Rose Garden for doctors to show their support of health care reform in 2009, President Obama's staff noticed that many doctors had ignored the suggestion on the invitation that they wear white lab coats to the occasion. Knowing that the visual image would be much more powerful if those supporting the president were obviously medical professionals in white coats, the White House staff scrambled to find white lab coats for those attendees wearing regular business suits. The resulting images from the rally speak for themselves—those are clearly doctors supporting the president's health-care reform measures.[92]

But in many cases, these conventions have become, in the words of Charles Baxter, "'tiresome clichés': the black background, the outraged voice-over, the accusations, the snow-infested distorted image of the opponent."[93]

The effectiveness of a political stereotype is based upon a consensus of meaning that is associated with the stereotype. To illustrate, Jane Squier Bruns relates a story in which her son Mark Squier, also a media consultant, told her about an upcoming project—a political spot for the Democratic Party designed to raise concerns about the Republicans' policy on Medicare. The commercial contained visuals of a grandmother tending her infant grandson, while the voice-over declared that Republican initiatives would jeopardize the health care of both the young (the baby) and old (the grandmother). Squier told his mother that his daughter Emma was being cast as the infant. Bruns, a vibrant, attractive woman who is also an actress, immediately volunteered to play the role of the grandmother. Squier responded that she "didn't look the part" of the grandmother. Bruns responded, "But Mark, I *am* the grandmother!" Instead, the role of the grandmother was played by an elderly, frumpy woman who wore a drab housedress. Ironically, Bruns was not cast for the part because she did not fit the stereotypical image of a grandmother—even though she is Emma's actual grandma.

In addition, the characters who appear in political spots often are stereotypes of the candidate's constituents. As a result, the characters in the ads often provide insight into the candidate's perception of the appearance and attitudes of his or her constituents.

Author Charles Baxter comments on the portrait of Minnesota voters in this 2004 Senate race ad produced by Mark Kennedy (R) in his race against Amy Klobuchar (D):

One such warm-and-fuzzy ad is instructive. In a staged conversation between a little old lady on a park bench and Mr. Kennedy, the Republican challenger is pestered with questions about why he keeps accusing Ms. Klobuchar of so many faults. "Because they're true," he says plaintively.

What's interesting about the ad is not the predictable subject matter. It's that the little old lady is straight out of Fargo—not the city in North Dakota, but the film by the Coen brothers. She wears a hideous pink cardigan sweater, a mismatched blouse, bright purple slacks and drugstore reading glasses. The actress playing the little old lady gives her a broad Minnesota accent, along with a slight dental-plate lisp. The ad is funny, but what is satirized, or plainly mocked, is the intelligence of the electorate.[94]

STRUCTURE

As discussed in Chapter 5, media companies are often beneficiaries of the political system. For instance, local television stations are beneficiaries of the election cycle. As an example, WJLA, the ABC affiliate in Washington, D.C., took in $33 million in election-related and issue advocacy advertising in 2012. Another Washington station, WTTG, even added an extra half-hour of news programming during the election to accommodate the demand for campaign advertising.[95] Moreover, as discussed earlier, special interests exercise particular influence over the policies of politicians.

In addition, because of the imperative to maintain strong ratings, the media often treats politics as a form of entertainment. Newspaper coverage of debates emphasizes dramatic exchanges between candidates, often entirely ignoring any substantive news. Even more alarming is the tendency of journalists to translate good conduct into a vice. To illustrate, in 2000, *The Daily Show* poked fun at presidential candidate Al Gore because he was "boring"—conduct that might be of some value for the chief executive of the nation.

FRAMEWORK: INTRODUCTION

Introduction as Foreshadowing Device

Campaign slogans are designed to generate immediate name recognition. For instance, "All the way with LBJ" was a memorable catchphrase. Slogans also encapsulate the central positions that the candidate wishes to stress. Ironically, however, a slogan occasionally contains revealing latent messages. Gerald Ford pinned his 1976 election hopes on national inertia: "He's Our President—Let's Keep Him." Richard Nixon's pre-Watergate motto "Nixon's the One!" foreshadowed his ouster. And Pat Buchanan's slogan for the 1996 and 2000 presidential campaigns contained this veiled threat: "America First."

Obama's 2008 slogan, "Change We Can Believe In," is a message that incorporates many positive messages: change as social progress, a collective mission ("we"), and the power of faith. However, this slogan is at odds with the deliberate character of the American system of governance. As a result, some supporters who expected immediate change grew frustrated, as reflected in the strong showing of the opposition Republican party in the 2010 midterm election.

Explicit Content

Examining the explicit content of political communications is a useful way to uncover fallacies, inconsistencies, and attempts to obfuscate issues or mislead the public.

Political communications teams employ the following rhetorical techniques that manipulate information in order to influence how the public responds to issues and candidates:

- *Selective facts.* In political communications, facts may be used arbitrarily to make a point. For example, during the 2012 U.S. presidential election, Republican candidate Mitt Romney presented isolated facts, without providing the context that determines the truthfulness of the statement. A highlight of the Republican candidate's stump speech was the promise that he would add 12 million jobs to the economy during the first four years of the Romney administration. But although this statement may have been factually correct, it did not tell the whole story. In August 2012, Moody's Analytics had issued a report predicting that 12 million jobs would be added to the U.S. workforce, *regardless of who would win the presidential election.*[96]

  In the face of this bewildering array of information, facts become meaningless. Truth has thus been reduced to a matter of *faith*— whose facts the public chooses to believe.

- *The front page/back page strategy* works on the principle that if enough time elapses, a corrected story will receive substantially less media attention. To illustrate, during the 2012 presidential election, when Mitt Romney's comments first appeared, they were given prominent positions in news programming—on the front page in newspapers or among the first stories in television news. As a result, this first news release contained information that either: 1) ran counter to their actual policies; 2) was untrue; or 3) was a denial of charges, even if they were guilty. Then later, the Romney campaign would "walk it back," as campaign advisors corrected the "misstatement." However, this follow-up story would be relegated to the back pages, behind breaking news.

  As an example, in October 2012, Romney spoke to a general audience on CNN, declaring that he was not in favor of any new antiabortion legislation. Immediately after this appearance, Romney's staff issued a disclaimer, asserting that Romney actually favors additional legislation to limit or prohibit abortions. However, this disclaimer was difficult to find, appearing toward the back of the news section and at the end of broadcast news programs. But although these "corrections" to Romney's moderate statements on abortion were consigned to the back pages of the mainstream media, the Romney campaign made sure that these stories were sent to his political base.

- *Innuendo* is a strategy in which the candidate raises doubts without necessarily providing evidence. For example, campaigning in Ohio during the closing stage of the campaign, Governor Romney declared that he had "read somewhere" that Chrysler, the company that makes Jeeps, was planning to send all of their manufacturing capabilities to China. This allegation was of major importance in Ohio, a state in which one out of eight workers is employed in the auto manufacturing business. Chrysler immediately issued a denial, responding that the company recently had added 19,000 American manufacturing jobs and planned an increase of an additional 1,100 jobs. Astonishingly, the Romney campaign responded by repeating its bogus claim in a campaign ad.

- *Misrepresenting a person's position and presenting it in a form that people will reject* occurred repeatedly during the 2012 presidential campaign. For instance, Governor Romney repeatedly made false statements about Obama's "apology tour for America," reinforcing the idea in the mind of the public. For example, during the third debate, he directed this claim directly at Obama:

> The reason I call it an apology tour is because you went to the Middle East and you flew to Egypt and to Saudi Arabia and to Turkey and Iraq. And by the way, you skipped Israel, our closest friend in the region, but you went to the other nations. . . . In those nations, and on Arabic TV, you said that America had been dismissive and derisive. You said that on occasion America had dictated to other nations.[97]

Obama responded by declaring that Romney's claim about an Obama apology tour "has been probably the biggest whopper that's been told during the course of this campaign."

CNN's nonpartisan Fact Check column provided the following assessment:

> Romney's claim is false. The president has mentioned past U.S. mistakes and flaws during speeches about the larger issues of building

bridges to other countries. But he has never apologized or gone on an "apology tour."[98]

But despite this disclaimer, Romney persisted in repeating this mischaracterization.

- *Taking an opponent's words out of context.* Without context, bare facts can be misleading. Campaign teams routinely comb through comments of their opponents to find comments that can be damaging when taken out of context. For instance, Romney often cited the statistic that 24 million people are unemployed—more than when President Obama took office. What remained unsaid was that:
  - When Obama took office, the economy was in free-fall, with 800,000 Americans per month losing their jobs.
  - It took nearly 15 months to turn that trend around.
  - For the final 38 months of Obama's first term, the number of private sector jobs in the United States had *increased.*
- *Absolute assertions* are pronouncements that politicians make without sufficient evidence. Ironically, Eleanor MacLean observes that "words like 'unquestionably' and 'indisputably' should be looked at very closely, as should such expressions as 'But the truth is' or 'The fact is.' . . . Can such statements be proven?"[99]
- *Evading the question.* In formats such as debates and press conferences, a reporter has only one opportunity to ask a question. This enables politicians to evade the question or respond with a nonanswer—that is, a response that does not properly address the question—before moving to the next question.
- *Shifting the argument.* If a particular rationale for a policy is no longer favorably received by the public (or never was popular), politicians can shift the argument. To illustrate, the Bush administration's rationale for the war in Iraq went through several incarnations:
  - Iraq possessed weapons of mass destruction
  - Saddam's complicity in the attack of 9/11
  - Bringing democracy to Iraq
  - Saddam was an evil man
  - Fighting in Iraq will prevent terrorism in the United States

This rhetorical technique is most effective when the public has forgotten the original rationale behind a policy. In this case, the function of the press is to provide the context that reminds the public of the chronology of the event (including the rationale for the event itself).

- *Questionable use of evidence.* When policies or issues are supported by clear-cut evidence, the politicians have an easy task. But when the evidence is ambiguous or supports the opposition, campaigns must rely on the following rhetorical strategies to contain the damage. Evidence can be manipulated in the following ways:
  - Downplaying the evidence
  - Using incriminating evidence to support the candidate's own position
  - Attacking the person, not the argument
- *Citing fabricated studies in support of a candidate's assertion.* As an example, throughout the campaign Romney cited "six studies" to support his assertion that his economic plan (a combination of increased military spending and cutting taxes on the wealthy) would reduce the deficit. But in reality, the six "studies" consisted of:
  - Two blog posts by a conservative think tank
  - A report by a conservative think tank
  - A paper by a former George W. Bush advisor
  - A blog post and *Wall Street Journal* op-ed by a Romney advisor
- *Language collectives* are a form of personification, ascribing human qualities to a large, all-encompassing organization or entity (e.g., "the Supreme Court said today," or "the White House claimed. . ."). However, it is impossible for an organization to talk or express remorse. This misuse of language sends several messages to readers. First, language collectives make absolute claims, overlooking individual dissent or disagreement among people within the organization. In addition, language collectives invest the organization with an aura of authority.
- *Qualifiers* are words or phrases that modify the meaning of the sentence. The use of qualifiers is designed to subtly introduce doubt in a statement. To illustrate, in 2013, the United States raised the issue about the Syrian government's possible use of chemical weapons against its rebel resistance troops. Because President Obama had declared that the use of chemical weapons constituted a "red line" that would necessitate a response from the United States, the government was very careful in the word choice of the announcement. A government spokesperson declared, "The U.S. Intelligence Community assesses *with some degree of varying confidence* that the

Syrian regime has used chemical weapons *on a small scale.* President Obama declared 'These are *preliminary assessments* based on our intelligence gathering. We have *varying degrees of confidence* about the actual use'. . ." (italics added).[100]

- *Implied agreement.* This technique uses future verb tense to suggest past agreement. To illustrate, in 2006, Representative Peter Hoekstra of Michigan, the Republican chairman of the House Intelligence Committee, sent a letter to President Bush charging that the administration may have violated the law by failing to inform Congress of some secret intelligence programs. Administration officials framed their responses in a way that subtly refuted these charges by Congress:
  - White House spokesman Frederick Jones: "We *will continue* to work closely with the chairman and other Congressional leaders on important national security issues." (Italics added)
  - Carl Kropf, a spokesman for National Intelligence Chief John Negroponte: "We value this dialogue with Congress, and we will *continue* to provide the committee with the information they need to fulfill their responsibilities." (Italics added)
  - Jennifer Millerwise Dyck, a spokeswoman for General Hayden: "The director believes in the important oversight role Congress plays, and he *will continue* regular and transparent interactions with members." (Italics added)[101]

The use of the verbs "will continue" subtly denies the charges by suggesting that the administration has complied with the law in the past, dodging any statement of disagreement.

- *Hasty generalizations* are a technique in which people make assertions based on only a few unrepresentative samplings, arguing that what may be true in one or more specific instances holds true for all cases. MacLean provides the following example:

> If someone says, "Both Bill and Terry were on the first string basketball team; therefore both their younger brothers will probably also be stars," this person has jumped to a conclusion. The generalization is based on only two examples. Besides, human beings are too complex to be reduced to many generalizations: they often differ as much within a family as not.[102]

Genre: Political Advertising

The functions of a political ad are:

- *To promote name recognition of the candidate*
- *To convince the uncommitted*
- *To give those who are committed the impetus to vote*
- *To present a positive, consistent image*
- *To appeal to the self-interest of the electorate*
- *To produce and maintain the enthusiasm of the voters*

Political ads share many of the defining characteristics of product advertising. These ads must be striking and dramatic in order to build name recognition for the candidate.

The ads also try to connect the candidate with his/her constituents. For instance, ads make generous use of inclusive pronouns (e.g., wanting to see "*our* kids get ahead") to underscore that the candidate shares his or her constituents' values and concerns.

Political advertising can be considered as a genre, with distinct and recognizable functions, plots, characters, structure, and conventions. Indeed, this genre has become so formulaic that media consultant Charles Guggenheim has complained about the "cookie-cutter" approach to producing political spots: "They take a technique that works in one state and apply it in another, changing only the name of the candidate."[103]

The structure of the political ad generally falls within the formula of order/chaos/order. From the relative serenity that the audience experiences before the appearance of the ad, a problem is introduced: inflation, despair, the inadequacies of the opposition. The candidate then is presented as a solution to the problem.

According to Jane Squier Bruns, the production of the political ad has become significantly more sophisticated since the 1952 Eisenhower-Stevenson presidential election:

Technically speaking, it's evolved tremendously. We no longer see sixty-second spots. We used to do five-minute spots. You just don't see those anymore. The kind of production values you see today are very different. You're into the whole glitzy thing. [Political spots] now take a stricter advertising approach.[104]

Because of the improvements in technology, political ads assume many of the characteristics of a dialogue, as candidates respond to criticisms, recent events, and the political ads of their opponents.

**MEDIA LITERACY TIPS: STAGES
OF CAMPAIGN ADVERTISING**

Edwin Diamond and Stephen Bates have identified four stages of campaign advertising:

- *Phase one: ID spots*
  The first stage of an advertising strategy is designed to instill the name of the candidate in the public consciousness. For instance, a 1978 ad for Paul Tsongas humorously featured children mispronouncing the name of the candidate as a means of insuring name recognition.
- *Phase two: Argument spots*
  This stage is intended to distinguish the candidate from others in the race; what a candidate stands for. However, these "position ads" are often vague slogan ads, in which the candidate expresses an emotional response toward an issue.
- *Phase three: Attack*
  After the candidate has been defined and promoted, it is time to tear down the opposition.
- *Phase four: "I see an America"*
- The last stage of a political campaign typically presents the candidate as dignified, thoughtful, and reflective—beginning to act the part of the elected official.

Sub-Genres

A number of formats—sub-genres, if you will—have emerged in political advertising:

- *Humor* is an effective approach to making messages memorable. In addition, ridicule is a socially acceptable means of undermining the accomplishments of an opponent.
- *Testimonial* ads generate the highest audience recall of all standard formats. Audience members respond to the sincerity and genuine quality of average citizens offering their views on candidates and issues. This approach flatters its audience, inferring that its opinions (and votes) matter. Moreover, a TV spot featuring the testimony of a member of a particular subculture can have a significant impact on members of that group.

A variation of the testimonial is the *just folks* ad, in which actors playing average citizens give a grassroots quality to the messages crafted by politicians and their staffs.

- *TV parodies.* As in advertising, political spots borrow heavily from established television genres. The most striking example of these TV parodies is broadcast news. Political scientist Larry Sabato declares, "The 'news look' format enhance[s] credibility by presenting political advertisements as mini-documentaries or press conferences, with nonpartisan, factual deliveries sometimes depicting the candidate in the role of an inquiring television news reporter."[105] In addition, political ads that parody game shows and sporting events tap into the common understanding and experience of the audience. And in some respects, political ad campaigns unintentionally have evolved into soap operas, since they are ongoing, episodic, and deal with character issues familiar to this genre: betrayal, romance, and credibility.

Negative Ads

Although the *negative ad* has been receiving a great deal of attention in recent elections, historian Thomas V. DiBacco reminds us that negative campaigning has long been a part of the American political process.

> No campaign was filthier than that of 1884, when Democrat Grover Cleveland was accused of fathering an illegitimate child and the GOP's James Blaine of being on the take. Republicans rushed to make up their verse about the wayward candidate: "Ma, Ma, Where's My Pa?" But Democrats responded, "Gone to the White House, Ha! Ha! Ha!"[106]

However, in recent years, political campaigns have relied more on these negative ads. In the past, candidates would resort to negative ads only if they were behind in the latter stages of the campaign. Today, however, negative ads are employed from the very beginning of a race, regardless of where the candidate stands in the polls.

Campaign staffs routinely include a team of opposition research specialists, who dig for damaging information on opponents that can be used throughout the campaign.

The objective of attack ads is not so much to convince the audience as to introduce doubt in their minds about the charges being made. Charles

Baxter observes that with negative ads, "You are not really being informed; you are, like a child witnessing a divorce, being asked to take sides."[107] Negative ads also are designed to put opponents in a defensive position, disrupting their ability to communicate their positions on issues, as they must spend their time denying allegations.

Although the public does not approve of negative ads, it tends to remember them more readily than less-controversial positive commercials.[108] However, this approach is not without risk. Indeed, the use of negative ads often discourages overall voter turnout. Furthermore, the "accuser" can alienate the viewers by appearing petty and mean spirited; people do not like a tattletale. Darrell West explains, "The trick is to attach negative information to your opponent without being blamed for having gone negative."[109]

In order to avoid voter backlash, candidates have devised a number of indirect negative ad strategies:

- *Using an opponent's own words or record against him (or her).* This approach absolves the candidate of direct responsibility. For instance, a 1960 ad for John F. Kennedy featured a film clip of President Eisenhower responding to a question about what policy contributions Vice President Nixon made to his administration. Eisenhower quipped, "I don't know. . . . If you give me a week, I might think of one." This off-hand statement by Nixon's boss was far more damaging than anything the Democrats could cook up.
- *Letting surrogates play the heavy.* Surrogates are useful, in that their reputations stand as endorsements of those people they are representing. Further, controversial positions are not accountable by the candidate if spoken by the surrogate. However, surrogates are, indeed, authorized to speak for the candidate. Consequently, unless the candidate states his objections to the comments of the surrogate, they can be considered the official position of the candidate. Thus, surrogate John Sununu represented Mitt Romney's position when he described Obama as "lazy" and charged that former Republican secretary of state General Colin Powell's endorsement of Barack Obama was motivated by race.
- *Exploit negative media commentary about the opposition.* During the 1992 presidential election, the George H. W. Bush campaign used a cover of *Time Magazine* that asked the question, "Why Don't Voters Trust Clinton?" Time/Warner Corporation sued the Bush campaign in an effort to stop the ad, claiming that the Bush people had not

received permission to use the cover and that the spot misrepresented the contents of the related article.

- *A variation of this strategy occurs when candidates* first *leak information to the press and* then *simply quote what was reported in the media.* For example, when the George W. Bush administration was engaged in generating support for the U.S. invasion of Iraq, Vice President Dick Cheney leaked information to the *New York Times* that under Saddam Hussein, Iraq had acquired weapons of mass destruction. Cheney then appeared on Sunday morning political "talk shows," quoting the *New York Times* as his source for this information.

- *Cry foul.* Because the public has become uncomfortable with the use of negative advertising, a candidate can paint an opponent in a negative light by decrying the other side's use of negative campaign tactics. Ramesh Ponnuru explains, "The method is simple: Call the other guy a dirty-trick artist; then shake your head sorrowfully about name-calling. The beauty of this self-serving accusation is that one can look altruistic while making it."[110]

PRODUCTION ELEMENTS

In political communications, sophisticated production techniques generally can clarify ideas, issues, and positions. But according to Kathleen Hall Jamieson, production values can also be used to *undermine* the electorate's ability to evaluate political messages:

> By flooding us with words, sounds, and images, these stimuli reduce the time that we have to respond and overload our analytic capacity. With that reduction comes a lessened ability to dispute the offered material, a lessened ability to counter-argue. Once these defenses are gone, a persuasive message that might otherwise have been challenged or rejected can slip by. Persuasion without benefit of analytic scrutiny of the message is the result.[111]

Editing

Inclusion and Omission

Given the time and space limitations of the news media, it is impossible to include all of the content of a political speech on the six o'clock news or in the newspaper. Consequently, news presentations extract a brief *sound bite* from a longer speech to bring pertinent information to the attention of the public. Throughout the years, the press has selected sound bites for the public; for instance, Franklin Roosevelt's famous line "The only thing to fear is fear itself" had been embedded in a longer address. Indeed, the restrictions of the sound bite anticipate the 160-character limit of Twitter messages.

This reliance on the sound bite has resulted in media communicators creating content with the sound bite in mind. As a result, John Tierney observes, "The public's attention span is inexorably shrinking in the age of MTV, which forces anyone in search of an audience—television producers, newspaper reporters, politicians—to deliver shorter, punchier quotes."[112]

Indeed, political speechwriters are now composing with sound bites in mind. Speeches are constructed around memorable, concise statements that present an idea or attitude in capsule form. Kathleen Hall Jamieson declares that voters should think carefully about messages contained in the sound bite: "It's quite possible to state a coherent position in a few seconds. . . . The problem with sound bites is that the one chosen for the news often doesn't have any substance."[113]

Editing Techniques

Editing techniques are generally employed to clarify the intended messages in political ads. At times, however, editing is also used in negative ads to remove important contextual information. The first television ad released by Romney displayed footage of Obama admitting, "If we talk about the economy, we're going to lose." However, upon investigation, it was revealed that Obama made that remark in 2008, not 2012. But even more damaging was the revelation that the first part of Obama's quote was deleted. In the complete transcript of his remarks, Obama stated, *"What John McCain actually said was,* "'If we talk about the economy, we're gonna lose.'" In the unedited version, then, it is clear that Obama was not discussing his own economic agenda but was quoting the 2008 Republican candidate, who was admitting that the *Republican* economic plan was a failure. (For further discussion of editing, see Chapter 7, Production Elements.)

Color

It should come as no surprise that the most common background colors employed in American politics are red, white, and blue. In addition to their patriotic connotation, these warm, uplifting colors evoke positive feelings in the audience. Bright colors are also common to positive political ads.

In contrast, dark colors are frequently employed in negative advertising. One common technique consists of a "dead shot." A black-and-white photograph of the candidate's opponent, often shrouded in a black frame, is inserted into the colorful ad, providing a stark visual contrast between the two candidates. (For further discussion of editing, see Chapter 7, Production Elements.)

Scale

In American politics, height is often associated with power and authority. As a result, political consultants manipulate the environment to give their clients the appearance of stature. For instance, a campaign spot for diminutive John Tower of Texas was filmed in an old, reconstructed Senate Chamber, using tiny furniture to make him appear larger.[114] (For further discussion of scale, see Chapter 7, Production Elements.)

Relative Position

The placement of stories sends distinct messages about political figures. For instance, on January 21, 2007, the *New York Times* carried a front-page story on Senator Hillary Clinton's announcement that she intended to run for president of the United States. At the same time, at the bottom of page 25, there was a story that Senator Sam Brownback had declared *his* candidacy for the presidency. The relative placement of these two stories conveyed the message that Senator Clinton was the favored candidate. (For further discussion of relative position, see Chapter 8, Journalism.)

Movement

Movement suggests a sense of direction, purpose, and leadership. This might explain why political ads depict the politicians walking in the woods, busily engaged in legislation and interacting with citizens. (For further discussion of movement, see Chapter 7, Production Elements.)

Proximity of the Camera

In political advertisements, the proximity of the camera can promote feelings of familiarity and trust with the audience. Close-up shots of the candidates create the illusion that we know the candidate well, and inspire public confidence, suggesting that they have nothing to hide. During the 2000 presidential campaign, the ads of George W. Bush emphasized close-ups of the candidate, with the camera moving even closer as he spoke, contributing to the impression that Bush was, indeed, a "compassionate conservative." In contrast, most of Al Gore's ads featured medium or wide-angle shots of the vice president, conveying the message that Gore was cold and uncaring.

Angle

Political communications make use of angle in presenting media messages. The camera is often tilted up at candidates in a gesture to evoke feelings of respect and competence. To illustrate, during the 2012 presidential campaign, two very different photographs of the same event began circulating in the media of Paul Ryan speaking at the Republican National Convention. The *Wall Street Journal* used a photograph in which Ryan was photographed from below, which gave him a look of power and decisiveness. The *New York Times* elected to use an image that was framed so that only Ryan's head and shoulders were visible at the bottom of the frame. The rest of the picture contains an uncomfortable amount of empty space, causing Ryan to look insignificant, immature, and ill prepared for the job.

WORD CHOICE

As societies evolve, new words are continually being invented in the political landscape. Lexicographer Grant Barrett provides the following examples of words that emerged during the 2012 U.S. presidential election:

- *47 percent.* The percentage of people who do not pay taxes, are dependent on government assistance, and would vote to re-elect President Obama no matter what, according to Mitt Romney, the failed Republican presidential candidate. His comments were captured on a video taken surreptitiously at a fundraising dinner for big campaign donors.
- *Binders full of women.* In explaining during a debate that he often sought to hire women while he was governor of Massachusetts, Mr. Romney said he was given "whole binders full of women" to consider as candidates for government jobs. The comment was widely

ridiculed, since it made it seem as though he knew so few qualified women that others had to find them for him.

- *Eastwooding.* Talking to an empty chair as if President Obama were sitting in it, as Clint Eastwood did at the 2012 Republican National Convention.
- *Legitimate rape.* A confirmed rape. In August, Representative Todd Akin of Missouri, the Republican Senate candidate, was asked whether he believed abortion was justified in cases of rape and replied that rape rarely resulted in pregnancy. "If it's a legitimate rape, the female body has ways to try to shut the whole thing down," he said. His comment drew widespread expressions of anger, as it questioned women's intentions in cases of forced sexual assault. Mr. Akin apologized for his remarks but lost.
- *Unskew.* To adjust data to suit one's beliefs or a desired outcome. The verb evolved from the name of the Web site unskewedpolls.com, which adjusted polling findings to reflect what the results would look like if more Republicans had been questioned.[115]

Politicians can shape public opinion through the choice of language. Reporter Peter Baker observes, "Every White House picks its words carefully, using poll-tested, focus-grouped language to frame issues and ideas to advance its goals."[116] For example, "affirmative action" is often referred to as "racial preference programs" by opponents. In a Fairness and Accuracy in Reporting (FAIR) survey, 70 percent of people polled said they favored "affirmative action," while only 46 percent favored "racial preference programs."[117]

In addition, word choice can be used to define (or redefine) a position, person, or issue. To illustrate, the term *commander in chief* was only occasionally used to describe the president of the United States until the administration of George W. Bush. The reliance on this term by the Bush administration can be traced back to May 2, 2003, when President Bush, in pilot gear, landed a fighter jet on the USS *Abraham Lincoln* to announce "Mission Accomplished" in Iraq. The exterior of the plane was marked with "Navy 1" in the back and "George W. Bush Commander-in-Chief" just below the cockpit window.

The usage of this term has an ideological context that resonated with the administration's belief in a strong executive branch of the government. The definition of the verb "to command" is "to have control or authority over; to dominate; to demand obedience on the part of the person or group addressed." Thus, the term "commander" suggests unlimited authority and power.

In contrast, an alternative synonym, *chief executive* is derived from the word "execute," which means "to carry out, or put into effect." Instead of simply being an executive who carried out the law of the land, Bush was positioned as a commander who exercised authority and control over the law.

The news media frequently adopts the vernacular of a politician, which promotes the agenda of the administration. For instance, CNN.com ran a story about the president landing on the aircraft carrier, using the headline "Commander in Chief Lands on USS *Lincoln.*"

Because of the extraordinary power of language, politicians must be careful to select words that have the greatest impact on their audience. To illustrate, after the events of 9/11, George W. Bush addressed an international audience, proclaiming that "this *crusade,* this war on terrorism, is going to take a while." But columnist William Safire explained that Bush's use of the word "crusade" was a colossal error, turning a political war into a religious conflict:

> [Crusade] has a religious root, meaning "taking the cross," and was coined in the 11th century to describe the first military expedition of the Crusaders, European Christians sent to recover the Holy Land from the followers of Muhammad. . . . In this case, a word that has traditionally been used to rally Americans was mistakenly used in the context of opposing a radical Muslim faction, and the White House spokesman promptly apologized.[118]

This choice of words reframed the conflict. In political wars such as World War II, winners and losers were declared, and the victors helped in the reconstruction of the defeated countries. But religious wars such as the Crusades last until the enemy is completely eliminated or converts to the religion of the victor.

Other lines of inquiry involving language can also provide insight into political media messages. Examining the *frequency* with which particular words appear in a media presentation can furnish perspective into the themes that the communications team has decided to emphasize. To illustrate, in 2011, as a conference call between influential Senate Democrats and reporters was scheduled to get underway on Tuesday morning, Charles E. Schumer (NY) was overheard instructing his fellow senators on how to talk to reporters about the contentious budget process: "I always use the word 'extreme.' That is what the caucus instructed me to use this week."

As the conference call proceeded, the senators made repeated use of this connotative word choice:

- Barbara Boxer (CA) said, "We are urging Mr. Boehner to abandon the extreme right wing."
- Thomas Carper (DE) referred to some House Republicans' "right-wing extremist friends."
- Richard Blumenthal (CT) referred to the "relatively small extreme group of ideologues" who are "an anchor" dragging down the budget negotiation process.[119]
- Benjamin Cardin (MD) criticized Mr. Boehner giving into "extremes of his party."

As applied to political communications, connotative terms fall into several categories:

- *Traditional vernacular* like "home" and "family" respond to the public's thirst for stability and meaning, given the uncertainties of contemporary culture. As such, these words are thrown around generously by politicians.
- *War rhetoric* has been applied to a variety of issues, from the "War on Drugs" to the "War on Terror." These references to war suggest a sense of mission, clear heroes and villains, and glory. At the same time, however, war rhetoric suggests a recognizable end goal, which can lead to public frustration when the situation is actually an ongoing struggle.
- *Drug rhetoric* is a very powerful metaphor to describe any social or political ill. To be "hooked" on anything conjures up images of immorality, dependency, and weakness on the part of the abuser.
- *Patriotic jargon* has always been a staple in American politics. All politicians want to reassure their constituents that they love their country.
- Although the Constitution guarantees separation of church and state, it is always a good bet to interject *religious rhetoric* into political speeches wherever possible.
- Words that *demonize* the enemy are a time-honored way to mount public opinion against one's adversaries. Thus, enemies of the United States from Saddam Hussein to Iranian President Mahmoud Ahmadinejad have been compared to Adolf Hitler.

- The *sports vernacular* in politics often reflects the male-dominated perspective of American culture. For instance, the coverage of political life often assumes the character of sporting events, with "frontrunners" and "knock-out blows." Moreover, this macho vernacular suggests that political leadership ability is defined by who is the biggest and strongest.

Euphemisms refer to neutral terms that are employed to minimize the impact of potentially damaging information. As an example, in 2013, the U.S. State Department announced that Secretary of State John Kerry had engaged in a "spirited" discussion with Iraqi Prime Minister Nuri Kamal al-Maliki about Iran shipping arms to Syria through Iraq. This use of this euphemism was a diplomatic way to state that Kerry was unsuccessful in convincing the prime minister to change this activity.

Other euphemisms found in political communications include:

- *Ordinance:* bomb or missile
- *Enhanced interrogation:* torture
- *Collateral damage:* civilian casualties
- *Depopulate:* to destroy towns and villages
- *Service the target:* destroy what you are aiming at
- *Transport tube:* body bag
- *Degrade (v):* to bomb
- *Overseas contingency operations:* war on terror
- *Man-caused disasters:* terrorist attacks

Some political euphemisms are not merely neutral, but in fact suggest a meaning that is diametrically opposed to the actual policies. To illustrate, in April 2011, President Obama gave a speech outlining his vision with regard to America's economic future. According to Obama, one way to reduce the debt is through "spending reductions in the tax codes"—his euphemism for "taxes." As political humorist Jon Stewart points out, the president framed the notion of a tax hike as a spending reduction: "Like saying, 'I'm not going on a diet, I'm going to add calories to my excluded food intake.'"[120]

Labels are words or phrases that describe a person or group. Labels such as "oil-rich," "arch-conservative," "liberal," and "special interests" often appear with such frequency in the media that they no longer simply *describe* but, in fact, *define* the group. In the process, adjectives (e.g., "liberal") are transformed into nouns ("a liberal").

Labels send very clear signals about candidates and issues. For example, "Socialism" is a label with a stigma that is derived from its association with Soviet-style Communism. As Charles Geisst, a financial historian at Manhattan College in the Bronx, explained, "The right would use 'socialist' against Franklin Roosevelt all the time in the 1930s. To hear him referred to as Comrade Roosevelt during that period was not unusual."[121]

This label, which was last employed in 2002 as part of the organized resistance against Bill Clinton's efforts to institute a national health care program, has resurfaced again, as Republicans attack Barack Obama. Mike Huckabee, former governor of Arkansas, decried the creation of "socialist republics" in the United States, declaring, "Lenin and Stalin would love this stuff."[122]

Sometimes a label can be used in a positive fashion. For instance, George W. Bush coined the label "compassionate conservative" to attract a new voter base consisting of members of both political parties. The term bridges the usual distinctions between the two political parties, combining the warmth and social concern generally attributed to Democrats with fiscal responsibility, a Republican bedrock.

But regardless of intent, Anthony Pratkanis suggests, "Be wary of anyone who gives you a label; ask, 'Why are they dividing the world up this way?' Do not succumb to hating vague categories of people; rather, think of people as individuals."[123]

Code words are terms that contain clear and distinct meaning for a sub-group within the general audience. For example, journalist Charles Blow has identified the term "patriot" as a code word that speaks to "antigovernment activists (who) believe that being well armed is a must. The militia movement engages in paramilitary training aimed at protecting citizens from this feared impending government crackdown."[124] To illustrate, James Yeager, the CEO of a Tennessee company that trains civilians in weapons and tactical skills, posted a video online in which he declared,

I need all you *patriots* to start thinking about what you're going to do, load your damn mags, make sure your rifle's clean, pack a backpack with some food in it and get ready to fight.[125]

Businesses that employ the term "patriot" (e.g., Patriot Real Estate) are signaling that they belong to this political movement—a message that would be unnoticed by the general audience.

MEDIA LITERACY TIPS: CODE WORDS

It sometimes requires a vigilant eye to discern the meaning behind the use of code words commonly employed in political discourse. For instance, American diplomat James A. Kelly described a stormy meeting between the United States and North Korea as "frank but useful"—a term that means "no progress."

- The *Glossary of Diplomatic Coverage* provides a definition for the following euphemisms:
  - *A frank exchange of views:* Negotiations stopped just short of shouting and table-banging.
  - *Making progress, but no breakthrough:* Still talking at cross-purposes.
  - *Regret (verb):* To care, but not enough to condemn. ("We regret the loss of life in Sierra Leone. We have no intention of doing anything to stop it, mind you, but we regret that it happened.")
  - *A mercurial, colorful, or controversial official:* An off-the-wall wacko.[126]

CONNOTATIVE IMAGE

Political connotative images fall into the following categories:

- *Primary personal experiences* show a political figure at home and play, surrounded by family members. Jane Squier Bruns observes, "The message is, 'Oh, he's a good family man and he cares about family values. . . . But really, it doesn't have anything to do with the major issues in the campaign."[127]
- *Place images* associate a politician with a setting that evokes positive responses. For example, one formulaic shot consists of congressional candidates in front of landmarks from their home states.
- *Bonding images* consist of photographs or videos in which the politician is posing with the elderly, middle class, or Hispanics, in order to become a symbolic member of the group—if only for the moment in which the photo is snapped. These images send this message: "I am with you, I share your concerns, I support you . . . now, please support me."
- *Embodiment images* feature individuals who exemplify the ramifications of political policies on human beings. Many politicians

now include these individuals at staged media events. For instance, throughout 2013, President Obama attended events with the parents of the victims of the mass killing of school children in Sandy Hook, Connecticut, to remind citizens of the need for "common-sense" gun control legislation.

- *Strength symbols* reflect the public's expectations that our leaders should be vigorous, courageous, and resolute in times of crisis. Thus, George W. Bush was frequently seen clearing brush on his land, riding a mountain bike, or exercising in the gym.

- *Sports* images of presidents jogging, throwing the first pitch of the major league baseball season, or congratulating winners of sports tournaments suggest that the talents and skills that are essential to success in sports are also vital in the world of politics. Bob Teeter, a Republican pollster, observes, "Sports plays a special role in our society. There are probably more people . . . who would say they would rather be sports stars than actors or other things."[128]

- *Warm images* inspire positive responses in the viewer that are then transferred to the politician. Ever since Vice President Richard Nixon brought his dog Checkers on national television as part of his defense against charges of graft in the 1950s, dogs have served as invaluable political props for politicians. Babies are also sure bets to evoke positive feelings on the part of the audience. No president was more adept at using *warmth and sincerity symbols* than Jimmy Carter. The connotative properties associated with Carter's cardigan sweater— the informality, warmth, and comfortable appearance—convinced the electorate of his sincerity and conviction.

- *Patriotic symbols* such as American flags and eagles are familiar props in political communications. Although these symbols remain in the background, they serve as reminders of the politician's loyalty and commitment to the country.

- Ever since the days of Caroline and John-John Kennedy, images of children have been a universal symbol of *innocence and hope* for the future.

- Politicians also make frequent use of *competency symbols*. Politicians are often shown in professional settings, busily engaged at work (for their constituents). Shots of offices, the Senate, White House, or official ceremonies are common. We often find candidates seated at desks, surrounded by bookcases filled with impressive-looking volumes. The implication is that the politician has actually *read* these books and is a wise and learned person.

- *Negative symbols* are often used in political ads against opponents. Montague Kern explains, "Showing opponents in limousines and expensive clothes is an effective way of depicting them as rich and pampered beneficiaries of the political system who are out of touch with the concerns of the average citizen."[129]

Photographs that appear in newspapers and magazines such as lighting the White House Christmas tree frequently are staged photo opportunities designed to convey specific messages. As Jane Squier Bruns observes, "The politician's staff asks, 'What would the message be if they took this picture?'"[130] But although these photos are, in the main, formulaic, former Reagan communications director Michael Deaver counseled, "Don't use anything that's inconsistent with the candidate or what's being said, or the history and character of the person."[131]

CONCLUSION

The mass media have transformed the American political process. Information about issues is readily available to the public; in fact, it is sometimes difficult to ignore. In addition, continuous media exposure gives constituents unprecedented access to public figures.

However, long ago Greek philosopher Plato warned of the danger in democratic societies that rhetoric (i.e., the persuasive use of language) will replace epistemology (i.e., knowledge) in the political process. And indeed, in today's mass-mediated environment, *how* something is communicated—style—can overwhelm *what* is being communicated. Modern politicians have learned to use the media to manipulate public attitudes and behaviors.[132] Consequently, people tend to become more concerned with what they believe than what is true.

Media literacy enables individuals to recognize how the mass media are used to discourage debate, conceal information, and mislead the public. At the same time, media literacy can be an important democratic instrument that empowers citizens to make independent choices, based upon a critical awareness of the information they receive through the media.

NOTES

1. Jeff Zeleny, "Testing the Water, Obama Tests His Own Limits," *New York Times,* December 24, 2006.
2. Paul Blumenthal, "Obama Campaign Fundraising Best in History," *Huffington Post* Politics, July 12, 2012, http://www.huffingtonpost.com/2012/12/07/obama-fundraising-campaign_n_2257283.html.

3. Barbara Ehrenreich, speech at the twentieth anniversary event for the media watchdog group FAIR, Fairness and Accuracy in Reporting, DemocracyNow.com.

4. Shir Haberman, "Vilsack Bows Out of Race; Says Finances Stretched Thin," *Portsmouth Herald,* February 24, 2007, http://archive.seacoastonline.com/news/02242007/nhnews-ph-vilsack.html.

5. *Rachel Maddow Show,* March 30, 2012, www.msnbc.com.

6. Eric Lipton and Ben Protess, "Banks' Lobbyists Help in Drafting Financial Bills," *New York Times,* May 23, 2013.

7. "How Much Are Super PACs Spending?" *Wall Street Journal,* http://projects.wsj.com/super-pacs.

8. "Sheldon Adelson Sets New U.S. Political Donation Record: Report," *Huffington Post,* September 24, 2012, http://www.huffingtonpost.com/2012/09/24/shel -don-adelson-donations_n_1910094.html.

9. Bob Herbert, "The Donor Class," *New York Times,* July 19, 1998.

10. Adam Nagourney, "For 'America's Mayor,' Tips to Take to the White House," *New York Times,* November 19, 2006.

11. Dana Wilkie, "Image Firms Try to Give Candidates Right Look," *The San Diego Union-Tribune,* August 16, 1999: A-1.

12. Montague Kern, *30-Second Politics* (New York: Praeger, 1989), 16.

13. Larry J. Sabato, *The Rise of Political Consultants* (New York: Basic Books, 1981), 144.

14. Ibid., 38.

15. Ibid., 26.

16. Colbert Nation, *The Colbert Report,* Comedy Central, Episode 09014, www .colbertnation.com/10/23/12.

17. Franco Ordonez, "Fox, MSNBC Viewers See World Differently," McClatchy Newspapers, July 27, 2012.

18. Roger L. Worthington, "The Polemics of Polls," *St. Louis Post-Dispatch,* November 2, 2004: B-7.

19. Don Van Natta, Jr., "Polling's 'Dirty Little Secret': No Response," *New York Times,* November 21, 1999.

20. Jack Rosenthal, "Precisely False vs. Approximately Right: A Reader's Guide to Polls," *New York Times,* August 27, 2006.

21. "Experts Guide Voters on Weighing Polls," *St. Louis Post-Dispatch,* October 30, 1992: C-4.

22. Jennifer LaFleur, "Media Used Good Methods, Bad Judgment in Election Call, Experts Say," *St. Louis Post-Dispatch,* November 15, 2000.

23. *Rachel Maddow Show,* MSNBC, August 5, 2013.

24. David Broder, "When Push Comes to Shove, Fake Polls Become Dirty Trick," *New York Times,* October 10, 1994: B-7.

25. The Faith and Freedom Coalition, http://ffcoalition.com/.

26. "Experts Guide Voters on Weighing Polls," *St. Louis Post-Dispatch,* October 30, 1992: C-4.

27. Mark Hertsgaard, *On Bended Knee* (New York: Farrar Straus Giroux, 1988), 51.
28. Ibid.
29. Austin Ranney, *Channels of Power* (New York: Basic Books, Inc., 1983), 95.
30. "Lawmaker Calls Electoral College 'Relic,'" *St. Louis Post-Dispatch,* September 7, 1997: E-5.
31. Margaret Sullivan, "Covering Clinton's Candidacy in Waiting," *New York Times,* August 17, 2013.
32. John Tebbel, *The Media in America* (New York: Thomas Y. Crowell Company, 1974), 180.
33. "Obama's Press List: Membership Shall Have Its Privileges," *Wall Street Journal,* February 11, 2009.
34. Steve Mistler, "LePage Issues New Policy: No More Talking to 3 Newspapers," *Portland Press Herald,* June 19, 2013, http://www.pressherald.com/politics/LePage-spokeswoman-.html.
35. Ibid.
36. Andrew Malcolm, *Los Angeles Times,* October 31, 2008.
37. Michael Barbaro, "Paul Cuts Off CNN, Again," *New York Times,* January 9, 2012.
38. Dan Rather with Mickey Herskowitz, *The Camera Never Blinks* (New York: William Morrow and Company, Inc., 1977), 222.
39. Barbaro, "Paul Cuts Off CNN, Again."
40. Mark Halperin, "Reporters Try the Silent Treatment," *New York Times,* September 30, 2002: A-25.
41. Hertsgaard, *On Bended Knee,* 108.
42. Ibid., 35.
43. Ibid., 27.
44. Ibid., 52.
45. Ibid., 53.
46. Bernard Weinraub, "'Disinformation' Risks Reagan's Credibility," *Saint Louis Post-Dispatch,* October 4, 1986: B-1.
47. John Tebbel and Sarah Miles Watts, *The Press and the Presidency* (New York: Oxford University Press, 1985), 184–5.
48. David Barstow, "Behind Analysts, the Pentagon's Hidden Hand," *New York Times,* April 20, 2008.
49. Kathleen Hall Jamieson, *Packaging the Presidency,* 2nd ed. (New York: Oxford University Press, 1992), 10.
50. Tony Schwartz, *The Responsive Chord* (Garden City, NY: Anchor Books, 1973), 103.
51. James David Barber, *The Presidential Character* (Englewood Cliffs, NJ: Prentice Hall, 1972), 13.
52. Ibid.
53. Roger Streitmatter, "The Impact of Presidential Personality on News Coverage in Major Newspapers," *Journalism Quarterly* (Spring 1985): 66–8.

54. Jim Rutenberg, "Look Ma, No Script: What That Says about Me," *New York Times,* July 23, 2006.

55. Zeleny, "Testing the Water, Obama Tests His Own Limits."

56. Howard Kurtz, "Stop Me before I Swoon," *Washington Post,* October 18, 1999.

57. Nancy Gibbs and John F. Dickerson, "The Power and the Story," *Time Magazine,* December 13, 1999: 40–50.

58. Ordonez, "Fox, MSNBC Viewers See World Differently."

59. Jane Squier Bruns, former vice president, the Communication Company, interview by author, February 24, 1992, St. Louis, Missouri.

60. Bill Moyers, "A Walk through the Twentieth Century: The Thirty-Second President," Public Broadcasting Service, August 8, 1984.

61. Martin Schram, *The Great American Video Game* (New York: William Morrow, 1987), 24–6.

62. Ibid.

63. Ibid.

64. Project Staff, "Internet Gains Most as Campaign News Source but Cable TV Still Leads," Pew Research Center's Journalism Project. October 25, 2012, http://www.journalism.org/2012/10/25/social-media-doubles-remains-limited/.

65. Charles M. Blow, "The Engagement Gap," *New York Times,* September 7, 2012.

66. Ibid.

67. Ibid.

68. Mike Flynn, "Windfall: Obama Raises $181 Million, Only around 2% of Donations Reportable," *Breitbart,* October 6, 2012, http://www.breitbart.com/Big-Government/2012/10/06/windfall-obama-raises-181-million-only-2-reportable.

69. "Mojo News Team, Full Transcript of the Mitt Romney Secret Video," *Mother Jones,* September 19, 2012, www.motherjones.com/politics/.../full-transcript-mitt-romney-secret-vide.

70. Ben Goad, "Online Campaigning Facing New Regulations," *Press Enterprise,* September 14, 2010. http://www.pe.com/local-news/local-news-headlines/20100914-online-campaigning-facing-new-regulations.ece.

71. Danny Sullivan, "Romney's 'Binders Full of Women' Takes Over Google Images," Search Engine Land, October 17, 2012, http://searchengineland.com/library/link-building/link-building-link-bombs.

72. Moyers, "A Walk through the Twentieth Century."

73. Nick Wadhams, "Mistaken Airstrike Kills at Least 5; U.S. Acknowledges Bombing Wrong Building," *Washington Post,* January 9, 2005.

74. David D. Kirkpatrick, "The Ad Campaign: A Fiery Warning against Taking Risks," *New York Times,* November 7, 2006: A-18.

75. Nicholas D. Kristof, "What? Me Biased?" *New York Times,* October 30, 2008.

76. Ibid.

77. Ibid.

78. Editors, "A Certificate of Embarrassment," *New York Times,* April 27, 2011.

79. Daniel Goleman, "Voters Assailed by Unfair Persuasion," *New York Times,* October 27, 1992: C-1, C-8.

80. Bruns, interview by author.

81. "In Changing News Landscape, Even Television Is Vulnerable: Trends in News Consumption: 1991–2012," Pew Research Center for the People & the Press, Section 4: Demographics and Political Views of News Audiences. Released September 27, 2012. http://www.people-press.org/2012/09/27/section-4-demographics-and-political-views-of-news-audiences.

82. Bruns, interview by author.

83. William Raspberry, "Convictions to Fit All Occasions," *Washington Post,* August 26, 1996: A-13.

84. Ibid.

85. Frank Bruni, "Who Needs Reporters?" *New York Times,* June 1, 2013.

86. Martha T. Moore, "Romney Avoids Entertainment TV," *USA Today,* October 25, 2012, http://www.usatoday.com/story/news/politics/2012/10/24/romney -obama-letterman-leno/1655251/.

87. David Bauder, "Young Get News from Comedy Central," Associated Press, February 11, 2009, http://www.cbsnews.com/2100-207_162-603270 .html.

88. James Hirsen, "Study: Late Night Jokes Target Romney Twice as Much as Obama," Newsmax, November 1, 2012, http://www.newsmax.com/TheWire/ romney-obama-late-jokes/2012/11/01/id/462420.

89. Gregory Ferenstein, "MTV Hopes Online Game Can Energize 2012 Youth Vote," CNN, April 24, 2012.

90. Bill Carter and Brian Stelter, "In 'Daily Show' Role on 9/11 Bill, Echoes of Murrow," *New York Times,* December 26, 2010.

91. Frederick Jackson Turner, *Encyclopedia Britannica,* Vol. 22 (Chicago: William Benton, 1983), 625.

92. Sheryl Gay Stolberg, "White Coats in the Rose Garden as Obama Rallies Doctors on Health Overhaul," *New York Times,* October 5, 2009.

93. Charles Baxter, "Divorce-Court Politics," *New York Times,* November 5, 2006, D-13.

94. Bruns, interview by author.

95. Baxter, "Divorce-Court Politics."

96. Brian Stelter, "Campaign Ad Cash Lures Buyers to Swing-State TV Stations," *New York Times,* July 7, 2013.

97. Trevor Hayes, "Economic Growth for the Next Four Years Optimistic on Jobs," 2012 Election Center, September 6, 2012, http://ivn.us/2012/09/06/ economic-growth-next-four-years.

98. Joe Sterling, "CNN Fact Check: Obama Went on an Apology Tour, Romney and Others Say," CNN.com, October 23, 2012, www.cnn.com/2012/10/23/ politics/fact-check-apology-tour.

99. Ibid.

100. Eleanor MacLean, *Between the Lines* (Montreal: Black Rose Books, 1981).

101. Gopal Ratnam, Terry Atlas, and Margaret Talev, "Obama's Syria Red Line Tested by Chemical Weapons Report," *Bloomberg Politics,* April 26, 2013, http://www.bloomberg.com/news/2013-04-25/hagel-says-syria-chemical -use-found-with-varied-confidence-1-.html.

102. Eric Lichtblau and Scott Shane, "Ally Told Bush Project Secrecy Might Be Illegal," *New York Times,* July 9, 2006: A-1.

103. MacLean, *Between the Lines.*

104. Edwin Diamond and Stephen Bates, *The Spot: The Rise of Political Advertising on Television* (Cambridge, MA: MIT Press, 1984), 301.

105. Bruns, interview by author.

106. Sabato, *The Rise of Political Consultants,* 123.

107. Thomas V. DiBacco, "Dirty Campaigns—So What's New," *St. Louis Post-Dispatch,* April 22, 1992: C-3.

108. Baxter, "Divorce-Court Politics."

109. Kern, *30-Second Politics,* 94.

110. Howard Kurtz, "In Campaign 2000, More Mr. Nice Guy," *New York Times,* November 24, 1999.

111. Ramesh Ponnuru, "Accentuating the Negative," *New York Times,* December 4, 1999: A-29.

112. Jamieson, *Packaging the Presidency,* 64.

113. Tierney, "Using Ads to Cast Star of White House Series."

114. Jamieson, *Packaging the Presidency,* 84.

115. Sabato, *The Rise of Political Consultants,* 163.

116. Grant Barrett, "Words of 2012," *New York Times,* December 22, 2012.

117. Peter Baker, "The Words Have Changed, but Have the Policies?" *New York Times,* April 3, 2009.

118. Simon Waxman, "Poll: Yes to Affirmative Action, No to Racial Preferences," *Boston Review,* August 9, 2013, www.bostonreview.net/.../poll-yes-affirmative -action-no-racial-preferences.

119. William Safire, "On Language; Words at War," *New York Times,* September 30, 2001: F-26.

120. Jennifer Steinhauer, "On a Senate Call, a Glimpse of Marching Orders," *New York Times,* March 29, 2011.

121. *The Daily Show, Comedy Central,* April 14, 2011, www.dailyshow.com.

122. Mark Leibovich, "'Socialism!' Boo, Hiss, Repeat," *New York Times,* March 1, 2009.

123. Ibid.

124. Editorial Desk, "Presidential Ecospeak," *New York Times,* October 18, 2003: A-12.

125. Charles M. Blow, "Revolutionary Language," *New York Times,* January 11, 2013.

126. Ibid.

127. Matthew Reed Baker, "Glossary of Diplomatic Coverage," *Brill's Content* (April 1999): 38.
128. Bruns, interview by author.
129. James Dao and Don Van Natta, Jr., "Bradley Finally Ready to Rub Tall Shoulders," *New York Times,* October 2, 1999.
130. Kern, *30-Second Politics,* 100.
131. Bruns, interview by author.
132. David Wallis, "Political Props and Campaigns That Take Off, or Crash," *New York Times,* April 18, 1999: D-3.

11

Digital Media Communications

OVERVIEW

Digital media communications has had a profound effect on the way that we think, process information, and interact with our globally connected world.

- Google creates as much data in two days—roughly five exabytes—as the world produced from the dawn of humanity until 2003, according to a 2010 statement by Eric Schmidt, the company's chairman, who later declared that he didn't "believe society understands what happens when everything is available, knowable, and recorded by everyone all the time."[1]
- Forty-six percent of parents said their children already prefer computers to their peers.[2]
- Fifty percent of teens view the cell phone as "key to their social life."[3]
- Increasing numbers of people suffer ill health due to the stress of information overload.[4]
- Thirty-six percent of parents worried that their children were overexposed to information.[5]

DEFINITION OF DIGITAL MEDIA COMMUNICATIONS

Digital media generally refers to a range of devices that we use every day, including the computer, cell phones, mobile devices (e.g., iPods and iPads), and digital still and video imaging devices.

A useful definition of digital media communications is as follows:

Digital media communications refers to communication between an initiator and a receiver in which established media systems are combined with computer technology through a transparent machine. Digital media communications emulate humans' patterns of thought and expression, enhancing the role of the participant (initiator and receiver) in the communication process.

It might be helpful to break down this complex definition and expand on its major features:

"Communication between an initiator and a receiver . . ."

Digital media is interactive; we both *retrieve* and *impart* information. As is the case with interpersonal communications, our role changes as we move from the *media communicator* (the person initiating the dialogue) to a member of the *audience* (the recipient of information—both solicited and unsolicited) and back again.

". . . , in which established media systems are combined with computer technology . . ."

Digital media is the ultimate hybrid: established media (i.e., print, photography, graphics, audio, and video) are combined with computer technology to create new, digitized applications of these media.

". . . through a transparent machine."

It wasn't long ago that computer technology was terribly intrusive. We had to attach the connection to an outside source (often through the phone line), boot up the computer, fiddle with the software, log on, and contend with technical delays and interruptions. Today, we don't really care about what "operating system" the machine uses; we are only concerned about retrieving and sending information.

We are moving into the stage of *ubiquitous computers,* in which computers are fully integrated into our physical environment. The next generation of interactive devices will contain *virtual presence systems,* which will monitor both private and public spaces. For example, artificially intelligent refrigerators and pantries will oversee your home food inventory. Equipped with your personal food preference profile, these computerized systems will track the perishables that you require (such as milk and cheese), coordinate delivery, and arrange for payment—freeing you to engage in other pursuits. Your automobile will monitor your fuel level, so that while driving along the highway, the in-dash system will know that you need to purchase fuel within the next few miles. The system will contact the fueling station and arrange for the purchase.

In addition, computers will monitor your personal space. Wearable microprocessors will check your heart rate and blood pressure and automatically contact emergency services if it detects any health irregularities. And when dining at a restaurant, an electronic menu will be able to help you order, taking into account your medical or dietary restrictions.

Moreover, microchips are being inserted into personal clothing and products. Indeed, fashion designers are creating "Stealth Fashion," with pockets that will safely—and stylishly—store monitoring devices.

These ubiquitous computers will contribute to a "cloud" of data that connects our environment. In 2008, for the first time, the number of devices (e.g., lights, heating systems, traffic systems) exceeded the number of human beings connected to the Internet. These ubiquitous devices will communicate with each other. For instance, information from a medical monitoring device might retrieve information that would automatically modify your food preference profile and trigger changes in home food delivery.

Moreover, these ubiquitous computers will contribute to a network of data accumulated by individuals and instantaneously accessible. What we are seeing now with "clouds" will become the standard expectation—that unconnected content areas will become integrated. As a result, people will discover patterns and connections that are currently invisible, such as linkages between the medical and economic worlds, forging new industries that are currently unimaginable.

Like no other mass medium, digital communications approach the dynamics of interpersonal communications. Print, film, radio, and television operate in a *linear* fashion, so that information is presented in a predetermined, established order. However, digital technology is uniquely capable of adapting to our nonlinear patterns of thought and expression. The communication style of human beings can best be

The UNIVAC computer was far from transparent, with the complete system taking up over 380 square feet of space. (AP Photo)

described as *dynamic* and *nonlinear,* jumping from one subject to another before focusing all of our attention on a particular topic. Digital communications enable us to move from subject to subject or go into one topic in depth.

Moreover, digital technology will recapture other features of interpersonal communications to overcome the limitations of distance. As we get deeper into Skype environments and project holography, we will once again have the advantage of seeing body language and gestures. Humor and irony will again be effective communication tools. In addition, closed captioning and audio translation will be incorporated into augmented reality devices such as Google glasses, so that language differences will no longer be an obstacle.

DIGITAL MEDIA LITERACY

Applying critical thinking skills to digital media presentations enables individuals to make independent judgments about the information they receive and communicate through this dynamic medium. A media literacy approach to the study of digital media focuses on the following areas:

- The ability to decode information in a variety of forms[6]

- The discursive style that is peculiar to each medium and that shapes its content[7]
- The ability to make independent choices about the selection and interpretation of content
- An understanding of the emerging structure of the Internet and its impact on content
- An awareness of the impact of digital media on the individual and society
- An awareness of digital content as a "text" that provides insight into our contemporary culture and ourselves
- The development of strategies with which to analyze and discuss media messages conveyed through digital media

As the digital medium continues to evolve, our critical analysis of this communications channel requires continuous attention.

The Keys to Interpreting Media Messages are designed to provide people with the tools to enhance their critical understanding of digital media. As discussed earlier, not all of the keys necessarily are applicable to the study of a particular digital media presentations. However, the keys can offer ways to access and discuss digital media and digital media presentations.

As with all established media, digital technology is simply a channel of communication that can be used in a variety of ways and for a variety of purposes. As such, digital media is neither good nor evil. Much depends on: 1) the media communicator; 2) the motives behind the communication activity; 3) how effectively the media communicator uses the medium to convey the message; and 4) how the audience receives the information.

Digital Communications Model

The digital communications model (discussed in Chapter 2) enables individual audience members to bypass the traditional media gatekeepers. Individuals can now produce their own media presentations, and edit and distribute them over the Internet.

This model empowers the audience as never before, as the individual has become a more immediate factor in the communication process. Moreover, the audience can interact directly with each other in this virtual world. Video "gamers" are connected to a vast network, playing games with people all over the world. And sites like eBay and craigslist are virtual flea markets in which individuals barter and sell goods free of corporate intervention.

Media Communicator

Identifying the Author of Information Posted on the Internet

The Internet can mask the identity of people who, for various reasons, are engaged in some form of deception. Because many messages are unsolicited and anonymous, identifying the author of information posted on the Internet has become an enormous challenge. Unfortunately, the name of the digital media communicator does not always appear on the site—and even if a name is included, it may be a pseudonym. When an authentic name does appear, there may not be any accompanying biographical information, such as the author's background and credentials.

Indeed, the people with whom you interact in the virtual universe may not even be human. "Socialbots" are virtual people who have been programmed to appear authentic. Reporter Ian Urbina provides the following example:

> [In 2013] computer scientists from the Federal University of Ouro Preto in Brazil revealed that Carina Santos, a much-followed journalist on Twitter, was actually not a real person but a bot that they had created. Based on the circulation of her tweets, two commonly used ranking sites, Twitalyzer and Klout, ranked Ms. Santos as having more online "influence" than Oprah Winfrey.
>
> These automated charlatans are programmed to tweet and retweet. They have quirks, life histories and the gift of gab. Many of them have built-in databases of current events, so they can piece together phrases that seem relevant to their target audience. They have sleep-wake cycles so their fakery is more convincing, making them less prone to repetitive patterns that flag them as mere programs. Some have even been souped up by so-called persona management software, which makes them seem more real by adding matching Facebook, Reddit or Foursquare accounts, giving them an online footprint over time as they amass friends and like-minded followers.[8]

But at the same time, digital research tools make it possible to discover the identities of "anonymous" media communicators. Armed with the name of the author, online research can reveal other works of the author, reviews of his/her publications, the affiliations of the author, and other places where the author has been cited as an authority. Reporter Brian Stelter explains,

> Not too long ago, theorists fretted that the Internet was a place where anonymity thrived. Now, it seems, it is the place where anonymity dies. . . The collective intelligence of the Internet's two billion users, and the digital fingerprints that so many users leave on Web sites, combine to . . . make the public sphere more public than ever before and sometimes forces personal lives into public view. . . . This erosion of anonymity is a product of pervasive social media services, cheap cell phone cameras, free photo and video Web hosts, and perhaps most important of all, a change in people's views about what ought to be public and what ought to be private.
>
> . . . This growing "publicness," as it is sometimes called, comes with significant consequences for commerce, for political speech and for ordinary people's right to privacy. There are efforts by governments and corporations to set up online identity systems. Technology will play an even greater role in the identification of once-anonymous individuals: Facebook, for instance, is already using facial recognition technology in ways that are alarming to European regulators.
>
> . . . In Middle Eastern countries like Iran and Syria, activists have sometimes succeeded in identifying victims of dictatorial violence through anonymously uploaded YouTube videos. They have also succeeded in identifying fakes: In a widely publicized case . . . a blogger who claimed to be a Syrian-American lesbian and called herself "A Gay Girl in Damascus" was revealed to be an American man, Tom MacMaster.[9]

Examining the exact relationship between a media communicator and the host organization can provide further clues about the ideology of the media communicator.

For instance, many Web sites allow contributions by anyone who visits the site. Thus, unless informed otherwise, it is best to consider the commentary to be the individual's personal opinion on a topic: a virtual "letter to the editor." Elizabeth Kirk advises,

> If you cannot ascertain either the author or publisher of the page you are trying to evaluate, you are looking at information that is as anonymous as a page torn out of a book. You cannot evaluate what you cannot verify. It is unwise to use information of this nature. Look for another source.[10]

Close inspection often provides clues about the ideology of a Web site. Look for the following points of information about the organization:

- A statement of the Web site's agenda, mission, and vision
- A listing of who sponsors, or provides funding for, the organization
- A way to contact the media communicator (e.g., an e-mail address or a direct link)
- References to people, issues, and events
- Information from external sources that provide information on the ownership of a Web site (of course, it is important to ascertain the point of view of this third-party information)
- Examining the *links* on a Web site: Links have been included in a Web site because they are considered to be associated in some fashion with the site. Consequently, checking these links can be another way to determine the character and orientation of a site

Function

Understanding the *function,* or purpose, behind an interactive communications exchange is a vital consideration—both on the sending and receiving end of the process. To illustrate, author Alex Soojung-Kim Pang discusses the value of "tweeting mindfully": "Tweeting mindfully means knowing your intentions; knowing why you're online right now and asking yourself if you're on for the right reasons."[11]

1 *Identifying Functions: When You Are the **Initiator** of Information*
As discussed earlier, one of the distinguishing characteristics of digital technology is that it emulates interpersonal communications. Thus, during a digital communication exchange, your role may shift from being the initiator of messages and information to being the receiver.

Communication may serve a variety of functions for the *initiator* of media messages (the individual at his/her computer or mobile device):

- *Information.* Thanks to the Internet, individuals have immediate access to an entire universe of knowledge. The Internet has become an invaluable resource for scholarship, reference information, and newsgathering. As a result, individuals have developed sophisticated research skills as part of their normal daily activities.

- *Exchange of Ideas.* The digital domain offers numerous arenas in which individuals can express their ideas. For instance, social networks like Facebook and Twitter offer opportunities for individuals to engage others.
- *Persuasion.* Digital technology is sometimes used to influence the attitudes and behaviors of others. Reporter Ian Urbina declares,

> Researchers say this new breed of bots is being designed not just with greater sophistication but also with grander goals: to sway elections, to influence the stock market, to attack governments, even to flirt with people and one another.[12]

Moreover, many racist groups use Internet sites to sway unsuspecting individuals: "It has become the propaganda venue of choice," declared Mark Potok, spokesperson for the Southern Poverty Law Center.[13]

- *Agenda-Setting.* As discussed in Chapter 2, if the media doesn't tell you what to think, it does tell you what to think about. To illustrate, *culturomics* is a quantitative research methodology made possible through digital software that identifies areas of cultural interest. Using 5.2 million digitized books as their database, researchers have catalogued 500 billion words contained in books published between 1500 and 2008 in English, French, Spanish, German, Chinese, and Russian, identifying the appearance of concepts over time. Researcher Erez Lieberman Aiden explains, "The goal is to give an 8-year-old the ability to browse cultural trends throughout history, as recorded in books."[14] Reporter Patricia Cohen declares,

> With a click you can see that "women," in comparison with "men," is rarely mentioned until the early 1970s, when feminism gained a foothold. The lines eventually cross paths about 1986. You can also learn that Mickey Mouse and Marilyn Monroe don't get nearly as much attention in print as Jimmy Carter; compare the many more references in English than in Chinese to "Tiananmen Square" after 1989; or follow the ascent of "grilling" from the late 1990s until it outpaced "roasting" and "frying" in 2004.[15]

- *Artistic Expression.* The digital domain has emerged as a distribution outlet for artists, circumventing the control of powerful media conglomerates. In the past, musicians have had to attract the interest of record companies in order for their work to be distributed to a mass audience. In the process, these musicians were often forced to compromise their artistic voice to become "marketable," as defined by the recording company. Today, however, musicians whose work is not considered mainstream enough for label consideration can generate interest in their work by offering samples of their music on their Web sites. In fact, some groups are now distributing their music exclusively online.

- *Entertainment.* A world of entertainment exists in virtual space. Entertainment programming is now streamed directly to cell phones and other mobile devices.
- *Commerce.* Shopping has become a primary reason that people go online. (See the discussion of e-commerce in this chapter.)
- *Creating and Maintaining Community.* Digital technology can create a sense of community among individuals throughout the globe. Social networks provide a means of cultivating relationships. Sites like Facebook offer virtual meeting places, where people can develop a network of friends. In addition, virtual matchmaking sites like Match.com and eHarmony provide venues for romantic relationships, relying on database profiling systems to identify compatible mates. Networks such as LinkedIn have significantly changed business practices, from the recruitment of personnel to the exchange of business information.

Digital technology also provides an opportunity for individuals to become members of a community centered around common interests and experiences. To illustrate, after he was diagnosed with a rare form of lymphoma, Louis Birenbaum joined an online discussion group that has provided essential information, support, and advice over the years:

I logged on to the Internet with the hope of learning about the condition. I not only found a plethora of information, but also located a support group of people from around the world who shared my experience.

To my relief, I met people who had far exceeded the official life expectancy cited by doctors. I did not feel self-conscious about asking questions, since I felt that they knew what I was going through. I learned about a variety of treatments, which enabled me to discuss alternative forms of treatment with my physician. I also learned about common symptoms and the emotional reactions that accompany the disease. We even share recipes and jokes. It has been the most successful therapy I could have received.[16]

- *Exploration.* The environment of the Web is liberating in that it enables individuals to go where their curiosity takes them. All too often, however, an individual may be engaged in an *undefined function.* This "impulse browsing" can be extremely informative and entertaining. On the other hand, this can also be an enormous waste of time.

  One of the goals of media literacy is to address the *indiscriminate* use of the medium. Before logging on, identify the function of this communications activity, as well as the amount of time that you anticipate spending on this activity. Thus, if you decide that you would like to play a video game for the next two hours—fine. However, going online without a defined function—and time schedule—can lead to a situation in which you are up all night and suffer the consequences the next day.

  Defining the function can also prevent you from turning to digital media out of boredom or habit and can help you use your time more productively.

2 *Identifying Functions: When You Are the **Receiver** of Information*
What are the *functions,* or purposes, behind the messages that are being sent *to* you?

- *Tracking.* Increasingly, we have become receivers of unsolicited information from the digital landscape. These unrequested messages may fulfill a latent function in which the initiator wants something from the receiver that is not immediately apparent to the participant.

  One latent function, unfortunately, involves sexual predators. Police detective Bova Conti suggests that children should be told never to give out any personal information online, such as age, gender, telephone number, address, school name, or names of sports teams the child may play on. Children also should never send pictures of themselves online. Conti declares that children should be alert to red flags in conversations:

Any time the conversation starts turning to what I call "adult things," kids should get off line. If they are asked about their body parts, or what color their panties are or whether they wear boxers or briefs. That has no place in an online conversation.[17]

- *Marketing*. Games for children that are available for "free" are often marketing surveys designed to identify players' interests and patterns of behavior that later will have commercial value.

  In addition, information retrieval services such as maps actually provide information that has been paid for by business concerns. For instance, you can use Google Maps to find businesses and services such as coffee shops. However, the stores that appear most frequently on these sites are likely paid advertisers.

- *Public Relations*. Some digital sites are designed to create a positive impression about the site's organization with the public. For instance, the FBI has set up a Web site for kids (www.fbi.gov/fun-games/kids) with games, safety tips, stories, and a cartoon character named "Special Agent Bobby Bureau." The cumulative message is that the FBI are "good guys." Another feature (since taken down) was an "FBI Adventure Game" that taught children that they could be "field agents" by monitoring and reporting suspicious behaviors to the FBI. And finally, the page encourages its young audience to consider careers in the Federal Bureau of Investigation.

Audience

In the early days of mass media, advertisers employed a *broadcasting* strategy, in which they used direct mail, radio, print, and television, hoping to interest some of the mass audience within this broad sweep. As print, radio, and television became more sophisticated, marketers were able to *narrowcast* their messages, in which they developed a demographic profile of their target audience and then devised a communication strategy to reach this intended audience.

Today, digital media technology has enabled media communicators to move audience identification to the next level: *microcasting*. Digital media communicators can highlight different aspects of their message that satisfy the particular interests and expectations of each member of the audience. As an example, a digital billboard instantly customizes its message to the drivers of oncoming vehicles.

Further, media communicators can trace your movements on the Internet. Reporter Somini Sengupta explains,

> These efforts speak volumes about the data trail that consumers leave every day, online and off—a trail that can follow them back to

Facebook or to any other advertising platform on the Web. They offer lucrative information every time they provide their e-mail address to a dressmaker or a doctor, and even when they give their ZIP code at the checkout counter. They use loyalty cards to buy snorkeling gear or antidepressants. They browse a retail Web site, leaving a detailed portrait of whether they are interested in ergonomic work chairs or nursery furniture.[18]

Thus, in the case of a message that has been microcast to you personally, examining the presentation can furnish perspective into what the digital media communicator knows (or thinks they know) about you. And conversely, an analysis of audience can provide insight into the communications strategy, style, and content of a digital media presentation. (For additional discussion, see Chapter 9, Advertising.)

Cultural Context

A digital media presentation can be regarded as a text that furnishes perspective into the attitudes, values, behaviors, preoccupations, and myths that define a culture. (For further discussion, see Chapter 4, Cultural Context.)

To illustrate, virtual venues provide opportunities for members of subcultures to discuss issues of particular interest and concern to their communities. Because the digital domain is a virtual melting pot, numerous ideologies are represented—from right-wing militia groups to anarchists. Thus, subcultures that were hardly visible in traditional media in the recent past are now a significant presence within the worldview of the digital domain. As an example, in 1999, over 2,000 Web sites were dedicated to issues involving the gay community. But by 2013, the same search yielded over *2,530,000 million* Web site results.

The Singularity

The evolution of the digital communications age has been accompanied by dramatic cultural changes. Futurist Ray Kurzweil eagerly awaits the coming of *the Singularity* in 2045, an era characterized as "a serious hypothesis about the future of life on Earth."[19] The world of the Singularity is defined by an intelligence explosion in the twenty-first century, brought about largely by digital technology. Although this scenario sounds fantastic, reporter Lev Grossman points to the transformative developments that have already occurred in the virtual landscape:

> Five years ago we didn't have 600 million humans carrying out their social lives over a single electronic network. Now we have Facebook. (In 2012, over 1.06 billion active users.) Five years ago you didn't see people double-checking what they were saying and where they were going, even as they were saying it and going there, using handheld network-enabled digital prosthetics. Now we have iPhones. Is it an unimaginable step to take the iPhones out of our hands and put them into our skulls?
>
> Already 30,000 patients with Parkinson's disease have neural implants. Google is experimenting with computers that can drive cars. There are more than 2,000 robots fighting in Afghanistan alongside the human troops.[20]

Kurzweil contends that in the twenty-first century, technological progress will be 1,000 times greater than that of the last century. Humans will emerge from their self-imposed "era of scarcity," with startling biomedical advances, as well as breakthroughs in energy, agriculture, industry, and environment. Lev Grossman explains,

> In Kurzweil's future, biotechnology and nanotechnology give us the power to manipulate our bodies and the world around us at will, at the molecular level. Progress hyperaccelerates, and every hour brings a century's worth of scientific breakthroughs. We ditch Darwin and take charge of our own evolution. The human genome becomes just so much code to be bug-tested and optimized and, if necessary, rewritten. Indefinite life extension becomes a reality; people die only if they choose to. Death loses its sting once and for all. . .
>
> This is, Kurzweil believes, our destiny as a species.[21]

The day is soon approaching when it is culturally acceptable for computers to be implanted *within* the human body for various purposes. Already, chips are being installed in pets that contain medical, identification, and tracking information. It is a short imaginative leap to introducing this technology into human beings. Monitoring devices are currently in development that an individual would swallow, like a pill. Once ingested, this device would monitor your health and send data to your doctor for ongoing analysis and treatment.

Kurzweil trumpets the innovation of *nanotechnology,* a process in which molecular-sized agents are injected into humans and directly repair cells or tap into computers outside of the body. This technology could soon be used in supervision of Alzheimer's patients, as well as in tracking convicted felons. But in addition, implanting a computer chip in a human being promises to endow individuals with immediate and startling capabilities. Bran Ferren declares,

> An internal computer that lets you, rather than your PC, hook up to the wireless information superhighway. Why risk it? Well, imagine that you could understand any language, remember every joke, solve any equation, get the latest news, balance your checkbook, communicate with others and have near-instant access to any book ever published without ever having to leave the privacy of yourself. Not bad.[22]

This technology promises to slow or even *reverse* the aging process and gives humans startling capabilities.

Computer-augmented human systems will be inserted into the human cranium that will assist memory retention in Alzheimer's patients, and implants will eliminate epileptic seizures. Computer assisted replacement limbs and optical sight enhancements are no longer in the realm of science fiction, but are science *fact.* To quote Arthur C. Clarke, "Any sufficiently advanced technology is indistinguishable from magic."[23]

If the merging of humans and machines sounds too much like science fiction, it should be noted that in 1988 Kevin Warwick participated in an experiment in which a computer chip was temporarily implanted in his arm. Warwick recalls,

> A surgeon burrowed a hole between the skin and muscle on my left biceps and implanted a silicon chip enclosed in a little glass capsule. . . . A computer would monitor my movements and various things would happen automatically. We programmed [my department] building to say "Hello" when I came in and to tell me how many emails I had. Different lights would switch on as I went through various doorways. Doors opened.[24]

Of course, injecting microcomputer chips into the human body raises a set of ethical questions: Does this step turn people into machines, depriving them of their humanity? The science and science fiction writer

John Brunner has predicted, "First we use machines, then we wear machines, then we become machines."[25]

At the same time, machines are becoming more like human beings. The first computers essentially were computation and retrieval devices—rather like an advanced calculator. But today, rather than simply gathering and processing information, some computers have the ability to draw *inferences* from information: in other words, to *think*.

Further, in 2012, experiments were successfully conducted in which paraplegics were able to operate robotic arms by detecting *thought* patterns. Thus, computers now possess *intuition* capabilities, responding to what people are thinking.

By 2030, computers will have taken over the design of subsequent generations of digital technology. Indeed, computers now have the capacity to "replicate" themselves, so that humans will no longer be involved in the design or production of computers. The current models of advanced computers are designing the next generation of machines. Dr. Hod Lipson, professor of mechanical and aerospace engineering at Cornell, who led the research, explains, "Self-replication is the ultimate form of self-repair."[26]

The genre of science fiction has long focused on this theme of a world in which "the machines" have taken over and punish human beings for their hubris of playing God, in the creation of these omnipotent computers. *Forbidden Planet* (1956), *2001, A Space Odyssey* (1968), *Blade Runner* (1982), *The Terminator* (1984), and *The Matrix* (1999) share this fear of the loss of control.

However, Kurzweil regards this development in an optimistic light. Grossman explains,

> All that horsepower could be put in the service of emulating whatever it is our brains are doing when they create consciousness—not just doing arithmetic very quickly or composing piano music but also driving cars, writing books, making ethical decisions, appreciating fancy paintings, making witty observations at cocktail parties.[27]

However, one area of legitimate concern facing consumers of digital technology is balancing personal security with the invasion of privacy. In this post-9/11 world, steps to insure your safety sometimes require the ability to obtain information produced by potential terrorists.

Innovations in communications technology have made it possible to keep track of an individual's whereabouts and activities. Global positioning systems (GPS) are promoted as safety features; however, they also function as location tracking devices. These GPS systems are now automatically installed in cell phones and automobiles; if you object to this feature, you must manually disengage the system, which has become increasingly more difficult to accomplish.

As mentioned earlier, companies collect personal data for use in customizing advertising messages. Moreover, media companies that have access to vast amounts of personal data, including Google and Facebook, have been selling personal data to companies, who then use the data to promote their products. But in addition, the National Security Agency (NSA) has been gathering private phone records and Internet activities of U.S. citizens, in hopes of uncovering terrorist activities. In 2013, Edward Snowden, a contracted employee of the NSA, alerted the public that the U.S. government has been spying on U.S. citizens without first obtaining a warrant.

Privacy has also become an issue in the workplace. Using monitoring software, employers can track Internet activities of their employees and read their e-mail and computer files without informing the employees that they are being watched. This information can be placed in an employee's personnel record and used as part of his or her performance evaluation. In addition, RFID technology enables employers to track the physical whereabouts and daily activities of their employees.

Significantly, we are witnessing the maturing of the "digital native generation"—the first generation of individuals who are unfamiliar with a world *before* computers. This generation is far less concerned with what they might consider "antique notions" such as privacy and personal security, and more concerned with free access to information and accessibility to the network itself. As Scott McNealy, CEO of Sun Microsystems, has declared, "Privacy is dead. Deal with it."[28] There are no secrets in this generation.

Thus, your best defense may begin with understanding that privacy is tenuous in this digital age. Individuals must assume that they are being monitored the moment they enter the network, and that they must take responsibility for their actions in the virtual universe. Reporter Pete Slover advises,

> Assume nothing is absolutely private or safe. That includes your e-mail, browsing habits, news group postings and to be safe the contents of the hard drive of many machines hooked to the Net. Any crucial information should be backed up and, if privacy is essential, should be scrambled using encryption software widely available on the Internet.[29]

MEDIA LITERACY TIPS: PRIVACY

The Federal Trade Commission has posted the following list of steps that parents can take to protect children by safeguarding the privacy of their children online:

- Look for a privacy policy
- Decide whether to give consent . . . authorizing the Web site to collect personal information from your child.
- Decide whether to approve information collection from your kids based on new uses for the information.
- Ask to see the information your child has submitted.
- Understand that you may revoke your consent at any time and have your child's information deleted.[30]

Cultural Trends in the Digital Age

The evolution of the communications age has been accompanied by dramatic cultural changes. Nicholas Negroponte observes that some of these cultural trends appear, on the surface, to be contradictory:

> All things digital get bigger and smaller at the same time—most things in the middle fall out. We'll see a rise in huge corporations, airplanes, hotels, and newspaper chains in parallel with growth in mom-and-pop companies, private planes, homespun inns, and newsletters written about interests most of us did not even know humans have.[31]

Indeed it is often the contradictory nature of these cultural trends that makes societies so complex and multifarious—perhaps mirroring the paradoxical nature of human beings.

To illustrate, when e-commerce first emerged in the 1990s, the ease of online shopping led some to predict that the Internet would become the principal mode of shopping, and that the mall would disappear from the cultural landscape. However, any speculation about the impact of e-commerce must also take into consideration the customs, lifestyle preferences, and the entrepreneurial spirit of human beings. Thus, although shopping at the mall has declined (as online shopping has increased), it has not disappeared altogether. Even though shopping in a store is not the most efficient strategy, shopping at the mall remains America's favorite pastime. As Julie Connelly explains,

The real experience that the Web cannot replicate is social. Shopping is something teenagers do with their friends, especially girls who want to show each other how cool they look in the blue sweater they just found under a load of awful green ones.

"The Net kind of takes away the whole experience—the hunt, the get and the buy," said Eva Kuhn, 13, of New York who browses on line but buys in the stores. "Web shopping is just too perfect. You type in 'gray cords' and there they are. It's not fun."[32]

Moreover, as with all forms of human achievement, technology creates new problems as it solves others. For instance, thanks to GPS systems, we can locate lost pets and navigate unfamiliar environs, but this technology also enables us to be tracked at will. *As with all technology, the computer creates new problems as it solves others.*

However, it is possible to identify the following cultural trends:

- *Globalization*
  Digital media promises to obliterate traditional boarders, moving the world further toward Marshall McLuhan's vision of the global village. The digital domain offers social, cultural, artistic, economic, and political linkages throughout the world, giving rise to an international class of urban, mass-mediated citizens. Thus, a resident of Bangkok may have more in common with a person living in Montreal or Moscow than with a relative who lives in the country.
- *Decentralization*
  At the same time, the communications age is playing a major role in the *decentralization* of countries. Negroponte contends that the global communications age threatens the current configuration of sovereign nations: "Nations, as we know them today, will erode because they are neither big enough to be global nor small enough to be local."[33] In fact, more than half of the world's 200 nations formed as breakaways after 1946. Many nations—including Brazil, Britain, Canada, China, France, Italy, and Spain—are *devolving* power to regions in various ways.[34]

  This trend toward decentralization is also occurring in the United States. For instance, the federal government has been largely ineffectual in addressing major issues such as global warming. Consequently, private companies are increasingly assuming responsibility for a range of services traditionally provided by government, including military units, infrastructure repair, police, and prisons.

In this decentralized world, global corporations have resources that are comparable to many nations. With employees and holdings spread throughout the world, corporations are no longer beholden to these individual nations. Indeed, it can be argued that corporations are becoming such significant global entities that they have assumed much of the power and influence formally held by nation-states.

Indeed, discussions have cropped up about replacing centralized government with regional territories within the United States. A study by economists Alberto Alesina of Harvard and Enrico Spolaore of Tufts University made a strong case that the sheer size of a government has hindered its ability to meet the needs of its dispersed population.[35] In 2009, Texas governor Rick Perry declared that Texans might at some point get so fed up with federal mismanagement that they would want to secede from the union.[36] Another 2012 presidential candidate, Congressman Ron Paul, declared that secession is "an American principle."[37] In 2013, residents in over 30 states signed petitions on the White House Web site calling on President Barack Obama's administration to allow the state to secede.

According to former California governor Arnold Schwarzenegger, California's ability to legislate initiatives in universal health care and global warming is evidence that the decentralization of power has already begun: "[California is] the modern equivalent of the ancient city-states of Athens and Sparta. We have the economic strength, we have the population and the technological force of a nation-state. . . . We are a good and global commonwealth."[38]

As an example of this trend toward regionalism in the United States, Berkshire County, a small community in Massachusetts, has begun printing its own currency, BerkShares, with the bills bearing the likeness of famous figures who made this county their home: a Mohican ($1), Robyn Van En, champion of community-supported agriculture projects ($5), W.E.B. Du Bois, a founder of the civil rights movement ($10), Herman Melville ($20), and Norman Rockwell ($50). Reporter Dan Barry explains,

> The central purpose behind it is to strengthen the local economy, perhaps even inoculate it against the whims of globalization, by encouraging people to support local businesses. . . .
>
> Several dozen businesses agreed to include an alternative currency in their daily transactions and give a discount to those who used it. Now people can pay for groceries, an oil change, and even dental

work with currency. . . . For example, the Berkshire Co-op Market took in an astounding 160,000 BerkShares in the first three months.[39]

Private entities have even begun to assume the role of governments in the conduct of foreign affairs. In 2013, a delegation made up of a corporate head (Eric Schmidt, CEO of Google) and a former elected official (Bill Richardson, ex-governor of New Mexico) conducted a diplomatic mission to North Korea, asking the government to put a moratorium on missile testing and requesting humane treatment for an American citizen detained in the country.

Increasingly, nongovernmental organizations (NGOs) are negotiating peace accords among nations. Paul Lewis explains,

That shift [to NGOs] is a result of the growing complexity of the international agenda, of a communications revolution that has enabled NGOs to mobilize public opinion and of reduced ambitions of governments everywhere since the end of the cold war.[40]

- *Cultural Divisions*
  One of the truly alarming prospects of the communications age is that digital technology is widening existing divisions within societies, based on differences in age, social class, and regions. Twenty percent of American adults do not use the Internet at home, work, or school, or by mobile device, a figure essentially unchanged since 2009. Although the United States is the world's largest economy, it is only ranked seventh among 20 major global economies in 2012 with respect to Internet usage among adults over 18 years of age, behind Britain, Canada, South Korea, Germany, France, and Australia, as well as nearly every other smaller country in Western Europe. Indeed, since 2000, the United States has slipped from fourth in this category in 2000, according to the International Telecommunication Union, a United Nations agency. As a result, 60 million Americans are shut off from jobs, government services, health care, and education.[41]
- *Generational Schisms*
  Approximately half of Americans 65 and older use the Internet; in contrast, three-quarters of people under the age of 65 use the Internet.[42] This disparity in media usage contributes to the schism between generations. Given how quickly cultural trends are disseminated throughout the culture, it is increasingly difficult for parents

to keep up to date with the new artists and movements embraced by their children.

In addition, the communication patterns that characterize different generations also contribute to the distance between generations. As an example, young people are far more likely to use text messaging than their parents and grandparents. As a result, these generations aren't likely to communicate with each other.

Indeed, the generational divide has accelerated so markedly that the phenomenon of the "generation gap" now exists between *siblings*. Studies show that many college students are out of touch with the media habits of brothers and sisters still in high school. Reporter Brad Stone explains, "According to a (2009) survey . . . teenagers are more likely to send instant messages than slightly older 20-somethings (68 percent versus 59 percent) and to play online games (78 percent versus 50 percent)."[43] As a result, Lee Rainie, director of the Pew Research Center's Internet and American Life Project observes,

People two, three or four years apart are having completely different experiences with technology. College students scratch their heads at what their high school siblings are doing, and they scratch their heads at their younger siblings. It has sped up generational differences.[44]

- *Regional Divisions.* Although the mass media is well established in the urban areas of many traditional cultures, the global network may not have reached the outlying villages and farms. To illustrate, the typical resident of Bangkok, Thailand, is plugged into the virtual universe. However, in outlying villages, access to the Internet may be rare—almost foreign. As a result, many young people are leaving these small villages to reside in urban centers, feeling out of touch with the unmediated lifestyle of the rural environment. In the United States, Internet use is lowest in the South, particularly in Mississippi, Alabama, and Arkansas.[45]
- *Class Divisions.* The disparity of income in the United States is wider than at any time since the 1920s. The annual income of the top one-hundredth of 1 percent of the population is $27 million. In contrast, the median income for the bottom 90 percent is $31,244.[46] Taking inflation into consideration, the income of the average wage earner in the United States has increased by 26 percent since 1970. Over this same period, the median annual income of the top 1 percent

of the population has increased by 430 percent.[47] This income disparity has contributed to a "digital divide," in which poor, uneducated
people have limited access to media and cannot enjoy the benefits of
digital culture. As a result, a considerable segment of the population
feels disenfranchised, with little hope for success. Futurist Jeremy
Rifkin has projected that the global communications economy could
result in an 80 percent unemployment rate within the next 50 years—
principally in the labor, distribution, and service sectors.[48] This pre-
diction is eerily mirrored by a 2013 study, revealing that 80 percent
of adults have struggled with joblessness, near poverty, or reliance on
welfare for at least parts of their lives.[49]

- *Racial Disparities.* In 2012, 76 percent of white American households used the Internet, as compared with 57 percent of African
  American households.[50]
- *Social Upheaval.* Historically, as societies have moved from one
  stage of cultural sensibility to another, traditional lines of authority
  and power have been disrupted, leaving individuals to face issues of
  meaning and survival. As criminologist Richard Rosenfeld observes,
  "Generally speaking, widening disparities will create disorder. This
  disorder can take the form of political process, or it can take a more
  individualized form such as street crime."[51]

Potential applications of this technology raise some significant concerns. At the same time that the technology enables you to navigate
around your environment, the system is able to find you without effort.
The information-collection capability of digital technology can also discover where and when you bought your clothes, and, through an immediate cross-check, determine your identity, financial records, where you
reside, and your current location.

If a governmental entity accumulated these personal data, individuals
would be rightfully concerned. However, since these intrusions are driven
by commercial interests, people don't view this as dangerous. But it is.
One of the fundamental tenets of media literacy is that a medium is
inherently neutral—just a channel of communication. What determines
whether it is a positive or negative influence is who is producing the
messages and what purposes are served by the communication. This
same principle applies to digital media technology. It is imperative that
citizens remain vigilant to insure that no one exploits digital technology
for political ends.

Worldview

Digital imagery creates a seamless reality that makes possible a world (and worldview) that originates from our imaginations rather than from natural laws. In the virtual universe, people can fly and ducks can sing. While this has been true nearly as long as there have been media (and certainly literature works on this same imaginative principle), the digitized world that we experience is astonishingly "real."

In former days, the "cut and paste" technique of tabloid newspapers made the manipulated images readily apparent to the audience. Now, however, it is increasingly difficult to distinguish between "reality" and what we *experience* as reality. Thus, although the images of models may be unattainable (even to the models themselves), they establish convincing standards of beauty.

And soon, as we get deeper into the age of digital media, the boundary between what is real and what is "augmented reality" will begin to collapse: we won't be able to tell the difference.

The seamless nature of this reality will surely challenge our critical faculties. Augmented reality is the first 4-D medium and adds touch and smell to the senses we will use to experience the world. Augmented reality places the individual *within* the computing environment itself, extending Marshal McLuhan's observation to the digital age, "The medium is no longer the message—you are."

The danger of being embedded in a machine is that you may not know where *you* end and the *machine* begins.

If we are to learn from the history of other media, we know that people will spend *increasing* time in this alternate universe. As Metaio, an augmented reality software company, declares in its slogan, it is "Always On. Always Augmented." This becomes enticing in a world that is ultra-pleasant for each member of the audience (thanks to microcasting), presenting a reality that we *want* to believe in. These universes will be customized for us, based on our personal interests, myths, preoccupations, and anxieties.

However, all of these alternate universes will share the following characteristics:

- *A utopian world.*
  An alternative reality offers a brighter and more gratifying environment than the world we would otherwise encounter.
- *A consumer-oriented world, characterized by products that enhance our lives.*
- *A seamless world.*

MEDIA LITERACY TIPS

The following Medial Literacy Tips are particularly useful in the critical analysis of an augmented reality, when considered as a *media presentation:*

- Media communicator: Who is responsible for designing this reality?
- What are the *functions* (or purposes) behind efforts to construct (or, at least, to shape) this reality?

Other questions involve children's preparedness to contend with augmented reality:

- At what stage of development is inhabiting augmented reality appropriate?
- What is the role of parents in monitoring and directing children?
- How can parents learn about the kind of world that their children inhabit?
- How can parents talk with their children about the alternate worlds that their children inhabit?
- How can parents talk with their children about ways in which augmented reality presentations depart from our everyday reality?

A wondrous 4-D world that shapeshifts; the past is brought into the present, and consumer items assume new meanings.

- *A world characterized by immediate gratification.*
  Information will be instantly available, superimposed over the buildings, people, and artifacts that you see.
- *A world enhanced by an entertainment sensibility.*
  This world will be punctuated by a multimedia soundtrack that dramatizes our daily interactions (consisting of a combination of media: video, audio, print, graphs), perhaps programmed by a database of likes, dislikes, and expectations.

Education

Digital media technology is revolutionizing our educational system. Online classes and programs have become integral parts of higher education. In addition, digital technology has been incorporated into classroom instruction at the primary and secondary levels.

Digital technology has also had an *indirect* influence on the educational process, affecting how students learn. Jeffrey Rosen, author of *Rewired: Understanding the iGeneration and The Way That They Learn,* points out that today's "iGeneration" processes information differently from prior generations of students, and therefore requires an alternative delivery method and setting: "If (educators) continue to try to reach them on our terms, using traditional teaching tools, we will fail them."[52]

Moreover, in the future, education will be largely based on *game theory.* Video games offer sophisticated, personalized interactive learning environments, in which participants learn at their own pace. These simulation learning modules apply the entertainment sensibility of video games, including a narrative structure, characters, and storyline. As an example, a marine biology course might begin with you, the student, supplying basic information about yourself, including a photograph. From there, you would be able to see yourself in a "wetsuit," making your way to the ocean floor. The narrative flow involves learning the environment to reach a "goal" or objective. Thus, each fish that you encounter would tell you (since in this world, fish can talk) about themselves, which is part of the puzzle. The "winners" of the game are the students who are able to apply the principles of marine biology toward the objective.

Another fascinating development is the establishment of MOOCs—free online courses that are being offered by prominent educators. Students grade each other's work and at the end of the course, receive a certificate acknowledging their mastery of the material.

These classes have been phenomenally successful. In its first four months of operation, the online education company Coursera attracted two million students—70,000 new students a week signing up for over 200 courses.[53]

The educators who have organized MOOC classes freely acknowledge that they haven't anticipated the implications of these courses. However, it is certain that these free online classes have the potential to revolutionize higher education.

Warfare in the Digital Age

The digital culture has drastically affected how countries wage war. Indeed, the very concept of adversaries has changed. The terrorism network is no longer centralized in one nation but is spread throughout the world.

Moreover, as reporter David Sanger explains, in this new geopolitical landscape, defining the "enemy" is not always an easy task:

> China is not an outright foe of the United States, the way the Soviet Union once was; rather, China is both an economic competitor and a crucial supplier and customer. The two countries traded $425 billion in goods last year, and China remains, despite many diplomatic tensions, a critical financier of American debt. As Hillary Rodham Clinton put it to Australia's prime minister in 2009 on her way to visit China for the first time as secretary of state, "How do you deal toughly with your banker?"[54]

Moreover, the objective of warfare is no longer the conquest of territory or the subjugation of the opposing army. Instead, the modern army seeks to acquire information or disrupt the enemy's communications networks. In February 2013, the Obama administration circulated to the nation's Internet providers a confidential list of computer addresses linked to "Comment Crew," a hacking group that has stolen terabytes of data from American corporations. According to reporter David Sanger, "[O]f the evidence that the People's Liberation Army is probably the force behind 'Comment Crew,' the biggest of roughly 20 hacking groups.[55]

Significantly, another major target of cyber attacks is media Web sites. For example, in April of 2013, the Syrian Electronic Army took responsibility for a false tweet at the Associated Press's Web site announcing two explosions at the Web site that injured President Obama. The message was "re-tweeted" 5,000 times within the first minute. Within the first three minutes, the stock market plunged by 140 points. That month, the Syrian terrorist group also hacked into the *Sixty Minutes* Web site, as well as the Twitter account of two newspapers, the *Guardian* and the *Financial Times*.

Terrorists strike civilian targets, the goal being to inspire *terror* in the population through surprise and disruption of everyday activities. Thus, terrorists strike mass transportation targets such as airplanes and subways. Fear is spread among the populace with the help of the media; otherwise, people would be unaware of these relatively small acts of destruction.

Rather than using conventional weapons, cyber attacks have emerged as a major threat to world security. John Markoff comments,

> The specter of simultaneous computer network attacks against banking, transportation, commerce and utility targets—as well as against the military—conjures up the fear of an electronic Pearl Harbor in which the nation is paralyzed without a single bullet ever being fired.[56]

As Steven Lukasik observes, "Preparing for cyberwar will force the nation to rethink the way it fights wars. . . . We've been trained to fight nuclear wars where static defenses are fatal, but in information warfare we have to rethink everything."[57]

In 2007, China successfully conducted a missile test, successfully "blinding" one of its older communications satellites. The implications of this test are far reaching and devastating to countries like the United States, which rely on communication satellites to mange their military forces. Also in 2007, the United States and Israel developed and then deployed the Stuxnet computer worm, which "infected" (and thus disabled) the Natanz uranium enrichment facility in Iran.[58]

The U.S. Pentagon has established a military center to coordinate the nation's cyber-warfare forces under the Air Force Space Command. Markoff explains,

> The new command's first mission will be to coordinate the defense of the military's computer networks against foreign threats and cyberterrorists. Soon after the mission will expand to include offense: Joint Task Force Computer Network Attack, in Pentagon jargon, designed to conduct wartime military operations against computer networks in enemy countries.[59]

Nuclear weapons assume a different role in cyber warfare. Instead of a huge arsenal used to destroy property and military forces, a small tactical nuclear weapon that releases a powerful electromagnetic pulse (EMP) can be deployed to destroy computer, telecommunications, and defense systems. And in cases calling for conventional combat, the U.S. military is increasingly reliant on military drones—pilotless planes guided by digital technology from a great distance.

Structure

Digital media technology has moved the economy from the industrial age into a *global, communications-based system.* This new economic model has revolutionized the way in which people conduct business.

To illustrate, let us imagine that you want to purchase a bicycle. In the system left over from the industrial age, you would drive to a nearby store, where they maintain an extensive inventory of bikes. If you were fortunate, you would find a model among the store's inventory that met your specifications (e.g., size, color), and you would complete your transaction.

However, in the global, communications-based economic model, you would submit your desired bicycle specifications to an Internet auction site, where companies compete for your business. You then select the best offer, arrange for payment, and activate the order. The bicycle is then manufactured and shipped to you within 36 hours.

This economic model offers several advantages for the consumer. Shopping is convenient, accommodates your schedule, and is free of pressure by salespeople. In addition, companies now are able to produce *customized products,* so that you can purchase a bicycle manufactured to your personal specifications ("I'd like dark blue paint on the top and high visibility yellow on the bottom, and my left leg is 1/8" longer than my right"). Further, the savings accrued by reducing inventory, labor, and marketing costs enables the manufacturer to sell this personalized bicycle for 30 to 60 percent cheaper than the mass-produced model sold at your neighborhood bike store.

Thus, this communications-based economic model offers many advantages for the consumer. Indeed, because Internet stores operate on an automated system, they are "open" 24 hours per day—whenever you feel like purchasing a product. And finally, the product will be delivered straight to your door—the ultimate convenience.

In addition, this model is advantageous for *businesses:*

- Internet commerce eliminates the real estate expenses associated with setting up local stores and outlets, such as acquiring a brick and mortar storefront for displaying and selling goods.
- This new economic model eliminates the need to maintain an inventory, which is a major business expense.

  In this new business model, however, a product is never manufactured until *after* it has been sold. Thus, the bike you have purchased online will not be assembled until you order it. At that point, the company automatically places the order over the Internet with their suppliers (e.g., bike frame manufacturers, tire and paint companies). The materials are immediately sent to a factory, where the bike is assembled and shipped directly to you.
- This new economic model reduces personnel costs.

  Sales, support, and managerial personnel are no longer required at local retail outlets. Further, because the bike can be primarily assembled by robots, the labor force has been reduced substantially.
- The digital domain offers expanded opportunities for promoting products.

Unlike the neighborhood store, all companies can have global outreach. Consequently, the new challenge for companies involves targeting their advertising message to individuals who are most likely to buy the merchandise.

However, because many customers prefer to try on clothing before purchasing a product, some companies have adopted a business strategy called "showrooming" that incorporates aspects of both economic models. These companies reduce their inventory, keeping just enough sizes and colors on hand at local outlets so that shoppers can get a general impression about the style and desirability of the item. Body scanners then record the exact measurements of customers, so that all future purchases ordered over the Internet, can be made to the exact specifications of the customer.

Another hybrid approach is *social shopping,* in which social media provides the collaborate experience that is missing from online purchases. Jenna Wortham explains,

The social shopping sites essentially compile stylish goods of similar sensibility from shops around the Web, and make it easy to share with friends what items they like and buy. Most of the sites have adopted the interface of pinning images on a virtual bulletin board popularized by Pinterest, one of the most popular social networks.

In addition, most social shopping sites let their users find and follow their friends and favorite brands or shops, which creates a feed akin to those on Instagram, Twitter or Facebook. The feed is filled with new items that they might like to buy.

Veronica Gledhill, 29, an editor at The Cut, a fashion blog, said that sites like Wanelo brought back the fun of trips to the mall with her friends that she remembered from her youth. "The last time I went shopping with friends was at the mall in my early 20s or maybe when I was a teenager," she said. On the Web, "shopping is an isolated experience," she said. "But you still want input."[60]

Online shopping grew during 2012's holiday period. Visits to retail Web sites increased by 27 percent on Christmas Day over the previous year. Online purchases also increased by 6 percent on Thanksgiving and 11 percent on the Monday after Christmas.[61]

Advances in digital technology have contributed to the success of this new economic model. For example, 3-D printing is a manufacturing process that builds, or "copies," three-dimensional solid replicates from a digital model, often at a distance from the original model.

NASA currently is experimenting with 3-D printing of food, thus eliminating the need to stockpile an inventory of goods on the ship. Reporter Douglas Quenqua explains,

> The road to Mars is long and fraught with danger. What it doesn't have is restaurants. So a mechanical engineer, Anjan Contractor, has won a $125,000 grant from NASA to build a 3-D printer that can take the basic building blocks of food—oil, water, protein and tomato powders—and turn them into edible items like chocolate and pizza, the online magazine *Quartz* reported last week.
>
> The hope is that the system can provide enough food to sustain astronauts during journeys to Mars and beyond. Presumably, the menu will expand to include healthier options. The device, to be developed on open-source software, drew instant comparisons to the "Star Trek" meals-on-demand machine, the replicator.[62]

In the medical field, researchers are using 3-D printers to create synthetic body parts. Quenqua provides the following example: doctors at the University of Michigan successfully "printed" a synthetic body part for a child with a rare birth defect, a part that enables him to breathe on his own.

Moreover, the 3-D printer promises to usher in a return to the age of *personalized products*—not unlike the cottage industries that emerged at the beginning of the Industrial Revolution. Rather than buying "off-the-rack" mass-produced goods, products will be customized to suit you.

As an example, experiments are underway with the "printing" of personalized 3-D medications. For instance, you may require a medication that is equivalent to one and one-fourth of the standard dosage. Through 3-D printing, pills can be manufactured that contain that dosage.

Moreover, designers will be able to produce personalized products in quantities that will enable them to compete in the mass marketplace, transforming artisans into manufacturers.

Regulation

The current efforts to regulate the content of and access to the digital domain originate from four sources:

- *The Individual's Relationship to Digital Content*
  The digital domain is a democratic medium that thus far has resisted central ownership. However, large Internet service providers (ISPS) like AT&T, Sprint, MCI, and Charter argue that they

should have the right to "prioritize" the information that is distributed through their networks. The criteria for this multitiered system would be based upon commercial considerations; the highest priority would be for those organizations conducting business with the ISP. In essence, the Internet would become a toll road. Those at the end of the line would consist of personal communications, academic traffic, and companies that are unable to pay the additional charges. Opponents of this measure favor a policy of Net neutrality, which calls for equal access. As of 2007, this measure was being considered by the U.S. Congress. Eric Schmidt, CEO of Google and an advocate of Net neutrality, declares, "Creativity, innovation, and a free and open marketplace are all at stake in this fight."[63]

Two related areas of regulation are *copyright* and *privacy protection*.

- *Copyright*

  A major question has emerged about ownership of the content that appears on a company's Web site: do you own the content that you post on an online site?

  In 2012, a lawsuit was filed over whether Instagram (or its parent company Facebook) could use pictures posted on the site to make money. Instagram's cofounder, Kevin Systrom, maintains that the individuals posting images on the site hold the copyright on the material. He points to the company's terms of use, which declares, "Instagram does *not* claim *any* ownership rights in the text, files, images, photos, video, sounds, musical works, works of authorship, applications, or any other materials (collectively, 'Content') that you post on or through the Instagram Services."

  However, although we might own our data, we may not always control what happens to those data. For instance, although Facebook, Instagram's parent company, informs its users that they own their data, their preferences for certain products—their "likes"—can be used in the service of a type of advertising known as sponsored stories. Reporter Somini Sengupta explains,

  > Instagram is a free service, and the business model of free Web services relies precisely on taking advantage of user data, including the "content" users produce. Facebook makes money by letting advertisers direct marketing messages at prospective customers, based on what they reveal about themselves and who their friends are. And even as Facebook too says it doesn't "own"

any of it, personal data is the company's most valuable asset. Advertising is its principal moneymaker. . . .[64]

In 2007, a Belgian court ruled that Google's news-aggregating service, Google News, has been violating copyright laws by providing links to French-language newspapers.

- *Privacy Protection*
  In 2012, the U.S. Congress reauthorized the Foreign Intelligence Surveillance Act, extending the government's authority to intercept electronic communications of spy and terrorism suspects in the United States without having to show "probable cause" that the suspect was working for a foreign power or a terrorist group.
- *Efforts by Individual Nations to Regulate Access to Content on the Internet*
  In this emerging global culture, a country's ability to enforce its own system of laws and regulations has become increasingly challenging. To illustrate, the United States has its own laws restricting pornography; however, an Internet user need only tap into a Web site originating in another, more permissive country to circumvent U.S. laws. However, individual nations are attempting to make digital companies conform to their legal regulations.

  To illustrate, China has developed an extremely sophisticated filtering system designed to prevent access to sensitive topics, including pornography, religious materials, and political dissent. Government censors also impose harsh restrictions on China's international Internet traffic.

  In 2006, the Chinese government entered into an agreement with search engine Google; in exchange for access to 100 million Chinese consumers, Google agreed to censor material that the government found objectionable. Thus, a Google search of "Tiananmen Square," site of the 1989 student protest that turned into a massacre, generates images of protesters and tanks, whereas a search through the Chinese filter produces benign images of happy tourists posing in the square.

  In December 2012, the Chinese government issued new regulations requiring that Internet users furnish their real names to service providers, making it more difficult for individuals to view overseas Web sites that the Chinese Communist Party regards as containing politically objectionable information. At the same time, this ruling makes Internet companies responsible for deleting forbidden post-ings and reporting them to the authorities.

Chinese authorities periodically detain and even jail Internet users for politically sensitive comments, such as calls for a multiparty democracy or accusations of impropriety by local officials. However, it is difficult to enforce these measures, given the growing number of Chinese citizens with access to the Internet. As a result, the govern-ment constructs technological barricades that block access to the Internet. However, savvy activists immediately begin to devise ways to circumvent these technological barriers. This game of *media pong* is an ongoing contest:

- first, the government imposes technological curbs on the Internet;
- enterprising citizens then devise ways to circumvent these techno-logical barriers;
- the government then develops new technology to control information and access;
- citizens then come up with new strategies to evade the restrictions;
- and so forth. . . .

To illustrate, in 2012 the Chinese government imposed a series of regu-lations in response to stories that appeared on the Internet about the accu-mulation of wealth by the families of China's leaders. Chinese activists also posted stories about sexual and financial abuses by local officials that led to a number of their resignations and dismissals.

In order to enforce these new regulations, the Chinese government began experimenting with ways to identify and block virtual private net-works (VPNs).[65] A VPN is a tool for encrypted computer communication that is widely used by businesses and individuals in China to protect them-selves against intrusion by the government, as well as to provide access to international Web sites that have been prohibited by the government.

But in this game of media ping pong, the young Chinese journalists are doubtless preparing strategies to "return serve" and circumvent these latest technological government restrictions imposed by the government.

Iran, Saudi Arabia, the United Arab Emirates, Tunisia, Yemen, and Sudan also employ commercial filtering products—all developed by U.S. corpora-tions. Nart Villeneuve warns, "In effect, U.S. corporations are in a position to determine what millions of citizens can and cannot view on the Internet."[66]

Countries are also encountering obstacles in the enforcement of laws regu-lating e-commerce. Governments must contend with "virtual" corporations that can change their official "residence" within minutes. The *London Economist* observes, "Every day, $1.5 trillion moves around the world's foreign-exchange markets. Companies merge across national borders and even talk of changing nationality completely."[67] In this environment, the commercial regulations of one country have very limited authority.

Kim Gordon provides the following illustrative scenario involving the difficulty for individual governments to assess taxes on global business transactions:

> I live in the United States. I open a new business. I do not manufacture a product but, instead, provide an information service. It is entirely online. The monetary transactions are credited to my account in the Netherlands. I bypass the local, national, and the international tax structure. In fact, I don't pay taxes anywhere. How can the United States government require me to pay business taxes if the machines, information, and accounting transaction systems are physically located in South Africa?

- *Multinational Companies' Efforts to Control Content*
  Internet companies have struggled to adapt to the political climates of individual countries.

- In 2006, Google established Google.cn in China to adapt to the strict censorship imposed in that country. But in 2010, saying the security of its e-mail had been breached in a campaign to spy on Chinese dissidents, Google announced that it would stop censoring Google.cn and might have to withdraw from China altogether.
- In 2009, Google blocked its YouTube video service in South Korea from uploading material after the government imposed laws requiring contributors to register with their real names. Reporter Eric Pfanner observes, "Ostensibly, the law was intended to curb anonymous abuse that is said to have contributed to suicides, but critics say it stifles political dissent."[68]
- In Italy, four Google executives have been charged with privacy violations in a case involving a video posted on YouTube showing schoolboys bullying an autistic classmate. Google says a guilty verdict could make it hard for YouTube to continue operating in Italy because it might mean the site is responsible for its content; currently YouTube relies on users to flag anything potentially inappropriate.

- *International Consortiums' Transnational Regulatory Efforts*
  International organizations have endeavored to devise regulations that transcend national boundaries. One measure consists of
  designating additional *domain names* that appear at the end of the
  URL. These domain names identify the function of communication, informing the audience about the intent of the message. For
  instance, educational institutions affix the suffix ".edu," commercial enterprises are designated ".com," and government Web sites
  are ".gov."

  The Internet Corporation for Assigned Names and Numbers
  (ICANN), a nonprofit entity that coordinates the Internet address
  system, has opened the process of expanding the domain names.
  ICANN vetted and initially approved 1,574 applications for new
  "top-level domains."[69] In 2014, ICANN anticipates signing contracts
  with companies and organizations to manage the registries for the
  new top-level domains.

  Some companies have applied for multiple suffixes. Donuts Inc.,
  a domain registry company in Bellevue, Washington, filed the most
  applications, asking for 307—including .love, .family, .health, and
  .plumbing.[70] Google and Amazon have submitted applications for
  numerous suffixes, including .app, .book, .cloud, .game, .movie, and
  .search. L'Oréal, the cosmetics conglomerate, has requested .beauty,
  .hair, and .skin. And, not surprisingly, Johnson & Johnson has applied for .baby.

  However, as reporter Natasha Singer points out, these current
  plans place this process under the control of individual companies,
  which is a dangerous precedent:

Advocates of Internet freedom contend that such an expanded
address system effectively places online control over powerful commercial and cultural interests in the hands of individual companies,
challenging the very idea of an open Internet. Existing generic
domains, like .net and .com, overseen by Verisign Inc., a domain registry, have an open-use policy; that means consumers can buy domain
names ending in .com directly from retail registrars like GoDaddy.
With a new crop of applicants, however, ICANN initially accepted
proposals for closed or restricted generic domains, a practice that
could limit competing views and businesses.

. . . Charleston Road Registry, a unit of Google, has indicated on
its Web site that it plans to open certain of its new suffixes—like .ads,

.boo, .dad and .how—to public registration. But in applications to manage other generics like .app, the company has laid out a more restrictive approach, saying it planned to employ its own criteria to assess and approve entities seeking to use those suffixes.

. . . "It's a very legitimate competition concern," says Jon Leibowitz, a former chairman of the Federal Trade Commission who recently joined the law firm Davis Polk & Wardwell in Washington as a partner. "The public at large, consumers and businesses, would be better served by no expansion or less expansion" of domains.[71]

Introduction

The homepage serves as the introduction to a Web site. In this capacity, the homepage serves the following functions:

- *Attracting attention.* A Web designer relies on glitzy media (graphics, photos, video, and audio), as well as attractive colors to draw visitors to the site. At times, however, production elements can actually *interfere* with the message. The latent function of fancy graphics and animation may be to impress the audience with the designer's technical wizardry rather than to communicate a message.
- *Creating a first impression.* The homepage affects our attitudes about the site's credibility and value. In addition, the homepage provides information about the Web site's focus and mission.
- *Establishing the "personality" of the Web site.* Because Web sites strive to develop an identity with which the intended audience feels comfortable and familiar, examining the "personality" of the Web site can furnish some valuable clues about its intended audience.
- *Drawing audience members deeper into the site.* The homepage is designed to convince the audience that additional information of interest can be found deeper in the site. At times, however, a homepage is a teaser designed to *redirect* your initial interest. For instance, you may hit a site looking for a vacation to Scotland, only to have a "pop-up" ad attempt to convince you that you would rather invest in a new set of tires. It is important to remain clear about your initial purpose for visiting the site so that you can be alert to efforts to redirect this interest. You will then be in a position to

make a conscious decision about whether to pursue this new direction or find a site that provides the information you were originally seeking.

- *Serving as a guide to the Web site.* The homepage directs the audience to points of interest or importance in the site. In the process, the menu of information serves as an indicator of the priorities of the digital media communicator.

Explicit Content

How do you evaluate the information that is available in the digital universe?

In traditional print publications, much of what appears is subjected to a review process to verify the validity of the content. Copyeditors and editors review the text to insure clarity and accuracy. Scholarly articles generally go through a rigorous peer review process. However, no such guarantee exists with respect to the content that appears on the digital network. Because of the open nature of the network, the available information is, to be kind, uneven. Consequently, it has become a real challenge to evaluate the information that appears in virtual arenas. The criteria that should be used to evaluate content include:

- *Timeliness.* Information presented in digital media presentations can be continually revised and updated. Technology, science, medicine, politics, media, and business are disciplines that are constantly evolving. For these topics in particular, critical questions include:
  - When was the information first published?
  - When was the site updated?

  The date of the last revision sometimes appears at the bottom of the homepage. If you are unable to determine the currency of the information, it could be outdated and therefore should be researched further or discarded.
- *Verifiability.* Is the information supported by evidence? Can it be replicated?
- *Reputable Sources.* Does the author use sources? If so, what do you know about these sources? (For further discussion of sources, see Chapter 8, Journalism.)
- *Point of View.* What is the point of view of the content? How is this point of view supported? (For further discussion of point of view, see Chapter 2, Process.)

Production Elements

As discussed earlier, digital media represents a unique combination of print, photography, graphics, audio, and video. These media can complement and support each other to present information clearly and effectively. For instance, video footage can show an event unfolding, supplemented by print material that furnishes background, details, and context of the event.

Production elements serve the following functions:

- *Production elements can be used to reinforce messages, and in some cases can convey independent messages.*
- *The digital communicator is able to customize the style of the presentation to cater to the audience member's tastes and interests.*

  For instance, a Web site might present a conservative appearance for one visitor, and a wild look for the next one.
- *Style can also express an attitude about the content being presented.*

  For instance, the production elements may suggest that the site is hip, exciting, and contemporary, and that the information contained in the site is worth examining.
- *Production elements can draw the target audience to the Web site.*

  For instance, many Web sites designed for children are designed to attract their attention through colorful graphics or a fun interactive approach.

As discussed earlier, production elements such as the title, graphics, photos, and slogans can furnish perspective into the intended target audience. For instance, colorful graphics establish a fun interactive environment designed to attract the attention of a young audience. (For more discussion of audience, see Chapter 2.)

Because the audience assumes a major role in retrieving information, the editor must develop navigation strategies to present information in a clear, easily accessible manner. As an example, Web sites designed for an older audience use larger fonts, a simple graphic design, and clear navigational instructions.

Sophisticated media technology that was beyond the reach of individuals and small companies during the 1990s is now in the hands of anyone with a laptop computer. These technical advances have decentralized the artistic process; individuals now can shoot, edit, and distribute professional-level materials to a global audience. As of 2013, video accounts for 60 percent of the traffic on the Internet.[72] As a result, independent videos have emerged as an alternative entertainment format; young people are watching (and producing) independent videos on venues like YouTube .com, instead of the predictable genres that appear on the major broadcast networks.

Digital media programming is never "completed"—meaning that information can be updated minute by minute if the budget allows. Moreover, a Web page contains considerably more information than the conventional print layout. A "pull down" feature enables the digital media communicator to embed related topics for further consideration. In addition, audience members can click on "hyperlinks" that embellish the idea mentioned in the original article.

The following elements are common to most commercial Web sites, or graphical user interfaces (GUIs):

- Site-specific search engines that allow you to find information on the site.
- Comprehensive toolbar, a logical way to maneuver through the digital environment
- Advertising, pop-up or embedded on the page
- Multiple language option
- Archive
- Video/audio components
- Link to the author(s)
- Ancillary "hot links," or links embedded in the copy that provide additional information
- E-mail address of "author"
- Option to forward the content/site through e-mail
- Links to graphics and maps
- Blog link
- Podcast link
- Specific links to associated sites (either through commercial contract or mutual ownership sites
- "Opt in" notification system (so that you can request up-to-date information or sales)
- Online surveys

It is essential to look closely at the elements of the Web page to make certain that the page is authentic. Unscrupulous thieves engage in "phishing" expeditions, in which they fraudulently acquire passwords and credit card details by masquerading as a legitimate business enterprise that the customer has used. These phishers construct Web sites that are nearly identical to the actual business using "screen scraping" software. Even the links send the initiator to the identical sites. The only distinguishable difference between the phony and legitimate Web sites is the "Web address" that appears at the top of the browser.

NOTES

1. Pamela Jones Harbour, "The Emperor of All Identities," *New York Times,* December 18, 2012.
2. "Some Get Internet 'Data High': Parents Fear Kids Prefer PCs to Peers, Others Overwhelmed by Info," *St. Louis Post-Dispatch,* December 9, 1997.
3. Harris Interactive, "A Generation Unplugged," September 12, 2008, http://fles.cria.org/pdf/HI_TeenMobileStudy_ResearchReportpdf.
4. "Glued to the Screen: An Investigation into Information Addiction Worldwide," 1996 Reuters Survey.
5. "Some Get Internet 'Data High': Parents Fear Kids Prefer PCs to Peers, Others Overwhelmed by Info."
6. Kathleen Tyner, *Literacy in a Digital World* (Hillsdale, NJ: Lawrence Erlbaum Associates, 1998).
7. Ibid.
8. Ian Urbina, "I Flirt and Tweet: Follow Me at #Socialbot," *New York Times,* August 10, 2013.
9. Brian Stelter, "Upending Anonymity, These Days the Web Unmasks Everyone," *New York Times,* June 20, 2011.
10. Elizabeth Kirk, "Practical Steps in Evaluating Internet Resources," Milton's Web Page 423.99, http://milton,mse.jhu.edu:8001/research/education/practical.html.
11. Alex Soojung-Kim Pang, "The Distraction Addiction," *San Francisco Chronicle,* August 16, 2013.
12. Urbina, "I Flirt and Tweet: Follow Me at #Socialbot."
13. "Group Cites Alarming Rise of Hate Sites on Internet," *St. Louis Post-Dispatch,* February 24, 1999: A-4.
14. Patricia Cohen, "In 500 Billion Words, New Window on Culture," *New York Times,* December 16, 2010.
15. Ibid.
16. Lou Birenbaum, interview with author, September 14, 1999, St. Louis, Missouri.
17. Deborah Peterson, "Three Recent Cases Show Cyberworld Has Dark Side: Watch Young Surfers, Experts Urge," *St. Louis Post-Dispatch.* July 29, 1998: B-1.
18. Somini Sengupta, "What You Didn't Post, Facebook May Still Know," *New York Times,* March 25, 2013.

19. Lev Grossman, "2045: The Year Man Becomes Immortal," *Time Magazine,* February 10, 2011, http://content.time.com/time/magazine/article/0,9171, 2048299,00.html.
20. Ibid.
21. Ibid.
22. Bran Ferren, "The Intercranial Internet," *New York Times Magazine,* March 15, 1998: 28.
23. Arthur C. Clarke, "Hazards of Prophecy: The Failure of Imagination in *Profiles of the Future*" (1962 [rev. 1973]), 14, 21, 36.
24. "Questions for Kevin Warwick," *New York Times Magazine,* October 4, 1998: 27.
25. John Brunner, *Stand on Zanizibar* (New York: Ballantine Books, 1969), 262.
26. Kenneth Chang, "Now There Are Many: Robots That Reproduce," *New York Times,* May 17, 2005.
27. Grossman, "2045: The Year Man Becomes Immortal."
28. Polly Sprenger, "Sun on Privacy: 'Get Over It,'" *Wired News,* January 26, 1999, www.wired.com/politics/law/news/1999/01/17538.
29. Pete Slover, "Web 'Cookies' Are Hot on the Internet," *St. Louis Post-Dispatch,* July 22, 1998.
30. Kidz Privacy Resource Materials Federal Trade Commission, http://www .ftc.gov/kidzprivacy.gov.
31. Nicholas Negroponte, "Beyond Digital," *Wired Magazine,* December 1998.
32. Julie Connelly, "A Ripe Target for Web Retailers, Teens Keep Heading to the Mall," *New York Times,* September 22, 1999.
33. Negroponte, "Beyond Digital."
34. Parag Khanna, "The End of the Nation-State?" *New York Times,* October 12, 2013.
35. Gar Alperovitz, "California Split," op-ed, *New York Times,* February 10, 2007: A-27.
36. "Gov. Rick Perry: Texas Could Secede, Leave Union," *Huffington Post,* May 16, 2009, http://www.huffingtonpost.com/2009/04/15/gov-rick-perry-texas-coul _n_187490.html.
37. Jana Kasperkevic, "Rick Perry Might Not Want Texas to Secede, but Ron Paul Believes 'Secession Is an American Principle,'" *Houston Chronicle,* November 14, 2012.
38. Alperovitz, "California Split."
39. Dan Barry, "Would You Like That in Tens, Twenties or Normans?," *New York Times,* February 25, 2007: A-1.
40. Paul Lewis. "Not Just Governments Make War or Peace," *New York Times,* November 28, 1998: A-19.
41. Edward Wyatt, "Most of U.S. Is Wired, but Millions Aren't Plugged In," *New York Times,* August 18, 2013.

42. Brad Stone, "The Children of Cyberspace: Old Fogies by Their 20s," *New York Times,* January 9, 2010.

43. Ibid.

44. Wyatt, "Most of U.S. Is Wired, but Millions Aren't Plugged In."

45. Dave Gilson and Carolyn Perot, "It's the Inequality, Stupid," *Mother Jones,* March/April 2011, http://www.motherjones.com/politics/2011/02/income -inequality-in-america-chart-graph.

46. Peter Whoriskey, "Studies Cite CEO Pay as Significant Cause of Wealth Inequality," *Washington Post,* June 21, 2011, http://www.jsonline.com/business/ 124329979.html.

47. Jeremy Rifkin, *The End of Work* (New York: Putnam Publishing Group, 1996).

48. Hope Yen, "Exclusive: Signs of Declining Economic Security," AP, *The Big Story,* July 29, 2013, http://bigstory.ap.org/article/exclusive-signs-declining -economic-security.

49. Wyatt, "Most of U.S. Is Wired, but Millions Aren't Plugged In."

50. Richard Rosenfeld, interview with author, September 29, 1999, St. Louis, Missouri.

51. Larry D. Rosen, *Rewired: Understanding the iGeneration and the Way That They Learn* (New York: Palgrave Macmillan, 2010), 16.

52. Tamar Lewin, "Students Rush to Web Classes, but Profits May Be Much Later," *New York Times,* January 6, 2013.

53. David E. Sanger, "A New Cold War, in Cyberspace, Tests U.S. Ties to China," *New York Times,* February 24, 2013.

54. Ibid.

55. John Markoff, "Blown to Bits: Cyberwarfare Breaks the Rules of Military Engagement," *New York Times,* October 17, 1999.

56. Ibid.

57. Misha Glenny, "A Weapon We Can't Control," *New York Times,* June 24, 2012.

58. David E. Sanger and Eric Schmitt, "N.S.A. Imposes Rules to Protect Secret Data Stored on Its Networks," *New York Times,* July 18, 2013.

59. Markoff, "Blown to Bits: Cyberwarfare Breaks the Rules of Military Engagement."

60. Jenna Wortham, "Hanging Out at the E-Mall," *New York Times,* August 16, 2013.

61. Shelly Freierman, "Shopping after Santa," *New York Times,* December 31, 2012.

62. Douglas Quenqua, "3-D Help for Breathing, Vanishing Amphibians and More," *New York Times,* May 27, 2013.

63. Eric Schmidt, "A Note to Google Users on Net Neutrality," Google, February 17, 2007, www.google.com/help/netneutrality.

64. Somini Sengupta, "Instagram Flap Shows Confusion over Control of Content," *New York Times,* December 27, 2012.

65. Keith Bradsher, "China Toughens Its Restrictions on Use of the Internet," *New York Times,* December 28, 2012.

66. Nart Villeneuve, "The Filtering Matrix," *First Monday,* www.firstmonday .org (*First Monday* is the first peer-reviewed Internet journal).

67. Max Frankel, "A More Perfect Future," *New York Times Magazine,* January 24, 1999: 18.

68. Eric Pfanner, "In War against the Internet, China Is Just a Skirmish," *New York Times,* January 18, 2010.

69. "ICANN-Internet Corporation for Assigned Names and Numbers," www .icann.org.

70. Ibid.

71. Natasha Singer, "When You Can't Tell Web Suffixes without a Scorecard," *New York Times,* August 17, 2013.

72. Jason Pontin, "Millions of Videos, and Now a Way to Search Inside Them," *New York Times,* February 25, 2007: C-3.

PART 4

ISSUES AND OUTCOMES

12

Issues in Media Communications

This chapter examines the following media-related topics from a media literacy perspective:

- Media and Violence
- Media and Children
- Media and Social Change
- International Communications

MEDIA AND VIOLENCE

Everyone has heard or read about incidents in which violent media programming has led to violence in real life. However, violence in the media is a complex issue that does not offer any simple explanations or solutions.

There is a high degree of violence throughout almost all popular media programming:

- The average American child sees 200,000 violent acts on TV by age 18.[1]
- By the age of 18, Americans witness 16,000 "murders" on television.[2]
- Nearly two out of three TV programs contain violence, averaging six violent acts per hour.[3]
- There are more than twice as many violent incidents in children's programming than in other types of programming. The average child who watches two hours of cartoons a day may see more than 10,000 violent acts a year.[4]

- In nearly 75 percent of violent scenes on television, the characters show no remorse and face no criticism or penalty for the violence in the scene.[5]

Why does so much violent programming appear in the media? Possible explanations include the following:

Human Nature

From birth, human beings are both attracted to and repelled by violence. While children find it enjoyable to build something with blocks, it is often even *more* fun to knock them over. In the American market-driven media system, the audience exercises enormous influence over programming. For instance, if people didn't watch violent television programs, they would be taken off the air. But despite public protestations, these programs are popular; clearly, people enjoy watching violent programming.

Media Violence as Reflection of Culture

Violence is deeply ingrained in American culture. Richard Rosenfeld, coauthor of *Crime and the American Dream,* declares, "The U.S. is in a category by itself among developed nations in terms of homicide and serious interpersonal violence. American culture is saturated with violent images and examples that reflect the violent nature of U.S. culture."[6]

However, the media still present an exaggerated picture of violence in America.

Although 1 in 10 television characters is involved in violence in any given week, the chances of an individual being a victim of a violent crime is no more than 1 in 100 *per year.*[7]

Industry Considerations

In order to attract the largest possible audience, media programs generally feature unusual and exciting stories. Nobody wants to watch police officers involved in the uneventful routine of their jobs, like filling out forms, walking the beat, or selling tickets to the police officers' ball. As a result, successful action/adventure films are packed with shootouts, car chases, and mass destruction—to the point that the audience regards violence as a part of a police officer's typical day.

In addition, violent programming is highly exportable to international markets. While dialogue-driven programming can present translation challenges, blowing something up remains a universal language.

Moreover, there is evidence that the marketing strategy of film studios is designed to entice young people to circumvent the restrictive ratings and see R-rated films. An internal memo from one movie studio declared that the promotional goal was "to find the elusive teen target audience and make sure everyone between the ages of 12–18 was exposed to the film."[8] Another document outlined a plan to distribute fliers and posters about an R-rated movie to organizations like the Campfire Boys and Girls in Kansas City.[9] Similarly, the study found that music with explicit content labels and violent mature-rated video games targeted underage audiences.

Characteristics of Media

One of the chief characteristics of film and television is the illusion of motion. Consequently, these media often emphasize people *doing* things through external action, or plot. And since plot generally involves some conflict between characters or events, the action that takes place is often violent in nature.

Cumulative Messages: Media Violence

Audiences have been inundated with programs that, when seen as a whole, present some very clear cumulative messages about violence:

- *The world is a violent place*
  Violence in entertainment media programming, coupled with the news media's extensive coverage of violent events, can affect an individual's perception of the amount of violence in society. Although mass murders are statistically rare, these events, which are covered extensively in the media, have an enormous impact on students' perceptions of violence in schools.
  During the 1990s, the rate of violence in U.S. high schools decreased significantly—but at the same time, only 37 percent of high school students felt safe in school. Further, over half of American teenagers believed that a murderous rampage could erupt at their own schools.[10]

- *Violence is an effective solution to problems*

  This is an adolescent world that is defined by absolutes: good versus evil. In this world, direct action is the best way to combat "evildoers."

  In police dramas, the protagonist often faces two adversaries: the criminals that he or she is trying to catch and the bureaucrats who frustrate his or her efforts to get the job done. In this world, laws and regulations only get in the way.

- *The ends justify the means*

  In many media presentations, the moral issue is not whether violence is right or wrong, but rather is it *justifiable.* Significantly, nearly 40 percent of the violent incidents on television are initiated by the heroes of the story—those characters most likely to be perceived as role models.[11] The retribution film is a popular sub-genre that plays off of this notion. Initially, the hero is either personally mistreated or discovers a social injustice. In their effort to restore order, the protagonists become the primary perpetrators of violence. Thus, within the context of these films, the violence is justifiable: the end justifies the means.

- *A world without consequences*

  Action heroes are never held accountable for the damage they inflict on people and property in the course of their films. Indeed, only 16 percent of programs show the long-term consequences of violence.

- *Violence is associated with masculinity, power, and sexual energy*

  Real men are distinguished by their ability to inflict violence. Women are attracted to the strength and power of protagonists engaged in violence.

  Significantly, in entertainment programs, acts of violence are frequently followed by lovemaking scenes.

  In addition, violence can serve as an opportunity for male bonding between male protagonists as they fight together to defeat a common enemy.

- *Violence is fun*

  Entertainment programs often feature a type of comedic violence. This type of violence operates on an adolescent level; fighting among men is depicted as a way to let off steam and impress the girls. These scenes are accompanied by bouncy, upbeat, or silly music, which signals that there is no danger or threat of bodily harm to the protagonists.

- *The value of human life is minimized*

    Within the course of a narrative, the victims of violence function like chess pieces, removed from the board and forgotten in the flow of the story. For instance, westerns routinely include scenes in which Indians pursue a wagon filled with white passengers. One of the cowboys shoots a pursuing Indian, who takes a spectacular fall from his horse. Immediately thereafter, the camera resumes the chase, and the condition of the Indian warrior and his horse are quickly forgotten. The death of the warrior only represents one less obstacle threatening the settlers.

    Taking this a step further, in George Lucas's *Star Wars: Episode I—Phantom Menace* (1999), the army of the Trade Federation is made up entirely of robots. As a result, the mass destruction of these soldiers during the battle scenes has been completely depersonalized.

- *Some people are more important than others*

    As noted above, characters in supporting roles (who are often members of minority groups) are often killed without much attention or sympathy. However, even a minor injury to the protagonist (who generally is a member of the dominant culture) is treated as a crisis that commands the attention of the other characters—and the audience as well.

- *Violence is painless*

    Acts of violence never hurt members of the audience.

- *Violence is sanitary*

    Film director Sam Peckinpah, whose work included *The Wild Bunch* (1969) and *The Straw Dogs* (1971), was often criticized for the explicit scenes of violence in his films. For instance, Peckinpah would include scenes in which characters who were shot were thrown back against the wall by the force of the gunshot. The camera would then show a trail of skull fragments and blood as the character slowly slid to the floor. Peckinpah's defense was that the violence in his films was not gratuitous—he was simply presenting an accurate picture of violence.

- *Violence is a glamorous spectacle*

    Killings and bombings are frequently shot in slow motion, from many angles. The explosions resemble a fireworks display.

- *Violence is gratifying*

    In many media presentations, the primary message is a celebration of violence. Plot and character merely provide context and rationale that lead up to a violent climax. As media scholar Mark Crispin Miller observes, violence in the media engenders a sense of pleasure and excitement in the audience:

> Screen violence is now used primarily to invite the viewer to enjoy the feel of killing, beating, mutilating. There is no point to Rambo's long climactic rage . . . other than its open invitation to become him at that moment—to ape that sneer of hate, to feel the way it feels to stand there tensed up with the Uzi.[12]

The Effects of Media Violence

Six theories offer a range of perspectives on the effects of media violence on individuals.

- *The arousal theory.* The classic research of Bandura, Ross, and Ross (1963), Liebert and Baron (1972), Lukesch (1988), and Bushman and Geen (1990) supports the proposition that violent programming stimulates aggression in audience members that can lead to violent behavior.

Studies show that the likelihood of screen-triggered aggression is increased if the violence depicted on screen:

- Is realistic and exciting, like a chase or suspense sequence that sends adrenalin levels surging.[13]
- Succeeds in righting a wrong, like helping an abused or ridiculed character get even.[14]
- Includes situations or characters similar to those in the viewer's own experience.[15]

A graphic illustration of the arousal theory of media violence occurred in Aurora, Colorado, in 2012, when a mass shooter opened fire in a movie theater, killing 12 people and injuring 70 others. The massacre took place during the showing of *Batman: The Dark Knight Rises.* The killer timed the incident to coincide with a similar event on screen, suggesting that the film violence "inspired" the brutal incident.

- *The cathartic theory.* Paradoxically, violent programming may at times provide a healthy release for our aggressions. After watching a violent program, the audience may feel drained and purified, purged of violent impulses. Within this context, media violence can be construed as positive and constructive.

Supporting this perspective, a study found that that on days with a high audience for violent movies, violent crime is actually *lower* than average. From 6:00 p.m. to midnight on weekends—when the largest numbers of people are in theaters—violent crimes decreased by 1.3 percent for every million people watching a strongly violent movie. Thus, violent crimes declined by 1.1 percent for every million people attending a mildly violent film. Further, violent crimes dropped even further after theaters closed (between 12:00 a.m. and 6:00 a.m.)—by 1.9 percent for every million people at a strongly violent movie, and by 2.1 percent for every million at mildly violent film.[16]

- *The desensitizing theory.* Some researchers have found that frequent exposure to media violence can have a *numbing* effect on the audience. Daniel Linz, Edward Donnerstein, and Steven Penrod found that men who watched movies depicting violence against women regarded them as significantly less violent than subjects who were not exposed to these types of films, and considered them to be significantly less degrading to women.[17]

- *The opiate theory.* After watching enough programming, people may become passive and incapable of feeling *anything.* Fred and Merrelyn Emery found that watching television is a dissociative medium that "as a simple, constant, repetitive visual stimulus gradually closes down the nervous system of man [sic]."[18] Couch potatoes who fall asleep on Sunday afternoons while watching the brutality of NFL football would illustrate this theory.

- *Cumulative effects theory.* Most researchers have focused on the immediate effects of media-carried violence. However, some studies suggest that cumulative media messages regarding violence may have *long-term, indirect* effects on individuals. As reporter Peter S. Goodman explains, "Critics of violent media worry that the study, with its focus on immediate effects, could distract policy makers from troubling signs of long-term harm to society and leave parents thinking that violent films may be the least bad way for their adolescent children to occupy leisure hours."[19] For example, Malamuth and Check found correlations between exposure to sexually violent media content among male college students and aggressive attitudes, as reflected in the belief that women enjoy forced sex.[20] Studies also suggest that exposure to violence in media presentations can have long-term effects on individuals in the following ways:

- Becoming less sensitive to the pain and suffering of others.
- Being more fearful of the world around them.
- Being more likely to behave in aggressive or harmful ways toward others.[21]
- Thinking of aggressive behavior as normal.[22]
- *The no-effects theory.* This theory holds that media violence has a minimal effect on audiences: what we see and hear in the media is just entertainment and should not be taken seriously. Thus, watching a violent movie is simply an entertaining experience that will not dramatically change your life.

Which of these theories about the effects of media violence on individuals is correct? *All of them.*

As you have seen, studies can be found that support each of these theories. In truth, many factors contribute to an individual's particular response to media violence, including:

- *Psychological makeup.* Some studies suggest that aggressive children may be attracted to media violence, which causes them to be even more aggressive.[23] Other personality variables that may influence response to media-carried violence include:
  - Introverted personality vs. extroverted personality
  - Stable vs. unstable personality
  - Tender vs. tough-minded emotional constitution
- *Identification with media content.* A study by Frost and Stauffer found that people respond markedly to a media program if the content is "congruent" with their real-life experiences. Thus, the reaction to filmed violence can depend upon a person's identification with the characters.[24] For example, you might react more strongly to the way that a character behaves if the character resembles your ex-boyfriend or ex-girlfriend.
- *Recent experiences.* What kind of a day did you have today? If you are in a foul mood, you might react differently to a program than if you were in a jolly frame of mind.
- *Immediate environment.* Is someone sitting directly in front of you in the movie theater, blocking your view? Is someone behind you talking on a cell phone, so that you can't hear the dialogue in the film?

Sometimes what is going on around you can affect how you react to a media program.

- *Gender.* Some studies suggest that gender may be a factor in determining how people respond to violent programming.[25] In addition, the gender of the perpetrators and victims of violence played a role in how viewers responded. Viewers reacted dramatically when the content depicted men inflicting violence on women. However, Frost and Stauffer caution that these results must be seen in a broader societal context: "Since the great majority of violence in the real world is committed by males, their arousal responses to dramatized violence may differ from those of females."[26]

- *Social class.* Frost and Stauffer's study found that subjects who were members of the lower class were significantly more aroused by viewing violent programming than a sample of middle-class college students. The researchers concluded that because the environment of the lower-class subjects is often more violent than that of the college students, their significantly higher arousal levels in response to violent stimuli may be connected to their real-life surroundings.[27]

- *Content attributes.* Barry Gunter found that a number of specific program characteristics can affect how the audience responds to violent content in the media presentation:
  - *A realistic portrayal.* Violent acts committed within a realistic setting are more disturbing than similar acts depicted in fictional entertainment genres, such as westerns, science fiction, or cartoons.
  - *The type of violent act being depicted.* Some forms of violence are more disturbing than others. Shootings and stabbings are regarded as more "serious" forms of violence than explosions or unarmed combat.
  - *The amount of attention on the suffering of victims.* Visibly harmful violence was deemed to be more disturbing to viewers than violence with no observable consequences.[28]

Given all of these theories, the most accurate statement about the effects of media violence is as follows:

Under certain circumstances, some people may respond to violent media content in a particular way.

To illustrate, in 1981 John Hinkley attempted to assassinate President Ronald Reagan. After seeing the film *Taxi Driver,* Hinkley gleaned the message that he would impress actress Jodie Foster (on whom he had a crush) by killing the president. But though theaters filled with people watching *Taxi Driver,* Hinkley was the *only* one among them who was moved to attack the president. Other members of the audience may have felt purged, drowsy, or simply entertained. Jack Valenti, former president of the Motion Picture Association of America, commented,

> I'm not saying that movies don't have an impact [on violence in society]. All I know is that other countries whose children watch the same movies and [TV] shows as we do here have crime rates that are much lower. There must be other factors going on that we don't know about.[29]

Conclusion

No completely satisfactory solution exists to the issue of violence in American media. Obviously, there is no universal agreement on the effects of violent content in the media. Adding to the complexity of the regulatory issue, questions remain about how to define violence in media programming. In the current ratings system, subtle forms of violence routinely appear in children's programming, such as acts of emotional abuse and long-term violence against self (e.g., alcohol or drug abuse). Moreover, the issue of "sanctioned" violence (e.g., sports) is also not addressed in the ratings system. Thus, the ratings system would not consider a violent sport such as a football game or boxing match inappropriate for children.

Indeed, the *style* of a presentation can convey violent messages. Mabel L. Rice, Altha C. Huston, and John C. Wright note,

> Rapid action, loud music, and sound effects are often associated with violence in children's programs. . . . The forms themselves may come to signal violence or sex typing to children, even when the content cues are minimal or nonexistent.[30]

Moreover, in a democracy, it is always dangerous to censor information. Ultimately, audiences must assume responsibility by developing a sensitivity to media messages about violence and making thoughtful choices about what media programming to select. Frank Rich observes,

> To get real results in a society with free speech and a free market, we have to vote not for pious politicians but with our pocketbooks for

the culture we say we want. No one is forcing American families to subscribe to the pay-cable services that program violent movies; no one requires adults to watch Jerry Springer in eye-popping numbers (and then abandon him the moment his show is stripped of violence by a circumspect TV mogul); no one has mandated that every household purchase a bloody video or computer game (90 percent of which are bought by adults).[31]

Regulatory Steps

The Telecommunications Act of 1996 made built-in V-chips mandatory in all television sets, enabling the consumer to block out selected programs, so that parents can eliminate violent programming from their children's menu of programming choices. The V-chip has been designed to work in tandem with a voluntary ratings system created by broadcast executives in accordance with the TCA mandate.

However, these regulatory steps have not resolved the issue of children being exposed to violence in the media. Today most young people consume media through digital means. As a result, there is no real gatekeeper dictating what they can and cannot see. Moreover, many parents are unaware of how much violent content appears in online presentations like YouTube.

Although the FCC regulates sexual content and the use of language in television programming, there are no specific prohibitions with regard to violence. Instead, the FCC leaves it up to the networks to police themselves through their standards and practices departments. However, the standards are subjective, shifting over time. Kurt Sutter, creator of the violent dramatic series *Sons of Anarchy,* declares, "For me the frustration is that (the boundaries are) so arbitrary, and it changes from season to season."[32]

MEDIA AND CHILDREN

Overview

No discussion of media literacy would be complete without some discussion of the influence of media in the lives of children and some strategies through which youngsters can develop a critical independence from what they read and watch.

The media have emerged as a major factor in the lives of children. In 2010, children under the age of 18 consumed more than 53 hours per week—or 20 percent more than the equivalent of a full-time job. Secondary media consumption increased the daily total to 10 hours and 45 minutes per day.[33] Much of the time that children spend with media is unsupervised. Nearly half of children aged five to eight have a television in their bedroom. One-third of children below the age of one have a TV in their room. Digital video recorders are present in 29 percent of the bedrooms of children aged under eight, and 11 percent of that same age group have video game consoles in their rooms.[34]

However, young children can be instructed through an understanding of strategies that correspond to children's stages of development. Applying the principles of developmental psychologist Jean Piaget, Warren Buckleitner, editor of *Children's Technology Review,* has found that young children can be instructed through an understanding of strategies that correspond to children's stages of development:

> If he were alive today, Piaget would probably advise parents that for a young child, everything—whether it has batteries or not—is a discovery waiting to happen. But toys work best when they are matched to a child's level of development.[35]

Piaget has identified four elements that work together to influence children's development and shape their understanding of the world: maturation, experience, emotion, and social instruction. Aside from the natural maturation process, the media contribute strongly to Piaget's developmental elements:

- *Experience* is an important part of development because without it a child cannot develop and function normally. The media have emerged as a major aspect of a child's experience. Reporter Nick Bilton provides the following example:

> I recently watched my sister perform an act of magic.
>
> We were sitting in a restaurant, trying to have a conversation, but her children, 4-year-old Willow and 7-year-old Luca, would not stop fighting. The arguments—over a fork, or who had more water in a glass—were unrelenting.
>
> Like a magician quieting a group of children by pulling a rabbit out of a hat, my sister reached into her purse and produced two shiny Apple iPads, handing one to each child. Suddenly, the two

were quiet. Eerily so. They sat playing games and watching videos, and we continued with our conversation.

After our meal, as we stuffed the iPads back into their magic storage bag, my sister felt slightly guilty.

"I don't want to give them the iPads at the dinner table, but if it keeps them occupied for an hour so we can eat in peace, and more importantly not disturb other people in the restaurant, I often just hand it over," she told me. Then she asked: "Do you think it's bad for them? I do worry that it is setting them up to think it's O.K. to use electronics at the dinner table in the future."

"Conversations with each other are the way children learn to have conversations with themselves, and learn how to be alone," said Sherry Turkle, a professor of science, technology and society at the Massachusetts Institute of Technology, and author of the book *Alone Together: Why We Expect More from Technology and Less from Each Other.* "Learning about solitude and being alone is the bedrock of early development, and you don't want your kids to miss out on that because you're pacifying them with a device."

Ms. Turkle has interviewed parents, teenagers and children about the use of gadgets during early development, and says she fears that children who do not learn real interactions, which often have flaws and imperfections, will come to know a world where perfect, shiny screens give them a false sense of intimacy without risk.

And they need to be able to think independently of a device. "They need to be able to explore their imagination. To be able to gather themselves and know who they are. So someday they can form a relationship with another person without a panic of being alone," she said. "If you don't teach your children to be alone, they'll only know how to be lonely."[36]

- *Emotion.* As Piaget observes, emotions inspire and motivate learning. As discussed in Chapter 2, visual and aural media such as film, television, and components of the Internet operate on an *affective* (or emotional) level that influences how children respond to media programming.
- *Social Instruction.* Interaction with parents, teachers, peers, and the media influences how children perceive and understand the world around them. But in addition, as educator Larry Rosen observes, the

media also provide a context in which children learn how to make decisions and how to interact socially with others.[37]

Children are more susceptible to media messages than adults because they process information differently. Piaget's studies on language comprehension indicate that young children cannot distinguish the boundaries between media programming and the real world: "The ability to differentiate probability from possibility crystalizes during early adolescence."[38]

Thus, young children often attribute human qualities to inanimate objects. Moreover, although five- to seven-year-olds are aware that their favorite show is not real, they are not aware that the characters don't keep their roles off-screen. And lacking the ability to understand different levels of realism, school-age children are not likely to understand the differences between a news program and a scripted series.

Media Literacy Strategies

The following guidelines and approaches are designed to provide tools for young people to decipher the information in the media industry and specific media presentations. Young students of media literacy may find that identifying media messages is more enjoyable than passively taking in the actual program. Nobody likes to think of themselves as being "played" by the media. Consequently, these strategies empower young people, giving them an independence from the information being presented by the media.

Guidelines for Media Use

The following guidelines can help children develop a critical distance from media programming and become more aware of media messages:

Moderation. The Roman comic dramatist Plautus surely could have been thinking about media when he declared, "In everything the middle course is best: all things in excess bring trouble to men."[39] Thus, too much media consumption prohibits other activities.

The following tactics can combat the overuse of media:

- *Do not use media programming as background noise.*
  Adults often leave the TV set on as "background" noise, even though they are not watching. As a result, TV watching becomes accepted as a normal part of the daily routine.

- *Watch by the show, not by the clock.*

  In its excellent educational packet, *Parenting in a TV Age* (PTA), the Center for Media Literacy recommends that parents and children make clear choices *in advance* about what program the child should watch: "If you've set limits, they'll learn to prioritize and watch what they *really* like."[40]

  This strategy also sends the message that people should be in control of the television. The individual can decide when to watch, what to watch, and how to watch.

- *Set limits.*

  Parents should establish clear limits on how much TV their children should watch per day. Moderation can also be a wise policy with respect to children's use of digital media. Police detective Bova Conti regards anything over one and a half to two hours a day on the Internet as excessive. He also suggests some other good-sense guidelines, such as forbidding late-night or excessive use.[41]

  The Center for Media Literacy also recommends that parents should incorporate time in the schedule to discuss sensitive content like violence and sex in advance.[42]

- *Participate with your child.*

  Shared media time furnishes opportunities for discussions between parents and children. Talking back to the television transforms a passive activity into an active, two-way interaction that encourages critical viewing on the part of the child. Later, this common reference point can serve as a springboard for further discussion.

TV Postulates

Parenting in a TV Age suggests that parents stress the following postulates about TV. However, it should be noted that these postulates can be applied to other media as well, including film, satellite radio, and digital media:

- *You are smarter than your TV*

  While it may be marginally entertaining to watch TV programming, it is infinitely more fun to pick it apart. Point out inconsistencies in content. Ask how the program compares to their personal experiences and understanding of the world. This healthy skepticism encourages children to come to independent conclusions about the information presented on television.

- *TV's world is not real*

  PTA suggests that parents and children watch a cartoon together and list all the things that could not happen in real life. This exercise reinforces the notion that much of what we see on television is true only on the tube. This activity can also be applied to other genres of media programming, such as situation comedies.

Dorr, Graves, and Phelps recommend that parents raise the following issues about the reality/fantasy of television content:

- *Entertainment programs are made up.*
- *Plots are made up.*
- *Characters are actors.*
- *Incidents are fabricated.*
- *Settings are often constructed.*
- *Entertainment programs vary in how realistic they are.*
- *Viewers can decide how realistic they find entertainment programs.*

Television content may be evaluated by comparing it to one's own experience and that of other people, and consulting other media sources.[43]

- *TV keeps doing the same things over and over*

  By encouraging children to look for patterns in programming, children learn to anticipate these occurrences in future programming. For instance, once a child becomes sensitive to the introduction of ominous music in a program, he/she is less likely to become frightened by it. Moreover, discovering patterns together can be a useful starting point for discussion: *Why* does this type of music always appear during particular moments in a program?
- *TV teaches us that some people and ideas are more important than others*

  The PTA suggests an activity in which children identify patterns in television programming, such as the number or kinds of children on-screen at a time or the gender and race of "bad guys" in shows.
- *Encourage an active selection of programming*

  The digital domain offers a wide range of options with regard to media programming. The selection process requires that the children become active, critical viewers before they watch. In addition, this process enables parents and children to select a program or tape that both would enjoy watching together.

Children and the Internet

Buckleitner has found Piaget's work to be particularly enlightening with respect to children's aptitude with digital technology:

AGES 0–2 Babies and toddlers cannot use a mouse until at least age 2 ½, and flat monitors do not offer much in the way of stimulation in Piaget's first stage, "sensorimotor." To work at this age, technology products must act like a busy-box, with lights or sounds that respond to a child's actions. Toys (that have) doors and switches for a baby to explore and a crawl-through doorway, fit well with this stage.

AGES 3–5 "Preschoolers today are growing up in a digital world, and they see their parents using devices like cell phones and computers," said Prof. Sandra Calvert, director of the Children's Digital Media Center at Georgetown University. "They like to play with pretend cell phones as if it were the real thing." This pretend-play is actually an important part of the Piaget "preoperational" stage, when children first understand that they can control the events on a flat screen.

Digital cameras, interactive television Web sites, and videogames are well suited to this stage of development.

AGES 6–11 At the age a child can ride a bicycle comes the ability to search the Web, and the whole digital world starts to open up. Suddenly they are hooked on favorite video games and watching funny videos on YouTube. But Piaget labeled this stage "concrete operations" because children still have trouble with abstract ideas. Professor Calvert reminds parents that electronic devices should be used to "supplement rather than replace real experiences," and encourages them to "make sure there's an overall sense of balance" in activities during this stage of life.

This is a time when parents need to keep an eye on the screen and steer children toward good sites. Fortunately the number of video games with redeeming qualities is growing. [Some video games offer collaborative problem-solving opportunities and promote] reading skills and exercise. By age 10, many children can start editing videos.

AGES 12 AND UP Besides being much harder to wake up, middle and high schoolers are reaching the cognitive functioning of an adult. They have entered Piaget's "formal operational" stage, able to juggle synchronous streams of information from phones, MP3 players, and laptops. Communicating with friends is on par with breathing, to the delight of your wireless provider.

In fact, cell phones are now more or less mandatory for children at this age. Besides providing a social advantage, phones can reduce parental stress in a crowded mall, get children in touch for homework help, serve as a call to dinner—and be withheld as punishment that really works. . . .[44]

Of course, these stages of development are general categories that do not account for the strengths, learning styles, and rates of development that distinguish individual children. But the categories at least provide points of reference for the assessment of individual children.

Selected Keys to Interpreting Media Messages

As discussed in Chapter 1, not all of the Keys are necessarily suitable for the analysis of particular media presentations. Further, individuals may find that they are more comfortable with the application of certain Keys. In like fashion, some Keys are particularly useful for young people, and lend themselves to particular learning styles or a certain stage of development. The following Keys are particularly helpful for younger people as they interpret media messages.

Function. By the age of three, children understand the intent of television commercials.[45] Consequently, asking a child *why* an ad has been produced can make him/her a more critical consumer.

Audience. By the age of three, children understand the concept of *audience segmentation*—that advertisements are targeted to specific groups.[46] Thus, with some guidance from adults, children are able to identify the target audience. Having identified the target audience, discussion can then focus on how the communication strategy, style, and content have been developed to reach the intended audience.

As an example, it has been estimated that 90 percent of children's viewing time is devoted to watching programs designed for adults.[47] (This statistic does not include instances in which younger children are watching programs geared for *older kids*.) Consequently, discussion can focus on how the program reflects its manifest audience. (For further discussion of audience, see Chapter 2.)

Worldview. A useful way to spark discussion about a media presentation is to ask, "What kind of world is being depicted?"

In general, children's programming conveys the following cumulative messages about the world:

- A *homogeneous world.* The world of children's programming offers a distorted picture of the composition of American society. As discussed earlier, the world depicted on primetime television is predominately comprised of white males. Whites make up 63 percent of the American population,[48] but comprise 75 percent of the television characters on prime time.[49] In like fashion, although Latinos make up 17 percent of the population,[50] they are only represented by 5 percent of the primetime TV characters.[51]
- A *world populated by stereotypes.* Professor Linda Holtzman of Webster University conducted a class that examined stereotypes in children's Saturday morning television. After monitoring children's Saturday morning television programs, the class discovered that of 75 major characters, only 6 were women. Only one of those six female characters exhibited qualities that were not categorized as "traditional"—and she was a villain![52]
- A *violent world.* Significantly, children's programs have been found to be far more violent than programming directed at adults. In the world of children's programming, violence is depicted as a natural part of life and justifiable to achieve a worthwhile goal.
- An *absolute world.* The worldview of children's programming is characterized by conflicts between good guys and bad guys. Issues are clearly divided into right and wrong. Programs offer simple solutions to complex problems.
- A *material world.* In the world of children's programming, consumer goods are often more highly regarded than people. Heroes and heroines are fashionably dressed and own lots of material possessions. Conversely, children also see a world in which people are presented as objects. Heroes and heroines are generally more attractive than secondary characters and are the center of attention. It is no coincidence that boys and girls think that being attractive is the most important attribute for male and female characters.[53]
- A *youthful world.* Adult characters are depicted as ignorant, close minded, and inept, incapable of understanding or participating in the extraordinary adventures of the children. Indeed, a popular genre

now consists of presentations in which adult males are essentially big kids. Consequently, in media presentations, the kids are best served by bonding together with their peer group and keeping information from their parents. (For more discussion of worldview, see Chapter 4, Cultural Context.)

Structure. A general discussion about the economic structure of the American media system can focus on the following points:

- Programs are produced to make a profit.
- Media companies rely on advertisements for revenue.
- The economic structure influences media content and style (what we see and how the information is presented).

Introduction. As discussed in Chapter 6, the introduction is a microcosm of the entire media presentation. If the opportunity presents itself (for example, when watching television, during the first commercial break), parents and children can discuss what they have learned about the program's characters, worldview, plots, and themes, based on the information provided in the introduction.

Illogical Premise. Programming directed at children may be founded on a set of assumptions that are embedded in the premise. These assumptions play an important role in shaping the messages contained in the program.

To illustrate, approximately 500 newspapers carry a weekly syndicated "Mini Page" for kids, written by Betty Debman, which covers a range of topics. One installment on "South American Countries" contains a number of ideological assumptions that affect the content (see accompanying page):

- Progress is defined largely in terms of economic (specifically capitalistic) advancement. Debman declares that South America's future looks better because "many natural resources . . . are yet to be developed to the fullest . . . (including) minerals, forests, and fertile farmlands."[54] However, the economic development of this region has been an environmental disaster, including the devastation of the rain forests, ecological imbalances, and loss of habitat for animal life.
- The capsule description of each South American country is another extension of the premise of the article. The capsule summary describes each country in economic terms (i.e., its "important exports").

- Another premise of the article is that a country's success is measured in terms of its relationship with the United States. A major reason cited for the progress of the region is "better opportunities for trade with the United States and the rest of the world."[55]
- The article regards illegal drugs as a major problem in South America. However, the source of the problem is identified as the poor farmers who "make money by raising crops from which illegal drugs are made."[56] This statement shifts the blame away from the capitalists and government officials who have grown rich through the manufacturing and distribution of drugs.

Given this example, it is imperative that adults encourage kids to challenge the underlying assumptions contained in the premise of media presentations.

Plot: Explicit Content. As discussed in Chapter 6, W. Andrew Collins found that young children lack the capacity to identify the "essential content" of a story being conveyed through the media. The short attention span of young children affects their ability to decode content:

- Six-month-old infants gaze at the set but only sporadically.
- One-year-olds watch about 12 percent of the time that the set is on.
- By the age of two, children watch about 25 percent of the time that the set is on.
- Between the ages of two and three, children's attention spans jump to 45 percent of the time that the set is on.
- By the age of four, children are watching 55 percent of the time that the set is on, "often even in a playroom with toys, games, and other distractions."[57]

Indeed, five-year-old children have difficulty deciding what is real or fantasy on film. The children embellish stories with their own ideas, add people and objects not in the film, and have a hard time telling when a story ends. In addition, young children have difficulty deciding whether situation comedies are real or make-believe.[58] Nearly half (14 of 30) of the children thought a person on television had spoken directly to them and six had actually answered back.[59]

Asking a child to give a plot synopsis of the story ("what happened") provides an excellent opportunity for adults to clarify any misconceptions that they may have about a media presentation and gives children an opportunity to ask questions. In addition, because young children often focus attention on those aspects of a story that interest them, having a child reconstruct what happened in the presentation is a way to learn about the child's interests and concerns.

Plot: Implicit Content. In addition, young children often have difficulty understanding *implicit content:* those elements of plot that remain under the surface. Consequently, discussing elements of implicit content can serve as a useful springboard for discussion with children.

- *Ask why things occurred in the story.* Examine the *motives* of characters. ("Why do you think he behaved like that?") As mentioned in earlier discussions, young children are often unable to identify the motives behind an act of violence. (See Chapter 9.) As a result, they may not judge media violence on the basis of any moral standard but rather on whether or not the behavior is successful. As media scholars David Considine and Gail Haley observe, "The media, therefore, potentially provide a model that tells children 'might is right' and 'the end justifies the means.'"[60]
- *Discuss the connections between the characters that occur in the plot.*
- *Discuss connections between events in the plot.*
- *Discuss the consequences of characters' actions.* Frequently, the heroes do not face any consequences, even if they are responsible for destruction of property and people in the narrative. A good question to ask children to consider is what consequences *they* would face if they were in the same position.

Affective Response. Asking children to tune into their feelings can be a very useful springboard for discussion about a media presentation:

- How did you feel during particular points of the story?
- How did you feel about certain aspects of the program? For instance, "Did you like (a particular character)? Why?"
- Do your affective responses provide insight into *your* personal belief system? Explain.

These questions can lead to a discussion about personal feelings and values.

Another line of inquiry involves asking the children to *empathize* with the characters:

- How do you think (the character) felt at particular points in the narrative?
- How would you feel if you were in that situation?

Identifying with characters can give children perspective into the experience of the characters in the presentation. Specifically, asking children to empathize with characters they ordinarily wouldn't identify with (such as supporting characters, members of subcultures, or a character of the opposite sex) can give a child valuable insight into the experience of the members of that group.

Illogical Conclusion. Media communicators often insert artificial endings into media presentations that make those in the audience leave the theater with smiles on their faces (see discussion in Chapter 6). These illogical conclusions provide an excellent way to draw children into a discussion about the presentation:

- Did you like the ending? Why or why not?
- Does the conclusion of the presentation follow logically from the established premise, characters, and worldview?
- If not, how *should* the program have ended? Why?
- How would you have *preferred* for the program to end? Why?

Using this key furnishes perspective into the messages in the media presentation (both intended and unintentional), as well as providing an opportunity for children to examine their own values systems.

Children and Advertising

In 2012, American teens spent $208.7 billion.[61] In addition, children under the age of 12 influence adult spending to the tune of $700 billion a year.[62] As a result, companies spend $17 billion annually marketing to children.[63]

Because children represent the future adult consumer market, it is not surprising that marketing researchers think of children as "consumers in training." As James McNeal observes, "All of the skills, knowledge, and behavior patterns that together we call consumer behavior are purposely taught to our children right along with toilet training, toddling and talking."[64]

Among the production elements most likely to capture the attention of a young audience are humor, music, animals (real or computer generated), and animation.[65]

In addition, the distribution of promotional paraphernalia is an extremely effective form of advertising with young people. Teenagers who own a gym bag or sports clothing with a tobacco manufacturer's logo are twice as likely to become smokers as those who do not.[66]

Buy Me That: A Kid's Survival Guide to TV Advertising, produced by Public Media, Inc., raises some essential questions about advertising for children to consider. Significantly, many of the strategies employed in children's advertising are also in evidence in advertising that targets adult consumers. As a result, the following questions also may be applied to analysis of ads for adults:

- *Do commercials use tricks?*
  Commercials sometimes exaggerate the capabilities of toys to make them appear more enticing. For example, some products may appear more sturdy in ads than they really are.
- *Can toys really talk (move or sing)?*
  If they move or talk on TV . . . don't be so sure. This may only be a way of dramatizing the imaginative possibilities of the product.
- *How do they make food look so good?*
  Food stylists are often used to make food in magazine ads and television commercials look appetizing. In some cases, the product itself is not even used in the demonstration; for instance, the ice cream that appears in television ads is actually a combination of shortening, sugar, and food coloring.
- *How do they make games look so easy?*
  In television commercials, product demonstrations always appear effortless. Through skillful editing, nobody ever makes a mistake. Consequently, children may be frustrated once they attempt to use the product on their own.
- *What does "parts sold separately" mean?*
  Young children who cannot read the fine print at the end of an ad may be disappointed when they do not receive all of the accessories displayed in the ad.
- *Are celebrity sneakers better?*
  The relationship between a product and its celebrity spokesperson can be confusing to children. Ads suggest that a celebrity's use of a product is the secret to his/her performance; for instance, Nike ads featuring Kobe Bryant suggests that his spectacular dunks are made possible by his choice of sneakers. However, it must be made clear that buying these sneakers will not turn a youngster into another Kobe Bryant.[67]

MEDIA LITERACY TIPS: CHILDREN'S ADVERTISING

John Lyons offers some additional suggestions that will help children analyze advertisements:

- *Resist cereals named after monsters or cartoon characters.*
- *Resist anything that insinuates that it's made with fruit when it isn't.*
- *Be wary of little girl doll commercials shot through pink and green filters.*
- Beware of toy figures shot at severe angles that distort the scale and make a tiny toy appear huge.
- *Scorn any product whose commercial . . . makes one kid look "out of it" to his peers if he doesn't have the toy. Scorn . . . companies who work guilt trips on parents . . . .*[68]

MEDIA AND SOCIAL CHANGE

The media have been criticized at various times both for taking too active a role in promoting social change and obstructing needed societal change. As discussed earlier, however, the media are merely channels through which a communicator can reach his/her audience. The media's role with regard to social change is determined by the following factors:

- *The intentions of the communicator*
- *The predilections of the audience*
- *The capabilities of the medium*

The Media and the Feminist Movements

A comparison of the media coverage of the two twentieth-century women's movements provides insight into the factors that determine whether the media accelerates or inhibits social change.

It may come as a surprise that there were *two* women's movements in America during the twentieth century: the woman's suffrage movement, which began in 1908, and the feminist movement, which originated in 1968. Francesca M. Cancian and Bonnie L. Ross tabulated the number of articles devoted to women and women's issues appearing in the press during the time period surrounding these two movements in order to address the following questions:

- What is the causal relation between the movement and the media?
- Which changes first, the quantity of news coverage or the strength of the movement?
- What is the time lag between the two events?[69]

During the rise of the women's suffrage movement, the increase in media attention was almost immediate and played a direct role in the success of the movement. Several factors can account for the responsiveness of the press. First, the movement was characterized by dramatic tactics, such as open-air meetings and parades, which lent themselves to media coverage. In addition, the leaders of the suffrage movement made a devoted effort to cultivate the favor of the media. Finally, the authors note that the suffrage movement did not threaten the male-dominated society: "The suffrage movement was not revolutionary . . . but focused on the single goal of getting the vote."[70]

In contrast, the 1960s feminist movement was at first largely ignored by the press; media coverage lagged behind the movement by several years. The authors offer several explanations for the initial lack of attention by the press:

- *The 1960s movement emphasized issues rather than events*
  The feminist movement originated largely through the organization of conscious-raising groups and women's liberation organizations. These activities did not lend themselves to media attention (the more dramatic bra-burning demonstrations occurred later in the history of the movement).
- *The feminist movement was perceived to be anti-news organizations*
  Some of the leaders of the feminist movement were openly hostile toward the media, feeling that coverage was biased, demeaning, and exploitative. Consequently, these leaders were far from receptive to media attention.
- *The feminist movement posed a threat to the power elite*
  The authors maintain that the media only covers those movements and issues that are acceptable to the establishment: "Once a movement is accepted by the government, big business, labor leaders, and other members of the political establishment, it will receive considerable media coverage."[71]

- *News organizations were anti-movement*

  News organizations, which were dominated by males, were threatened by the radical goals of the feminist movement. M. B. Morris contends that the press attempted to subdue the movement in its early stages—first by ignoring it, then by undermining its serious intent through frivolous coverage, and finally by "publicizing its least offensive goals and de-emphasizing its revolutionary aims."[72]

By late 1969 and early 1970, media coverage of the women's movement began to increase. Cancian and Ross suggest that by that time the movement had gradually grown in popularity and notoriety, until it crossed some "threshold level" of respectability. At that point, the authors note that the media coverage contributed to the growth of the movement: "There is considerable support for believing that the media blitz caused the movement to grow much faster than it had previously."[73]

Cancian and Ross's study underscores the paradoxical role of the media with regard to social change. Under some circumstances, a social movement is covered promptly by the press, *promoting* public awareness. At other times, media coverage may lag behind the beginning of a movement, *inhibiting* social change. However, once a movement has become mainstream and nonthreatening, media attention often follows, which further contributes to the popularity of the movement.

Media as Agent of Social Change

The history of the founding of the United States is tied to the role of the media as an agent of social change. It is no coincidence that founding of the American democracy occurred at a time when the media began to influence public attitudes. Indeed, media historian John Tebbel argues that the activity leading to the American Revolutionary War was, in many respects, a media event, led by the press as manipulators of public opinion.[74]

By 1750, newspaper publishers in the colonies had grown so numerous that the English crown had given up trying to license them. At the same time, newspapers were becoming closely allied with the business community. Circulation and advertising had made the publishers reasonably rich. As a result, newspapers were increasingly invested in the growth of the economy and of colonial society.

In 1765, England imposed the Stamp Act on the colonists. Britain had drained much of its financial reserves during the French and Indian war, which "saved" the Protestant colonies from Catholic France. Consequently, England felt that the colonies should assume some of the financial burden.

The stamp tax was levied on all segments of the population but was most damaging to businesses relying on newsprint and legal documents. Ironically, then, the two most offended segments of the population were those capable of doing the most harm to England—newspaper publishers and lawyers.

In protest, some publishers suspended operations, upsetting the business community (which had grown reliant on newspapers for advertising), as well as the general readership. However, the majority of publishers simply evaded the law. Some published without the customary newspaper masthead or title. Others published without the required tax stamp on each issue, explaining editorially that the publisher had tried to buy stamps but had found none available.

Motivated by self-interest, these young editors mounted an effective media campaign against the British, charging that the Stamp Act was an assault on the freedom of the press. Tebbel observes, "They argued with fervor and dedication, if not with much devotion to the truth."[75] To illustrate, one paper claimed that the British were planning to impose a tax on kissing.

This public relations effort on the part of the publishers was crucial to the revolutionary movement. Newspapers kindled revolt in cities, where British tax collectors, civil servants, and soldiers were visible. These papers were also delivered in wagons to the isolated settlers in the "frontier" regions of the Ohio Valley, who otherwise would not have received news for weeks or months. As a result, the English presence in the colonies began to meet with an organized resistance, leading to the American Revolution.

Prosocial Impact of Media

The channels of mass communication can have a *prosocial impact,* working on several levels. Social media are uniquely structured to facilitate the process of *shared intentionality*—that is, the ability to form a plan with others for accomplishing a joint endeavor—that distinguishes humans from other species.[76] To illustrate, during the 2011 earthquake and tsunami in Japan, digital media technology provided a range of emergency services. Google quickly assembled a Person Finder site that helped people learn of the status of missing persons.

In addition, popular media programming can bring social issues to public attention. For instance, Dr. Phil focuses on issues of social importance, including body image and females, global child prostitution rings, and communication techniques for dysfunctional families.

Video games can also raise awareness of social issues among young players. Stephen Friedman, general manager of mtvU, a subsidiary of MTV, declares, "It's the next generation of activism."[77] As an example, "Food Force" is a popular game created by the United Nations World Food Program as an interactive tool to educate about world hunger. Players assume the role of a humanitarian worker stationed on a famine-stricken island. Since its release in 2005, the game has been adapted for social media sites such as Facebook, where the money players spend for supplies in the games now goes to fund real-world World Food Program school meal projects. The game has proven a success with another 6 million downloads and 10 million estimated players.

"Games for Change" is an ongoing social movement in which video games promote social change. Some of the games showcased by the "Games for Change" conference include:

1. "Ayiti: The Cost of Life," in which players manage a rural family of five over four years.
2. "Guess My Race," in which players take a quiz designed to encourage critical thinking about race and diversity.
3. "A Closed World," a game prototype with a focus on the challenges of LGBTQ youth.

Asi Burak, co-president of Games for Change, believes that larger companies will be willing to invest in these game-based projects:

I believe we are in a transition to the new phase, in which we no longer ask "why games" but much more "how games": understand and share best practices, strengthen the sector with publishing entities and sophisticated funders, and create models that derive from the tech industry or the film industry, but include the unique ingredients that this sector needs. Gaming for good is here to stay with better support and stronger engagement of consumers.[78]

Moreover, media programming can contribute to long-term prosocial behavior in the real world. A 2013 study found that playing immersive virtual reality games in which players are endowed with superpowers leads to proactive behaviors in the video games that increase their helping behaviors.[79]

The Internet has emerged as a powerful tool that can be used to energize and organize grassroots political movements. According to a 2013 Pew report, 72 percent of Americans have taken part in an online political participation activity, which included posting links to political stories or following elected officials. However, although there has been an increase in online political activism by 39 percent over the last five years, 17 percent of political online users do not engage in politics outside of social media. The subset on average is "young, less affluent, and less educated," and has been pinned with the term "slacktivism" to label the behavior.[80]

To illustrate, in June 2013, Turkish youths gathered in Taksim Square, ostensibly to protest the bulldozing of a public green space as part of a project orchestrated by Turkish prime minister Recep Tayyip Erdogan. But on a broader level, the protest was a response to Erdogan's despotic 11-year reign, during which he used a range of steps to stifle dissent. Columnist Thomas L. Friedman described the protest as follows:

> The Turks are engaged in an act of "revulsion." They aren't (yet) trying to throw out their democratically elected Islamist prime minister, Recep Tayyip Erdogan. What they're doing is *calling him out*. Their message is simple: "Get out of our faces, stop choking our democracy and stop acting like such a pompous, overbearing, modern-day Sultan."[81]

CNN Turk at first declined to cover the protests, instead showing a documentary on penguins. So in response Turkish youths used Twitter as their own news and communications network. Friedman explains,

> In doing so, they sent a message to Erdogan: In today's flat world, nobody gets to have one-way conversations anymore. Leaders are now in a two-way conversation with their citizens. Erdogan, who is surrounded by yes-men, got this lesson the hard way. On June 7, he declared that those who try to "lecture us" about the Taksim crackdown, "what did they do about the Wall Street incidents? Tear gas, the death of 17 people happened there. What was the reaction?" In an hour, the American Embassy in Turkey issued a statement in English and Turkish via Twitter rebutting Erdogan: "No U.S. deaths resulted from police actions in #OWS," a reference to Occupy Wall Street. No wonder Erdogan denounced Twitter as society's "worst menace."[82]

Turkish interests in America started a funding campaign on Indiegogo .com that bought a full-page ad in the *New York Times* supporting the protests. According to Forbes, they received donations "from 50 countries at

A Turkish youth laughs as he reads protesters' notes during a rally at the Taksim square in Istanbul on June 9, 2013. (AP Photo/Thanassis Stavrakis)

a clip of over $2,500 per hour over its first day, crossing its $53,800 goal in about 21 hours."[83]

Media as Impediment to Social Change

At the same time, however, the transition to a global communications age may very well be accompanied by a period of radical social upheaval that *obstructs* social change.

Edward Herman and Noam Chomsky argue that the U.S. media operate according to a propaganda model that supports the status quo: "The propaganda model traces the routes by which money and power are able to filter out the news fit to print, marginalize dissent, and allow the government and dominant private interests to get their messages across to the public."[84]

This propaganda model consists of the following elements:

- *Size, ownership, and profit orientation of the mass media*
  The American mass media industry prospers within the current system. As a result, media conglomerates benefit from the policies of the status quo policies of business and government.
- *The advertising license to do business*
  Because the American media system is market driven, media communicators are dependent upon sponsorship to produce

programming. Consequently, media executives are reluctant to present content that might offend powerful advertisers. Herman and Chomsky declare, "In addition to discrimination against unfriendly media institutions, advertisers also choose selectively among programs on the basis of their own principles. With rare exceptions, these are culturally and politically conservative."[85]

In addition, because advertisers are selective about the types of presentations they choose to support, they can exert enormous influence over programming decisions.

- *Sourcing mass media news*

  Stories told through the media are shaped through the use of sources, who often represent government and corporate interests. (For further discussion, see Chapter 8, Journalism.)

- *Flak*

  "Flak" refers to responses to media content, which can take the form of letters, phone calls, petitions, lawsuits, and legislative initiatives. Herman and Chomsky distinguish between individual feedback and "serious flak"—organized efforts by groups with political agendas. Indeed, some groups (e.g., the American Legal Foundation, the Capital Legal Foundation, the Media Institute, the Center for Media and Public Affairs, and Accuracy in Media) have been formed with the expressed purpose of influencing media content. The authors observe, "the ability to produce flak, and especially flak that is costly and threatening, is related to power."[86]

  These groups are often well funded and can produce "serious flak" through contacts with the White House, heads of networks, or ad agencies. These groups may also generate their own media campaigns in response to programming, or back politicians who support their points of view.

- *National security as a control mechanism*

  Since the 1950s, America has used the ideology of anticommunism to control the information that reaches the public. Since the terrorist attack of 9/11, this rationale has been replaced by a broader appeal of national security.

INTERNATIONAL COMMUNICATIONS

International communications is an established area of study within the discipline of media communications that can be approached from a media literacy perspective. International communications typically considers the histories and characteristics of media systems around the world. However, a media literacy approach to international communications also teaches students how to make sense of information being conveyed through the international channels of mass communications.

In addition, a media literacy approach to global communications also furnishes insight into the cultures that produce the media. Consequently, the ability to analyze and discuss the information being conveyed over the international channels of mass communication can lead to a broader understanding of issues and events that shape our lives.

Several factors account for the sparse international news coverage in U.S. news programming. Only a limited amount of attention is devoted to international news, which conveys the message that the United States is the only country that matters. As discussed earlier, many newspapers focus predominantly on local and community issues. The international stories that are included are picked up from wire services such as AP or UPI.

Moreover, television news operates on a crisis sensibility; that is, it commits its resources (crews and equipment) to events in countries involving the United States or its allies—often war scenarios.

Time and space constraints also require editors to select foreign news carefully. Each country has a complex story to tell on a daily basis. For instance, if a paper provided comprehensive coverage of events in the Netherlands, we would be reading a section nearly as large as a Dutch newspaper. If you multiply this by the 248 nations, dependent areas, and other global entities in the world, it would take the American reader a week to digest one day's worth of international news. Consequently, it is impossible to provide complete international coverage without omitting news of national and local interest.

Financial considerations further restrict foreign news coverage. Many news organizations have reduced their overhead by consolidating their foreign bureaus. The remaining correspondents, who are responsible for a large region, lack the familiarity with a single country—and the contacts—integral to insightful reporting.

In addition, the continental United States is only bordered by two countries, and consequently is not directly affected by events taking place on foreign shores. As a result, many Americans remain indifferent to and uninformed about other countries.

The world, as defined by American media coverage, is very small indeed:

- Some countries, like Afghanistan or Syria, have become the focus of national attention because of a crisis, such as a war, political upheaval, or natural disaster.
- According to Philip Gault, certain countries and regions receive sustained coverage in the American press because of their political, commercial, and ethnic linkages with the United States:
  - *Political Interests:* Russia, Central America, Southeast Asia, China
  - *Commercial Ties:* Taiwan, Japan
  - *Ethnic Identification:* Britain, Germany, Italy, Ireland, Israel[87]
- Herbert Gans observes that much of the international news that *does* appear in U.S. newspapers consists of *American* activities in other countries, such as:
  - Implementation of U.S. foreign policy
  - Stopovers by U.S. officials
  - American entertainers on tour
  - International events that affect Americans and American policy.[88]

Global media presentations have become increasingly available to international audiences through the Internet. However, universal *access* to the media should not be confused with media literacy, a field of study in which individuals develop the ability to analyze *media messages* (that is, the underlying themes or ideas contained in a media presentation).

Media Literacy Strategies

A media literacy approach to international communications familiarizes students with a range of strategies with which to analyze and discuss international media messages. The following strategies are particularly useful in the analysis of media and media presentations in other cultures.

Media Communicator

The point of view of the media communicator may appear in the text through such production techniques as editing decisions and connotative words and images.

The challenges of identifying the media communicator are compounded in the arena of global communications. The sheer number of reporters, editors, filmmakers, and Web masters makes it impossible to be familiar with all of their backgrounds, credentials, and orientations, or have an acquaintance with all the educational institutions where foreign media communicators received their training. Although an article or television program often cites the sponsoring organization, there is rarely any accompanying information that provides information on who funds this organization and its mission or orientation.

Function

Understanding the function of, or purpose behind, a media presentation is a particularly useful key to interpreting international media messages. The functions of global communications include:

- *Fostering global community.* Media technology brings different cultures together. One of the first instances of this "global village" concept occurred in 1952, when the coronation of England's Queen Elizabeth was broadcast overseas and celebrated worldwide. A more recent example occurred in 2010, when a mine collapsed in Copiapo, Chile, trapping 33 miners underground for 69 days. A small video camera was delivered to the trapped miners that kept the worldwide audience abreast of the situation. As a result, the worldwide audience provided one-third of the US$20 million cost of the rescue, support for the rescue operation, as well as help for the individual miners.
- *Disseminating information.* Enormous differences exist in the way that various countries produce and distribute the news. Comparing the coverage of a current event in a variety of international newspapers reveals dramatic differences in presentation and content, and even different cultural definitions of news. For example, in Western papers, news about the Third World and Asia tends to be sensational, while coverage of Western items shows more balance between political coverage and sensational stories.[89]
- *Propaganda* refers to the systematic development and dissemination of information to propagate the views and interests of a particular group. Harold D. Lasswell identified four principal strategic aims of propaganda in war:
  - To mobilize hatred against the enemy
  - To preserve the friendship of allies
  - To preserve the friendship and, if possible, to procure the cooperation of neutrals
  - To demoralize the enemy[90]

Significantly, American entertainment programming has been one of the most effective forms of propaganda. International audiences are decidedly fans of American films, television, and music. The unbridled energy and freedom of expression convey positive cumulative messages about America. International audiences have been fans of American films, television, and music.

- *Profit.* Regardless of the manifest function of a media presentation (e.g., entertainment or information), profit has emerged as a significant latent function in Western media. The emergence of the transnational media industry as a for-profit enterprise has had an enormous impact on the production and dissemination of media messages across the globe. In recognition of international markets, companies are developing communications strategies to cultivate markets and influence consumer patterns abroad.

  A related function involves the use of the media *to promote economic development* in a region. For instance, Ecuadorian native villagers are now able to sell their crafts over the Web.[91]

Audience

The audience for a media presentation is influenced by cultural, economic, and historical factors that in turn influence the audience's response to media content.

Questions for students to consider in the analysis of audience include:

- What is the audience's interaction with the media?
- What medium is used most frequently?
- Does the audience seek particular media for certain kinds of information?
- Does audience behavior vary between certain segments of the population?

Historical Context

A country's media programming often reflects its particular point of view with respect to a historical event. For instance, what Americans refer to as the "Viet Nam War" is thought of in Viet Nam as "The Great American War." Clearly, the historical assumptions on which media content is based differ between these two countries.

The historical sensibility of a country also has an impact on its coverage of current events. Historian Nikolai Zlobin explains, "Each nation has its own historical memory and mentality." To illustrate, the reaction of the Chinese media to the Iraq War was tempered by its own historical experience. Zlobin observes, "In its five thousand year history, China has seen dozens of dictators like Saddam Hussein come and go. They were not about to panic over one more."[92]

Cultural Context

Because the media have become such an integral part of a nation, a media system reflects the political, historical, cultural, and economic orientations of that country. Consequently, understanding a nation's media system can furnish valuable perspective about that country. And conversely, examining these aspects of a nation can provide insight into its media system.

Cultural Sensibility. Media presentations serve as a text that provides insight into a country's cultural sensibility. Every country has its own distinctive customs, informal codes of conduct, norms, and mores, which affect the content of its media programming. Zlobin provides the following example: "I once asked an Italian journalist if he could write an article criticizing the Pope. He said, 'No way. There is no law. However, it would never occur to me to do it.' It was outside of his cultural mentality."[93]

To illustrate, *The Yacoubian Building,* a film adaptation of the novel by Egyptian Alaa Al Aswany, focuses on the lives of residents both rich and poor of the Yacoubian, an actual apartment building in downtown Cairo. Journalist Peter Kenyon comments,

> *The Yacoubian Building* describes a country that is corrupt, unfair and thuggish. . . . Yacoubian takes a look at sometimes uncomfortable truths about life in contemporary Egypt. It tackles subjects considered taboo in traditional Egyptian society, such as homosexuality, and even features a corrupt imam.[94]

Wahid Hamed, who wrote the screenplay for *Yacoubian,* observes, "I think [the movie] will be like a document of the time we live in," noting that the movie says in public what many citizens are thinking in private.[95]

Reporters' ignorance of the cultural nuances of a country can cause errors in coverage. For instance, Zlobin recounts that in 1999, the international press reported that Russian President Boris Yeltsin had issued a warning that a military strike against Iraq by a U.S.-led coalition would lead to a "world war." This story caused understandable consternation within the global community. But according to Yeltsin spokesperson Sergei Yastrzhembsky, the Western media had overreacted because they misinterpreted Yeltsin's use of Russian slang. (*Naryvatsya,* which means "run-in," was interpreted by the Western media as signifying a much more serious confrontation.)[96]

International advertisers have also been disadvantaged by their insensitivity to the cultural nuances of its foreign market. To illustrate, Gillette mounted an expensive ad campaign in France promoting its shaving accouterments. But to the surprise of the company, the ads were ineffective. However, as Zlobin explains, the demonstration of the product made no sense to the French audience: "The commercials showed men shaving in the morning before going to work. However, in France, it is customary to shave at night before retiring."[97]

National Stereotyping. Media programming is a principal means by which people from different cultures learn about one another. Unless you have personally visited another country, what you know about that culture is derived primarily from the media depictions of other cultures. *National stereotyping* refers to the generalized conception associated with members of a particular country. These stereotypes generally are not very flattering.

For example, a Wendy's Hamburgers ad campaign portrayed Russians as ugly, ignorant peasants; the message is that Americans are blessed with both the taste and the freedom of choice to buy Wendy's Hamburgers.

Media and Cultural Identity. In some traditional cultures, the channels of mass communications have introduced new and different ideas that have disrupted the established values system. To illustrate, in his study of the effects of Western media on Indonesia, Asep Sutresna found that younger Indonesians are losing touch with traditional Indonesian culture: "Young Indonesians are not familiar with traditional cultures anymore, such as ephics which contain Indonesian ancestors' philosophy of life. They are not familiar with the figures in those ephics or traditional stories. They tend to view these cultures as being for rural people's consumption."[98]

The widespread presence of the media has led to a schism between generations. Sutresna explains, "Young Indonesians tend to view the traditional values and ethics as too strict and obsolete. Those are their parents' values and ethics."[99] Instead, the younger generation has adopted Western

values, including the definition of success: "The success for young Indonesian are rich (materialistic), popular, independent, and individualistic."[100]

In 2006, Playboy Enterprises announced plans to publish a version of the
magazine in India, reflecting the rapid Westernization of the country. The
Indian version of the magazine would focus on topics related to high living,
pop culture, celebrity, and fashion. Reporter Anand Giridharadas explains,

> [India is] overflowing with ambition, as a small but growing class of
> young, urban, world-traveling men with disposable income find their
> way to a new upper class. The democratization of affluence is creat-
> ing would-be male connoisseurs, keen for tutelage in ways of the
> high life.[101]

Because the mores of the country prohibit the graphic Western type of
sexuality, the Indian version of the magazine contains no nudity. However,
Venkatesh Abdev, a top official of the World Hindu Council, a conservative organization, declared. "They are going to spoil our culture. We are
not giving as much importance to sex as them. Free sex is not allowed in
our culture."[102]

Moreover, Indian law prohibits the sale or possession of material that is
"lascivious or appeals to the prurient interest" and that is without redeeming artistic, literary, or religious merit. And on a more practical level, even
though the younger generation welcomes this new version of sexuality,
they tend to live at home with their parents, who definitely are not comfortable with the "new" sexuality. N. Radhakrishnan, editor of *Man's
World,* explains, "In urban India, the concept of single men living alone is
quite new. Here, most men, until they're married, live at home. Once
you're married, your wife wonders what you're reading."[103]

Indeed, some media systems that are considered repressive by Western
standards are actually designed to protect and preserve their traditional
culture. For instance, in Thailand, billboards present images of the Thai
king and queen to honor the royal family. In 2007, the Thai government
blocked public access to YouTube after a clip appeared on the site that
showed graffiti-like elements superimposed over photographs of the king,
including pictures of feet over the king's image—a major taboo.

Economic Structure

Proponents of media reform in the United States are primarily concerned
about the concentration of media ownership in the hands of a few

mega-conglomerates. (See Chapter 5, Structure.) However, private owner-ship is but one of three global media ownership systems, each of which exercises a discrete effect on media content:

- *State-Owned System.* In authoritarian countries such as Cuba and North Korea, the media industry is controlled by the government. Under this system, television programs, radio shows, films, and newspapers, as well as books and magazines, are owned, produced, and distributed under the close supervision of the government.
- *Public Ownership.* Under this system of ownership, the media are owned by the public but operated by the government. In countries such as Sweden, the Netherlands, and Kazakstan, the revenue re-quired to cover the operating costs of newspapers, television stations, and radio stations is generated through public taxes.
- *Private Ownership.* In countries such as the United States, almost all of the newspapers, magazines, radio stations, film studios, and television stations are privately owned—either by individuals or, increasingly, by large multinational corporations. Under this market-driven system, the primary purpose, or function, is to generate the maximum possible profit.

Currently, the private ownership model is encroaching on the estab-lished media model of many countries. Thus, many countries now operate on a *hybrid media system,* in which several ownership systems coexist. For instance, in the United States the media are predominantly privately owned. However, National Public Radio (NPR) and the Public Broadcasting Sys-tem (PBS) are a publicly owned radio and television system, respectively.

The economic framework of a country plays a major role in the content of its media. For instance, in state-owned media systems, independent sources of information are not available. Consequently, stories are diffi-cult to substantiate, which undermines public confidence in the media. In England, the broadcast media are owned by the government and financed through public taxes. The staff of the British Broadcasting System (BBC) are civil employees who are not subject to market-driven pressures. In this system, the content of the programs is not determined by the audience; thus, although the quality of their programming may be superior, they may not be as successful in attracting an audience as American-style programs.

Moreover, although a country's policy with respect to freedom of the press is shaped by its political system, the economic structure of a country also can restrict media content. Zlobin explains,

If you ask a British journalist who has more freedom, you or an American journalist working for a private company, he [sic] will say, "No question, me . . . because I am defended by law. They can't kick me out, my salary is guaranteed. I am working for the British government—not the particular administration that might happen to be in power at the moment."

In this case, the British government protects the media from the pressures of the market and foreign influence. In contrast, the U.S. media maintains a strict independence from government. However, the American media industry struggles with freedom from market-forces which shapes the coverage of issues.[104]

Changes in a country's media system can bring about broader changes in the cultural, political, and economic life of the nation. This helps explain the significance of the announcement in 2012 of media reforms in Myanmar, which is beginning the process of moving the country toward democracy. Mr. Thiha Saw, editor of two Myanmar private weekly publications, sees media freedom as a "barometer for the reform process" in the country.[105]

Applied Areas of Analysis

International media literacy examines media formats such as journalism, advertising, and political communications and considers a range of issues, including violence in the media, media and children, and media and social change.

Journalism

The ready access to primary source material provides opportunities to compare the points of view of journalists, news organizations, and national perspectives. Media literacy students have the opportunity to compare the coverage of issues by news organizations throughout the globe by focusing on:

- What information is included and omitted
- Connotative word choice and images
- Order of presentation
- Use of quotes
- Point of view

Online journalism also provides invaluable research opportunities for media literacy scholarship. Students can compare how different countries cover the same issues and events. By using digital databases, researchers can instantly record and track the number of times that a word appears in the media, providing insight into emerging areas of cultural interest and concern. And in addition, social media provides immediate public response to historical and cultural events.

Advertising

Some international advertising campaigns have a *universal* appeal. As an example, beer ads take advantage of the fact that everyone gets thirsty. Thus, regardless of culture, beer commercials emphasize the refreshing quality of the product. In contrast, other ads are *localized,* which are effective only in a particular country or region. Thus, students can analyze ads to discover whether they reflect a standardized or localized approach.

Other lines of inquiry include:

- Identifying the values, attitudes, and preoccupations that are reflected in localized ads.
- Comparing national ads for the same brand or product as a reflection of each culture.
- Examining how specific products are advertised, such as alcohol and tobacco. What messages are conveyed about these products in different countries?
- Analyzing a sample of ads produced in one country, focusing on the following:
  - Who is the target audience?
  - What appeals and themes are used in these ads?
  - What are the worldviews of the advertisements?
  - What do the ads reveal about the country's cultural preoccupations, attitudes, values, behaviors, and myths?

Political Communications

Another area of study involves examining a country's media system as a way to assess the political landscape of a nation. Examining the *function,* or process, of the media can provide insight into a country's political system. The possible functions of the media range from *informing* to *controlling* citizens.

Every country's media system is shaped by its political framework—particularly its definition of freedom of the press:

- What kinds of information are permitted?
- What kinds of information are prohibited?

In a number of countries, journalists face serious repercussions for reporting the news. In 2012, 121 journalists were killed worldwide while reporting the news, an increase of 13 percent from the previous year. The deadliest countries for journalists were Syria, where 35 journalists were killed, and Somalia, which reported 18 deaths.[106]

Lucie Morillon, Washington director of Reporters without Borders, declares, "There has never been a more dangerous time to be a journalist. But even more deplorable was the lack of interest, and sometimes even the failure, by democratic countries in defending everywhere the values they are supposed to incarnate."[107]

In addition, media literacy analysis can furnish perspective into the distribution of power among nations, called *global hegemony.* The flow of global information has long been dominated by Western culture—particularly the United States. Four of the five major news agencies are Western; these agencies account for 90 percent of the global news flow. The Western dominance of international communications has long come under criticism by the international community. Developing countries in particular have accused the United States of promoting its ideology by monopolizing media programming on a global scale. In 1976, the United Nations Educational, Scientific and Cultural Organization (UNESCO) called for a new world information and communication order to respond to the following inequities:

1. *The flow of information is unequal, with too much information originating in the West and not enough representing the developing nations.*
2. *There is too much bias against, and stereotyping of, the developing or "less developed" countries.*
3. *Alien values are foisted on the Third World by too much Western (mainly American) "communication imperialism."*
4. *Western communication places undue emphasis on "negative" news of the Third World—disasters, coups, government corruption and the like.*
5. *Finances are unequally distributed around the world for technology and communication development.*

6. *The Western definition of "news" (meaning atypical and sensational items) is unrealistic and does not focus enough attention on development news (items helping in the progress and growth of the country).*
7. *Communication and journalism education in universities is too Western-oriented, and too many textbooks used in the Third World are authored by First-World writers, especially by Americans.*
8. *Too much of the world's information is collected by the big five news agencies, all but one representing the First (advanced capitalist) World.*[108]

However, American popular culture no longer has quite the influence of the past, for several reasons. As discussed in Chapter 4, at long last, the domestic media systems in many countries are catching up to those of the United States. As an example, India makes well over a thousand movies a year—more than a fourth of the world's films.[109] Moreover, in an effort to preserve cultural integrity, countries such as Canada, Israel, and France have imposed quotas on the amount of foreign media presentations (i.e., music, films, and television programs) that can be imported into the country. In addition, digital media technology "levels the playing field," enabling individuals to produce, edit, and distribute media around the globe.

The international community has developed initiatives designed to contend with the inequality of global information systems. UNESCO has adopted a strategy of providing support for individual countries as they develop their own communication systems. In addition, numerous countries support domestic media production through government subsidies to artists and media communicators, including Norway, Denmark, Spain, Mexico, Canada, and South Africa.

And finally, private organizations are working to provide digital access to remote communities so that individuals throughout the globe will be able to participate fully in the opportunities presented by unlimited access to information. For instance, nonprofit organizations such as One Laptop Per Child have developed a laptop computer at a cost of $150 U.S. dollars, which is designed to connect 1.2 billion children in the developing world to the resources of a global network.[110]

NOTES

1. Frank Baker, "Media Use Statistics," Media Literacy Clearinghouse, http://www.frankwbaker.com.
2. Ibid.

3. Henry J. Kaiser Family Foundation, "Fact Sheet: TV Violence," 2003, Menlo Park, CA.
4. Ibid.
5. Lawrie Mifflin, "An Increase Is Seen in the Number of Violent Television Programs," *New York Times,* April 17, 1998: A-16.
6. Richard Rosenfeld, Associate Professor of Criminology, University of Missouri–St. Louis, interview by author, August 12, 1992, St. Louis, Missouri.
7. Ibid.
8. David Rosenbaum, "Panel Documents How Violent Fare Is Aimed at Youth," *New York Times,* September 12, 2000.
9. Ibid.
10. Carey Goldberg with Marjorie Connelly, "Polls Find Decline in Teen-Age Fear and Violence," *New York Times,* October 20, 1999: A-1.
11. Mifflin, "An Increase Is Seen in the Number of Violent Television Programs."
12. Mark Crispin Miller, "Hollywood: The Ad," *Atlantic Monthly,* April 1990: 53.
13. Robert M. Liebert and Joyce Sprafkin, *The Early Window: Effects of Television on Children and Youth,* 3rd ed. (New York: Pergamon Press, 1988), 140–1.
14. Ibid., 157.
15. Ibid., 147.
16. Peter S. Goodman, "Economists Say Movie Violence Might Temper the Real Thing," *New York Times,* January 7, 2008.
17. Daniel Linz, Edward Donnerstein, and Steven Penrod, "The Effects of Multiple Exposures to Filmed Violence against Women," *Journal of Communication* 34.3 (Summer 1984): 130–47.
18. Fred Emery and Merrelyn Emery, *A Choice of Futures* (Leiden, NL: Martinus Nijhoff Social Sciences Division, 1976), 82.
19. Goodman, "Economists Say Movie Violence Might Temper the Real Thing."
20. Neil M. Malmauth and J.V.P. Check, "The Effects of Mass Media Exposure on Acceptance of Violence against Women: A Field Experiment," *Journal of Research in Personality* 1981, 15.
21. G. S. Lesser, *Children and Television: Lessons from Sesame Street* (New York: Vintage Books, 1974), 4.
22. Ibid., 3.
23. Charles W. Turner, Bradford W. Hesse, and Sonja Peterson-Lewis, "Naturalistic Studies of the Long-Term Effects of Television Violence," *Journal of Social Issues* 42.3 (1986).
24. Richard Frost and John Stauffer, "The Effects of Social Class, Gender, and Personality on Psychological Responses to Filmed Violence," *Journal of Communication* (Spring 1987).

25. Charles W. Turner and Leonard Berkowitz, "Identification with Film Aggressor (Covert Role Taking) and Reactions to Film Violence," *Journal of Personality and Social Psychology* 21.2 (1972): 256–64.

26. Warren Buckleitner, "So Young, and So Gadgeted," New York Times, June 12, http://2008.www.nytimes.com "_blank"2008.www.nytimes.com.

27. Ibid., 4l.

28. Ibid.

29. Miller, "Hollywood: The Ad," 53.

30. Mabel Rice, Altha C. Huston, and John C. Wright, "The Forms of Television: Effects on Children's Attention, Comprehension, and Social Behavior," in *Television and Behavior: Ten Years of Scientific Progress and Implications for the Eighties,* Vol. 2, *Technical Reviews,* ed. David Pearl, Lorraine Bouthilet, and Joyce Laza (Rockville, MD: National Institute for Mental Health, 1982), 26.

31. Frank Rich, "Washington's Post-Littleton Looney Tunes," *New York Times,* June 19, 1999: A-27.

32. Scott Collins, "Acceptable Level of TV Violence Is Ever Shifting for Viewers, Execs," *Los Angeles Times,* February 15, 2013, http://articles.latimes.com/2013/feb/15/entertainment/la-et-st-violence-tv-20130217.

33. Henry J. Kaiser Foundation, *Generation M2, Media in the Lives of 8–18 Year Olds: A Kaiser Family Foundation Study,* January 2010, kff.org/other/poll-finding/report-generation-m2-media-in-the-lives/.

34. Common Sense Media: Media Research Study, Fall 2011, http://vjrconsulting.com/storage/ZerotoEightFINAL2011.pdf.

35. Warren Buckleitner, "So Young, and So Gadgeted," *New York Times,* June 12, 2008.

36. Nick Bilton, "The Child, the Tablet and the Developing Mind," *New York Times,* March 31, 2013.

37. Larry D. Rosen, *Rewired: Understanding the iGeneration and the Way That They Learn* (New York: Palgrave Macmillan, 2010), 164.

38. J. Piaget and B. Inhelder, *The Origin of the Idea of Chance in Children* (New York: W.W. Norton, 1983).

39. Deborah Peterson, "Three Recent Cases Show Cyberworld Has Dark Side: Watch Young Surfers, Experts Urge," *St. Louis Post-Dispatch,* July 29, 1998.

40. Center for Media and Values, *Parenting in a Television Age: A Media Literacy Workshop Kit™ on Children and Television* (Los Angeles: Center for Media and Values, 1991), Handout #1.

41. Peterson, "Three Recent Cases Show Cyberworld Has Dark Side: Watch Young Surfers, Experts Urge."

42. Center for Media and Values, *Parenting in a Television Age: A Media Literacy Workshop Kit.*

43. Amiee Dorr, Sherryl Browne Graves, and Erin Phelps, "Television Literacy for Young Children," *Journal of Communication* (Summer 1980), 73.

44. Buckleitner, "So Young, and So Gadgeted."

45. "National Study Reveals Kids Favorite TV Ads," *Advertising Age* (March 1998).

46. Ibid.

47. D. Sweet and R. Singh, "TV Viewing and Parental Guidance," *Education Consumer Guide,* April 2, 1997, http://inet.ed.gov/pubs/OR/Consumer/tv .html.

48. U.S. Census Bureau, www.quickfacts.uscensus.gov.

49. Elizabeth Monk-Turner, Mary Heiserman, Crystle Johnson, Vanity Cotton, and Manny Jackson, "The Portrayal of Racial Minorities on Prime Time Television: A Replication of the Mastro and Greenberg Study a Decade Later," *Studies in Popular Culture* 32.2 (Spring 2010).

50. U.S. Census Bureau, www.quickfacts.uscensus.gov.

51. Elizabeth Monk-Turner, Mary Heiserman, Crystle Johnson, Vanity Cotton and Manny Jackson, "The Portrayal of Racial Minorities on Prime Time Television: A Replication of the Mastro and Greenberg Study a Decade Later."

52. Linda Holtzman, "Content Analysis-Cartoons," unpublished Webster University class project, Summer 1992, 1–22.

53. Megan Rosenfeld, "Girls Find Less to Like on the Tube, Survey Says," *Washington Post,* carried in the *St. Louis Post-Dispatch,* January 17, 1996: E-1.

54. Betty Debman, "Mini-Page: South American Countries," *St. Louis Post-Dispatch,* October 1999: C-3, C-4.

55. Ibid.

56. Ibid.

57. W. Andrew Collins, "Cognitive Processing in Television Viewing," in *Television and Behavior: Ten Years of Scientific Progress and Implications for the Eighties,* Vol. 2, *Technical Reviews,* ed. by David Pearl, Lorraine Bouthilet, and Joyce Lazar (Rockville, MD: National Institute for Mental Health, 1982), 11.

58. Ibid.

59. Ibid.

60. David Considine and Gail Haley, *Visual Messages: Integrating Imagery into Instruction* (Englewood, CO: Teacher Ideas Press, 1992), 80.

61. Marketingvox, Rand Youth Poll, Seventeen, Packaged Facts. September 8, 2012, www.marketingvox.com.

62. Ibid.

63. Adriana Barbaro, Jeremy Earp, directors, "Consuming Kids," Media Education Foundation, October 29, 2008, www.mediaed.org.

64. James McNeil, quoted in B. Horovitz, "Six Strategies Marketers Use to Make Kids Want Things Bad," *USA Today,* November 22, 2006: B-1. http:// www.usatoday.com/money/advertising/2006-11-21-toy-strategies-usat.

65. National Study Reveals Kids' Favorite TV Ads," *Advertising Age* (March 1998).

66. Paul M. Fischer et al., "Brand Logo Recognition by Children Aged 3 to 6 Years," *Journal of the American Medical Association,* December 11, 1991: 3145.

67. *Buy Me That: A Kid's Survival Guide to TV Advertising,* produced by Public Media, Inc. (Chicago: Films Incorporated Video, 1990).

68. John Lyons, *Guts: Advertising from the Inside Out* (New York: AMACOM, 1987, 292).

69. Francesca M. Cancian, M. Francesca, and Bonnie L. Ross, "Mass Media and the Women's Movement," *The Journal of Applied Behavioral Science* 12.1 (1981), 11.

70. Ibid., 18.

71. Ibid., 25.

72. Ibid., 18.

73. Ibid., 30.

74. John Tebbel, *The Media in America* (New York: Thomas Y. Crowell Company, 1974).

75. Ibid., 39.

76. Nicholas Wade, "Supremacy of a Social Network," *New York Times,* March 14, 2011.

77. Sylvester Brown, Jr., "Some Video Games Make a Point with Their Violence," *St. Louis Post-Dispatch,* July 2, 2006.

78. World Food Programme, http://www.wfp.org/stories/online-game-food-force -puts-players-front-lines-hunger.

79. R. S. Rosenberg, S. L. Baughman, and J. N, Bailenson, "Virtual Superheroes: Using Superpowers in Virtual Reality to Encourage Prosocial Behavior," *PLoS ONE* 8.1 (2013): e55003, doi:10.1371/journal.pone.0055003.

80. Pew Internet: Civic Engagement in the Digital Age, http://pewinternet.org/ Reports/2013/Civic-Engagement/Summary-of-Findings.aspx.

81. Thomas L. Friedman, "Postcard from Turkey," *New York Times,* June 18, 2013.

82. Ibid.

83. Ibid.

84. Edward Herman and Noam Chomsky, *Manufacturing Consent* (New York: Pantheon Books, 1988), 2.

85. Ibid., 17.

86. Ibid., 26.

87. Philip Gault, *Choosing the News: The Profit Factor in News Selection* (New York: Greenwood Press, 1990), 127.

88. Herbert Gans, *Deciding What's News* (New York: Pantheon Books, 1979), 31–7.

89. W. James Potter, "News from Three Worlds in Prestige U.S. Newspapers," in *Current Issues in International Communications,* edited by L. John Martin and Ray Eldon Hiebert (New York: Longman, 1990), 280.

90. Harold D. Lasswell, *Propaganda Technique in the World War* (New York: Peter Smith, 1927), 195.

91. Simon Romero, "When Villages Go Global," *New York Times,* April 23, 2000.

92. Zlobin, interview with author, July 20, 1999, St. Louis, Missouri.

93. Ibid.

94. Peter Kenyon, "Provocative 'Yacoubian' Film Opens in Cairo," *All Things Considered,* National Public Radio, June 21, 2006.

95. Ibid.

96. Zlobin, interview.

97. Ibid.

98. Asep Sutresna, "International Communication and Popular Culture in Indonesia," paper presented to MED 531, Media and Culture, Webster University, May 1993, 6.

99. Ibid., 7.

100. Ibid., 13.

101. Anand Giridharadas, "Playboy Makes Move in India, but without the Centerfold," *New York Times,* January 2, 2006.

102. Ibid.

103. Ibid.

104. Zlobin, interview.

105. Thomas Fuller, "Myanmar to Curb Censorship of Media," *New York Times,* August 20, 2012.

106. Mark Sweney, "121 Journalists Killed in 2012," *The Guardian,* December 31, 2012, http://www.guardian.co.uk/media/2012/dec/31/121-journalists-killed-2012-syria.

107. Doreen Carvajal, "1,000 Journalists Killed . . . and More Than 140 Were Jailed—Its Highest Level in a Decade," *Forbes.com,* http://www.forbes.com/feeds/ap/2007/02/01/ap3386569.html.

108. John C. Merrill, John Lee, and Edward J. Friedlander, *Modern Mass Media* (New York: Harper & Row, 1990), 428.

109. Pankaj Mishra, "Hurray for Bollywood," *New York Times,* February 28, 2004: A-15.

110. Cherlynn Low, "One Laptop Per Child Launches $150 Tablet," *NBC News Technology,* July 17, 2013. http://www.nbcnews.com/technology/one-laptop-child-launches-150-tablet-6C10660697.

13

Outcomes

It is now appropriate to consider the "quintessential so what"—that is, given what you know about the media, what steps can be taken to improve our communications environment? The Aspen Institute National Leadership Conference on Media Literacy has considered this critical issue of possible *outcomes:*

> Is media literacy important only to the extent that it enables one to be a better citizen in society? What is the role of ideology in the process? To what extent is an individual "media literate" if she just appreciates the aesthetics of a message without going further with it?[1]

The range of possible outcomes fall into the following categories:

Personal Responses

The most immediate outcome is that you are now in a position to make independent personal choices about your media consumption. Digital media technology gives you unprecedented control over your personal media usage as well as access to a range of perspectives on issues.

Your personal decisions include:

- Becoming well informed on matters of media coverage
- Maintaining a "balanced media diet" with regard to:
  - Different ideological perspectives; and
  - Different media (e.g., print, television, Internet), which emphasize different aspects of content.
- Becoming aware of your everyday contact with the media and media influence on your lifestyle, attitudes, behaviors, and values.

- Applying media literacy analysis tools (Keys to Interpreting Media Messages) to media presentations to derive insight into media messages.
- Examining media programming to learn about cultural attitudes, values, behaviors, preoccupations, and myths.
- Developing an awareness of programming as a text that furnishes perspective into cultural changes.
- Keeping abreast of patterns in ownership and government regulations that affect the media industry.
- Promoting discussions about the media industry, media programming, and issues with friends, colleagues, and children.

Becoming Involved in the Media Literacy Community

Media literacy organizations promote the field of media literacy by collecting and disseminating media literacy information. They also sponsor programs and conferences throughout the country. Examples of media literacy organizations include:

- Center for Media Literacy
- Center for Media Education
- About Face
- National Telemedia Council
- Gateway Media Literacy Partners (GMLP)

Many other organizations promote goals that are associated with media literacy. Some of these organizations include:

- Children Now
- Action for Children's Television
- Children's Advertising Review Unit
- National Alliance for Non-Violent Programming

Media Activism

Media activists are committed to finding ways to democratize the communications environment, both nationally and globally. *Media justice* has emerged as a movement designed to enable the voice of the masses to be heard in the media. According to the media justice organization *Reclaim the Media*, the work of the media justice movement is "pursuing a more just society by transforming our media system and expanding the communication rights of ordinary people through grassroots organizing, education, networking and advocacy."[2]

The following activities are designed to develop awareness within communities and work for change in the media landscape.

Individual Activism. Individuals may make the following personal choices in response to media programming:

- Cancel your subscription or turn off objectionable programming
- If you have concerns about a newspaper article, write a letter to the editor
- If you have concerns about a television or radio program, write to the general manager of the station or register a complaint with the Federal Communications Commission (FCC). The FCC can respond to public complaints by investigating broadcast stations. On the basis of its findings, the FCC is authorized to levy fines on stations. In extreme cases, the FCC can suspend station operations, refuse to renew a station's broadcast license, or even withdraw a station's current license. However, the first amendment (freedom of speech) provides considerable latitude for the expression of ideas—even those that are in "poor taste."

    Federal Communications Commission regulations require that stations keep all public correspondence on file. Consequently, station management must make a formal acknowledgement of your point of view.
- Meet in person with the staff of the newspaper, TV, or radio station.

Grassroots Organizing. These activities begin at the local level and focus on organizing community resources. Digital technology has updated traditional strategies such as letter writing and petition drives. To illustrate, in 2012, Sarah Kavanagh, a 15-year-old girl from Hattiesburg, Mississippi, and her little brother gathered almost 200,000 signatures on Change.org, an online petition platform, designed to persuade Gatorade's parent company PepsiCo to eliminate brominated vegetable oil from its formula. (They were successful.)

Contacting Advertisers. Media organizations are very sensitive to the concerns of their advertisers, who in turn strive to maintain the goodwill of the public. Consequently, explaining your concerns and listing the program's advertisers can be an effective action step. As an example, in 2009, after Fox News commentator Glenn Beck said on the air that President Barack Obama was a racist with a "deep-seated hatred for white people or the white culture," approximately a dozen companies withdrew their commercials from Beck's program, including ConAgra, Geico, Procter & Gamble, Progressive Insurance Company, RadioShack, and the Roche and Sanofi-Aventis pharmaceutical companies. The sponsors' shifts came after a campaign by ColorOfChange .org, a political coalition, urged individuals to contact sponsors of Mr. Beck's program (as opposed to contacting the producers of the Beck program).

In addition, Donny Deutsch, the advertising executive at CNBC and MSNBC, listed some of the "Glenn Beck" advertisers and told MSNBC viewers that people who objected to Mr. Beck's remark should write to the chief executives of the companies. Deutsch declared that corporate decisions about where to allot ad dollars were the "ultimate check and balance."[3] Soon thereafter, Fox News and Beck jointly announced that Beck's show would be taken off of the air.

- *Becoming an activist stockholder* can be an effective way to exercise some influence over the direction of media conglomerates. By purchasing as little as one share of a company's stock, you can become a shareholder and can bring issues of concern to the attention of other stockholders, as well as vote on policy issues.

  Becoming an activist stockholder is not simply a confrontational strategy, but is an approach designed to educate investors in the media conglomerate. The "other" stockholders of media conglomerates are often parents who are concerned about the impact of media programming on their children. Thus, this educational approach is designed to broaden stockholders' definitions of corporate success beyond quarterly profits to include responsible, quality programming.

- *Monitoring local media.* Groups that do not feel well served by the media in their communities can challenge the license renewal with the Federal Communications Commission (FCC). As an example, the members of the United Church of Christ in Jackson, Mississippi, monitored civil rights stories carried on local station WLBT-TV between 1953 and 1979. After the citizens demonstrated that the station's programming excluded a significant segment of the population, the station's license was not renewed.

Organizational Activism. National organizations with large memberships can most assuredly influence the policies of media corporations. Organizations such as Free Press (www.freepress.com) and *Action Coalition for Media Education* (ACME) are employing different strategies that share common goals of broadening and diversifying corporate ownership of the media industry. In 2006, thanks largely to an enormous grassroots movement organized by Free Press, language about "Net neutrality" was included as part of an agreement for a merger between AT&T and the Bell companies, and a two-year moratorium was established preserving the principle of "Net neutrality." (For more information on Net neutrality, see Chapter 5.)

At the 2013 Media Reform Conference in Denver, Colorado, participants brought forward a range of proposals intended to democratize the media environment in the United States, including:

- accurate representation of our communities and stories;
- balanced perspectives;
- more media in the hands of more people;
- community-owned broadband everywhere;
- a critical and media-literate viewership;
- free airtime to political candidates and less fundraising (for politicians), more time legislating;
- an effective, responsive FCC;
- media literacy required for all middle school students;
- requiring corporations to pay rent for use of our public airwaves;
- more environmental coverage;
- more news about labor;
- more women and people of color as owners; and
- more coverage of the poor.[4]

In addition, individual states, including Massachusetts, New Jersey, and Texas, have introduced bills that promote media literacy as an educational priority.

SECTORS

Media literacy is an area of study that prepares students for careers in a range of fields. In an opinion column in the *New York Times* entitled "Is a Cinema Studies Degree the New MBA?" Elizabeth Van Ness, Dean of the School of Cinema-Television at the University of Southern California, argued that cinema studies imbues students with the critical skills that make them sought after in the workplace:

> Rick Herbst, now attending Yale Law School, may yet turn out to be the current decade's archetypal film major. Twenty-three years old, he graduated last year from the University of Notre Dame, where he studied filmmaking with no intention of becoming a filmmaker. Rather, he saw his major as a way to learn about power structures and how individuals influence each other.
>
> "People endowed with social power and prestige are able to use film and media images to reinforce their power—we need to look to film to grant power to those who are marginalized or currently not represented," said Mr. Herbst, who envisions a future in the public policy arena. The communal nature of film, he said, has a distinct power to affect large groups, and he expects to use his cinematic skills to do exactly that.
>
> At a time when street gangs warn informers with DVD productions about the fate of "snitches" and both terrorists and their adversaries routinely communicate in elaborately staged videos, it is not altogether surprising that film school—promoted as a shot at an entertainment industry job—is beginning to attract those who believe that cinema isn't so much a profession as the professional language of the future.[5]

Substituting the term "media literacy" for "cinema studies" expands this theoretical and diagnostic focus to include all forms of media. As Elizabeth Daley observes, "The greatest digital divide is between those who can read and write with media, and those who can't. Our core knowledge needs to belong to everybody. . . . If I had my way, our multimedia literacy honors program would be required of every student in the university."[6] Indeed, today's geopolitical world requires that professionals in the public realm understand the nuances of media messages. Van Ness explains,

> Members of a Baltimore street gang circulated a DVD that warned against betrayal, packaged in a cover that appeared to show three dead bodies. That and the series of gruesome execution videos that have surfaced in the Middle East are perhaps only the most extreme face of a complex sort of post-literacy in which cinematic visuals and filmic narrative have become commonplace.[7]

Graduates of these programs have pursued careers in museums and leisure businesses, and in the public policy arena.

Media literacy is a discipline with career applications in the following sectors.

Media Literacy Education

Media literacy is an established field of study within the international academic community. Most significantly, in 2012, UNESCO, the United Nations' educational agency, declared that media and information literacy is a "fundamental human right." Indeed, media literacy has emerged as a twenty-first-century survival skill. An educated person is someone who can make sense of his or her environment; today, our environment is being formed by the media.

Among individual countries, Canada has long been a global media leader in media literacy education. Media literacy education pioneers John Pungente and the late Barry Duncan provide the following background information:

> Over the past few decades Media Literacy has become part of the basic curriculum for all elementary and secondary school students in Canada. Because of the research, teaching and promotion of Media Literacy by Canadian educators and the provincial ministries of education, Media Literacy has also become an essential building block for many post secondary areas of study, life-long learning programs, continuing education programs, professional development and training programs and specialized programs for the at-risk or marginalized population.[8]

England and Australia have emerged as leaders in the discipline of media education, with performance and content standards, norm-referenced tests, and preservice university training for a specialty in media education. In 2002, the UK passed a communications bill charging a new super-regulator, Ofcom, with the duty to encourage "a better public understanding of the nature and characteristics of material published by means of electronic media." It also allows for greater use of rating systems, filters, and other devices that block out objectionable content.[9]

Other countries have also made significant inroads into the field of media literacy education, including New Zealand, Chile, India, Scotland, South Africa, Japan, France, Italy, Spain, and Jordan.

In 1999, media educator Frank Baker and Rutgers University media professor Robert Kubey conducted the first national study of media literacy in state K–12 teaching standards and reported that for the first time "elements of media literacy" could be found in the teaching standards of almost every state.[10] These standards can be found in the curriculum requirements of several disciplines, including Language Arts, Social Studies, Health, and Performing Arts. Advocates of this *integrated approach to media literacy* use the analogy of foreign language instruction, pointing out that offering classes in Latin, French, or Chinese once or twice a week is not nearly as effective as becoming immersed in the language by traveling to a foreign country. And as a critical thinking skill, media literacy can actually *enhance* the instruction of these established disciplines.

However, many teachers ignore this mandate—in part because schools' certifications and teachers' promotions are predicated on students' performance on these tests. Consequently, as media literacy educator Frank Baker observes, "Teachers, who know what is on the test, teach only that material, and thus media literacy gets left out."[11]

In addition, teachers have not been instructed in how to teach media literacy.

However, in recent years, the media literacy movement has gained momentum in American colleges and universities. A 2002 survey found that 61 two-year and four-year institutions of higher education offered media literacy courses or programs.[12] A 2007 update of this survey found that the number of colleges and universities offering media literacy courses had tripled—to over 180 schools.[13] These course offerings are offered through a number of academic disciplines, although they can most often be found in departments of communication or education. In addition, a number of schools, including Webster University, Morehead State University, and Wesley College, have added media literacy courses to their general education requirements for all students. Further, a number of professional associations promote media literacy in the United States, including the Center for Media Literacy in Los Angeles, the National Telemedia Council in Madison, Wisconsin, and the New Mexico Media Literacy Project (NMMLP).

In addition, several *nontraditional educational avenues* introduce media literacy to audiences normally not reached through the conventional educational system. For example, media literacy classes have been offered through Oasis, a national organization for people above the age of 50 that subscribes to the mission of "promoting successful aging through lifelong learning, health plans, and volunteer engagement."[14] In addition, speaking to parents' groups such as parent/teacher organizations (PTOs) about the value of media literacy education has the added benefit of enlisting support for media literacy education in the schools. Administrators may not be attentive to the recommendations of teachers, but they are extremely responsive to parental concerns.

Homeschool is another nontraditional educational arena. Media literacy educator Debra Stieferman provides the following insights into homeschooling and media literacy:

> There is enormous potential for media literacy as a part of the curricula of homeschools.
>
> Homeschooling is an alternative educational approach, in which parents choose to educate their children outside of a traditional public or private school. Homeschooling appears to be the fastest-growing form of education in the USA. Statistics gathered from 2006–2007 estimate that 1.5 million students are homeschooled in the USA, an increase of 74 percent in the past 10 years.
>
> The three most common reasons why parents choose to homeschool their children are: 1) to provide religious or moral instruction; 2) concern about the school environment (i.e. alcohol and drug usage, etc.); and 3) dissatisfaction with academic instruction at public and private schools.
>
> The most formidable obstacle to teaching Media Literacy in a homeschool environment is that the homeschool community is thoroughly *decentralized*. To illustrate, there are more than thirty co-ops/ learning centers and support groups in the St. Louis City, County and surrounding area, without any central organization to reach them all. In addition, although homeschooling is legal in every state, each state has its own requirements. Some jurisdictions require that homeschoolers follow a state-mandated curriculum, while in others, including Missouri, there are few if any restrictions.
>
> However, the discipline of media literacy lends itself to homeschool education, in several respects:
>
> • Homeschooled children are not simply given information and knowledge by the parent but instead are taught *how* to acquire information and knowledge. This critical thinking approach is the essence of Media Literacy: learning to access, analyze and evaluate information. Moreover, because of their skepticism about formal education, it is important to stress Media Literacy as a *process;* Media Literacy

education doesn't teach people *what* to think; the discipline teaches people *how* to think.

- Media Literacy empowers individuals to develop a critical distance from the information they are receiving through the media. This emphasis on intellectual autonomy resonates with homeschool students and parents, who value independence of thought.
- A final point of convergence is the focus on the role of the media in *values formation.*[15]

Public Policy Sector

A number of educational institutions, community organizations, and media literacy associations are promoting legislative and regulatory reforms in media policy. Some of the areas of media policy legislation that are being addressed include:

- *Media Ownership*
  - Imposing limits on mergers that further concentrate media ownership
  - Restoring the FCC's fairness doctrine on the public airwaves, so that broadcast license renewals will determine whether a station has met its public interest obligations
  - Using the proceeds from the auction of the public airwaves and awarding broadcast licenses to support local and independent media operations
  - Extending the ownership base of the media industry to members of minority groups
  - Enforcing antitrust laws to break up media oligopolies
- *Political Campaign Reform*
  - Increasing public financing of political campaigns
  - Providing free television airtime for candidates during campaigns as part of its licensing agreement
- *Digital Media Protections*
  - Guaranteeing the principle of "Net neutrality" so that all users of the Internet will have equal opportunities to access and dissemi-nate information
  - Addressing the digital divide by taking steps to insure that the Internet is accessible and affordable
  - Taking steps to insure that intellectual property rights of individuals are protected
  - Supporting policies that protect the privacy of Internet users

- *Education*
  - ○ Implementing the education standards of states, which mandate the instruction of media literacy in schools at the elementary and secondary levels
- *Community Media*
  - ○ Urging local officials to demand public interest obligations and safeguards for PEG (public, education, and government) television in return for the cable companies' use of public rights of way
- *Media and Children*
  - ○ Requiring broadcasters to air a minimum amount of educational programming for children as part of their public service obligation
- *Public Broadcasting*
  - ○ Expanding the public broadcasting system (especially news)

Community Media

Community-based media organizations are distinctly local operations. Community radio and television stations are staffed by members of the community. Often, a large percentage of the positions are filled by volunteers.

These nonprofit stations are almost entirely supported by individual donations. Because their operation is free of the economic imperatives that characterize commercial stations, their programming reflects the interests of their audience (some of whom volunteer at the station). Community media stations produce programming that promotes an awareness of issues, challenges, and opportunities facing their communities. In addition, community stations promote the local arts; indeed, WWOZ is among the most popular radio stations in New Orleans, Louisiana. The station plays the music of local artists, as well as examples of their rich musical heritage, and promotes community events and festivals throughout the year.

Many community media organizations incorporate education in their missions. For instance, Double Helix, the community television and radio station in St. Louis, Missouri, offers media literacy classes, reaching audiences typically not in contact with academic institutions.

Media Arts

Media arts programs promote media literacy through both production and critical analysis. These programs are primarily directed at young people.

Media arts programs encourage self-discovery and growth through artistic expression. The topics of these films, videos, and Web sites examine issues rarely addressed in mainstream media. In addition, the process of producing media presentations can provide insight into how messages are constructed in the media.

Writing and Research

A number of publications, both in print and on the Internet, analyze media coverage and trends in the media industry. Some of these publications include *FAIR (Fairness and Accuracy in Media), Media Reality Check, American Journalism Review,* and the *Pew Research Center's Project for Excellence in Journalism.*

In addition, media literacy analysis can be found throughout the popular press. Many newspapers and magazines throughout the country include film and television critics on their staff who discuss cultural trends found in programming. In addition, features and entertainment journalism pieces often focus on trends in media programming that serve as a barometer of cultural attitudes.

As an example, journalist David Carr authored an article in the *New York Times* entitled "Hollywood Gives the Press a Bad Name," which looks at how journalists are depicted in popular films. Carr observes,

The movies in which the press is seen as holding business and government to account—how the press likes to think of itself—are far outnumbered by the films in which the news media come off as entirely unaccountable.

When Hollywood has a role requiring greasy self-interest, it knows it can insert a fast-talking guy with a notebook and soup stains on his tie. . . . *King Kong* offers a typical scenario. The poor gorilla is chained to a stage for the entertainment of others and photographers shower him with flashbulbs until he goes ballistic, flattens New York and then tumbles to his death. And, oh yeah, the journalists are there to climb atop the carcass for some more pictures. Not much has changed in public perception of the craft since the original *King Kong* was made back in 1933. In *Capote,* the journalist sells out his subject, while in *Munich* a frantic electronic press in pursuit of the story tips off the terrorists.[16]

According to Carr, this tarnished view of journalists is an indication of a lack of public confidence in journalists in the wake of examples of discreditable behavior by members of the press:

> The business in general seems to be playing to type. Myriad plagiarism scandals, most notably one involving *The New York Times* and Jayson Blair and CBS's failure to verify a memo related to President Bush's National Guard service, conjure their own images of journalistic malfeasance.
>
> There were the travails of Judith Miller, the former reporter for *The Times,* and now even Bob Woodward of *The Washington Post*—whose work with Carl Bernstein provided grist for *All the President's Men,* a journalistic paean—is starring in a far less praiseworthy role.[17]

PROFESSIONAL SECTOR

The professional media sector can be a very powerful and effective voice for media literacy. The newspaper, film, and television industries have established programs designed to promote critical understanding of media and media content. In some cases, media professionals work in partnership with educational institutions, community groups, or media literacy organizations. Organizations of media professionals with interests in media literacy include Creating Critical Viewers, Newspaper Association of America Foundation, Show Coalition, and the Taos Film Festival.

Geena Davis is a professional media practitioner whose firsthand experience as an actress makes her an effective spokesperson on the representation of women in Hollywood films. Ms. Davis has established the Geena Davis Institute on Gender in Media, whose mission is "to engage, educate, and influence the need for gender balance, reducing stereotyping and creating a wide variety of female characters for entertainment targeting children 11 and under."[18] Ms. Davis, a 1989 Oscar winner, has successfully brought this issue to the attention of Hollywood film executives, who are addressing the issue of gender representation in Hollywood productions.

In addition, many media professionals are producing responsible and informative programming that improves the industry. Documentary programs such as *Frontline* and *On the Media* heighten awareness of the impact of the media on our culture. And news programming like *Democracy Now* calls attention to issues and challenges its audience to think critically about the information that they receive through the mainstream media.

Independent video producers also promote media literacy by examining issues that are not covered by corporate media. One famous example is *An Inconvenient Truth* (2006), a film produced by former vice president Al Gore that brought the issue of global warming to public attention. Companies that produce independent media literacy programming include the Association for Independent Video and Filmmakers, the Foundation for Independent Video and Film, Boston Film and Video Foundation, and the Northwest Film Center.

Presentations produced for theatrical release also can bring social issues to the consciousness of the public. Most famously, *All the President's Men* (1976) dramatized how American investigative journalists Woodward and Bernstein uncovered the Watergate scandal. More recently, the film *Promised Land* (2012) tackled the contentious issue of *hydraulic fracking*. Fracking is a relatively new technique for extracting oil from shale rock by pumping water laced with chemicals and sand at high pressure into shale rock formations to break them up and unleash hydrocarbons. Critics worry that fracking fluids or hydrocarbons can leak into water tables from wells, or above ground. In the film, Matt Damon plays a corporate salesperson seeking land on behalf of a gas company. John Krasinski plays an environmentalist who challenges Damon and has the health and welfare interests of the local people as his priority.

In addition, popular music groups, including Christina Aguilera ("Beautiful"), Pink ("Mr. President"), and The Fray ("How to Save a Life") raise questions and call on their audiences to take action on social issues.

Business

As discussed in Chapter 1, many companies now place a value on employees who have the ability to interpret and construct messages using the different "languages" of media, such as film, television, audio, and the Internet. As an example, at MIT's annual entrepreneurial competition, contestants submitted their start-up ideas through "elevator pitches"—60-second videos on YouTube. MBA student Kourosh Kaghazian, who organized the contest, notes, "It's really important for start-ups that have limited resources to be able to use social media platforms to . . . promote their products or services, to recruit talent or raise funding."[19]

Further, the critical thinking skills inherent in the discipline of media literacy are also in demand in a business environment. Premier business schools such as Harvard, Stanford, and the Rotman School of Management at the University of Toronto have redesigned their curricula to emphasize *critical thinking*—the foundation of media literacy. Garth Saloner, Dean of Stanford's Graduate School of Business, declares, "If I'm going to really launch you on a career or path where you can make a big impact in the world, you have to be able to think critically and analytically about the big problems in the world."[20]

Steve McConnell, a managing partner of NBBJ, an architecture firm based in Seattle, has noticed a distinctly different approach in the Rotman students he has hired: "They seemed to be naturally free of the bias or predisposition that so many of us seem to carry into any situation. And they brought a set of skills in how you query and look into an issue without moving toward biased or predetermined conclusions that has led to unexpected discoveries of opportunity and potential innovation."[21] Recognizing this connection, business and management majors at Webster University can supplement their primary program of study with an 18-hour certificate in Media Literacy.

Media-Related Careers

Media literacy can provide a distinctive orientation that prepares individuals for careers in media-related professions such as advertising and marketing, journalism and broadcast journalism, and political media communication.

- *Marketing.* The quantitative and qualitative methodologies employed in the discipline of media literacy are used to identify audiences—the primary objective of marketing.
- *Advertising.* Media literacy approaches media presentations as a reflection of cultural attitudes preoccupations and behaviors. This information can help advertisers to determine which advertising approaches would be most effective.
- *Political Communications.* A background in media literacy can help media consultants develop effective and responsible media strategies for influencing the public.

NOTES

1. Aspen Institute, "National Leadership Conference on Media Literacy," Queenstown, Maryland, December 7–9, 1992.
2. "About RTM," Reclaim the Media, http://www.reclaimthemedia.org/.

3. Brian Stelter, "Host Loses Some Sponsors after an Obama Remark," *New York Times,* August 14, 2009.

4. 2013 National Conference for Media Reform, http://conference.freepress. net/sites/default/files/resources/ncmr13_0.pdf.

5. Elizabeth Van Ness, "Is a Cinema Studies Degree the New MBA?" *New York Times,* March 6, 2005.

6. Ibid.

7. Ibid.

8. John Pungente and Barry Duncan, "Media Literacy: Canada," in *Handbook of Media Literacy,* ed. Art Silverblatt (Santa Barbara, CA: ABC-CLIO, 2013).

9. Ofcom, www.ofcom.org.uk/.

10. Robert Kubey and Frank Baker, "Has Media Literacy Found a Curricular Foothold?," *Editorial Projects in Education* 19.9 (2000): 56, 38.

11. Frank Baker, e-mail to author, June 11, 2006.

12. Art Silverblatt, Frank Baker, Kathleen Tyner, and Laura Stuhlman, "Media Literacy in U.S. Institutions of Higher Education," July 25, 2002, http:// www.webster.edu/medialiteracy/survey/survey_Report.htm.

13. Ibid.

14. Oasis, www.oasis.org/AboutUs.aspx.

15. Debra Stieferman, "Homeschooling and Media Literacy," Gateway Media Literacy Partners, July 2013, www.gmlpstl.org.

16. David Carr, "Hollywood Gives the Press a Bad Name," *New York Times,* December 12, 2005: C-1.

17. Ibid.

18. Geena Davis Institute on Gender in Media, http://www.seejane.org.

19. Mitchell Hartman, "The Art of the Elevator Pitch," Marketplace.org, May 10, 2011, www.marketplace.org/topics/business/art-elevator-pitch.

20. Lane Wallace, "Multicultural Critical Theory. At B-School?" *New York Times,* January 10, 2010.

21. Ibid.

Suggested Reading

Alexander, Janet E., and Marsha Ann Tate. *Web Wisdom: How to Evaluate and Create Information Quality on the Web.* Hillsdale, NJ: Lawrence Erlbaum Associates, 1999.

Altheide, David L., and Robert P. Snow. *Media Logic.* Beverly Hills, CA: Sage Publications, 1979.

Arnheim, Rudolf. *Art and Visual Perception.* Berkeley: University of California Press, 1974.

Bagdikian, Ben. *The Media Monopoly,* 3rd ed. Boston: Beacon Press, 1990.

Braudy, Leo. *The Frenzy of Renown: Fame and Its History.* Oxford, UK: Oxford University Press, 1986.

Buckingham, David. *After the Death of Childhood.* Cambridge, UK: Polity Press, 2000.

Buckingham, David. *Moving Images.* Manchester, UK: Manchester University Press, 1997.

Collins, W. Andrew. "Children's Comprehension of Television Content," in *Children Communicating,* ed. Ellen Wartella. Beverly Hills, CA: Sage Publications, 1979.

Considine, David, and Gail Haley. *Visual Messages: Integrating Imagery into Instruction.* Englewood, CO: Teacher Idea Press, 1992.

Ewen, Stuart. *All Consuming Images.* New York: Basic Books, 1988.

Finnegan, Lisa. *No Questions Asked: News Coverage since 9/11.* Westport, CT: Praeger.

Gans, Herbert. *Deciding What's News.* New York: Pantheon Books, 1979.

Gault, Philip, *Choosing the News: The Profit Factor in News Selection.* New York: Greenwood Press, 1990.

Goffman, Erving. *Gender Advertisements.* New York: Harper & Row, 1976.

Holtzman, Linda. *Media Messages: What Film, Television, and Popular Music Teach Us about Race, Class, Gender, and Sexual Orientation.* Armonk, NY: M. E. Sharpe, 2000.

Jamieson, Kathleen Hall. *Packaging the Presidency.* New York: Oxford University Press, 1992.

Jenkins, Henry. *Textual Poachers: Television Fans and Participatory Culture.* New York: Routledge, 1992.

Klein, Naomi. *No Logo: No Space, No Choice, No Jobs.* New York: Picador, 2002.

Klinenberg, Eric. *Fighting for Air: The Battle to Control America's Media.* New York: Metropolitan Books, 2007.

Kress, Gunther, and Theo van Leeuwen. *Reading Images: The Grammar of Visual Design.* London: Routledge, 1995.

Lee, Martin A., and Norman Soloman. *Unreliable Sources: A Guide to Detecting Bias in the News Media.* Secaucus, NJ: Carol Publishing Group, 1990.

Lessig, Lawrence. *Free Culture: The Nature and Future of Creativity.* New York: Penguin, 2005.

MacLean, Eleanor. *Between the Lines.* Montreal: Black Rose Books, 1981.

Masterman, Len. *Teaching the Media.* London: Routledge, 1985.

McChesney, Robert. *Rich Media, Poor Democracy.* Champaign: University of Illinois Press, 1999.

McLuhan, Marshall. *Understanding Media: The Extensions of Man.* New York: McGraw-Hill, 1964.

Mitroff, Ian I., and Warren Bennis. *The Unreality Industry.* New York: Oxford University Press, 1989.

Parenti, Michael. *Make Believe Media.* New York: St. Martin's Press, 1992.

Sabato, Larry J. *The Rise of Political Consultants.* New York: Basic Books, 1981.

Saven, Leslie. *The Sponsored Life.* Philadelphia: Temple University Press, 1993.

Schwartz, Tony. *The Responsive Chord.* Garden City, NY: Anchor Books, 1973.

Silverblatt, Art, ed. *Handbook of Media Literacy.* Westport, CT: ABC-CLIO, 2013.

Silverblatt, Art, Jane Ferry, and Barb Finan. *Approaches to Media Literacy,* Armonk, NY: M. E. Sharpe, 1999.

Twitchell, James B. *Adcult USA.* New York: Columbia University Press, 1997.

Tyner, Kathleen. *Literacy in a Digital World.* Hillsdale, NJ: Lawrence Erlbaum Associates, 1998.

Wasko, Janet. *Understanding Disney: The Manufacture of Fantasy.* Cambridge, UK: Polity Press, 2001.

Wolf, Naomi. *The Beauty Myth.* New York: William Morrow, 1991.

Index

About the Authors

NIKOLE BROWN is a graduate student in media literacy/education at Webster University in St. Louis, Missouri.

DON MILLER is a faculty member at Webster University School of Communications, St. Louis, Missouri. He holds a master's degree in media communications.

ART SILVERBLATT, PhD, is professor of communications and journalism at Webster University in St. Louis, Missouri, and vice president of Gateway Media Literacy Partners (GMLP), a regional media literacy consortium. He is the author of numerous books and articles, including Praeger's *Media Literacy: Keys to Interpreting Media Messages*, Greenwood's *Dictionary of Media Literacy*, *The Praeger Handbook of Media Literacy*, and *Approaches to the Study of Media Literacy*. Silverblatt earned his doctorate from Michigan State University.

ANDREW SMITH is a full-time professor in the School of Communications at Lindenwood University in St. Charles, Missouri, teaching courses in media literacy, mass communication, film, and interactive media. Prior to joining Lindenwood's faculty, Smith taught film courses at Webster University, where he completed his master's degree in media literacy. His research and writing specializes in film/television analysis, media aesthetics, and video game theory. A pop culture enthusiast, he examines collective consciousness and correlates social phenomena such as memes, slang, and culture trends back to their origin to better understand the media's influence on our everyday lives.

JULIE SMITH is professor of media literacy at Webster University in St. Louis, Missouri, and holds a master's degree in mass communication from Southern Illinois University–Edwardsville.